FISHING
THE
CANADIAN ROCKIES
Second Edition

JOEY AMBROSI
an angler's guide to every lake, river & stream

hancock house

ISBN-13: 978-0-88839-425-5 [paperback]
ISBN-13: 978-0-88839-349-4 [epub]
Copyright © 2021 Joey Ambrosi

Library and Archives Canada Cataloguing in Publication

Title: Fishing the Canadian Rockies : an angler's guide to every lake, river & stream / Joey Ambrosi.
Names: Ambrosi, Joey, author.
Description: 2nd edition. | Includes index.
Identifiers: Canadiana (print) 20200181793 | Canadiana (ebook) 20200181815 | ISBN 9780888394255
(softcover) | ISBN 9780888393494 (EPUB)
Subjects: LCSH: Fishing—Canadian Rockies (B.C. and Alta.)—Guidebooks. | LCSH: Canadian Rockies
(B.C. and Alta.)—Guidebooks. | LCGFT: Guidebooks.
Classification: LCC SH572.A4 A62 2020 | DDC 799.1/109711—dc23

All rights reserved. No part of this publication may be reproduced, stored in a retrieval system or transmitted, in any form or by any means, electronic, mechanical, audio, photocopying, recording, or otherwise (except for copying permitted by Sections 107 and 108 of the U.S. Copyright Law and except for book reviews for the public press), without the prior written permission of Hancock House Publishers. Permissions and licensing contribute to the book industry by helping to support writers and publishers through the purchase of authorized editions and excerpts.
Please visit www.accesscopyright.ca.

Illustrations and photographs are copyrighted by the artist or the Publisher.

Printed in China

INTERIOR DESIGN: J. Ambrosi
Cover Design: M. Lamont
EDITOR: D. Martens

Front Cover Photo: Gary Enzsol fishing the West Castle River by Vic Bergman
Inside Cover Photo: Cutthroat Trout by Curtis Hall
Back Cover Photo: Bull Trout by Curtis Hall

We acknowledge the financial support of the Government of Canada through the Canada Book Fund and the Canada Council for the Arts, and of the Province of British Columbia through the British Columbia Arts Council and the Book Publishing Tax Credit.

Hancock House gratefully acknowledges the Halkomelem Speaking Peoples whose unceded, asserted and shared traditional territories our offices reside upon.

Published simultaneously in Canada and the United States by

HANCOCK HOUSE PUBLISHERS LTD.
19313 Zero Avenue, Surrey, B.C. Canada V3Z 9R9
#104-4550 Birch Bay-Lynden Rd, Blaine, WA, U.S.A. 98230-9436
Phone (800) 938-1114   Fax (800) 983-2262
www.hancockhouse.com   info@hancockhouse.com

TABLE OF CONTENTS

Foreword

In 2001, I completed *Fishing the Canadian Rockies*, an effort to accurately describe as many bodies of waters in the Canadian Rockies as possible. Over the years since the publication of that book, I have had many people ask me when I was going to do another edition. The 2001 version was such a monumental task I thought that I would never be able to do a second edition. However, I have done a lot of fishing since 2001, collecting information and photos, and in 2018 I decided I give it a go on a second edition. From 2018 through 2020, in an effort to keep things up to date, I visited every Region in the book and over 600 lakes, taking new pictures and catching a few fish here and there. Into the fall of 2020, I rewrote the text, redrew the maps and assembled new images (with the help of some great photographers and anglers). As with the 2001 version, every body of water described in the text can be found on a map. The maps in the new edition are much more accurate having been based on Google Map and Google Earth (and are in colour, making it easier to differentiate a road from a river!). Longitude and latitude coordinates for every lake will assist those who are not technology-challenged like me. The photos in the book are all in colour, with plenty of great fish pictures. *Fishing the Canadian Rockies, 2nd Edition* was as much a labour of love as the original. I hope that all anglers will find it useful and will be able to use it to explore new waters in our wonderful Canadian Rockies.

Joey Ambrosi
Crowsnest Pass, Alberta
January, 2021

Self-portrait of author, flood pants and all, fishing in Magog Lake below Mt. Assiniboine in the late 1970s

*Author with his son, Tyler, 2019
Photo: Grace Campbell*

Author with his son, Tyler, at Wall Lake, 1996

Acknowledgments

As with the original Fishing the Canadian Rockies, assembling this much information and images could not be done without the help of others. Jason Godkin, intrepid Rocky Mountain backcountry explorer and angler who also runs the excellent *OutdoorAlberta.com* website, provided valuable updates on many lakes. He also provided outstanding images of fish from many southern Alberta lakes. Vic Bergman of Crowsnest Pass and Curtis Hall of Fernie, both fishing guides and professional photographers, generously offered some brilliant images from their fishing collections. Jim Rennels of Calgary provide updated information on several lakes in southern Alberta as well as images. Author of Mountain Footsteps and acclaimed photographer Janice Strong (janicestrong.com) provided some great images of backcountry lakes in the Kootenays. A big thank you goes out to the Kootenay Trout Hatchery at Bull River who provided images of hard-to-reach lakes in the Kootenays. Leanne Jones at the Kootenay Trout Hatchery was particularly helpful in gathering information and images. Dallas Meidinger and Paul Harper from Parks Canada in Waterton Lakes National Parks were able to help with Kenow Fire images and information on invasive species and the Clean, Drain and Dry program. Robert Vanderwater, who runs an excellent blog for the Central Alberta Fly Tying Club (rdflytying.blogspot.com), rounded up some great fishing pictures by Steve Luethi and Ken Prowse. Thanks to the Frank Slide Interpretive Centre for the use of Friends Society photos.

A number of anglers provided images of their favourite waters or their big catch. Logan Urie, a young man out of Jasper with enormous fishing talent, provided information and pictures for many northern Rockies lakes. Other anglers who provided images include Jonathan and Patrick Shandrowsky, Fiore Olivieri, Chad Smith, Chaunce Olson, Mark Houze and Chris Mouriopoulos. Thank you to Dawn Rigby of Country Encounters in Crowsnest Pass (*countryencounters.com*) for directing me to Mark and Chris. Thanks for the great images from Wayne Pierce, Nick and Marla Schlacter from Wapiti Sports in Canmore (*wapitisports.com*), Craig Somers of Fortress Lake Wilderness Retreat (*fortresslake.com*), Anders at Banff Fishing Unlimited (*banff-fishing.com*), the Fischer-Olson clan, and *explorejasper.com*. Also a big thanks to those who caught fish and were willing to let me take their picture. I find these days that I usually end up fishing alone, which turns out to be great for the soul – and of course nobody to contradict my fishing stories at a later date. I do still try to get together with fishing buddy, Don Shandrowsky, or hiking buddy, Wayne Pierce, when I can. Great fun to get together with the Hideib family in the outdoors. However, the most enjoyable fishing time is still with my son, Tyler, whenever we can connect during fishing season.

This book is dedicated to my family: my wife Valerie, my son, Tyler, and my mother, Eileen. Without their loving support, this project would have never been completed.

INTRODUCTION

Fishing the Canadian Rockies, 2nd Edition is a comprehensive guidebook to the lakes, rivers and streams of the Rocky Mountains that straddle the British Columbia-Alberta border. This extends from the US border in the south, through Mt. Robson Provincial Park and Jasper National Park in the north. Virtually every lake or stream of any consequence in the Canadian Rockies is described within this book.

Regions

The area covered by *Fishing the Canadian Rockies, 2nd Edition* is divided into 26 geographical Regions. Each chapter of the book covers one of the 26 Regions. All Regions have been further subdivided into geographical Sub-Regions.

Maps

Each Region and Sub-Region has its own map, and each body of water described in the text can be found on a map. The Region map identifies the location of the corresponding Sub-Regions. The Sub-Region maps are more detailed and have been drawn from information from Google Maps and Google Earth, but are for general orientation only. All maps (Region and Sub-Region) in *Fishing the Canadian Rockies, 2nd Edition* are oriented with north at the top of the map. It is strongly recommended that topographic maps be used for any backcountry use. Topographic maps in a variety of scales can be purchased at many sporting goods stores or retail book outlets. Earth view and GPS apps are available online and aid immensely in scouting areas prior to heading out. With satellite connections, these apps can be used virtually anywhere in the Rockies. As an aid to those trying to find individual lakes, all lakes have been given longitude and latitude coordinates. These coordinates can be input into programs such as Google Earth to find the specific body of water. As a test, you can check out the author's absolute favourite fishing spot in the Canadian Rockies: 50°57'08"N 115°45'31"W.

Names

The official name, or most common name, for a body of water is given, plus any alternate or local name (aka – also known as).

Fishing Licenses

Three separate jurisdictions cover the waters described in *Fishing the Canadian Rockies, 2nd Edition*. These are the Province of British Columbia (BC); the Province of Alberta (AB); and the Government of Canada in the National Parks (NP). Each jurisdiction requires a separate license, and each jurisdiction has a completely different set of angling regulations. In the text, following the name of the body of water, the abbreviation for the appropriate jurisdiction is given (BC, AB or NP). Individual anglers must be aware of the regulations in effect of the body of water they are fishing. Regulations change each year and anglers must be aware of the changes. **This book is not a substitute for the regulations! Check the regulations before you go fishing!** Fishing regulations can be found online at:

B.C. regulations:
http://www.env.gov.bc.ca/fw/fish/regulations/#Synopsis
Alberta regulations:
http://www.albertaregulations.ca/fishingregs/
Parks Canada regulations:
https://www.pc.gc.ca/en/pn-np/ab/banff/activ/peche-fishing
(The Parks Canada (Banff) link will lead to fishing regulations for all other mountain National Parks)

Fish

Fishing the Canadian Rockies, 2nd Edition identifies the game fish that inhabit a particular body of water. The length and weight given for each species is for larger specimens that one would expect to catch in that body of water. The average size of individuals caught will generally be less than the stated sizes and is normally described in the text. Species recognition by anglers is essential. All angling regulations are based in some manner on species identification. The Regulation Synopses provided by all three jurisdictions provide good descriptions and/or illustrations of game fish species. *Fishing the Canadian Rockies, 2nd Edition* provides an accurate description of fish species present in specific bodies of water at the time of publication. Winterkill, new plantings, reproductive success and fish migration will undoubtedly change the status of many bodies of water over time.

Status: Quality of Angling

STATUS: QUALITY OF ANGLING

Good

A Author's Favourite

Limited

Doubtful

Devoid of fish

Closed to angling

? Unknown

Each body of water described in *Fishing the Canadian Rockies, 2nd Edition* has been assigned a status as to its quality of angling. A series of colour-coded symbols make it easy to understand the current status of any lake or stream. The status of each body of water is based on the author's most current information, whether from personal experience, reports from other anglers, government reports and/or stocking reports. Note that the status of any body water can change from season to season based on a number of factors, including winterkill, new plantings and changes in regulations. The seven levels of status used in *Fishing the Canadian Rockies, 2nd Edition* are Good (■); Author's Favourite (▲); Limited (□); Doubtful (▨); Devoid of Fish (■); Closed to Angling (⊗); and Unknown (?). *Good* indicates a healthy population of fish. However, this does not ensure fishing success. Catching fish will still come down to tactics, equipment, skill and usually a bit of luck. *Author's Favourites* are lakes that the author has enjoyed fishing above others over the years. They all fall within the *Good* category and have healthy trout populations. *Limited* indicates that there are fish within a body of water, but that their numbers are low and angling success will likely will be accordingly more difficult. Catch-and-release is essential to maintain fish populations in these waters. *Doubtful* indicates that fish were present in the body of water at some time in the past, but few if any fish remain. A lake listed as **Doubtful** may surprise on occasion as fish may have migrated into the body of water or have been re-planted. I have had great days at lakes that previously had nothing in them. Both the British Columbia and Alberta governments have online lists of bodies of waters that are stocked each year. **Devoid of Fish** indicates that there are no fish in a particular body of water. Again, stocking programs can change this status. **Closed to Angling** indicates that the body of water is closed to angling by regulation. Regulations change each year, so be sure to check to see if the body of water you are about to fish is open or closed to angling. **Unknown** indicates that no reports or records are available for a particular body of water and any available information is out-of-date. Some of these bodies of waters were stocked at one time, but usually require extremely difficult access and few, if any, anglers make it in to these locations.

Description

Every body of water is given a general description in the text, including access and physical characteristics. The expectations in terms of fish species, quantity and size are given, and general angling tactics are provided where applicable. The common name for each body of water is given, as well as the alternate names (aka – also known as). Alternate names are often local names given to lakes and streams.

Photographs

Photographs of selected bodies of water are provided as are images of fish taken in these bodies of water. Numerous anglers and photographers provided the author with outstanding images of lakes, streams and fish of the Canadian Rockies. Individual images are credited to the photographer. All images not credited were taken by the author.

Index

The Index at the back of *Fishing the Canadian Rockies, 2nd Edition* lists alphabetically every body of water in the text. Alternate names (aka – also known as) for bodies of waters are also listed. For locations with similar names, the Region and Sub-Region are identified for clarification.

Legend

The following is a common legend for all of the Region and Sub-Region maps.

Jasmine Hideib at Fish Lake

MAP LEGEND

Boundaries

- ▬ ▪ ▬ ▪ ▪ International
- ▬ ▪ ▬ ▪ ▬ ▪ Provincial
- — ▪ — ▪ — ▪ — Park

Roads/Trails

- ▬▬▬ Highway (Paved)
- ——— Gravel Road
- ▬ ▬ ▬ 4WD Road
- - - - - - - Trail
- 🛡 ㊵ ⑧⓪⓪ Highway number

Natural Features

- ⬭ Lake
- ～ River, Creek
- ⊣ Falls
- ⌣ Pass
- ▲ Mountain

Natural Features

- ⬤ Town
- • Point of Interest
- ⚂ Campground (vehicle accessible)
- ⚃ Backcountry campsite
- ⬆ Backcountry cabin/lodge
- ⚑ Backcountry warden cabin

Map Reference

- ◀ (Invermere Region) Adjoining Region
- ◀ (Tamarack Sub-Region) Adjoining Sub-Region
- 0 —— 1 —— 2 km All distances are metric
- ◁N North

Abbreviations (in maps and text)

BC = British Columbia	AB = Alberta
NP/Nat'l Park = National Park	FS = Forest Service
PP/Prov. Park = Provincial Park	2WD = Two wheel drive
US/USA = United States	4WD = Four wheel drive

FISHING THE CANADIAN ROCKIES

Second Edition

Photo Curtis Hall

WATERTON REGION

Each year hundreds of thousands of tourists flock to Waterton Lakes National Park to take in the magnificent scenery. In addition to its scenery, the park offers excellent fishing opportunities, with the Waterton Lakes and Waterton Townsite serving as the focal point of the Region. The park itself can be reached from Pincher Creek via Highway 6, from Cardston via Highway 5, and from the United States via the Chief Mountain Highway (Highway 6). The Waterton Townsite has a major campground, as well as motels, restaurants, gas stations and a variety of tourist-related stores, including stores selling fishing tackle and offering current fishing information. The Parks Canada Information Centre is located in the Townsite and the warden office (in the park compound) is located just east of the Townsite on Highway 5. The Region nicely divides into three Sub-Regions, with the Waterton Lakes being the focal point of the central Prince of Wales Sub-Region. The backcountry surrounding the Tamarack Trail is the westernmost Sub-Region. The rolling hills and grasslands around the small community of Mountain View outside the National Park form the eastern Sub-Region.

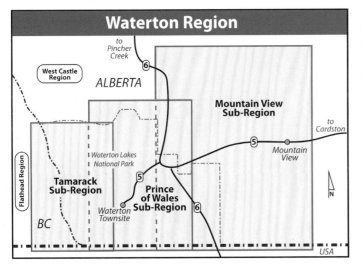

The Kenow Fire

In 2017, the colossal Kenow Fire burned over 38% of Waterton Lakes National Park. Following an intense lightning storm on August 30, 2017, a wildfire was detected 10 kilometres west of the park boundary, in British Columbia. Strong winds, hot weather and dry conditions fueled the fire. The Waterton Townsite was issued an evacuation alert on September 8. On September 11, the fire crossed the provincial boundary into Waterton Lakes National Park at the head of Cameron Creek valley. The fire rapidly descended northeast along the Akamina

Parkway, spreading quickly through the grasslands near the park entrance, then continued north and east out of the park, before eventually being extinguished by crews. Over 38,000 hectares (380 square kilometres) were eventually burned, including over 19,000 hectares in Waterton Lakes National Park. Two main roadways (Akamina Parkway and Red Rock Canyon Parkway) and over 80% of Waterton's trail network were affected by the Kenow Fire. Parks Canada has developed a long term strategy for the recovery of the areas of Waterton Park burned by the Kenow Fire. As a result, some roads and trails have been reopened, some will be reopened in the near future and some may not be opened for several years, if ever. This will directly affect access to many fishing locations in Waterton. Check with the Parks Canada office in Waterton for up-to-date information.

Prince of Wales Sub-Region

All three Waterton Lakes are readily accessible, and are very popular with anglers. Daily boat tours take sightseers down the entire length of Upper Waterton Lake and arrangements can be made with the operators for drop-offs and pick-ups at the Crypt Lake trailhead. From the Townsite, trails branch to Bertha Lake and to Alderson and Carthew Lakes via the Carthew Trail. Crandell Lake is located at the midway point, by trail, between the Akamina Highway and the Red Rock Canyon Road.

Invasive Mussels

To date, invasive mussels have not been detected in Waterton Lakes National Park. Parks Canada regularly tests for invasive mussels, following similar protocols as the U.S. National Parks Service in Glacier National Park and Alberta Environment and Parks. This includes visual testing for invasive mussels and active monitoring for invasive mussel veligers (larval stage).

Invasive mussels, such as quagga and zebra mussels, are aquatic invasive species introduced from Europe into North America in 1980s. The fingernail-sized freshwater mollusk can produce millions of eggs and easily attach itself to objects such as boats and trailers. Mussels can inadvertently be moved to a new location attached on boats, equipment and trailers. Standing or trapped water in boats is a concern because invasive mussels have a microscopic larval stage, allowing them to be present without being visible. Their numbers can reach tens of thousands per square metre. Prodigious filter feeders, they strip nutrients from the water leaving little or no food for native species. This affects the entire food web, impacting the plant and animal life in the region, and altering water chemistry and water clarity. They are permanent and irreversible. No method, technology or natural predator exists to remove invasive mussels once established in a water body.

Parks Canada would like visitors to Clean, Drain, Dry their watercraft and gear after every trip:

- **CLEAN** and inspect watercraft and gear (including fishing and SCUBA equipment).
- **DRAIN** buckets, ballasts, bilges, coolers, internal compartments, and other containers that may hold trapped or standing water.
- **DRY** the watercraft and gear completely between trips and leave compartments open and sponge out standing water.

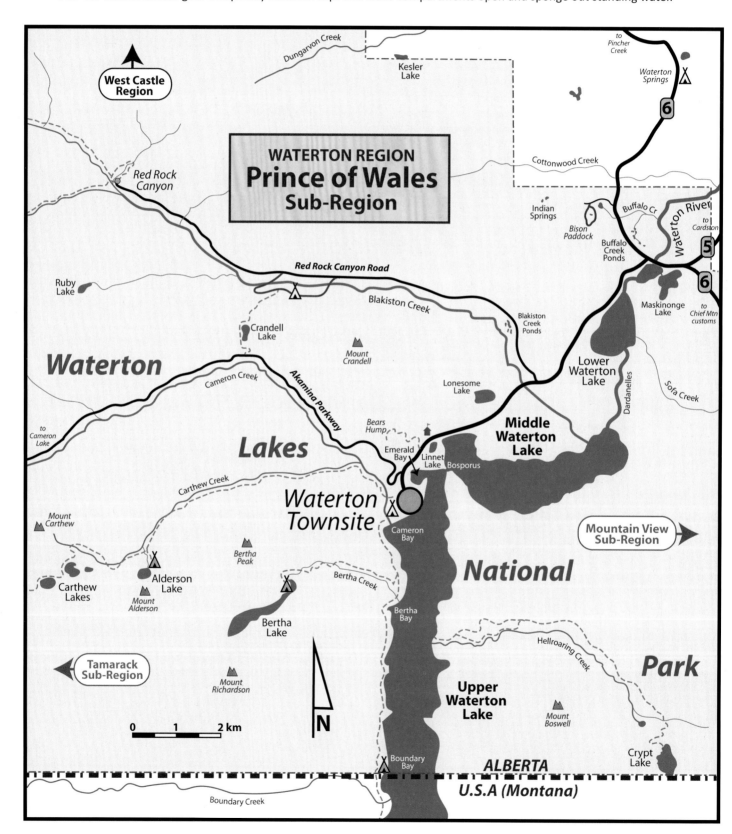

■ **Waterton Lakes [Upper and Middle] (NP)**
Upper: 49°01'20"N 113°54'10"W Middle: 49°03'17"N 113°52'44"W
Lake trout to 1 m (10.0 kg)
Rainbow trout to 65 cm (3.0 kg)
Cutthroat trout to 55 cm (1.5 kg)
Brook trout to 55 cm (1.5 kg)
Bull trout to 75 cm (5.0 kg)
Whitefish to 50 cm (1.5 kg)
The Waterton Lakes are world-renowned for their spectacular beauty, and offer good angling for a wide variety of fish. Although the sheer size of the lakes dictate that fishing from a boat will be the most effective method, fishing from shore can be productive from many locations. The Waterton record 24 kg lake trout was caught from shore by Elenora Hunter in July, 1920 (allegedly, her husband left her behind to go fishing with a friend in a boat). Areas around the numerous inlet creeks are generally the best waters, with Bertha Bay and Boundary Bay particularly noted for their good fishing. Today, large lake trout are the main quarry, and they can be caught in sizes up to 10 kg. Lakers are generally taken by those trolling in the deep waters. Whether casting from shore or trolling, rainbow, cutthroat, and brook trout can all be taken from Waterton Lakes. If fishing from shore, focus on areas where streams enter the main lake. Bull trout, suckers, chub, ling cod and the odd northern pike are also taken from the Waterton Lakes. In the fall, whitefish can be taken in good numbers from the Bosporus, the narrow channel that separates the Upper and Middle Waterton Lakes. Boat rentals are available in Waterton Townsite. Be aware that Waterton Lakes are well-known for their strong winds which will keep most small craft off the lakes and foil any attempts at fly fishing. Boaters and canoeists should pay particular attention to changing weather conditions, as storms can arrive very quickly.

Middle (left) and Upper (right) Waterton Lakes

■ **Lower Waterton Lake (aka Knight's Lake) (NP)**
49°05'31"N 113°51'13"W
Brook trout to 45 cm
Whitefish to 50 cm (1.5 kg)
Bull trout to 60 cm (4.0 kg)
Northern pike to 70 cm (5.0 kg)
Located two kilometres downstream from the outlet of Middle Waterton Lake, Lower Waterton Lake holds virtually the same variety of fish as the upper two lakes. However, since the Lower Lake is much shallower than either Middle or Upper Waterton, very few lake trout are present, while northern pike are more abundant. The inlet and outlet areas have the best potential for anyone fishing from shore.

Lower (Knight's) Lake

⊗ **Sofa Creek (NP)**
Status: Closed to angling
Sofa Creek enters the east side of Lower Waterton Lake and is closed to angling.

⊗ **Maskinonge Lake (NP)**
49°06'22"N 113°49'58"W
Status: Closed to angling
Northern pike
Maskinonge Lake has been closed to angling to protect the ideal pike spawning habitat.

■ **Waterton River (NP-AB)**
Brown trout to 65 cm (2.5 kg)
Rainbow trout to 45 cm
Cutthroat trout to 45 cm
Bull trout to 75 cm (5.0 kg)
Whitefish to 35 cm
The Waterton River offers some fine stretches of fishable water as it flows a short distance between Middle and Lower Waterton Lakes, and then, further downstream, out of Lower Waterton Lake. Particularly good for trout is the two kilometre section between Middle and Lower Waterton Lakes, referred to as the Dardanelles. The odd pike is taken in the river near Maskinonge Lake. In the fall, whitefish are taken regularly from all stretches of the river.

Vic Bergman photo

Waterton River brown trout

11

⬛ Crypt Lake (NP)

49°00'04"N 113°50'25"W

Cutthroat trout to 50 cm (1.5 kg)

A unique 9 km access trail, at one time rated as the #1 hike in Canada, which includes a boat crossing of Waterton Lake and a crawl through a 20 m tunnel, leads to a spectacular rocky amphitheater containing Crypt Lake. The lake's emerald green waters hold large numbers of wary cutthroat trout averaging 30–40 cm in length. If the water is not too choppy from wind, fish can be sighted from most locations around the lake. Due to the clarity of the water, however, the fish are spooked easily. Anglers with a little patience are generally rewarded in Crypt. Simply find a promising-looking location and have a seat. Within minutes a school of trout will cruise by. Fly fishing is the most effective tactic, and back-casting space is available along most of the shoreline. Due to its sheltered position, Crypt usually remains frozen into early July, and ice floes dot the lake for the entire summer.

Tyler Ambrosi at Crypt Lake

Crypt Lake cutthroat trout

⬛ Bertha Lake (NP)

49°01'29"N 113°56'22"W

Rainbow trout to 45 cm

Bertha Lake is nestled in a hanging valley 6 km from Waterton Townsite by trail and is very popular with hikers. Be forewarned that although the length of trail is not long, it is very steep over the final few kilometres. Much of the forest cover along the access trail was burned in the 2017 Kenow Fire. Fortunately, the Bertha Lake basin was not touched by the fire. Bertha's blue waters hold a fair number of rainbow trout, most averaging 25–30 cm in length. Although fly fishing is usually productive, most of Bertha's shoreline has heavy brush, and those spin casting will be able to fish from more locations. The waters around the log jam at the outlet creek invariably hold fish, regardless of the time of year or time of day.

Bertha Lake (post-Kenow Fire)

⬛ Alderson Lake (NP)

49°01'25"N 113°58'14"W

Cutthroat trout to 45 cm

Alderson Lake sits in a pleasant basin 8 km from Waterton Townsite along the Carthew Trail. Most hikers hurriedly bypass Alderson near the end of a long day on their way from Cameron Lake to Waterton Townsite. Those who do make the short detour to fish the stunning azure waters of Alderson will be rewarded with cutthroat trout averaging 25–35 cm in length. For those fly fishing, roll casting will be necessary from much of the shore, particularly in the deep waters along the scree slopes which form the northwest corner of the lake.

Alderson Lake

WATERTON REGION: Prince of Wales Sub-Region

◩Carthew Lakes (NP)

49°01'32"N 113°59'45"W

Cutthroat trout to 40 cm

Situated two kilometres beyond and almost 400 vertical metres above Alderson Lake on the Carthew Trail is a windswept alpine basin that holds the Carthew Lakes. The Carthew Lakes consist of Upper and Lower Carthew lake plus the diminutive Carthew Pond. Although all three lakes hold cutthroat trout ranging from 20 to 30 cm, the upper lake at one time also contained a few rainbow trout most of which have now been absorbed into the cutthroat population. The middle lake (Lower Carthew) holds the best angling possibilities, particularly in the bay near the outlet stream. However, brightly coloured cutthroat trout can be taken from most locations in both Lower and Upper Carthew. The alpine surroundings ensure reasonable fly casting room from most locations, although the strong winds which are very common will hamper fly fishing. Due to their lofty elevation, the lakes are usually frozen and access trails snowbound until early to mid July.

Carthew Lakes

◼Crandell Lake (NP)

49°04'57"N 113°58'01"W

Rainbow trout to 35 cm

Brook trout to 35 cm

Accessible by short hiking trails through the Kenow Fire burn from both the Akamina Highway and the Red Rock Canyon Road, Crandell Lake's crystal clear waters are a favourite of local anglers, especially in the early season. Both rainbow and brook trout are caught from Crandell, most averaging 20–25 cm in length. The open slabs of rock along the northeast shore are the most popular location for angling, although fish can be taken from most locations around the lake.

Crandell Lake (post-Kenow Fire)

Parks Canada photo

◼Lonesome Lake (NP)

49°04'28"N 113°53'30"W

Status: Devoid of fish

Lonesome Lake is located near the Waterton Golf Course and at one time was stocked with both rainbow and brook trout, but both species failed to reproduce.

◼Linnet Lake (NP)

49°03'41"N 113°54'18"W

Status: Devoid of fish

Linnet Lake is situated just north of Waterton Townsite and was stocked in the past with rainbow, cutthroat and brook trout, all of which failed to take hold. On occasion, when spring flood waters are high enough to connect Linnet Lake and Middle Waterton Lake, a few fish inevitably swim into Linnet and are trapped there when the high water recedes.

☐Buffalo Creek ponds (NP)

49°07'13"N 113°50'52"W

Rainbow trout to 25 cm

Brook trout to 25 cm

This series of beaver dams west of the park gates along Highway 6 contain small rainbow and brook trout. As with most Waterton's beaver ponds, extremely heavy brush dominates the shoreline; wet feet are a certainty if you want to get a clear cast.

◼Indian Springs (NP)

Status: Devoid of fish

These two small ponds located west of the buffalo paddock contain no fish.

◼Kesler Lake (AB)

49°10'52"N 113°55'59"W

Status: Devoid of fish

Kesler Lake is located on the northern boundary of Waterton Lakes National Park on a tributary of Dungarvan Creek. The shortest access is by ill-defined trail from Yarrow Creek. The lake's shallow waters reportedly held rainbow trout at one time.

Tamarack Sub-Region

The Kenow Fire devastated the forests in most of this Sub-Region. Parks Canada has a long-term recovery plan for this area. Check with Parks Canada regarding trail closures. This Sub-Region encompasses the western section of Waterton Lakes National Park, and is centred on the 36-km Tamarack Trail which prior to the 2017 fire, led hikers through some incredible backcountry from the Akamina Parkway to Red Rock Canyon. In addition to the promise of outstanding scenery, the trail passed close to several fine lakes, including Rowe, Lineham, Lone, Twin, Lost, and Goat. Red Rock Canyon is the northern terminus of the Tamarack Trail, as well as the Blakiston Creek access to Twin Lakes. Cameron Lake, at the western end of the Akamina Parkway, is popular with anglers throughout the summer and serves as a starting point for short hikes to Akamina and Summit Lakes. After crossing Akamina Pass into British Columbia, prospective anglers can hike to Wall or Forum Lake (see Flathead Region). Check with BC Parks regarding trails in the Akamina-Kishenina Provincial Park.

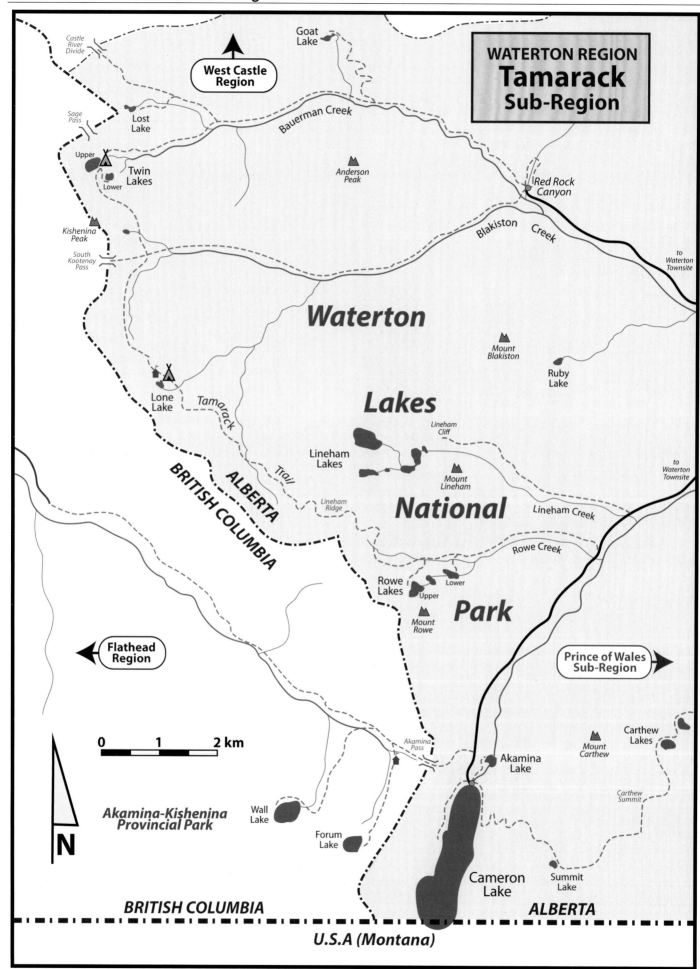

WATERTON REGION
Tamarack
Sub-Region

Castle River Divide

Goat Lake

West Castle Region

Sage Pass

Lost Lake

Bauerman Creek

Upper

Twin Lakes

Lower

Anderson Peak

Red Rock Canyon

Kishenina Peak

Blakiston Creek

South Kootenay Pass

to Waterton Townsite

Waterton

Mount Blakiston

Ruby Lake

Lone Lake

Tamarack

Trail

Lakes

Lineham Cliff

Lineham Lakes

Mount Lineham

to Waterton Townsite

National

Lineham Ridge

Lineham Creek

BRITISH COLUMBIA

ALBERTA

Rowe Creek

Rowe Lakes

Lower

Upper

Park

Mount Rowe

Flathead Region

Prince of Wales Sub-Region

Carthew Lakes

Mount Carthew

Akamina Pass

Akamina Lake

Carthew Summit

0   1   2 km

Akamina-Kishenina
Provincial Park

Wall Lake

Forum Lake

Cameron Lake

Summit Lake

N

BRITISH COLUMBIA

ALBERTA

U.S.A (Montana)

Cameron Lake (NP)

49°00'28"N 114°03'00"W
Rainbow trout to 50 cm (1.5 kg)
Brook trout to 50 cm (1.5 kg)

Cameron Lake is set in a large subalpine basin, 15 km from Waterton Townsite along the Akamina Parkway, and is one of the more popular fishing spots in Waterton Park, especially in the early season. Both rainbow and brook trout are caught regularly, with most fish averaging 25–35 cm in length. Fishing from shore is usually not overly productive due to the size of the lake, although areas around the larger outlet creek and the many small inlet creeks hold fish. Fortunately for perpetually shore-bound anglers, boat rentals are available. Trolling a fly or lure slowly behind a rowboat generally works well and requires little skill on angler's part. Take note that even though the fishing season at Cameron Lake technically opens on the long weekend in May, the lake itself can be often ice-bound well into June.

Cameron Lake (Pre-Kenow Fire)

Cameron Lake Valley (post-Kenow Fire)

Akamina Lake (aka Little Cameron Lake) (NP)

49°01'24"N 114°02'23"W
Rainbow trout to 30 cm
Brook trout to 30 cm

Pretty Akamina Lake sits in a marshy opening in the midst of heavy forest half a kilometre downstream from Cameron Lake. The lake can be reached by a half-kilometre trail that begins in the Cameron Lake parking area. Fishing of any kind is difficult in Akamina Lake, as Cameron Creek, which forms both the inlet and outlet stream must be forded to reach fish-holding waters. From the edge of the lake, shallows extend far out from shore, making long casts a necessity.

Akamina Lake (Pre-Kenow Fire)

Cameron Creek (NP)

Rainbow trout to 25 cm
Brook trout to 25 cm

Cameron Creek, which parallels the Akamina Parkway, flows for approximately 16 km from the outlet of Cameron Lake to Upper Waterton Lake. Reasonably accessible from the highway, the many pools along Cameron Creek's tumbling route hold small rainbow and brook trout. Take extreme caution if you are planning to fish any of Cameron Creek's canyons.

Cameron Falls on Cameron Creek at Waterton Townsite

Summit Lake (NP)

49°00'26"N 114°01'30"W
Status: Devoid of fish

Tiny Summit Lake, situated 4 km by trail from Cameron Lake on the Carthew Trail, was at one time stocked with cutthroat trout. However, the trout failed to take hold, likely due to winterkill.

Summit Lake (pre-Kenow Fire)

Parks Canada photo

15

Rowe Lakes (NP)
■ Upper Rowe 49°03'04"N 114°03'33"W
□ Lower Rowe 49°03'15"N 114°03'03"W
Brook trout to 30 cm (Lower Lake only)
These three small lakes nestled on the flank of Mt. Rowe all contained populations of brook trout at one time. However, reports indicate that the two Upper Lakes are devoid of fish, and the Lower Lake may contain a very limited population of small brook trout. Lower Rowe Lake, 4 km by trail from the Akamina Highway, has sparse vegetation around its shoreline while the Upper Lakes are set in an alpine basin reached via a steep 1 km spur trail from the Rowe Meadow, a total distance of 6.5 km from the trailhead.

Rowe Lakes (Pre-Kenow Fire)

Lone Lake (NP)
49°05'19"N 114°07'53"W
Cutthroat trout to 35 cm
Diminutive Lone Lake is situated close to the midway point on the Tamarack Trail, in the heart of the area hit by the 2017 Kenow Fire. Lone Lake holds plenty of small cutthroat in its emerald green waters. Most of the fish average 25–30 cm in length, and are generally very eager to take a fly. Except for a break around the area of the outlet stream, the lake is encircled by forest and requires reasonable roll-casting abilities from those fly fishing.

Lone Lake (pre-Kenow Fire)

Lineham Lakes (NP) (Known individually as Lineham North, Lineham South, Lineham; also known as individually as Water Cugel, Hourglass, Ptarmigan, Channel, Larch)
Lineham North: 49°04'37"N 114°04'12"W
Cutthroat trout to 50 cm (1.5 kg)
Trail access to the magnificent Lineham Basin, which holds the Lineham Lakes, is extremely hazardous, at one point requiring the hiker to negotiate a narrow ledge across the top of a 100 m-high cliff. Anglers using this route must register out with the warden service. For those unwilling to risk their life on the cliff, an alternate route exists which leads from Lineham Ridge on the Tamarack Trail down a steep, ill-defined trail into Lineham Basin. This route is very arduous, and also requires registering with the warden service. Those who do make it to Lineham Lakes are rewarded with some of the best backcountry fishing in Waterton Park, with all of the lakes holding plenty of cutthroat trout in the 25–35 cm range. Adequate fly casting room is available around all of the lakes. Due to their high elevation and sheltered location, the Lineham Lakes are seldom ice-free until mid-July. Accordingly, spawning often occurs into late-July.

Lineham Lakes basin from Lineham Ridge

Lineham South

▢ Twin Lakes (NP)

Upper Lake: 49°08'04"N 114°09'27"W

Lower Lake 49°07'56"N 114°09'06"W

Brook trout to 35 cm

Rainbow trout to 40 cm (Upper Lake only)

These two small lakes, situated 11 km by trail from Red Rock Canyon, were, prior to the Kenow Fire, very popular with backpackers, many working their way along the Tamarack Trail. Both lakes contain brook trout, with the Upper Lake also reported to be still holding a few rainbow. Lower Twin Lake serves as an ideal training ground for novice fly fishers, as it has plenty of small (15–25 cm) brook trout eager to bite. Fly casting room is available around much of the shore, and short casts of only 5–10 m are usually all that is required to reach the fish. The fish in Upper Twin Lake are somewhat larger and are usually a little more difficult to catch. Fly and lure will both work effectively in either lake.

Upper Twin Lake

Lower Twin Lake

▢ Lost Lake (NP)

49°08'50"N 114°08'43"W

Status: Doubtful

Tiny Lost Lake is located 2 km by trail from the Snowshoe Fire Road (a misnomer, as the Fire Road is itself a 10 km trail from Red Rock Canyon). Lost Lake was been stocked in the past with cutthroat, brook and rainbow trout, all of which, according to Park records, failed to reproduce. For those eternal optimists wishing to test the waters of Lost Lake, be forewarned that fishing will be a difficult proposition as the lake is completely surrounded by very thick brush.

▲ Goat Lake (NP)

49°09'47"N 114°05'27"W

Cutthroat trout to 35 cm

The jade-green waters of Goat Lake are set in a splendid hanging valley 7 km by trail from Red Rock Canyon. The lake hold hordes of small cutthroat trout that are eager to bite. The crystal-clear waters will allow the angler to see fish far out in the lake, particularly near the outlet where the lake is shallower. Casting ahead of cruising trout with a lure or fly is your best bet. If the fish are beyond your casting range, try the little pond just below Goat's outlet. It usually holds a few fish, although they tend to be spooky.

Goat Lake

▢ Ruby Lake (NP)

49°05'34"N 114°01'10"W

Status: Doubtful

Ruby Lake is nestled high in a basin beneath the east face of Mt. Blakiston and is seldom visited and seldom fished. A topographic map is recommended, as only ill-defined game trails lead steeply for 5 km up the north side of Ruby Creek to Ruby Lake. Although it was stocked in the past with rainbow trout, reports indicate that few, if any, trout exist in the lake today.

Ruby Lake

⊗ Blakiston Creek, Bauerman Creek (NP)

Status: Closed to angling

Both Blakiston Creek and its major tributary, Bauerman Creek, are currently closed to angling.

Mountain View Sub-Region

This Sub-Region literally sits in the evening shadow of the Rocky Mountains, and dramatic vistas are present at every turn. From Waterton Lakes National Park, the primary access to fishable waters is via Highways 6 (to Pincher Creek and Chief Mountain Border Crossing), Highway 5 (to Cardston) and Highway 800 (to Hill Spring). There are some excellent rainbow trout lakes in the Sub-Region, including Police Outpost and Payne lakes. For those boating, be aware of strong west winds that regularly whip across the open prairie. The Belly and Waterton rivers also provide fine angling opportunities, particularly in the fall.

⊗ **Belly River (NP)**
Status: Closed to angling
◼ **Belly River (AB)**
Rainbow trout to 40 cm
Whitefish to 40 cm
Cutthroat trout to 40 cm
Brown trout to 55 cm (1.5 kg)
Bull trout to 70 cm (4.0 kg)
The Belly River enters the extreme southwest corner of Waterton Lakes National Park and flows north and east, eventually joining the Waterton River. Within Waterton Lakes National Park, the Belly River is closed to angling. Outside the National Park, the Belly River offers some excellent stream fishing in deep pools holding a variety of trout. To the north, outside the National Park boundary, the river can be accessed from Highways 5 and 800. Historically, the Belly River and its tributaries provided outstanding angling for huge bull trout. The over-harvesting of bull trout eventually took its toll, and their numbers began a dramatic decline. In recent years, with the protection of the bull trout (all bull trout caught in Alberta must be released), numbers have begun to improve significantly. The Belly holds a variety of trout, with rainbow trout or whitefish in the 20–35 cm range the most likely catch. However, don't be surprised if you hook into a big bull in one of the deeper pools. As one fishes further downstream, the likelihood of catching brown trout increases, with a few pike in the river as well.

Belly River

■ **Giant's Mirror (NP)**
49°03'07"N 113°41'09"W
Status: Devoid of fish
The Giant's Mirror is a small pond located a short distance north of Highway 6 as it re-enters Waterton Lakes National Park from the Blood Indian Reserve. The outlet dam has been breached and the Giant's Mirror has dried up to the point of no longer being able to hold fish. The few small ponds between the Belly River and the Giant's Mirror site may hold a few rainbow or brook trout.

▲ **Police Outpost Lake (aka Police Lake, Outpost Lake) (AB)**
49°00'41"N 113°27'24"W
Rainbow trout to 55 cm (2.0 kg)
Police Outpost Lake and its lovely campground are located in a provincial park approximately 18 km southeast of Mountain View. The lake is quite shallow and is prone to winterkill on occasion. Weed growth is rampant in the lake by mid-summer, and it is only the centre of the lake that is free of weeds. Although it is possible to fish from shore from numerous locations, a boat will significantly increase the angling quality. Bait, lures and flies are all effective at Police Outpost Lake. Chironomid fishing with a strike indicator tends to be the most productive, especially in the early season. Hard-fighting rainbow trout ranging from 30 to 40 cm in length will be the normal catch. The fish grow rapidly due to the abundant feed, and if they survive a winter or two, they can easily top the 2 kg mark.

Police Outpost Lake

Larry Prowse with Police Outpost rainbow trout

■ **Lee Creek (AB)**
Rainbow trout to 35 cm
Cutthroat trout to 35 cm
Whitefish to 35 cm
Northern pike to 60 cm (3.0 kg)
Lee Creek is a tributary of the St. Mary River and is accessible from a number of gravel roads southeast of Mountain View. The creek holds rainbow and cutthroat trout in small sizes, with few larger than 30 cm in length. The odd lunker pike can also be caught.

☐ **Tough Creek (AB)**
Rainbow trout to 35 cm
Cutthroat trout to 35 cm
Whitefish to 35 cm
Northern pike to 60 cm (3.0 kg)
Tough Creek is a tributary of Lee Creek, is of similar character and holds the same variety of fish as Lee. Access is from gravel roads southeast of Mountain View.

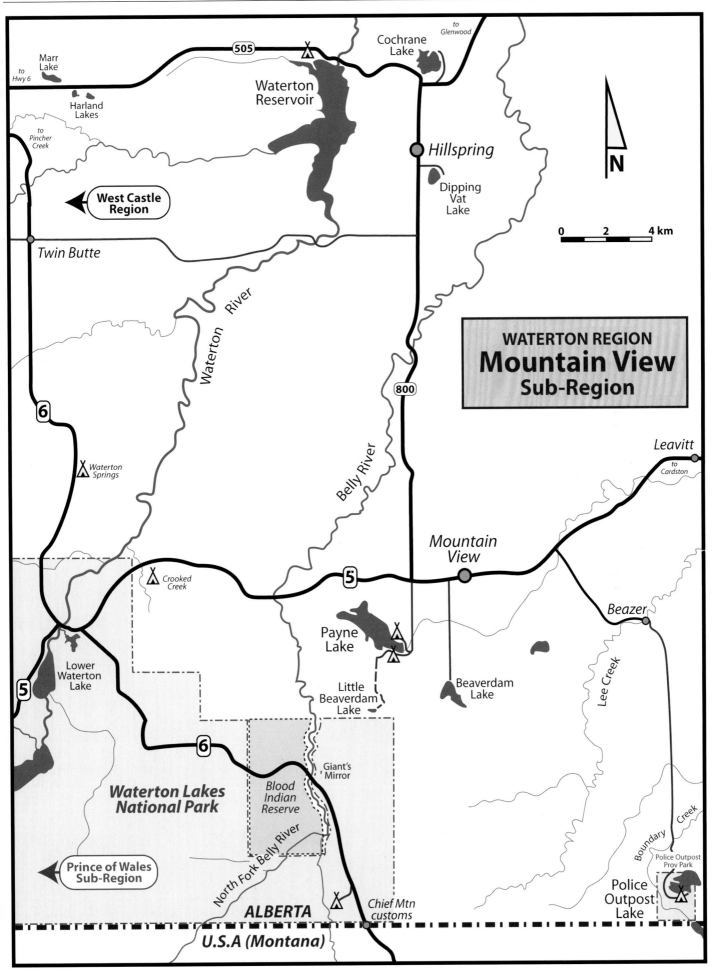

☐ **Boundary Creek (AB)**
Northern pike to 60 cm (3.0 kg)
Boundary Creek crosses into Alberta from Montana in Police Outpost Provincial Park, then does a short 15 km loop before recrossing the border back into Montana. Fishing in Boundary Creek is marginal at best, with northern pike found in some of the slower sections.

"Put-and-Take" Lakes

The Fisheries Society of BC and Alberta Environment and Parks both have hatchery facilities and extensive fish stocking programs to keep many lakes and streams populated with trout and other species. Many lakes that are stocked on a regular basis are known as "put-and-take", in which fish are stocked, or "put", into lakes and then the fish are caught by anglers, or "taken." These put-and-take lakes actually fall into two broad categories. In lakes where food is adequate and there is a good chance the fish will survive the winters, small fish are stocked and allowed to grow to catchable size. These are called "put-grow-and-take" fisheries. In other lakes and ponds, where fish cannot survive the winter because of inadequate oxygen (winterkill) or other factors, larger fish are stocked. These waters in which catchable trout are planted are referred to as "put-and-take" fisheries.

Zach and Everett Lowe with a nice "take" from Payne Lake

🅰 **Payne Lake (aka Paine Lake, Mami Lake) (AB)**
49°06'42"N 113°39'19"W
Rainbow trout to 55 cm (2.0 kg)
This large reservoir, a classic "put-grow-and take" lake, is the most popular fishing spot in the Mountain View area. The two campgrounds at the lake are active during spring, summer and fall. Payne Lake is very shallow and has lots of feed, making for ideal trout growing conditions. Rainbow trout are stocked annually in large numbers, and despite the heavy fishing pressure, fish are still plentiful in the fall. Rainbow trout caught in Payne Lake will average 25–35 cm in length, with larger ones taken regularly. Bait fishing from shore is very popular and is generally successful. Fishing from a boat and simply trolling a lure or fly is also very effective at Payne Lake.

Payne Lake

■ **Little Beaverdam Lake (AB)**
49°04'46"N 113°39'20"W
Brook trout to 35 cm
Little Beaverdam Lake is located approximately 2 km due south of the main campground at Payne Lake. Drive past the Payne Lake boat launch and continue on the gravel road to the T-intersection at a large house, where you turn left. A rough, pot-holed road leads to within half a kilometre of Little Beaverdam Lake. Although the semblance of a road does lead up a steep hill to the lake, it has been closed to motorized vehicles to prevent further erosion. Little Beaverdam Lake is man-made, not beaver-made, and serves as a watering hole for range cattle. There is a reproducing population of brook trout in the lake, and most brookies caught will be in the 20–30 cm range. There are numerous locations to fish from around the entire lake.

Little Beaverdam Lake

☐ **Beaverdam Lake (AB)**
49°05'13"N 113°36'31"W
Brook trout to 35 cm
Beaverdam Lake is a large, shallow reservoir situated 5 km south of Mountain View. Access to much of the shoreline is limited by private property. Fishing is generally poor, although there are reportedly still some brook trout in the lake.

Beaverdam Lake

◻ Waterton River (AB) (Downstream from National Park boundary)
Rainbow trout to 55 cm (1.5 kg)
Brown trout to 60 cm (2.5 kg)
Cutthroat trout to 50 cm
Whitefish to 45 cm
Bull trout to 75 cm (5.0 kg)
Northern pike to 70 cm (4.0 kg)
After leaving Waterton Lakes National Park, the Waterton River flows northeast to Waterton Reservoir, and beyond that joins the Belly River. Between the park boundary and the reservoir, the Waterton River offers good fishing for a variety of trout. Rainbow trout predominate, although brown trout are also found in good numbers. Trout caught in the river will average 25–35 cm in length. Some very nice browns are caught each year downstream from the reservoir. Pike are also in the river below the reservoir. The Waterton River is crossed by Highway 5/6 at the park boundary and by a number of secondary roads farther downstream. The fall, when water levels are at their lowest, is the most popular time of year to fish the river.

Waterton River

Nathan Bond with Waterton River rainbow

Vic Bergman photo

◻ Cottonwood Creek (AB)
Rainbow trout to 30 cm
Brown trout to 30 cm
This small tributary of the Waterton River flows south from the foothills, joining the main river near the park boundary. Cottonwood Creek is crossed by Highway 5 approximately 4 km north of the park boundary. Most of the creek flows through private property, although there are a few places where it can be accessed. Small rainbow and brown trout in the 15-25 cm range are the average catch, with browns more likely in the lower section and rainbows in the upper reaches.

◻ Waterton Reservoir (AB)
49°18'08"N 113°40'43"W
Brown trout to 60 cm (2.5 kg)
Rainbow trout to 55 cm (1.5 kg)
Lake trout to 65 cm (4.0 kg)
Whitefish to 50 cm (1.5 kg)
Northern pike to 80 cm (6.0 kg)
The Waterton Reservoir, located 5 km northwest of Hill Spring, is very much an irrigation reservoir. Water levels are dictated by agricultural water needs. As such, water levels in the reservoir fluctuate wildly during the year, making it very unstable as a fishery. There are a variety of fish in the reservoir, but the quality of angling is not particularly good. Depending on the time of year, brown, rainbow or even the odd lake trout can be taken from the reservoir. Pike and whitefish are also present.

Waterton Reservoir

◻ Dipping Vat Lake (AB)
49°17'02"N 113°36'52"W
Status: Doubtful
Dipping Vat Lake was not so long ago renowned for its rainbow trout fishery. With large amounts of feed, the trout grew rapidly to large sizes. However, significant water level issues exist and massive algae blooms now occur annually. The fish population has suffered accordingly. Few, if any, rainbow trout remain in the lake.

◻ Cochrane Lake (AB)
49°19'41"N 113°36'58"W
Northern pike to 60 cm (3.0 kg)
Cochrane Lake is a large irrigation reservoir located 2 km north of the community of Hill Spring. Northern pike are the only game fish that are present in substantial numbers. Pike can be take from shore in the spring, soon after ice out.

Cochrane Lake

◼ Marr Lake (AB)
49°19'18"N 113°51'16"W
◼ Harland Lakes (AB)
49°19'03"N 113°49'47"W
Status: Devoid of fish
These small ponds alongside Highway 565 do not hold any fish.

FLATHEAD REGION

The mighty Flathead River flows south from headwaters in the upper Flathead Valley in British Columbia to Flathead Lake in Montana. All of the fishing opportunities in this Region are part of the Flathead River watershed. The main access to the Region is via logging roads from Highway 3 in British Columbia. River and stream fishing attract most anglers' attention, although there are some fine alpine lakes in the region. However, the Region is much more suited to explorers and those who want to get away from civilization, as many of the lakes have little or no defined trails. Akamina-Kishinena Provincial Park, in the southeast corner of the Region and bordering on Waterton Lakes National Park, merits description on its own. The rest of the waters are spread throughout the Flathead Valley proper. The Kenow Fire of 2017 destroyed the forests in much of the upper Akamina and Kishenina watersheds.

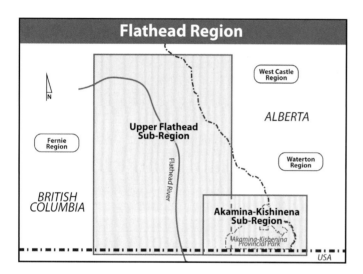

Akamina-Kishinena Sub-Region

This Sub-Region's boundaries conform to those of Akamina-Kishinena Provincial Park in the extreme southeastern corner of British Columbia. Much of the park is beyond the reach of unmotivated anglers, requiring a long (120+ km) drive on rough gravel and dirt roads from Morrissey on Highway 3 just to reach the park. Once at the park, lakes including Polar and Ledge are protected by some very difficult terrain and an absence of trails. Wall and Forum Lake are the park's most visited locations, as access is over shorter trails from paved roads in Waterton Lakes National Park. The Kenow Fire of 2017 did tremendous damage to the Provincial Park and some access trails still may not be fit for travel.

◢ Wall Lake (BC)
49°00'53"N 114°05'32"W
Cutthroat trout to 45 cm
Wall Lake is situated on the south side of the Akamina Valley beneath a spectacular headwall. It offers some fine cutthroat trout fishing and is a popular destination for anglers from nearby Waterton Lakes National Park. Fish can be taken from shoreline locations all around the lake, with the area near the main inlet creek on the west side always being productive. Most fish taken from Wall Lake are 25-30 cm in length. A well-maintained 5 km

trail leads from the Akamina Pass trailhead on the Akamina Parkway in Waterton Park to Wall Lake. Much of the forest along the access trail was burned in the Kenow Fire of 2017.

Wall Lake

◢ Forum Lake (BC)
49°00'37"N 114°04'30"W
Cutthroat trout to 50 cm (1.5 kg)
Forum Lake is set in a rocky amphitheatre at the head of Akamina Creek and is overlooked by most hikers who are intent on Wall Lake, despite the promise of good cutthroat trout fishing in Forum. Access is via a steep 4 km trail that begins at the Akamina Pass trailhead in Waterton Lakes National Park, the same trailhead as Wall Lake. Turn left (south) at the junction where the warden cabin used to be prior to the Kenow Fire. Hard-fighting cutthroat trout averaging 30–40 cm can be taken from Forum, with the late season (August and September) much more productive than the early season. Ice-out is slow on Forum due to its sheltered location, and ice floes are on the lake well into summer. Lake levels fluctuate during the year, continually dropping to a low point in the late fall.

Forum Lake

Forum Lake cutthroat

▢ Akamina Creek (BC)
Cutthroat trout to 35 cm
Bull trout to 70 cm (4.0 kg)
Flowing west from Akamina Pass at the Alberta-BC border, Akamina Creek joins Kishinena Creek as a major tributary. Small cutthroat trout are plentiful in the creek's pools, with very large bull trout present as well in the fall. An abandoned road leads from Akamina Pass and parallels Akamina Creek downstream for its entire length.

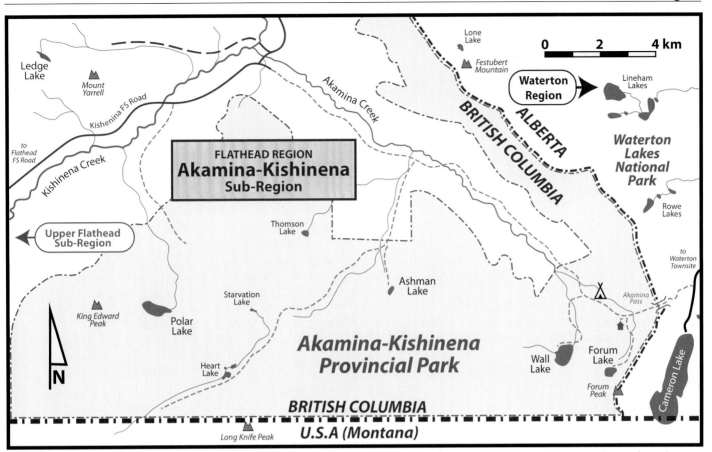

Kishinena Creek (BC)

Cutthroat trout to 50 cm
Bull trout to 80 cm (6.0 kg)
Whitefish to 35 cm

A tributary to the Flathead River, Kishinena Creek receives some enormous bull trout each year during the fall spawning season. Many of these monsters have made it all the way from Flathead Lake in Montana. In years past, the large bull trout were fished unmercifully, especially below waterfalls where they congregated, and their numbers subsequently declined dramatically. New regulations on the Flathead River and its tributaries were put in place to protect the bull trout. Nice cutthroat trout in the 25–35 cm range can be taken throughout the summer from Kishinena Creek's numerous pools and whitefish become plentiful in the fall.

Kishinena Creek

Ashman Lake (BC)

49°01'49"N 114°09'28"W
Cutthroat trout to 30 cm

Tiny Ashman Lake is set in the heart of prime grizzly bear habitat, just off appropriately named Grizzly Gulch and receives few visitors each year. An 8 km hike leads to Ashman from logging roads at the confluence of Akamina and Kishinena creeks. The lake holds plenty of cutthroat trout, but most are very stunted, with large heads and small bodies, due to the large number of fish and limited food supply. A large cutthroat from Ashman will seldom exceed 25 cm. Fly casting room is available around most of the lake. Be sure to keep an eye on the surrounding terrain for four-legged visitors.

Ashman Lake

❓ Thomson Lake (BC)

49°02'38"N 114°11'24"W
Status: Unknown

Tiny Thomson Lake, at the head of See Creek, has no access trails and is strictly for explorers. The lake has never been stocked, although cutthroat trout may have made their way in from See Creek. Have a look if you have the time and band-aids to spare.

☐ Starvation Lake (BC)

49°01'32"N 114°12'38"W

Cutthroat trout to 40 cm

This diminutive tarn at the head of Starvation Creek is reached by a 15 km trail from Akamina Creek through Grizzly Gulch and over an unnamed pass. Other than hunting parties that work this area in the fall, few humans make their way into Starvation Lake. The lake holds cutthroat trout in the 20–30 cm range. Like Grizzly Gulch, its companion valley to the east, the Starvation Creek valley holds a healthy population of grizzly bears. Obviously, they're not the ones starving.

☐ Heart Lake (BC)

49°00'42"N 114°13'04"W

Cutthroat trout to 35 cm

Situated on Starvation Creek, petite Heart Lake and its two accompanying ponds hold small cutthroat trout. Access is very long and difficult, either from the west via a trail along Starvation Creek from logging roads on the lower Kishinena, or from the east via the Grizzly Gulch trail. In either case, expect plenty of solitude. Winter avalanches occasionally rumble down onto Heart Lake, prolonging ice-out into the early summer.

☐ Polar Lake (aka Beavertail Lake) (BC)

49°01'34"N 114°14'53"W

Status: Unknown

Cutthroat trout

Polar Lake is set high on a ledge on Kishinena Ridge and is accessible to only the most determined hikers. No formal trails lead into Polar, and the final two kilometres are guarded by a very steep headwall. It was stocked in the past with cutthroat trout, but out-of-date reports indicated poor fishing.

Polar Lake

Frank Slide Centre photo

☐ Ledge Lake (BC)

49°07'22"N 114°14'51"W

Status: Unknown

Cutthroat trout

Ledge Lake is in a location similar to but even more dramatic than Polar Lake and is virtually inaccessible to anglers. A sheer cliff protects Ledge Lake from the most direct line of ascent, and any would-be visitors will have to do an inordinate amount of bushwhacking and scrambling to reach this remote lake. As would be expected, fishing reports on Ledge Lake are non-existent. Stocked with cutthroat trout, this lake is for explorers only.

Upper Flathead Sub-Region

Great cutthroat and bull trout fishing typify the Flathead River and its tributary streams. Individual lakes are scattered at tributary headwaters along the entire length of the valley, and few if any, have maintained access trails. Procter Lake and Frozen Lake are two of the few lakes that are accessible to vehicles. Most anglers confine themselves to the Flathead River and the more easily reached streams. Intrepid hikers and horse parties are the only ones who frequent the Flathead's pristine backcountry. All visitors should note that the Flathead Valley is prime grizzly bear habitat and they should take the appropriate precautions.

▲ Flathead River (BC)

Cutthroat trout to 50 cm (1.5 kg)

Bull trout to 1 m (10.0 kg)

Whitefish to 40 cm

The Flathead River flows for 65 km in British Columbia before crossing the border into neighbouring Montana and provides some outstanding river fishing opportunities. For virtually all of its length in B.C., the Flathead is close to logging access roads. Typical of rivers in the Rockies, the Flathead experiences major runoff in mid-June, followed by a gradual clearing of the waters. By mid-summer, the Flathead is usually crystal-clear, and fishing picks up and continues to improve into the fall. The river is characterized by long stretches of fast water with the occasional nice pool. Cutthroat trout in the 25–35 cm range are plentiful and are the normal catch in the river, although big bull trout are making a comeback, thanks to protective legislation. At many locations in the valley, beaver dam complexes are connected to the main river, and most hold a few trout.

Chad Smith photo

Chad Smith with Flathead River cutthroat

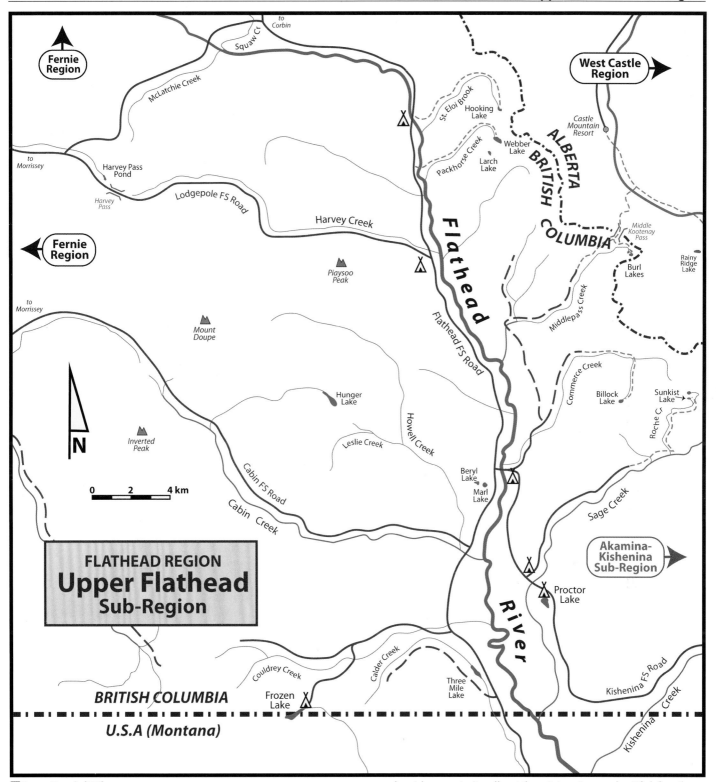

◻ Sage Creek (BC)

Cutthroat trout to 40 cm
Bull trout to 75 cm (6.0 kg)
Whitefish to 35 cm

Sage Creek is one of the major tributaries of the upper Flathead River, beginning high in the Clark Range and flowing south to join the Flathead just south of the Canada-US boundary. Logging roads allow for reasonable access to most of Sage Creek, although a bit of bushwhacking may be required to reach the actual stream bed. The campsite at the Kishinena Forest Service Road bridge over Sage Creek is popular, and fishing pressure is accordingly high, especially downstream from the campground, where the creek widens out. Small cutthroat trout are plentiful for those who get away from the most accessible points.

◻ Harvey Creek, Squaw Creek, McLatchie Creek, St. Eloi Brook, Packhorse Creek, Middlepass Creek, Commerce Creek, Howell Creek, Cabin Creek, Couldrey Creek (BC)

Cutthroat trout to 30 cm
Bull trout to 35 cm
Whitefish to 30 cm

These tributaries of the Flathead River generally hold cutthroat trout in small sizes. Most of the creeks are in valleys that have been logged in the past or are currently being logged, and are at least in some manner accessible. Reaching the fishable waters may require some walking. The confluence of the smaller creeks with the Flathead River is usually a good fish-holding spot, especially when the tributaries are clearer than the main river.

☐ Procter Lake (BC)
49°03'19"N 114°26'46"W
Cutthroat trout to 40 cm

Procter Lake is located on a flat, forested bench above Sage Creek, two kilometres south of the Kishinena Forest Service Road crossing of Sage Creek. A rough, half-kilometre 4WD road leads off the main road into a primitive campsite at the north end of Procter Lake. The lake is very shallow and reeds circle the entire lake, making fishing from shore a difficult proposition. For those with a boat or float tube, the best fishing can be found around the island on the south side of the lake. The lake's few deep holes are in the vicinity of the island, and cutthroat trout in the 20–30 cm can be caught, although the numbers are somewhat limited. Patient anglers will be able to take cruising fish from the shallower waters as well.

Procter Lake

■ Marl Lake (BC)
49°07'27"N 114°30'53"W
■ Beryl Lake (BC)
49°07'29"N 114°31'11"W
Status: Devoid of fish

These two shallow lakes are located approximately one kilometre west of the junction of the Flathead and Kishinena Forest Service roads. They have never been stocked and contain no fish.

☐ Three Mile Lake (BC)
49°01'25"N 114°31'19"W
Cutthroat trout to 40 cm

Three Mile Lake is located, appropriately enough, approximately three miles north of the B.C.-Montana border crossing at Flathead. Three Mile Lake has been stocked in the past with cutthroat trout, which now reproduce naturally. The lake is very shallow, and fishing where Calder Creek enters and exits Three Mile Lake can be productive. Access is difficult, with the 1 km bushwhack up Calder Creek being the best option.

☐ Frozen Lake (BC)
49°00'09"N 114°40'13"W
Cutthroat trout to 55 cm (1.5 kg)
Bull trout to 60 cm (3.0 kg)

A long, long drive of well over 100 km on gravel and dirt roads from Highway 3 at Morrissey leads to Frozen Lake, which straddles the Canada-U.S. border. On the Canadian side, the road reaches the lake and the small Forest Service recreation site. From the American side of the border, there is trail access only. Although cutthroat trout upwards of 50 cm in length are present, you are more likely to hook into one of the lake's plentiful bull trout, which average 40–50 cm in length. The lake is long and narrow and forest-bound. Angling from shore can be productive from many locations for those using lures or bait.

Frozen Lake

☐ Hunger Lake (BC)
49°10'13"N 114°38'42"W
Status: Doubtful

This isolated lake, set in the Leslie Creek drainage, receives few visitors each year as there are no formal access trails. Hunger Lake is the catchment basin for Leslie Creek and has no outlet. As such, there are major fluctuations in the lake level during the year. The lake likely drains underground, as Leslie Creek reappears a kilometre below the lake. The lake has not been stocked, and it is doubtful if it contains any trout.

☐ Sunkist Lake (BC)
49°09'49"N 114°20'09"W
Cutthroat trout to 30 cm

This tiny lake is located beneath Sunkist Mountain, at the head of a tributary of Roche Creek. Access is via a poor 8 km trail that begins from the Sage Creek Forest Service Road and ascends the Roche Creek drainage. How far you can travel up the Sage Creek FSR by vehicle can change from year to year, potentially making this hike an even longer one than anticipated. Water levels in Sunkist Lake are highest after spring runoff is complete, and then drop throughout the summer and fall. Cutthroat trout in the lake are small but plentiful, most in the 20–25 cm range. A forest fire from years past has denuded half the tree cover that surrounds the lake.

◬ Burl Lakes (aka Middlepass Lakes) (BC)

49°14'52"N 114°23'20"W

Cutthroat trout to 35 cm

The three Burl Lakes are situated in a stunning alpine basin below Rainy Ridge and the Continental Divide. The new Castle Provincial Park and motorized vehicle restrictions have added 8 km of road walk to the access. Once you have made your way (non-motorized) from Castle Mountain Resort to Middle Kootenay Pass, the route to the lakes from the pass is via an ill-defined 3 km trek over game trails. In the past, many anglers bypassed the Burl Lakes on their way to the "golden" waters of Rainy Ridge Lake, back over the border in Alberta. The Burl Lakes are definitely worth a visit in their own right. All three Burl Lakes hold stunted cutthroat trout in the 20–30 cm range, which can be taken from shore with ease. Fly fishing is the preferred method, although spin casting will also be effective. The upper lake is the largest and offers the most angling opportunities. The small, shallow middle lake holds a few trout that are easily spooked, while the rockbound lower lake allows for some fine sight fishing. A few informal backcountry campsites can be found in the stands of larch along the upper lake's west shore. A big plus in the fall is the innumerable huckleberry patches along the route in, the downside being the numerous bear that feed on said huckleberries.

Burl Lakes from Rainy Ridge

Upper Burl Lake

▪ Billock Lake (BC)

49°11'02"N 114°22'46"W

Cutthroat trout to 40 cm

Billock Lake is set in a scenic amphitheatre below massive Commerce Peak at the headwaters of Commerce Creek. Trail access begins on the Commerce Creek Forest Service Road. The trail is used by hunting parties annually and is decent in the lower valley, deteriorating as one begins the climb into Billock Lake basin. Fishing is reported to be good for cutthroat trout in the 25–35 cm range.

▪ Webber Lake (BC)

49°18'33"N 114°30'07"W

Cutthroat trout to 40 cm

Webber Lake is the larger of the two lakes in the upper Packhorse Creek watershed. Webber, and nearby Larch Lake, can be reached on trails that begin at a major ford on the Flathead River, approximately four kilometres below the bridged crossing of the river above St. Eloi Brook. The rockbound basin and dramatic cliff face along Webber's south side make for an unforgettable setting. The cutthroat trout that inhabit Webber average 30–35 cm in length, although larger ones are present.

▫ Larch Lake (BC)

49°18'08"N 114°30'32"W

Cutthroat trout to 35 cm

Located in a splendid larch-filled subalpine valley just south of the basin holding Webber Lake, tiny Larch Lake is stocked with cutthroat trout. Trout in the lake are not large, with most in the 20–25 cm range.

▪ Hooking Lake (BC)

49°19'33"N 114°30'01"W

Cutthroat trout to 40 cm

Hooking Lake is set in a forest fire–ravaged basin near the headwaters of St. Eloi Brook. Access is via abandoned seismic roads and horse trails from the Flathead River Forest Service Road, a distance of 10 km. The final pitch up into the lake is very steep. The lake itself has two deep, connected holes and fish can be taken from the area separating the shallower waters from the deep. Fish feed in the shallows, but are easily frightened. Cutthroat trout in Hooking Lake average 25–35 cm in length. Scree slopes make up the majority of the lakeshore, with a few stands of forest cover.

Curtis Hall photo

KOOCANUSA REGION

The Koocanusa Region is one of the most unique in all of the Canadian Rockies. Spring comes very early to this Region, as it is at the southern end of the Rockies and at a very low elevation. Snow is generally gone by March, and many of the lakes will be free of ice by late March or early April. The fish species available to the Region are also unique. Kokanee are found in great numbers in Lake Koocanusa and largemouth bass can be caught in many lakes. The Region's focal point is Lake Koocanusa and its source, the Kootenay River. Highway 3 provides east-west access and Highway 93 provides north-south access. The Region divides into four distinct Sub-Regions, all centred on small communities: Elko to the south and east; Jaffray in the middle; Wardner to the west; and Fort Steele to the north and west.

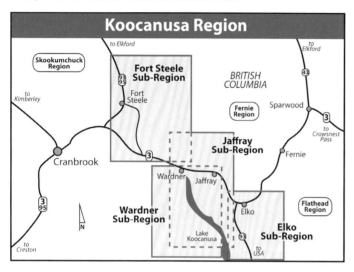

Elko Sub-Region

The small logging community of Elko on Highway 3 is the hub of this Sub-Region, which extends south along Highway 93 to Grasmere and the United States border at Roosville. The Elk River, flowing west to Kookanusa Lake, is fishable above and below major canyons around Elko. The Wigwam River, a major tributary to the Elk, is an outstanding catch-and-release cutthroat and bull trout fishery. Closer to Elko, Silver Spring Lakes provide some great fishing for large rainbow trout, and Burton Lake holds some fine brook trout. Near the small community of Grasmere, chunky rainbow trout thrive in both Loon and Edwards lakes.

▇ Elk River (Elko to Lake Kookanusa) (BC)
Cutthroat trout to 55 cm (1.5 kg)
Bull trout to 80 cm (6.0 kg)
Whitefish to 40 cm
Kokanee to 35 cm
Downstream from Elko, the Elk River drops into Phillipps Canyon, which is virtually impenetrable to all but the hard-core anglers. Whitewater raft companies regularly pass through the canyon in summertime with tour groups, but seldom stop to fish. Road access above the canyon is limited, and anglers will have to make a significant trek even before attempting the difficult climb down into the canyon. For those who do make it down to the Elk River, the fishing is excellent, as there is little or no fishing pressure. Cutthroat trout of 30–40 cm are the regular catch. Bull trout, whitefish and kokanee can also be caught, and there may

be the odd rainbow or brook trout as well. The canyon finally opens up as it nears the Highway 93 bridge, and it is a little more accessible, although it will still require walking upstream along the river amid heavy forest cover and a lot of high-water debris. Less than a kilometre below the Highway 93 bridge, the Elk River flows into Lake Koocanusa. Fishing can be good where the river enters the lake, but the lake level fluctuates massively during the year, and this will affect the quality of fishing. Fishing at the lake can be hit-or-miss – plenty of fish one day, and none a week later. Boating on Lake Koocanusa where the Elk River enters can be very dangerous due to floating and submerged debris.

Phillipps Canyon, Elk River

Curtis Hall photo

Elk River cutthroat trout

◮ Silver Spring Lakes (BC)
49°17'44"N 115°04'28"W
Rainbow trout to 55 cm (2.0 kg)
The Silver Spring Lakes are a series of lakes and ponds of various sizes that stretch for approximately 5 km down a narrow, cliff-walled side valley above the Elk River. A short, but steep, 0.5 km hike leads from a trailhead on the Elko-Morrissey Road to the first and largest Silver Spring Lake, a stunning blue-green

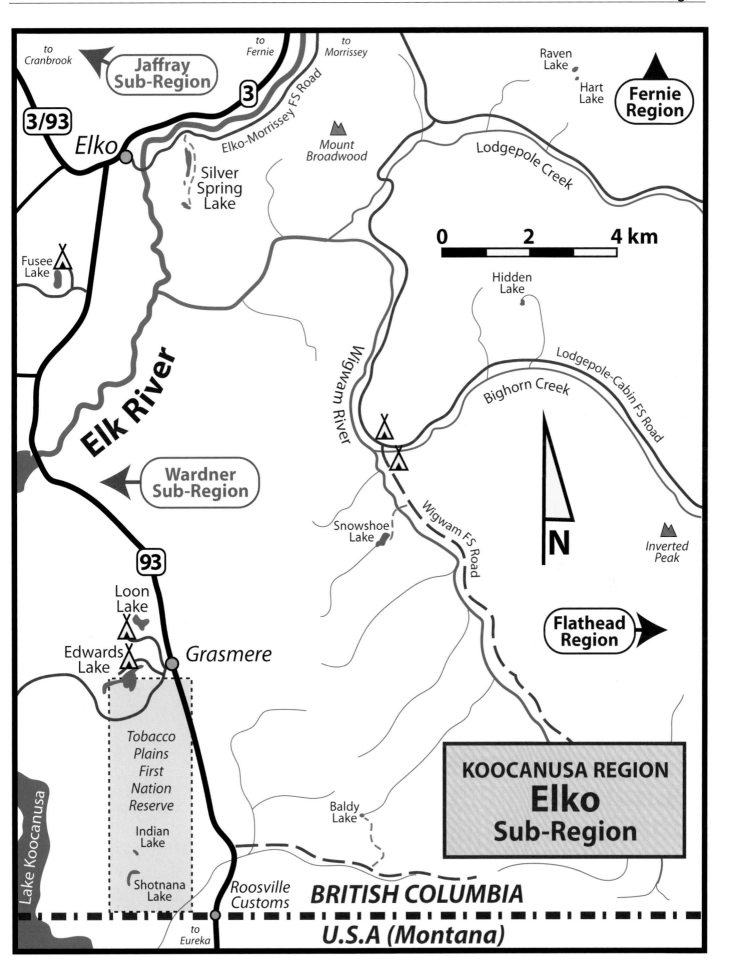

body of water. The rainbow trout in the first lake grow to good sizes, with the average being 30-40 cm in length. Fishing is very productive off of the scree slopes along the east shore, and at the shallows at the south end of the lake. The shallows can be especially tantalizing during low-light periods, when many of the larger fish move there to feed. A well-worn trail continues past the end of the first lake to the second and third Silver Spring Lakes. The second lake, half a kilometre beyond the first, is a shallow pond that does not hold any trout. Fifteen minutes of hiking past the second lake brings one to the third lake, a dark body of water with high cliffs on several sides. Forest cover and extended shallows make shore fishing difficult. One of the better options is to fish off of the 5m–high rock bluffs, where you can at least cast to fish-holding waters. The difficulty arises when you hook a big one and have to figure out how to land it. There are other ponds beyond the third lake, but none has been stocked.

Silver Springs Lakes (First Lake)

Silver Springs Lakes (Third Lake)

Burton Lake (BC)

49°19'01"N 115°08'57"W
Brook trout to 45 cm
Rainbow trout to 45 cm

Burton Lake is located just west of Elko, and is accessed by a gravel road off Highway 3. From the parking area, it's a steep walk down to the lakeshore. Casting room is at a premium due to forest cover and a series of cliffs. Burton's cheerful green waters are home to a population of brook and rainbow trout, most of which run in the 25-35 cm range. Lures and spinners are very effective at Burton.

Burton Lake

Wigwam River (BC)

Cutthroat trout to 50 cm (1.5 kg)
Bull trout to 70 cm (4.0 kg)
Whitefish to 40 cm

The Wigwam River is a major tributary to the lower Elk River and was one of the East Kootenay's first experiments with catch-and-release fishing. Catch-and-release has been an unqualified success on the Wigwam, with fish stocks as healthy as anywhere in the Rockies. The primary access to the Wigwam River is over lengthy logging roads from Morrissey at Highway 3. The upper reaches of the Wigwam Forest Service Road tend to vary between rough 2WD and 4WD in quality. Cutthroat trout in the Wigwam River are plentiful and generally range from 25–35 cm in length. Virtually every likely looking spot will have a trout lurking about. Large bull trout also make their way up the Wigwam River in summer from the Elk River to spawn. Many anglers plan fishing expeditions around their annual return.

Curtis Hall photo

Wigwam River

Curtis Hall photo

Wigwam River bull trout

■**Snowshoe Lake (BC)**
49°08'49"N 114°57'20"W
Cutthroat trout to 40 cm
Snowshoe Lake is hidden in a side valley off of the Wigwam River. Finding Snowshoe Lake is usually an angler's first problem. To reach the lake, one first must ford the Wigwam River, approximately 4 km above its confluence with Bighorn Creek. Once across the Wigwam, it's a matter of finding a rough trail that leads up to the lake. Normally, the outlet creek of a lake would be a good landmark, but Snowshoe's outlet flows underground and is of no help. One kilometre up from the Wigwam River, Snowshoe Lake is found amid its pleasant forest and meadow surroundings. The lake fills up after runoff in late spring, and then gradually drops in level over the summer to a low point in the fall. The cutthroat trout in Snowshoe Lake average 25–35 cm in length, and can be taken from most locations along the shore.

Snowshoe Lake

☐**Baldy Lake (aka Thomas Lake, Ted's Lake) (BC)**
49°03'52"N 114°58'45"W
Cutthroat trout to 35 cm
This tiny pond is located high in the Galton Range, at the head of an unnamed tributary of the Wigwam River. Although the lake is in the Wigwam River watershed, it is reached by a 5 km trail from roads in the Phillipps Creek drainage. Baldy Lake has been stocked in the past with cutthroat trout, which are reported to be present in small sizes and limited numbers.

Baldy Lake
Janice Strong photo

■**Lodgepole Creek, Bighorn Creek (aka Ram Creek) (BC)**
Cutthroat trout to 40 cm
Bull trout to 60 cm (3.0 kg)
Whitefish to 35 cm
These two main tributaries to the Wigwam River are easily accessed from Forest Service Roads that parallel the creeks for their entire length. Small cutthroat trout, in the 20-30 cm size range, are the normal catch.

☐ **Harvey Pass pond (BC)**
49°17'38"N 114°43'34"W
Cutthroat trout to 25 cm
This small lake, which drains westward into Lodgepole Creek, is located alongside the logging just west of Harvey Pass (the pass between Lodgepole and Harvey Creeks). Heavy brush surrounds the lake, and just finding an opening to make a cast is very difficult. The lake holds small cutthroat trout, few larger than 20 cm in length.

Harvey Pass pond

■**Hidden Lake (BC)**
49°14'23"N 114°52'19"W
Cutthroat trout to 40 cm
Located north of Bighorn Creek at the head of a steep, narrow valley below Overfold Mountain, Hidden Lake does not attract many anglers due to its very difficult access. The lake contains cutthroat trout that are small (20–30 cm) and easy to catch. There is heavy forest cover and lots of deadfall around the shoreline at Hidden Lake.

☐ **Raven Lake (BC)**
49°20'38"N 114°52'54"W
☐ **Hart Lake (BC)**
49°20'32"N 114°52'59"W
Cutthroat trout to 35 cm
These two tiny lakes, located less than kilometre from each other, are found in the Lodgepole Creek watershed. Both lakes are on a bench at the top of Flathead Ridge and can be reached by hiking reclaimed mining roads that traverse the length of the ridge. Cutthroat trout have been stocked in both lakes, with the size of most trout caught being in the 20–30 cm range.

Illegal introduction of non-native species

Two popular lakes in the East Kootenay are now closed to sport fishing because of the introduction of largemouth bass and yellow perch. Both Fusee Lake and New Lake (near Cranbrook) have been stocked illegally by a person or persons who a provincial fish biologist has described as being from "the low end of the gene pool." The stocked trout in the lakes cannot compete with the bass and perch and subsequently suffer drastic decline in numbers. The invasive fish also eat native amphibians and could introduce new parasites or diseases. Authorities have a "zero tolerance" policy for illegal introductions and the closing of the lakes is meant as a disincentive to further introductions. The lakes will be assessed and a plan will be developed to eradicate or suppress the perch and bass.

⊗ Fusee Lake (aka Fussee Lake) (BC)

49°14'36"N 115°09'42"W
Status: Closed to angling
Brook trout
Rainbow trout
Largemouth bass
Fusee Lake is a small, shallow lake off Highway 93 that was good for brook and rainbow trout. Illegal plantings of largemouth bass and yellow perch into Fusee have forced authorities to close the lake to angling.

◪ Loon Lake (BC)

49°06'52"N 115°06'23"W
Rainbow trout to 60 cm (2.5 kg)
Loon Lake is located on a wooded bench, approximately 2 km west of Highway 93 and the small community of Grasmere. A large forestry campground is at the lake. A boat is recommended for fishing, as the lake is fairly large, and the trout tend to stay in the deeper waters, other than late in the evening. The rainbow trout in Loon Lake are Blackwater Lake stock, which tend to do well when there is baitfish around. Loon Lake has red-sided shiners and the rainbow trout feed on them and grow rapidly. Trolling is the most popular technique on Loon Lake, although fly fishers who use a sinking line and a streamer will also do well. Loon Lake and its nearby counterpart, Edwards Lake, are generally ice-free by late-March, which is much sooner than most lakes in the Rockies.

Loon Lake   *Loon Lake rainbow trout*

▣ Edwards Lake (BC)

49°05'36"N 115°06'45"W
Rainbow trout to 60 cm (3.5 kg)
Edwards Lake is located south of Loon Lake, approximately 2 km west of Grasmere. Fishing from shore is possible at Edwards, particularly at the east end, where the lake narrows significantly. The rainbow trout in Edwards Lake grow quickly on the abundant feed, and trout caught from the lake average 25–40 cm in length, with some big, fat lunkers in the 2-3 kg weight class taken regularly. The lake is not very deep and is susceptible to winterkill on occasion. Fly fishing is great at Edwards, whether tossing a dry fly to rising trout or trolling a nymph through the deeper waters.

Edwards Lake

▣ Shotnana Lake

49°01'04"N 115°05'47"W
☐ Indian Lake
49°01'28"N 115°06'09"W
(Both lakes on Tobacco Plains First Nation Reserve)
Brook trout
The two lakes on the Tobacco Plains Reserve were stocked in the past with brook trout. Today, Shotnana Lake is little more than a dried-up slough. Permission is required to fish either lake.

Jaffray Sub-Region

The town of Jaffray, situated just south of Highway 3, is the main centre of human activity for this Sub-Region, which stretches east from the shores of Lake Kookanusa. Lake Koocanusa is the dominant physical feature of the area and has been increasing exponentially in terms of angling attention in recent years due to the popularity of its kokanee fishery. Many of the Sub-Region's lakes, including Surveyors, Baynes, Suzanne, Tie and Rosen, are unique in that they contain largemouth bass. Virtually all of the Sub-Region's lakes can be reached by vehicle on paved or gravel roads.

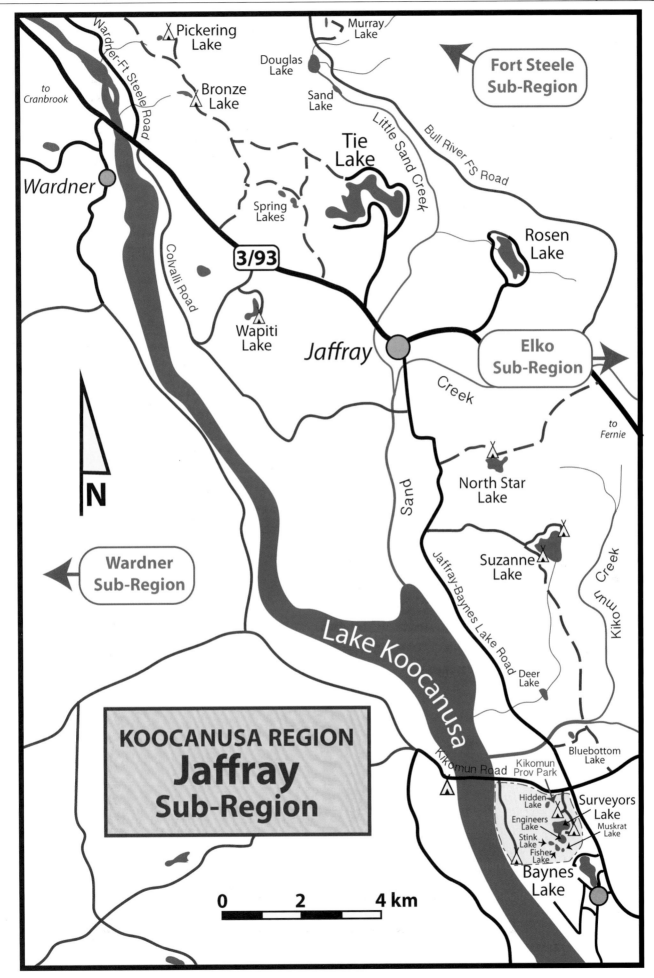

Fort Steele Sub-Region

Elko Sub-Region

Wardner Sub-Region

KOOCANUSA REGION
Jaffray
Sub-Region

Pickering Lake

Murray Lake

Douglas Lake

Bronze Lake

Sand Lake

Tie Lake

to Cranbrook

Wardner

Wardner-Ft Steele Road

Little Sand Creek

Bull River FS Road

Rosen Lake

Spring Lakes

Colvalli Road

3/93

Wapiti Lake

Jaffray

Creek

to Fernie

North Star Lake

Sand

N

Suzanne Lake

Kikomun Creek

Lake Koocanusa

Jaffray-Baynes Lake Road

Deer Lake

Bluebottom Lake

Kikomun Road

Kikomun Prov Park

Hidden Lake

Surveyors Lake

Engineers Lake

Muskrat Lake

Stink Lake

Fisher Lake

Baynes Lake

0   2   4 km

33

■ Lake Koocanusa (BC)

49°17'17"N 115°17'25"W
Kokanee to 40 cm
Bull trout to 80 cm (6.0 kg)
Cutthroat trout to 55 cm (2.0 kg)
Rainbow trout to 65 cm (3.0 kg)
Whitefish to 45 cm

Lake Koocanusa is the large man-made reservoir that extends for 150 km from the Libby Dam on the Kootenai (Kootenay) River in Montana to Wardner, BC, and Highway 3. The name Koocanusa is derived from "Koo" for Kootenay River, "can" for Canada, and "usa" for United States of America. The reservoir is subject to massive drawdowns, and by springtime the upper 10 km of the lake in some years can be little more than the Kootenay River meandering through mud flats. In June, runoff waters from snow melt fill the reservoir and the lake level rises, in some years, upwards of 20 m. Lake Koocanusa's popularity with anglers is derived from its dynamic kokanee population. These landlocked sockeye salmon were stocked following the reservoir's creation, and they have flourished. Kokanee live for four years in the lake before heading upstream to spawn and die. In the lake, these beautiful silver salmon range from 25 to 35 cm in length and are most effectively caught using trolling gear. Gang trolls followed by a bright pink flatfish or lure such as a Wedding Ring or Kokanee Killer are the standard rig for kokanee. Bull trout in the lake feed on the kokanee and grow to very large sizes. Cutthroat and rainbow trout have also been stocked in Lake Koocanusa, but are not present in numbers anything close to the kokanee population. Cutthroat and rainbow trout taken from the lake average 30–35 cm in length. The rainbow trout in the lake include Gerrard-strain, which have grown to enormous sizes in other lakes with bountiful kokanee stocks. Anglers in boats using fish finders and down riggers tend to catch more kokanee.

Lake Koocanusa

Lake Koocanusa kokanee

■ Kootenay River (Fort Steele to Lake Koocanusa) (BC)

Cutthroat trout to 55 cm (1.5 kg)
Bull trout to 80 cm (6.0 kg)
Rainbow trout to 55 cm (1.5 kg)
Whitefish to 45 cm
Kokanee to 40 cm

The section of the Kootenay River upstream from Lake Koocanusa to Fort Steele has never gained a good reputation among anglers. In contrast, nearby Lake Koocanusa is busy with anglers during the summer. The river remains murky for much of the summer, seldom clearing until well into the fall. Although some of the river's reputation as mediocre fishing is deserved, those who take the time to work the river may be pleasantly surprised. Cutthroat trout in the 25–35 cm size range are the normal catch, with a few rainbow trout present as well. More and more anglers now target the large bull trout in the spring before runoff begins.

Kootenay River

▲ Baynes Lake (BC)

49°14'00"N 115°13'28"W
Largemouth bass to 50 cm (2.0 kg)
Rainbow trout to 50 cm (1.5 kg)
Kokanee to 35 cm

Baynes Lake is located just south of Kikomun Creek Provincial Park and west of Highway 93. The lake is a popular destination in the summer, and many people have built recreational and permanent homes on its shore. Largemouth bass are present in good numbers and can be taken throughout the summer. Spin casting with a jig or worms, or fly fishing with a big deer hair mouse will bring the bass a runnin'. Largemouth in Baynes Lake average 20–30 cm in length, with big 2 kg+ whoppers caught on occasion. Work areas around the boat docks for the big boys. Rainbow trout are also stocked in Baynes Lake, and they grow quickly because of the plentiful food supply in the lake. Rainbow trout in the lake average 30–40 cm in length but are normally caught in lesser numbers than largemouth bass. Kokanee are a recent introduction to Baynes Lake. If relegated to shore, fishing off a dock is a popular way to fish at Baynes (assuming you have a dock to fish off). Bass can be taken from shore at many locations, but if you are after the lake's rainbow trout, a boat is strongly recommended.

Baynes Lake largemouth bass

Baynes Lake

◼ Surveyors Lake (BC)

49°14'44"N 115°14'07"W
Brook trout to 55 cm (1.5 kg)
Largemouth bass to 50 cm (2.0 kg)
Rainbow trout to 50 cm

Surveyors Lake is the crown jewel of Kikomun Creek Provincial Park, located 15 km south of Jaffray. The large campground at Surveyors Lake is extremely popular and is filled to the brim throughout the summer. Two sandy beaches on the lake attract hordes on sunny days. The beach bunch always far outnumber anglers at Surveyors Lake, even though the lake does hold some very nice fish. Brook trout and largemouth bass predominate, although there are a few decent rainbow trout around as well. The brook trout grow to large sizes, with many specimens exceeding the 1 kg weight class. Normally, trout are caught in the deeper waters and the bass are caught in the shallows. The largemouth bass like to hide under lily pads, deadfall, or overhanging tree branches – just about anything your hook is likely to get caught on. Most of the bass are in the 20–25 cm range, but there are always bigger ones around. Sight fishing is very effective as long as you can get your lure in a position to attract the bass that you can see. Take a rod and make a circuit of the lake on the fine hiking trail. As you are walking along, keep a sharp eye on the water – you will undoubtedly see some bass.

Surveyors Lake

◼ Engineers Lake (BC)

49°14'32"N 115°13'59"W
Largemouth bass to 50 cm (2.0 kg)

Engineers Lake is a small lake attached directly to Surveyors Lake by a narrow channel. Although there may be the odd brook or rainbow trout present, largemouth bass tend to prefer the shallow, warm waters of Engineers Lake. A tangle of brush surrounds the lake and makes casting difficult.

Engineers Lake

☐ Muskrat Lake (BC)

49°14'11"N 115°14'02"W
☐ Fisher Lake (BC)
49°14'20"N 115°14'10"W
☐ Stink Lake (BC)
49°14'26"N 115°14'23"W
Largemouth bass

These three small lakes are located north of Engineers Lake. Largemouth bass may be present in the lakes in limited numbers.

☐ Hidden Lake (BC)

49°15'06"N 115°14'26"W
Largemouth bass to 40 cm

Hidden Lake is located in a small basin alongside the paved road that leads from Surveyors Lake campground to the Koocanusa boat launch. Hidden Lake's population of turtles likely exceeds any bass that may present.

☐ Deer Lake (BC)

49°17'10"N 115°14'58"W
Rainbow trout to 40 cm

This small lake is located just east of the Jaffray-Baynes Lake Road on Suzanne Creek. The lake's rainbow trout, which average 20–30 cm in length, are best fished in the springtime.

◼ Bluebottom Lake (BC)

49°16'15"N 115°13'51"W
Brook trout to 40 cm

Bluebottom Lake is located approximately 3 km north of the entrance to Kikomun Creek Provincial Park and is reached on rough roads that lead east from the Jaffray-Baynes Lake Road. Bluebottom Lake has been stocked with brook trout, which average 25–35 cm in length. Fishing is generally difficult due to extended shallows and heavy brush around the lake.

Bluebottom Lake

North Star Lake (BC)

49°20'37"N 115°15'52"W

Rainbow trout to 55 cm (2.5 kg)

This popular lake and campground is located approximately 5 km south of Jaffray, west of the Jaffray-Baynes Lake Road. The lake contains Blackwater-strain rainbow trout, among others, which prey on the red-sided shiners in the lake. Rainbow trout in North Star average 30–40 cm in length, and large trout over 50 cm are caught often. Trolling the deeper water works well at North Star, although patient fly fishers will be very effective.

North Star Lake

Suzanne Lake (aka Manistee Lake) (BC)

49°19'13"N 115°14'21"W

Rainbow trout to 60 cm (3.0 kg)

Largemouth bass to 55 cm (2.5 kg)

Suzanne Lake can be reached on good dirt roads west from the Jaffray-Baynes Lake Road. Two nice campgrounds are located at the lake. Suzanne has a substantial bass population, and there have been problems in the past with the bass eating the stocked rainbow fingerlings. To alleviate the problem, two-year-old Gerrard-strain rainbow trout were stocked in Suzanne. The hope was that the rainbows would not be eaten by the bass and would be able to grow to large sizes. The lake itself is big and requires a boat for any quality fishing opportunities. The rainbow trout in the lake average 30–40 cm in length and are generally taken from the deeper water. Largemouth bass can be taken from the shallows wherever there is sufficient cover for the bass to hide.

Suzanne Lake

Wapiti Lake (aka Warm Lake) (BC)

49°23'11"N 115°21'54"W

Rainbow trout to 55 cm (1.5 kg)

Brook trout to 55 cm (1.5 kg)

Wapiti Lake is located on a bench east of Lake Koocanusa, approximately 5 km west of Jaffray. Wapiti is actually two small, interconnected lakes. The lakes are very shallow and tend to winterkill regularly. Fish are stocked annually and grow very quickly due to the massive amount of food available in this productive pond. Catchable-size rainbow trout have been stocked in recent years, with brook trout also stocked on occasion. Trout in the lake average 25–35 cm by mid-summer and many will reach 50 cm by late fall. Extensive reeds along virtually the entire shoreline will hamper most shorebound anglers.

Wapiti Lake

Sand Creek, Kikomun Creek, Caithness Creek (BC)

Rainbow trout to 35 cm

Cutthroat trout to 35 cm

These three creeks in the Jaffray Sub-Region are easily accessed from good gravel roads. Fishing is decent for small rainbow and cutthroat trout, which average 20–25 cm in length. Kikomun Creek is stocked regularly with rainbows.

Douglas Lake (BC)

49°28'44"N 115°21'40"W

Sand Lake (BC)

49°27'47"N 115°20'50"W

Rainbow trout to 30 cm

Cutthroat trout to 30 cm

Douglas and Sand Lakes are located north of Jaffray and can be reached from the Galloway-Bull River road. Fishing has been reported as poor in both lakes.

Murray Lake (aka Mirror Lake) (BC)

49°28'58"N 115°20'32"W

Rainbow trout to 40 cm

Murray Lake is situated east of the Galloway-Bull River road and is reached via a confusing series of rough tracks. Murray contains stocked rainbow that average 25–35 cm in length.

Rosen Lake (aka McBaines Lake) (BC)

49°23'58"N 115°15'25"W

Largemouth bass to 55 cm (2.0 kg)

Rainbow trout to 40 cm

Kokanee to 35 cm

Rosen Lake is situated just northeast of Jaffray and can be reached on paved and gravel roads from Highway 3. A boat is essential at Rosen, as shore fishing is restricted by private property that surrounds virtually the entire lake. Largemouth bass and rainbow trout both inhabit Rosen's waters, but the fishing is fair at best. The lake warms up significantly in the summer and the few trout present seem to disappear into the deeper, cooler waters. Bass averaging 25–35 cm in length can be caught in the shallower waters throughout the season. Yellow perch and sunfish are in the lake, and kokanee have been recently stocked.

Rosen Lake

◻ Tie Lake (BC)

49°25'02"N 115°18'46"W
Largemouth bass to 55 cm (2.0 kg)
Located directly north of Jaffray and accessible by paved road, Tie Lake has much in common with nearby Rosen Lake. Private property also encircles much of Tie Lake, cutting the shoreline off from prospective anglers. A boat is the only reasonable alternative for fishing on Tie Lake unless you own lakeshore property. As with Rosen Lake, largemouth bass will be the catch of the day. A variety of trout have been stocked in the lake in the past, but few if any are present in the lake. Largemouth bass tend to be 20–35 cm in length, with large ones taken regular. Yellow perch and sunfish can also be caught in Tie Lake.

Tie Lake

◻ Spring Lakes (BC)

49°25'02"N 115°21'28"W
Brook trout to 40 cm
Rainbow trout to 40 cm
The Spring Lakes can be reached via rough 2WD roads that lead north off Highway 3 just west of the Highway 3 junction to the US. The lakes are fed by springs and hold brook trout in fair numbers. Trout taken from the larger of the two lakes will average 25–35 cm in length.

◻ Pickering Lakes (aka Crowsnest Lakes) (BC)

49°27'28"N 115°24'30"W
Brook trout to 45 cm
Rainbow trout to 40 cm
The Pickering Lakes can be reached via rough 2WD roads that lead north off Highway 3 just east of the Wardner-Fort Steele Road junction. The name is a bit of a misnomer, as one of the two lakes is virtually dried up. The main Pickering Lake (the one with the water in it) is completely encircled by reeds, making fishing from shore rather troublesome. Stocked brook trout in good numbers and the odd rainbow live out beyond the reeds, requiring a long cast if fishing from shore. The trout caught will average 25–35 cm in length, with some larger, fatter models available as well.

Main Pickering Lake

◻ Bronze Lake (aka Weatherhead Lake) (BC)

49°26'39"N 115°24'30"W
Brook trout to 45 cm
Rainbow trout to 45 cm
This small lake can be reached by driving on a rough 2WD road for approximately 3 km southeast from the Bull River bridge on the Wardner-Fort Steele Road. Casting room is available around the entire lake, although stumps and deadfall in the lake will undoubtedly claim a few lures. Bronze Lake contains stocked brook trout, which thrive in the nutrient rich environment. Brook trout in the lake average 25–35 cm in length and can be taken with equal effectiveness by lure or fly. Rainbow trout have also been stocked in the past. If fishing is poor, sit back and watch the numerous turtles that like to sun themselves on logs along the lakeshore.

Bronze Lake

Wardner Sub-Region

The Wardner Sub-Region extends south and west from the small community of Wardner along the western side of Lake Koocanusa. To the immediate west of Wardner, along the Ha Ha Creek Road, is a cluster of lakes that include Lund, Ha Ha, Bednorski and Edith. To the south of Wardner in the Caven Creek drainage, Cherry Lake is the most popular of the mountain lakes.

■ Lund Lake (BC)
49°25'46"N 115°27'01"W
Rainbow trout to 45 cm
Brook trout to 45 cm

Lund Lake is situated less than two kilometres west of Wardner on the Ha Ha Creek Road. This small lake is beside the road and easily accessed. Lund Lake has been stocked in the past with rainbow and brook trout and may even hold a few largemouth bass. Using a boat or float tube and venturing out into the middle of the lake will enhance angling results. Flies and lures are both effective at Lund Lake.

Lund Lake

■ Ha Ha Lake (aka Rothwell Lake) (BC)
49°25'44"N 115°29'24"W
Brook trout to 45 cm

Ha Ha Lake is a shallow body of water alongside Ha Ha Creek Road, a few kilometres west of Lund Lake. Waterfowl seem more at home at Ha Ha Lake than do trout. The lake is stocked with brook trout that average 20–30 cm in length. A boat or float tube is essential for fishing this lake, as reed growth and very shallow water will inhibit shore-bound anglers. There may also be illegally planted largemouth bass in Ha Ha.

Ha Ha Lake

■ Bednorski Lake (aka Simon's Lake) (BC)
49°26'28"N 115°30'19"W
Brook trout to 55 cm (1.5 kg)
Cutthroat trout

Bednorski Lake is similar in character to nearby Ha Ha Lake. Bednorski Lake is very shallow and ringed by substantial reed growth. Fishing from shore is generally unproductive. Although most of the lake is surrounded by private property, there is a small public boat launch area on the south side of the lake. The brook trout in Bednorski Lake average 25–35 cm in length, although there are larger fish present. Cutthroat trout were also stocked in Bednorski in years past. Illegally planted largemouth bass may be in the lake as well.

Bednorski Lake

□ Edith Lake (BC)
49°26'02"N 115°30'47"W
Brook trout to 45 cm

Edith Lake is reached by branching west of the Ha Ha Creek Road onto a side road at Bednorski Lake. Even though Edith Lake is visible from the access road, private property must be crossed to reach the lakeshore. Be sure to gain permission before crossing any private property, here or elsewhere. Edith Lake holds a limited number of brook trout in the 25–35 cm range.

□ Ha Ha Creek (BC)
Brook trout to 30 cm

Ha Ha Creek flows through both Bednorski Lake and Ha Ha Lake before passing through Wardner and emptying into the Kootenay River. Small brook trout can be taken from the upper reaches of the creek.

◭ Cherry Lake (BC)
49°10'51"N 115°32'50"W
Rainbow trout to 55 cm (1.5 kg)

Cherry Lake is situated amid heavy forest cover in the upper Caven Creek watershed and is reached from the Caven Creek Forest Service Road. At Km 41.5, turn right onto Haller Creek road (not left onto Cherry Road). The Forest Service Recreation Site and boat launch are only 200 m from the Haller/Cherry intersection. Cherry Lake sits in a sunken basin, and although there is forest all around the lake, the shoreline has receded to the point that there is generally a 20–30 m wide swath around the lake that is free of vegetation. Water levels at Cherry Lake rise in the spring and early summer with the runoff and then continue to decline during the late summer and fall. Fishing from shore is possible around the entire lake, with some deep holes visible in the clear water. If fishing from shore, watch for rising fish and make your way to that location. A boat will be most helpful at Cherry Lake, as it seems that the fish tend to keep to that point just beyond

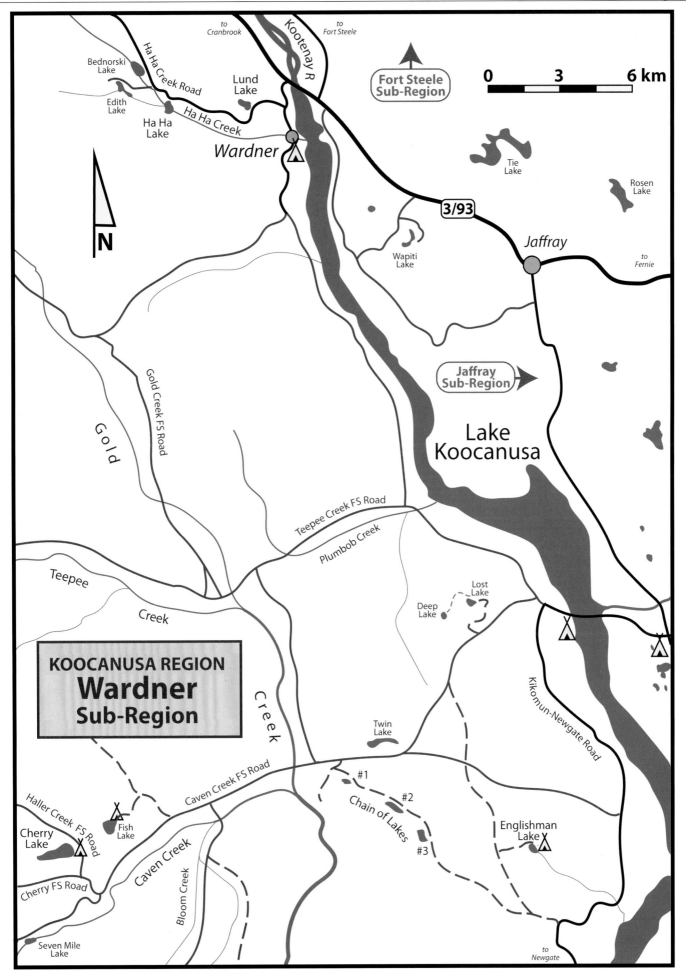

to Cranbrook

to Fort Steele

Kootenay R

Bednorski Lake

Ha Ha Creek Road

Lund Lake

Edith Lake

Ha Ha Creek

Ha Ha Lake

Wardner

Fort Steele Sub-Region

0   3   6 km

Tie Lake

Rosen Lake

3/93

Jaffray

to Fernie

N

Wapiti Lake

Gold Creek FS Road

Jaffray Sub-Region

Lake Koocanusa

Gold

Teepee Creek FS Road

Plumbob Creek

Teepee

Lost Lake

Deep Lake

Creek

KOOCANUSA REGION
Wardner
Sub-Region

Creek

Kikomun-Newgate Road

Twin Lake

Caven Creek FS Road

#1

Haller Creek FS Road

#2

Chain of Lakes

Fish Lake

Englishman Lake

Cherry Lake

#3

Caven Creek

Cherry FS Road

Bloom Creek

Seven Mile Lake

to Newgate

39

your longest cast from shore. The rainbow trout in Cherry Lake are plentiful, and most will average 25–35 cm in length. There may also be the odd cutthroat trout present from previous plantings.

Cherry Lake

Fish Lake (BC)
49°11'03"N 115°31'42"W
Cutthroat trout to 40 cm
Fish Lake is located in the small valley just to the northeast of Cherry Lake and is also accessed from the Caven Creek Forest Service Road. The most prominent access road into Fish Lake leads to private property. The Forest Service Recreation Site is only a few hundred metres down the lakeshore on a rough road. Although Fish Lake is relatively small, it has extensive shallows, and long casts will be required to reach the fish-holding waters. The best fishing for the lake's small cutthroat trout is along the deeper waters on the opposite side of the lake from the Recreation Site.

Fish Lake

Seven Mile Lake (BC)
49°08'31"N 115°36'15"W
Cutthroat trout to 40 cm
Seven Mile Lake is found at the headwaters of Caven Creek. There is a Recreation Site at the small lake. Seven Mile Lake is stocked regularly and holds cutthroat trout in the 20–30 cm range.

Chain of Lakes (aka Twin Lakes) (BC)
(#2) 49°12'00"N 115°22'29"W
Brook trout to 50 cm (1.5 kg)
Chain of Lakes are three lakes located just of a secondary road that branches south near the intersection of the Caven Creek and Plumbob Creek Forest Service roads. The two southern lakes have been stocked with brook trout. Deadfall in both lakes affords good fish habitat. Brook trout in the lakes average 25–35 cm in length and can be taken from shore with lures.

Chain of Lakes #3

Twin Lake (BC)
49°13'16"N 115°23'06"W
Status: Doubtful
Twin Lake is a large, shallow two-headed pond that is located just north of the Caven Creek Forest Service Road at Km 26, approximately ten kilometres west of Lake Koocanusa.

Englishman Lake (BC)
49°11'12"N 115°18'13"W
Rainbow trout to 45 cm
This small lake is set in a pleasant forest at the head of Englishman Creek and is accessed via a number of confusing and rough roads from the Kikomun-Newgate Road. Englishman Lake is stocked regularly with rainbow trout, and anglers will catch trout averaging 25–35 cm in length in good numbers.

Lost Lake (BC)
49°15'59"N 115°20'15"W
Brook trout to 40 cm
Lost Lake is reached by taking a short, but very nasty 4WD road north off the Caven Creek Forest Service Road. New logging roads will add to the confusion of finding the lake. Although Lost Lake is relatively shallow, there are a number of deeper pools that can be accessed by intrepid anglers who fight their way around the underbrush to the far side of the lake. Brook trout in Lost Lake average 20–30 cm in length and are very limited in number. Although unlikely, there may be a few rainbow trout from past plantings.

Lost Lake

Deep Lake (BC)
49°15'45"N 115°20'58"W
Rainbow trout to 40 cm
To reach Deep Lake, one must first navigate the bad road into Lost Lake. From Lost Lake, a rough trail around the northwest side of Lost Lake leads in 15 minutes to Deep Lake, a small, but not surprisingly, deep body of water. Rainbow trout are stocked regularly and have done well in Deep Lake, likely due to the general absence of fishing pressure. Cutthroat trout were also stocked several years ago. Expect to catch rainbow trout averaging 25–35 cm in length, with larger ones present in decent numbers.

◼ Gold Creek, Caven Creek, Plumbob Creek, Teepee Creek, Bloom Creek (BC)

Cutthroat trout to 35 cm

All of the major creeks to the west of Lake Koocanusa hold trout in good numbers in their upper reaches. Forest Service roads and/or logging roads ascend most of the drainages. Rainbow trout, bull trout, brook trout, whitefish and kokanee may be present in the lower sections of Gold and Plumbob Creeks at various times of the year.

Gold Creek

◼ Mud Lake (BC) (Note: Lake is off south end of Wardner map)

49°03'11"N 115°13'44"W

Brook trout to 40 cm
Rainbow trout to 40 cm

Mud Lake is located off Alta Road, which splits west off the Kikomun-Newgate Road approximately 3 km north of Newgate. As would be expected, the water can be murky at times. Stocked rainbow in the 20–30 cm range are the average catch at Mud Lake. Brook trout are present as well.

Mud Lake

Kootenay Trout Hatchery photo

Fort Steele Sub-Region

This Sub-Region is concentrated around Fort Steele Heritage Town, a popular tourist attraction on Highway 93/95. The paved Fort Steele-Wardner Road branches off Highway 93/95 at Fort Steele, and leads to several fine lakes in and near Norbury Lake Provincial Park. Logging roads up the Bull River drainage allow access to some excellent stream fishing, as well as to secluded mountain lakes. The Kootenay Trout Hatchery at Bull River provides an interesting perspective on fish management and angling in southeastern BC and is definitely worth a visit.

Kootenay Trout Hatchery at Bull River

The Freshwater Fisheries Society of BC is a private, non-profit organization whose mandate is to enhance and conserve freshwater fisheries for public benefit. The Society owns and operates six major fish hatcheries in BC, including the Kootenay Trout Hatchery at Bull River. The Kootenay Trout Hatchery rears up to 3 million baby trout each year, specifically rainbow, cutthroat and brook trout plus kokanee. White sturgeon is also raised at the hatchery for conservation purposes. The Kootenay Trout Hatchery is open daily to visitors, with a tour guide on hand from May through August. Check out the big trout in the moat outside the entrance (if local otters have not got to them). The Hatchery is absolutely worth a visit if you're in the area.

Kootenay Trout Hatchery photo

Staff at Kootenay Trout Hatchery

Learn to Fish Program

There is also a stocked pond near the hatchery for new anglers to practice their catch-and-release angling skills. Rods are available for loan and a guide can help visitors get set up. For more information on the Learn to Fish Program, contact the Kootenay Trout Hatchery at 250-429-3214 or visit *gofishbc.com*.

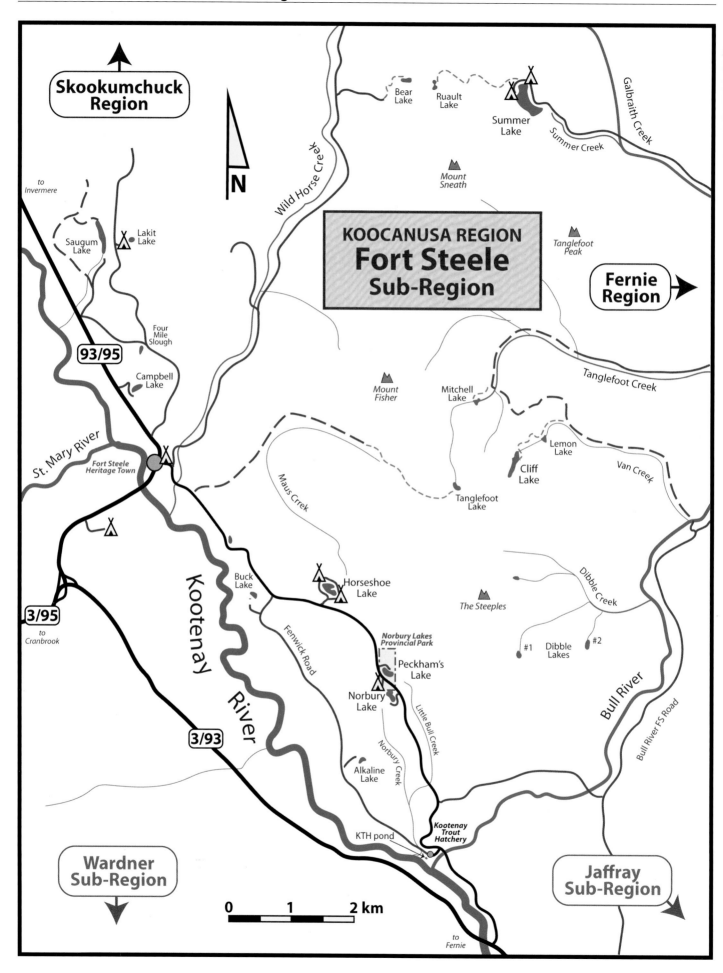

Skookumchuck Region

N

to Invermere

Saugum Lake

Lakit Lake

93/95

Four Mile Slough

Campbell Lake

St. Mary River

Fort Steele Heritage Town

3/95

to Cranbrook

Kootenay River

3/93

Wild Horse Creek

Bear Lake

Ruault Lake

Summer Lake

Summer Creek

Galbraith Creek

Mount Sneath

KOOCANUSA REGION
Fort Steele
Sub-Region

Tanglefoot Peak

Fernie Region

Tanglefoot Creek

Mount Fisher

Mitchell Lake

Lemon Lake

Cliff Lake

Van Creek

Maus Crrek

Tanglefoot Lake

Buck Lake

Horseshoe Lake

Fenwick Road

The Steeples

Dibble Creek

#1 Dibble Lakes #2

Norbury Lakes Provincial Park

Peckham's Lake

Norbury Lake

Little Bull Creek

Bull River

Bull River FS Road

Norbury Creek

Alkaline Lake

KTH pond

Kootenay Trout Hatchery

Wardner Sub-Region

0   1   2 km

to Fernie

Jaffray Sub-Region

■ Kootenay Trout Hatchery Pond (aka KTH Pond)
49°28'20"N 115°28'06"W
Rainbow trout to 30 cm

The small, stocked KTH pond is located a short walk from the hatchery parking lot. It's a great place for kids to learn to fish. Small rainbow trout can be caught and released.

Kootenay Trout Hatchery Pond

■ Kootenay River (Wasa to Fort Steele) (BC)
Cutthroat trout to 55 cm (1.5 kg)
Bull trout to 80 cm (6.0 kg)
Rainbow trout to 50 cm
Whitefish to 45 cm
Kokanee to 40 cm

The Kootenay River flows south from Wasa to Fort Steele, en route to Lake Koocanusa. This section of the river receives light fishing pressure for its cutthroat and bull trout populations. The water remains mud-coloured for most of the year, clearing in the fall. Although fishing is fair at best, cutthroat trout averaging 25–35 cm in length can be taken from most stretches of the river. Bull trout, kokanee and whitefish, as well as the occasional rainbow trout, can also be caught. In the spring before runoff begins, big Kootenay River bull trout are targeted by anglers.

Kootenay River

■ Wild Horse Creek (BC)
Cutthroat trout to 35 cm

Wild Horse Creek was the scene of a frantic gold rush in the 1860s, and the streambed was utterly destroyed in the search for gold. With over 100 years to recuperate, the stream now looks normal in most respects. The flow is generally turbulent, although there are nice pools along the length of Wild Horse Creek. Small cutthroat trout can be taken from the creek, with most fish averaging 15–25 cm in length.

■ Bull River (BC)
Cutthroat trout to 50 cm
Bull trout to 70 cm (5.0 kg)
Whitefish to 45 cm
Kokanee to 40 cm

The Bull River is the major tributary to this segment of the Kootenay River. The Bull River experiences very high stream flow during runoff in June and early July, but then clears quickly. Logging roads extend to the upper reaches of the Bull River drainage, offering good access to the river. Cutthroat trout fishing is excellent in the Bull River's many fine pools, with fish averaging 20–35 cm in length. Big bull trout in the 3-4 kg range can also be found in the deeper pools. The Bull River has a great whitefish run each fall. Fall also brings spawning kokanee salmon into the lower river in great numbers.

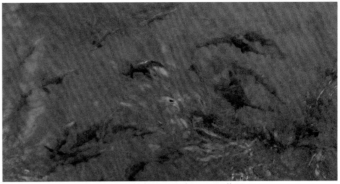
Spawning kokanee in lower Bull River

Bull River

Bull River whitefish

■ Galbraith Creek, Summer Creek, Tanglefoot Creek, Quinn Creek (BC)
Cutthroat trout to 40 cm

These tributaries of the Bull River are all noted for their good stream fishing for cutthroat trout. Logging roads have been built up each drainage, allowing anglers relatively easy access. The cutthroat trout tend to be small, in the 20–30 cm range, but are plentiful. Bull trout and whitefish may also be present in the fall.

■ Norbury and Little Bull Creeks (BC)
Rainbow trout to 35 cm
Cutthroat trout to 35 cm
Kokanee to 35 cm

Norbury Creek, which flows beside the Kootenay Trout Hatchery at Bull River, is formed by the joining of Norbury and Little Bull Creeks a kilometre above the hatchery. Hatchery staff at one time regularly released surplus trout into the creek near the hatchery, a practice that is no longer continued. Rainbow and cutthroat trout are the most likely species to be caught, although kokanee are now stocked in large numbers. These creeks have an age restriction on them, so be sure to check the fishing regulations.

▲ Summer Lake (BC)
49°45'40"N 115°23'55"W
Cutthroat trout to 55 cm (1.5 kg)

Summer Lake is reached by taking a series of Forestry Service Roads up the Bull River, Galbraith Creek and Summer Creek, respectively. Camping sites are available along the lake at several locations. The lake itself is a blue-green gem, set in a crown of fine peaks. Water levels rise with the melting of the snow into early summer, and then recede for the rest of the year. Hard-fighting cutthroat trout are plentiful in the lake, and average 30–40 cm in length. Fishing from shore is possible from almost any location once the lake level begins to recede, but shorebound anglers should concentrate on areas around inlet creeks and near drop-offs. If the lake is calm, watch for rising fish. Many times, they will be close enough to cast to. If fishing from a boat, you can either troll a lure through the deeper water, or anchor and try fly fishing in the shallows where feisty cutthroat cruise back and forth.

Summer Lake

Summer Lake cutthroat trout

▣ Ruault Lake (BC)
49°46'10"N 115°27'20"W
Status: Doubtful

This tiny lake is located approximately 4 km west of Summer Lake and is accessed by a steep trail. Cutthroat trout were present at one time in the lake, but their status is precarious at best. It is likely that the lake dries up to the point of being unable to hold fish. Reports indicate no fish are present in the lake.

Ruault Lake

▲ Bear Lake (BC)
49°46'10"N 115°28'25"W
Cutthroat trout to 40 cm

Bear Lake is located in a basin above Wild Horse Creek and can only be reached by trail. A 2 km trail climbs up the valley of the outlet stream from the Wild Horse Creek Forest Service Road. A second, much more difficult route crosses the ridge above Ruault Lake before descending to Bear Lake. Bear Lake holds numerous cutthroat trout, few growing much larger than 30 cm in length. Fish can be taken from virtually any location all around the lake, with the inlet creek particularly productive.

Bear Lake

Bear Lake cutthroat trout

▣ Lemon Lake (BC)
49°37'54"N 115°23'18"W
Cutthroat trout to 35 cm

Lemon Lake is the first of two lakes reached by trail at the head of the Van Creek Valley. Vehicle access to the trailhead is off the Bull-Van Forest Service Road. A mix of forest, meadow and rock around Lemon Lake affords adequate casting room. Cutthroat trout in the lake are small, most being 20–25 cm in length.

Lemon Lake

Cliff Lake (BC)

49°37'18"N 115°24'25"W

Cutthroat trout to 40 cm

A steep and rocky headwall protects Cliff Lake from most intruders who venture beyond Lemon Lake. Cliff Lake lies a little over 2 km and 400 vertical metres above Lemon Lake. For those who do reach Cliff Lake, colourful cutthroat trout can be taken from most locations along its rocky shoreline. The cutthroat trout in the crystal-clear waters average 25–35 cm in length and are particularly susceptible to fly fishing.

Cliff Lake

Tyler Ambrosi with Cliff Lake cutthroat
Tyler Ambrosi photo

Frank Slide Centre photo

Mitchell Lake (BC)

49°38'44"N 115°25'45"W

Cutthroat trout to 35 cm

This small forest-bound lake can be reached by taking a 1 km trail up Tanglefoot Creek from the Tanglefoot Forest Service Road. Fly casting room is at a premium due to the dense forest cover. Cutthroat trout in the lake are plentiful but small, with the average being 15–25 cm in length.

Mitchell Lake

Tanglefoot Lake (BC)

49°36'44"N 115°26'29"W

Cutthroat trout to 35 cm

This lovely subalpine lake sees more hikers than anglers during the season due to the challenging access via a steep 6 km access trail. The route to Tanglefoot Lake can be combined with a great alpine route to Cliff Lake. Tanglefoot is reported to hold cutthroat trout in the 20–30 cm range. Scree slopes allow for good casting room around much of the lake.

Frank Slide Centre photo

Tanglefoot Lake

Dibble Lakes (BC)

49°36'25"N 115°23'38"W

Cutthroat trout to 40 cm

The two Dibble Lakes are situated in pretty basins to the south of Dibble Creek. Access to Dibble #1 (the more westerly one) is on abandoned logging roads and rough trail. Access to Dibble #2 is more difficult, following a poor trail up from Dibble Creek. Both lakes hold cutthroat trout that average 20–30 cm in length. Fly fishing with a sinking line and nymph is normally very productive.

Kootenay Trout Hatchery photo

Dibble Lake #2

Norbury Lake (aka Garbutt Lake) (BC)

49°31'55"N 115°28'55"W

Rainbow trout to 50 cm (1.5 kg)

Norbury Lake is located alongside the Fort Steele-Wardner Road, partially within appropriately named Norbury Lake Provincial Park. Shore fishing is restricted by private land, but those with boats or float tubes will have no problems. Rainbow trout in the lake grow quickly, with the average trout caught being in excess of 30 cm. Large brood stock rainbow are dropped in the lake regularly. There may be a few cutthroat trout in the lake as well. Sight fishing in the shallows is possible, and the area around the inlet creek is usually productive. During most of the day, the larger trout are in the deeper water, and a lure or sinking fly line will be needed in order to drum up any action.

Norbury Lake

◪ Peckham's Lake (BC)
49°32'28"N 115°29'04"W
Rainbow trout to 50 cm (1.5 kg)

Peckham's Lake is in Norbury Lake Provincial Park, just off the Fort Steele-Wardner Road. A nice picnic and day use area covers much of the lake's east shore. Expect lots of people enjoying the shoreline on warm summer days. Fishing is especially productive in the springtime at Peckham's Lake, and many anglers show up for the first few weeks of the season. Even though the lake is relatively small and a good cast will reach halfway across the lake, many anglers prefer watercraft when fishing Peckham's. Rainbow trout are stocked regularly, and they have plenty of food to get fat on. Trout caught in the lake average 30–35 cm in length, with larger fish caught often. The hatchery often drops lunker brood stock into the lake, so don't be shocked if you tie into a 2–3 kg fish!

Peckham's Lake

▣ Horseshoe Lake (BC)
49°34'21"N 115°31'08"W
Rainbow trout to 60 cm (2.5 kg)

Horseshoe Lake is located less than a kilometre north of the Fort Steele-Wardner Road in an open Ponderosa pine forest. A popular forestry campground encircles the entire lake. Tree cover does not extend down to the lakeshore, so fishing from shore is quite easy. Horseshoe Lake is relatively shallow and has extensive weed beds, which produce plenty of food for the lake's fat rainbow trout. Trout taken from Horsehoe Lake tend to be on the chunky side and average 30–40 cm in length. Trolling a fly

slowly over the weed beds will produce well on most occasions. Fishing tends to slow significantly in the summer months, but picks up well again in the fall. Water levels at Horseshoe seem to be dropping each year and at some time in the not too distant future the lake will be unable to sustain fish.

Horseshoe Lake

☐ Alkaline Lake (BC)
49°30'19"N 115°29'57"W
Brook trout

Alkaline Lake is a shallow body of water located southwest of Norbury Lake Provincial Park. Brook trout have been stocked in the past, but problems with the lake's water level and it alkalinity have affected productivity. Although trout are likely to still inhabit Alkaline Lake, their numbers are very limited.

◼ Buck Lake (BC)
49°34'14"N 115°34'04"W
Status: Devoid of fish

Tiny Buck Lake is located northwest of Norbury Lake Provincial Park. It has never been stocked and likely holds no fish.

◼ Campbell Lake (aka Campbell Meyer Lake) (BC)
49°38'52"N 115°38'44"W
Brook trout to 45 cm
Rainbow trout to 45 cm

Campbell Lake is conveniently located at a Rest Area north of Fort Steele on Highway 93/95. The lake is prone to winterkill and on occasion loses its entire trout population. However, Campbell Lake is normally stocked each spring with catchable-sized rainbow or brook trout, which grow rapidly during the year. By the fall, most of the fish are close to 40 cm in length. The lake is relatively small and fishing from shore is usually productive, although a boat will allow you to fish the deeper waters in the middle of the lake. The Kootenay Trout Hatchery occasionally drops a few retired lunkers into Campbell, sure to give heart palpitations to a lucky but unsuspecting angler.

Campbell Lake

☐ Four Mile Slough (BC)

49°40'27"N 115°38'47"W

Brook trout to 40 cm

Four Mile Slough is located south of Holmes Road, a gravel road off of Highway 93/95. The shallow lake holds small brook trout, most in the 15–25 cm range.

◼ Lakit Lake (BC)

49°42'22"N 115°38'53"W

Rainbow trout to 35 cm

This petite pond on Lakit Creek is located east of Highway 93/95 off of Holmes Road. The bottom of the shallow lake is completely covered with deadfall and logs, which makes for good habitat for fish. Rainbow trout are present in small sizes, with few larger than 30 cm in length.

Lakit Lake

◼ Saugum Lake (BC)

49°42'32"N 115°39'40"W

Brook trout to 60 cm (2.0 kg)

Rainbow trout to 40 cm

Largemouth Bass to 50 cm

Saugum Lake is located on Saugum Creek, east of Highway 93/95 along Holmes Road, due west of Lakit Lake. The primary access to the lake leads to private property. A convoluted, roundabout route over rough roads from farther north off Highway 93/95 leads to public access at the north end of the lake. This shallow lake primarily holds brook trout in good numbers and size, with rainbow trout and largemouth bass in the lake as well.

Saugum Lake

Saugum Lake brook trout

Kootenay Trout Hatchery photo

Curtis Hall photo

WEST CASTLE REGION

This Region encompasses the foothills and mountain valleys between Waterton Lakes National Park and the Crowsnest Pass. Variety is foremost, with excellent stream and river fishing opportunities, as well as heavily fished foothill lakes and pristine alpine tarns. The western, mountainous Beaver Mines Sub-Region centres on the Castle and West Castle River drainages south of the hamlet of Beaver Mines. Farther to the east, mountains give way to the rolling foothills of the Pincher Creek Sub-Region.

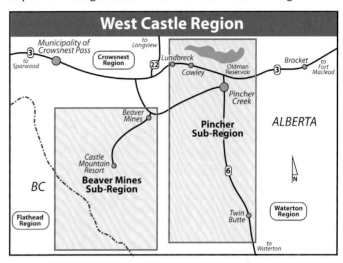

Castle Provincial Park and Castle Wildland Provincial Park

In 2017, the Government of Alberta created Castle Provincial Park and Castle Wildland Provincial Park, an area of more than 100,000 hectares, encompassing some of the most spectacular foothill and mountain landscapes in the Rockies. The creation of the two parks has significantly affected access to a number of river, streams and backcountry lakes in the Castle and South Castle River drainages. Restrictions on vehicular access beyond Castle Mountain Resort will add many kilometres of hiking or biking on roads to reach former trailheads. *Note: Alberta's current UCP government continues to review motorized access restrictions to the park.*

Beaver Mines Sub-Region

Outstanding stream fishing and secluded mountain lakes typify the Beaver Mines Sub-Region. The Castle and West Castle Rivers, both noted for their fine angling for cutthroat trout, flow from south to north through the heart of the area. Vehicle access is from either Pincher Creek or Highway 3 at Burmis, and then through the hamlet of Beaver Mines and along Highway 774 to the Castle Mountain Resort ski area. The creation of the new Castle Wildland Provincial Park has significantly changed access to the upper reaches of both the Castle and West Castle Rivers, adding kilometres of road walk/bike to several hikes. Beaver Mines Lake, accessible by a good gravel road, has a provincial campground and receives heavy fishing pressure throughout the summer. The Southfork Lakes and Rainy Ridge Lake contain stocked populations of golden trout, the only lakes in the southern Canadian Rockies where this rare species has been successfully planted. Grizzly, Lys and South Scarpe Lakes, all backpacking adventures, are highly regarded fishing destinations.

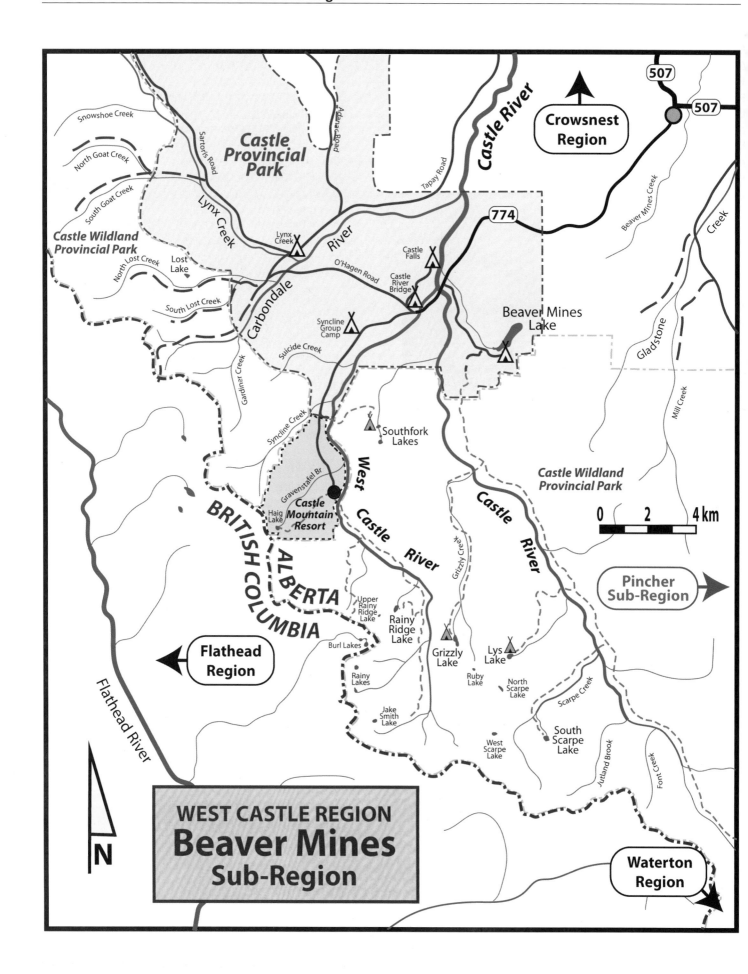

Snowshoe Creek
North Goat Creek
South Goat Creek
Castle Wildland Provincial Park
North Lost Creek
Lost Lake
South Lost Creek
Sartoris Road
Adanac Road
Castle Provincial Park
Lynx Creek
Carbondale River
Lynx Creek
O'Hagen Road
Suicide Creek
Gardiner Creek
Syncline Group Camp
Castle Falls
Castle River Bridge
Tapay Road
Castle River
774
507
507
Crowsnest Region
Beaver Mines Creek
Creek
Gladstone
Mill Creek
Beaver Mines Lake
Syncline Creek
Gravenstafel Br
Haig Lake
Castle Mountain Resort
Southfork Lakes
West Castle River
Castle River
Castle Wildland Provincial Park
0 2 4 km
Pincher Sub-Region
BRITISH COLUMBIA
ALBERTA
Flathead Region
Flathead River
Upper Rainy Ridge Lake
Burl Lakes
Rainy Ridge Lake
Rainy Lakes
Jake Smith Lake
Grizzly Creek
Grizzly Lake
Ruby Lake
Lys Lake
North Scarpe Lake
West Scarpe Lake
Scarpe Creek
South Scarpe Lake
Jutland Brook
Font Creek
Waterton Region

WEST CASTLE REGION
Beaver Mines
Sub-Region

N

▲ Castle River (aka South Castle River) (AB)

Cutthroat trout to 55 cm (1.5 kg)
Rainbow trout to 55 cm (1.5 kg)
Bull trout to 60 cm (4.0 kg)
Whitefish to 35 cm

Renowned locally for excellent fishing, the Castle River receives the attention of many anglers each season. Flowing gently along the valley floor, the Castle's pools and riffles provide long stretches of fishable water. The lower Castle, below the confluence of the Castle and West Castle Rivers, is crossed at several locations by highways and secondary roads. Reaching the better pools will often require a hike along the bank from the main access points. The upper Castle, upstream of the Castle-West Castle junction, is referred to by locals as the South Castle River. With new motorized vehicle restrictions in place, the upper Castle can only be reached by hiking a rough dirt road that branches south off of the Beaver Mines Lake road. Cutthroat trout in the 20–30 cm range predominate in the Castle River, with specimens in excess of 3.0 kg having been taken in the past, including the current Alberta record. Rainbow and bull trout, as well as whitefish, are also taken from the Castle. Spring runoff is usually complete by early July, and as water levels on the Castle subside, fishing picks up tremendously. The upper reaches of the river tend to be fished less and accordingly have more and larger trout. The stretch near Castle Falls holds trout but is fished to its limits during the summer. The lower river has some real beauties in its big holes notably in the area around the old Canyon Bridge site, off Highway 507.

Castle River

Castle River cutthroat trout

Castle River bull trout

■ West Castle River (aka Westcastle River) (AB)

Cutthroat trout to 45 cm
Rainbow trout to 45 cm
Bull trout to 60 cm (3.0 kg)
Whitefish to 35 cm

The West Castle River is very similar in character to the upper (South) Castle River and provides many kilometres of superb stream fishing. The West Castle River is paralleled by Highway 774 from its confluence with the Castle River upstream to Castle Mountain Resort (ski hill). Beyond the ski area, vehicular access is restricted, and those going past the ski area are limited to foot, horseback or mountain bike. As with the upper Castle River, fine cutthroat and bull trout can be caught in the West Castle, with rainbow trout and whitefish taken on occasion as well. After spring runoff is complete, the West Castle can easily be forded, and anglers who do a little searching away from the main access points will be rewarded with lots of beautiful cutthroat trout in the 25–35 cm range. West Castle River Falls, at the upper end of the valley is particularly outstanding.

Gary Enzsol fishing the West Castle River

Vic Bergman photo

West Castle River cutthroat trout

■ Beaver Mines Lake (aka Beaver Lake) (AB)

49°22'16"N 114°17'52"W
Rainbow trout to 55 cm (2.0 kg)
Bull trout to 60 cm (4.0 kg)

Beaver Mines Lake is situated beneath the impressive form of Table Mountain, two kilometres west of the Castle River Ranger Station on Highway 774 and is busy with anglers all season. The accompanying provincial campground is always crowded with tents and RVs. The lake's popularity arises from its abundance of hard-fighting rainbow trout that average 25–35 cm in length. A few large bull trout are also present in Beaver Mines Lake and the occasional cutthroat from past plantings may still exist.

Vic Bergman photo

Trolling is the usual method of fishing at Beaver Mines, although both spin casting and fly fishing can be productive. Weed growth chokes many parts of the lake by mid-summer, making trolling difficult for those who aren't familiar with the lake. For those without a boat, try the area alongside the access road near the outlet. Trout can be taken very close to shore in this area. Beaver Mines Lake is well-known for both its ravenous insect population and its strong winds. No wind: too buggy. No bugs: too windy. Camp Impeesa, a Boy Scout camp at the west end of the lake, is busy throughout the summer, and there will invariably be swimmers and canoes near the camp. As one would expect, fishing is not as good in this part of the lake, unless you are planning to catch a Boy Scout.

Beaver Mines Lake viewed from Table Mountain

Beaver Mines Lake rainbow trout

■ **Mill Creek, Gladstone Creek, Beaver Mines Creek, Screwdriver Creek (AB)**
Rainbow trout to 30 cm
Cutthroat trout to 30 cm
Brook trout to 30 cm
Bull trout to 60 cm (2.0 kg)
Whitefish to 30 cm
These tributaries of the lower Castle River contain a variety of game fish but are dominated by cutthroat and rainbow trout in small sizes. However don't be surprised if you catch a bull or brook trout or a whitefish. These are typical foothill creeks, with nice pools and long stretches of fishable water. All of these creeks are crossed by either Highway 507 or gravel secondary roads.

Mill Creek bull trout

■ **Grizzly Creek, Scarpe Creek, Font Creek, Jutland Brook, Syncline Brook, Suicide Creek, Gravenstafel Brook (AB)**
Cutthroat trout to 30 cm
These tributaries are located in the headwaters region of the upper Castle and West Castle Rivers but do not offer the quality of angling that is available in the lower Castle tributaries. These creeks generally have a much steeper gradient and fish are unable to make it far beyond the confluence with the Castle. An exception is Grizzly Creek, where the better fishing is in the kilometre or so below Grizzly Lake, and small brook trout can be taken. When the Castle River is still murky with run-off, cutthroat trout can often be taken where a tributary joins the main river.

▲ **Rainy Ridge Lake (AB)**
49°15'31"N 114°22'16"W
Golden trout to 45 cm
Set against the backdrop of the continental divide, delightful Rainy Ridge Lake offers much for the prospective angler. The lake contains beautifully coloured golden trout, originally stocked in the late-1950s and now able to maintain their population through natural reproduction. Most golden trout taken from Rainy Ridge are in the 25–35 cm range, although much larger ones are taken on occasion. Fly fishing is the most successful method of fishing, and casting room is available around most of the lake with the area along the scree slopes on the south shore generally the most productive. Patient anglers can work the shallows near the outlet with success. Two different routes lead into Rainy Ridge. New Castle Park regulations require a 10 km road walk from Castle Mountain Resort to a difficult-to-locate traihead. A 4 km trail then climbs steeply up into Rainy Ridge Lake basin. A second, somewhat longer route, begins at Middle Kootenay Pass at the end of an 8 km road walk from Castle Mountain Resort. This ill-defined 6 km route from Middle Kootenay Pass skirts Burl Lakes, before climbing to a pass and dropping down to Rainy Ridge Lake. Despite the difficult access, expect company at Rainy Ridge Lake.

Rainy Ridge Lake

Rainy Ridge Lake golden trout

Vic Bergman photo

◼ Upper Rainy Ridge Lake (AB)

49°15'26"N 114°23'02"W

Status: Devoid of fish

This small pond is located approximately 1 km above Rainy Ridge Lake and is tucked in a forested basin below Rainy Ridge. The lake is visible to those who cross the ridge above Burl Lakes and is often mistaken for Rainy Ridge Lake. The lake fills in the spring and is usually dry by fall. There are no fish in Upper Rainy Ridge Lake.

◼ Rainy Lakes (AB)

(Upper) 49°14'18"N 114°23'48"W

Status: Devoid of fish

Set in a fine subalpine basin below Three Lakes Ridge, these two tarns have never been stocked and contain no fish.

◼ Jake Smith Lake (AB)

49°13'14"N 114°22'23"W

Status: Devoid of fish

Jake Smith Lake is located on a ridge east of Scarpe Mountain and has never been stocked and contains no fish. The lake dries up completely in some years.

◼ Haig Lake (AB)

49°17'46"N 114°26'33"W

Status: Devoid of fish

Haig Lake lies nestled in a cirque four kilometres above Castle Mountain Resort, immediately below the foreboding east face of Mt. Haig. Haig Lake has never been stocked, and it is impossible for fish to enter the lake from Gravenstafel Brook as Haig Lake drains underground.

Haig Lake

◼ South Scarpe Lake (aka East Scarpe Lake) (AB)

49°12'35"N 114°16'29"W

Rainbow trout to 50 cm (1.5 kg)

South Scarpe Lake is set in a large cirque high on the flank of Jutland Mountain and attracts anglers each summer despite its remote location. Reaching the trailhead requires a substantial effort. Vehicular access beyond Castle Mountain Resort may be restricted, making this a 15 km one-way overnighter. The hiking trail part of the route (after a 12 km road walk) begins just downstream from the confluence of Scarpe Creek and the Castle River on an abandoned seismic road. Two kilometres up from the Castle River, a steep, less-defined side trail heads up into the forest along South Scarpe Lake's outlet creek. One heart-pounding kilometre later, a primitive campsite and the outlet of the lake are reached. South Scarpe Lake and its basin are a verdant delight, with the emerald green waters of the lake blending with the grass-covered slopes and dark forest. Other than at the outlet, where shallows and a major log jam are present, the steep sides of the basin continue down into the lake. Fishing deep with a fly or lure is generally successful. Rainbow trout are in the lake in good numbers, and most average 30–40 cm in length. Many of the fish in the lake appear to be rainbow-cutthroat hybrids, with general rainbow characteristics but having a bright red throat slash.

South Scarpe Lake

☐ West Scarpe Lake (AB)

49°12'25"N 114°18'34"W

Rainbow trout to 35 cm

West Scarpe Lake is situated on the southern end of Lys Ridge two kilometres above Scarpe Creek. It was stocked a number of years ago with golden trout, which apparently failed to reproduce, and West Scarpe was long though to be incapable of sustaining fish. However, plantings of rainbow trout have reportedly been successful, and rainbows are present in fair numbers. As access from Scarpe Creek is difficult because of a lack of defined trails over the final 2 km (not to mention the long road walk from Castle Mountain Resort), this lake can only be recommended to the most adventurous.

◼ North Scarpe Lake (AB)

49°13'49"N 114°18'13"W

Status: Devoid of fish

This small tarn is situated in the middle of a high, rocky basin above Scarpe Creek and below Lys Ridge. Access is by bushwhacking up from Scarpe Creek or over Lys Ridge from Lys Lake. North Scarpe Lake is very shallow and incapable of holding trout.

◻ Lys Lake (AB)

49°14'36"N 114°17'49"W

Rainbow trout to 45 cm

Lys Lake is set in a narrow basin off the southeastern end of Lys Ridge and receives relatively little fishing pressure due to its isolated location. Outfitter parties use the area regularly, but few anglers make the effort to hike 7 km up into the pretty, larch-filled valley from the Castle River (after the 17 km road walk). Lys Lake holds rainbow trout in the 30-35 cm range in good numbers. Fish can be taken from most locations around the lake with lures being notably successful.

Lys Lake

◪ Grizzly Lake (AB)

49°14'58"N 114°19'55"W

Brook trout to 50 cm (1.5 kg)

A tiring 13 km trail hike up Grizzly Creek valley from the Castle River (after a 4 km road walk) leads to Grizzly Lake, situated at the south end of Barnaby Ridge. Grizzly's striking green waters are popular with anglers despite its lengthy access, and the lake provides some of the Southern Rockies finest brook trout fishing, with many trout in the 40 cm+ range. Fly fishers will enjoy sight fishing in the shallows near the outlet. Other areas, particularly along the scree slopes in the lake's southwest corner, are also very productive.

Grizzly Lake

Grizzly Lake brook trout

◼ Ruby Lake (AB)

49°14'17"N 114°19'13"W

Status: Devoid of fish

Ruby Lake is set in a basin near the treeline one kilometre above Grizzly Lake. The lovely waters of Ruby Lake have never been stocked and contain no fish.

◻ Barnaby Lake (AB)

49°20'15"N 114°22'57"W

◻ Lower Southfork Lake (AB)

49°19'57"N 114°22'44"W

◻ Upper Southfork Lake (AB)

49°19'52"N 114°22'47"W

(collectively aka Barnaby Ridge Lakes/Southfork Lakes)

Golden trout to 40 cm

These three lakes are set in an exquisite subalpine basin immediately beneath Southfork Mountain and stand out collectively as the gem of the entire region in terms of natural beauty. Along with nearby Rainy Ridge Lake, these lakes are the only lakes in the Southern Rockies where golden trout have been successfully planted. Access is by a steep 4 km trail that leads up open hillsides after an easy ford of the West Castle River. Barnaby Lake, the first one encountered as one approaches by trail, is at a lower elevation than the other two lakes. Fishing is generally less successful in Barnaby, although there definitely are fish present. Half a kilometre by trail above Barnaby Lake is Lower Southfork Lake, the smallest of the three lakes. It is circular in shape and has shallows that extend out for 10–15 m all the way around the lake. These shallows make fly fishing from shore a difficult proposition, unless the intrepid angler wades out in the ice cold water on the rocky, thigh-deep shelf surrounding the main body of the lake to improve one's casting position. Until a substantial winterkill in the winter of 2017–18 eradicated many fish, Lower Southfork Lake always seemed to hold the most trout. Golden trout in all three lakes range from 20–35 cm in length, with larger specimens present. As golden trout are generally spooky by nature, and the water is extremely clear in all three lakes, anglers must be very cautious when approaching the lakes. Although reduced catch limits are in place for Barnaby and the Southfork Lakes, catch and release is strongly recommended in order to maintain fish stocks.

Southfork Lakes

Upper Southfork Lake   *Middle Southfork golden trout*

Steve Luethi photo

Carbondale River (AB)

Cutthroat trout to 35 cm
Rainbow trout to 35 cm
Bull trout to 50 cm
Whitefish to 35 cm

The Carbondale River is the major tributary of the Castle River and begins in alpine meadows below North Kootenay Pass along the Continental Divide. The river is turbulent in its upper reaches and provides excellent stream fishing below its confluence with Gardiner and Lynx Creeks all the way to its junction with the Castle. Cutthroat trout are the dominant species, most averaging 15–25 cm in length. Bull or rainbow trout, along with whitefish, are also taken. The Carbondale River road, the major route into the Carbondale drainage is accessible from Hillcrest in the Crowsnest Pass via Adanac Road or from Highway 507.

Lynx Creek, Gardiner Creek, Macdonald Creek, Lost Creek, Goat Creek, Snowshoe Creek (AB)

Cutthroat trout to 30 cm
Bull trout to 40 cm

These tributaries of the Carbondale River or Lynx Creek all contain small cutthroat trout in good numbers. Gardiner and Lynx Creeks, in particular, offer excellent stream fishing and will be busy with anglers all summer and fall.

Lost Lake (AB)

49°27'03"N 114°35'00"W
Status: Devoid of fish

This promising-looking lake in the North Lost Creek drainage has never been stocked and contains no fish.

Lost Lake

Pincher Sub-Region

This Sub-Region encompasses the sweeping foothill country to the south and west of the community of Pincher Creek. Access is west from Pincher Creek off of Highway 507, or south from Pincher Creek off Highway 6. Beauvais Lake, set in its namesake provincial park, is the main attraction for visitors, both in terms of scenery and angling. Farther south, the man-made duo of Butcher and Bathing Lakes offer easily accessible fishing opportunities. Bovin Lake is the region's sole backcountry angling destination.

Beauvais Lake (AB)

49°24'40"N 114°06'14"W
Rainbow trout to 50 cm (1.5 kg)
Brown trout to 50 (1.5 kg)

Lovely Beauvais Lake is set in the foothills west of Pincher Creek and can be reached by taking Highway 775 eight kilometres south from Highway 507. In addition to the summer cottages that line the lake's east shore, a large campground and an excellent picnic area within the park attract many families each summer. Seldom is there any time of the day when there aren't at least a few boats out on Beauvais. Landlubber anglers should not be deterred, however, as there are many places where fish can be taken in close proximity to the shore, particularly near the picnic area at the south end of the lake. Rainbow trout are caught in much greater numbers from Beauvais than brown trout. Rainbows are stocked annually in large numbers, and over a typical summer are taken in great numbers as well. Most rainbow trout taken from Beauvais average 20–35 cm in length. Brown trout are stocked annually as well, and browns in the lake tend to be larger, but are more difficult to catch. If you're after a big brown, try a dry fly in the late, late evening. Trolling seems to be the preferred method of angling on Beauvais, but fly fishing and spin casting will work very well also. If boating on Beauvais, take note of signs restricting access to the section of the lake where waterfowl nest in the spring.

Beauvais Lake

Beauvais Lake brown trout

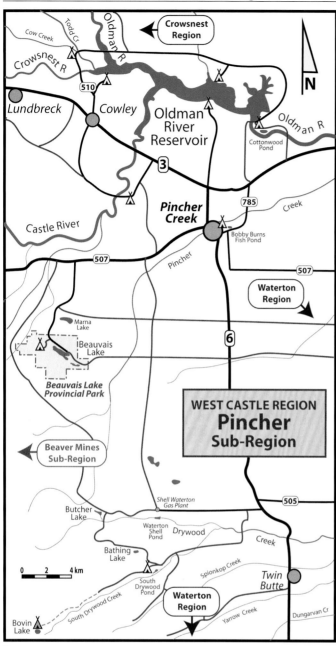

Marna Lake (AB)
49°25'58"N 114°05'38"W
Status: Devoid of fish
This shallow lake just off the Highway 775 access road to Beauvais Lake Provincial Park has never been stocked and is unlikely to sustain fish over the winter.

Pincher Creek (AB)
Rainbow trout to 35 cm
Cutthroat trout to 35 cm
Bull trout to 45 cm
Whitefish to 30 cm
Pincher Creek has maintained a good reputation among anglers in Southern Alberta for many years. Even though the massive flooding in 1995 and 2013 damaged the stream severely, it always seems to recover. Pincher Creek still ranks among the better foothill streams. Over its entire course, from headwaters between Pincher Ridge and Mount Victoria, to its confluence with the Oldman River near Brocket, Pincher Creek offers excellent creek fishing for small rainbow and cutthroat trout.

Bobby Burns Pond (AB)
49°29'34"N 113°55'48"W
Rainbow and Cutthroat trout to 35 cm
Diminutive Bobby Burns Pond is located in Bobby Burns Park in Pincher Creek (named for locals Janet and Robert Burns, who donated the property for the park, not for Robert Burns, Scottish poet). The park and pond are found within the town of Pincher Creek, just north of Macleod Street, beside the ball diamonds. Rainbow or Cutthroat trout are regularly stocked and the pond is open to seniors and handicapped anglers only. Several locations offer handicapped access to the pond. Most trout caught will be small, in the 15–25 cm range.

Bobby Burns Pond

Waterton Shell Pond (AB)
49°18'03"N 113°59'51"W
Brook trout to 35 cm
Rainbow trout to 35 cm
The Waterton Shell Pond is on Drywood Creek immediately below the Waterton Shell Gas Plant, approximately eight kilometres west of Highway 6. This man-made lake at first glance appears to be some sort of water storage facility for the gas plant. However, closer inspection will generally reveal trout rising in good numbers. Small brook trout in the 20-30 cm range are the normal catch, although rainbow trout and the occasional cutthroat are present as well. A good cast from the parking area can reach most corners of the lake, so there is no need to walk to far to fish. The water level in the lakes changes significantly depending on usage by the nearby gas plant. Due to the pond's close proximity to the plant, there are potentially issues with water quality, so it would be prudent to release all fish you catch.

Waterton Shell Pond

Butcher Lake (aka Prairie Bluff Lake) (AB)
49°18'14"N 114°03'40"W
Brook trout to 40 cm
Man-made Butcher Lake is located alongside the road, approximately 5 km west of the Waterton Shell Gas Plant, on

a small tributary of Drywood Creek. The outflow of the small creek was dammed, forming the lake. Brook trout are stocked regularly in Butcher, and most fish from the lake will be 25–30 cm in length, although there are undoubtedly a few larger specimens as well.

Butcher Lake

Butcher Lake brook trout

Bathing Lake (AB)

49°16'43"N 114°01'28"W

Rainbow and Cutthroat trout to 40 cm

Bathing Lake, another of the region's small lakes, is located between the Waterton Gas Plant and Butcher Lake. The lake holds plenty of rainbow and cutthroat trout that average 25-35 cm in length, but they can be finicky at times, especially if you are fly fishing and trying to match the hatch. The shoreline can be a bit soggy in spots, but anglers should be able to make their way around the entire lake. The lake is an open area and strong winds whip through regularly.

Bathing Lake

South Drywood Pond (AB)

49°16'22"N 114°01'03"W

Rainbow trout to 30 cm

Cutthroat trout to 30 cm

Brook trout to 30 cm

South Drywood Pond is little more than a widening of a small spring-fed tributary of South Drywood Creek. The pond usually receives attention from anglers camped nearby. The lake holds plenty of small rainbow trout, although the trout will often move into nearby South Drywood Creek if the lake level drops too much during the summer. Rainbow trout in South Drywood Pond average 15–25 cm in length, and the odd cutthroat or brook trout may be present as well.

Bovin Lake (aka Blue Lake) (AB)

49°13'27"N 114°07'41"W

Brook trout to 40 cm

Bovin Lake is reached by a 5 km road walk from gas well maintenance roads in the South Drywood Creek drainage. Bovin contains plenty of brook trout, few stretching beyond the 35 cm mark. The lake itself is a large, circular sink hole, with no permanent inlet or outlet creek. The water level in the lake fluctuates during the year, reaching its high point after runoff is complete and dropping throughout the summer and fall. The changing water levels wreak havoc on the lake's littoral zone, where the fish should be getting most of their food. Fishing is usually the most productive at the far end of the lake, where the scree slopes reach the shoreline and there is deep water within casting distance.

Bovin Lake

Drywood Creek, South Drywood Creek, Spionkop Creek, Yarrow Creek, Dungarvan Creek (AB) ⊗ Dungarvan Creek (NP)

Cutthroat trout to 35 cm

Rainbow trout to 35 cm

Brook trout to 35 cm

Brown trout to 35

Bull trout to 50 cm (1.5 kg)

Whitefish to 30 cm

All of these foothill tributary streams of the Waterton River hold trout in good numbers. Fishing pressure on these creeks is light, with most angling attention near the most accessible locations. Small cutthroat trout are the normal catch, although rainbow, brook, and bull trout as well as whitefish are all present as well. Note that Dungarvan Creek within Waterton Lakes National Park is closed to angling.

■ Oldman Reservoir (AB)

49°35'15"N 114°58'46"W
Rainbow trout to 60 cm (2.5 kg)
Bull trout to 70 cm (5.0 kg)
Cutthroat trout to 55 cm (2.0 kg)
Brown trout to 60 cm (2.5 kg)
Whitefish to 45 cm

The Oldman Reservoir is the backwater created by construction of the Oldman Dam. There is paved access from Highway 3 at Cowley and Pincher Creek and several nice campgrounds around the reservoir. The dam flooded the junction and several kilometres of the Oldman, Castle and Crowsnest Rivers. In its first few years of existence, the dam was not very productive in terms of fish habitat. However, rainbow trout seem to have taken hold, in large part due to regular stocking programs. Having a boat on the Oldman Reservoir is a priority. Trolling is the preferred technique among most anglers on the reservoir, although bait fishers working the shoreline are usually successful. The area around the inlets of the major feeder streams and river, notably Todd Creek, is the best place for those on shore to try. Rainbow trout in the 35–45 cm range are the normal catch, even though there is a mixed bag of fish in the lake. Be aware that the lake is very prone to extremely strong west winds that will make boating, much less fishing, impossible.

Oldman Reservoir

Oldman Reservoir rainbow trout

■ Cottonwood Pond (aka Oldman River Campground Pond) (AB)

49°33'30"N 114°53'07"W
Rainbow trout to 45 cm
Brown trout to 45 cm

Cottonwood Pond is a small pond within the Oldman River Campground, which is located below the dam. The pond is stocked on occasion and will contain whatever has been stocked or whatever has made its way in from the river during high water. Some nice rainbows are taken each year from the pond. In periods of low water, the pond can dry up completely.

Cottonwood Pond rainbow trout

■ Todd Creek, Cow Creek (AB)

Rainbow trout to 45 cm
Cutthroat trout to 45 cm
Brown trout to 45 cm
Whitefish to 30 cm

These two creeks enter the Oldman Reservoir at its western end. Although both creeks tend to be murky during much of the year, they hold trout in good numbers. Seldom will be a day when you don't see trout rising. Trout in the lower portions of the creeks, near the reservoir, will average 25–35 cm in length, with rainbow trout being the most likely catch.

■ Oldman River (downstream from Oldman Reservoir) (AB)

Rainbow trout to 55 cm (2.0 kg)
Brown trout to 60 cm (2.5 kg)
Bull trout to 80 cm (5.0 kg)
Whitefish to 45 cm

Below the Oldman Dam, the Oldman River flows eastward towards its confluence with Bow River. In the tailwaters below the dam, and for a few kilometres downstream, fishing is generally good. Rainbow trout are the vast majority and can generally be taken in the 25–35 cm size range. There is also a small population of bull trout that annually congregate below the dam in a fruitless effort to reach their former spawning beds far upstream. Some nice brown trout waters can be found further downstream, just west of the Piikani Nation at Brocket.

Vic Bergman photo
Oldman River (below Oldman Reservoir)

Curtis Hall photo
Oldman River brown trout

56

CROWSNEST REGION

The Crowsnest River and Crowsnest Mountain lend their name to this Region which centres on the Municipality of Crowsnest Pass (an amalgamation of the towns of Blairmore, Coleman, Bellevue, Frank and Hillcrest). Highway 3 cuts through the middle of the Region, leading east to Fort Macleod and west to Sparwood in British Columbia. The Crowsnest River, which begins near the Alberta-B.C. boundary and parallels Highway 3 as it flows east to the Oldman Reservoir, is regarded by many as one of the premier fly fishing streams in Western Canada. The numerous minor tributaries of the Crowsnest hold trout and are sought out by creek fishing enthusiasts. There are also many well-stocked lakes, making the Crowsnest a mecca for anglers. The Region is split geographically east-west, with the town of Blairmore being the dividing line: the Coleman Sub-Region to the west; and the Bellevue Sub-Region to the east.

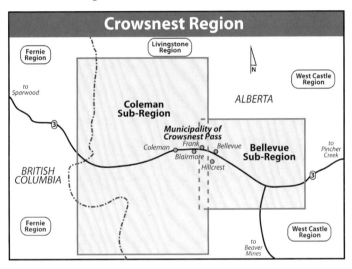

Coleman Sub-Region

The western half of the Crowsnest Region extends from the BC-Alberta boundary west to Blairmore. Crowsnest Lake, Island Lake and Emerald Lake at the head of the Crowsnest River are popular with local anglers. Chinook Lake, located just off the Allison Creek Road, has a large campground, which is very busy during the summer. Window Mountain Lake, a short hike off the upper Allison Creek Road provides one of the region's few backcountry fishing opportunities

▪ Crowsnest River (Crowsnest Lake to Blairmore) (AB)
Rainbow trout to 50 cm (1.5 kg)
Cutthroat trout to 45 cm
Bull trout to 60 cm (3.0 kg)
Whitefish to 35 cm
The Crowsnest River is renowned as one of the finest fly fishing streams anywhere in the Rockies. It flows passively eastward from headwaters at Crowsnest Lake. The upper section of the river, between Crowsnest Lake and Blairmore receives much less fishing pressure than the lower section downstream from Bellevue. The upper Crowsnest is very slow and meandering, typified by gentle riffles and wide sweeping corners with undercut banks. Access can be difficult due to adjoining swampland and willow thickets. Not as nutrient-rich as the lower river, the

upper Crowsnest contains fewer fish in generally smaller sizes. Rainbow trout averaging 20–25 cm in length predominate and are generally very susceptible to the fly or a spinner.

Crowsnest River

Crowsnest River rainbow trout

▪ Island Lake (North) (AB)
49°37'48"N 114°40'50"W
☐ Island Lake (South) (AB)
49°37'36"N 114°41'11"W
Rainbow trout to 40 cm, Cutthroat trout to 35cm
Brook trout to 35 cm
Constituting the headwaters of the Crowsnest River, Island Lake is located just east of the B.C.-Alberta boundary, and is divided in half by Highway 3. Island Lake is stocked regularly and contains a good population of rainbow and cutthroat trout, most averaging 25–35 cm in length, as well as a few brook trout. Angling is much better in the waters on the north side of the highway, and a boat is suggested, although fish can be taken from shore. Monster trout from the Allison Creek Brood Station who have outlived their usefulness for the brood stock program are on occasion put into (north) Island Lake, giving fortunate anglers who hook one a 3 kg, line-screaming thrill ride.

Island Lake (North)

57

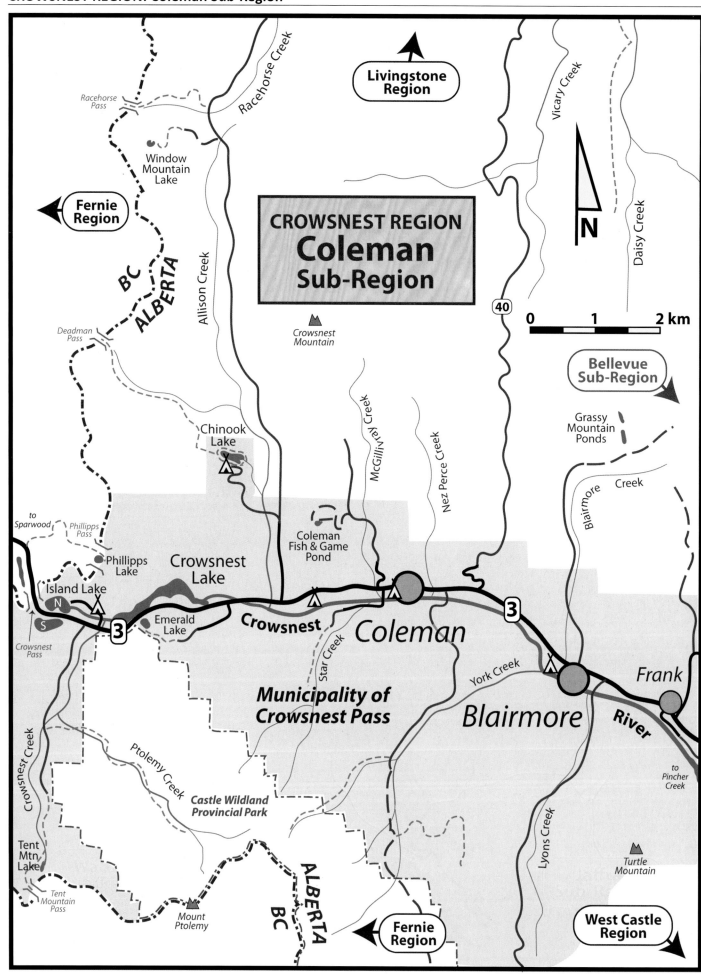

◼ Crowsnest Lake (AB)

49°37'53"N 114°38'34"W

Rainbow trout to 55 cm (1.5 kg), Cutthroat trout to 55cm (1.5kg)
Lake trout to 70 cm (6.0 kg)
Bull trout to 60 cm (4.0 kg)
Whitefish to 45 cm

Crowsnest Lake, one kilometre east of Island Lake, is the largest lake in the Region and has the Crowsnest River as both the inlet and outlet creek. Crowsnest Lake's dark waters hold rainbow and cutthroat trout that average 25–40 cm in length. The lake also holds lake trout ranging from 35–50 cm in length, with some brutes reaching over 60 cm in length and 5 kg in weight. The best time of year for lakers is very early or very late in the season, immediately after ice-out in April, or near freeze-up in November. Bait fishers who patiently work the shoreline are often productive. Trolling can also work well on Crowsnest Lake, but boaters should be aware that howling west winds usually sweep down the lake on an almost daily basis.

Crowsnest Lake

◼ Emerald Lake [aka Hart Lake] (AB)

49°37'37"N 114°38'31"W

Cutthroat trout to 50 cm
Lake trout to 90 cm (8.0 kg)

The pretty green waters of Emerald Lake are situated on the south side of Highway 3 opposite Crowsnest Lake, approximately 8 km west of Coleman. Despite its relatively small surface area, Emerald Lake has been identified as the Region's deepest lake, surprisingly surpassing even nearby Crowsnest Lake in depth. Cutthroat trout are the predominant species in Emerald Lake, most being in the 25–35 cm range. Emerald also holds some big lake trout, which attract local anglers, especially during ice fishing season. The odd rainbow or brook trout may even be present in the lake. As with neighbouring lakes, strong winds can be a major problem at Emerald Lake.

Emerald Lake

Mark Houze with Emerald Lake lake trout

Mark Houze photo

◼ Allison Creek, McGillivray Creek, Nez Perce Creek, Blairmore Creek, Crowsnest Creek, Ptolemy Creek, Star Creek, York Creek, Lyons Creek (AB)

Cutthroat trout to 30 cm
Rainbow trout to 30 cm
Brook trout to 30 cm

All minor tributaries of the Crowsnest River, these creeks hold small trout in fair numbers. Rainbow and brook trout generally predominate in the lower portions of the creeks and cutthroat in the upper. Catching a trout longer than 25 cm would be very much of a surprise in any of these creeks. Despite the small size of the trout, these tributaries of the Crowsnest remain very popular, especially with local youngsters. Active and abandoned industrial roads extend up the valleys drained by most of these creeks and provide access for anglers. (Note: Lyons Creek generally dries up completely by mid-summer in its lower reaches within the town of Blairmore.)

◼ Grassy Mountain Ponds (aka Rainbow Ponds) (AB)

49°40'06"N 114°25'40"W

Status: Devoid of fish

Located at the base of the former Grassy Mountain coal mine on former Scurry Rainbow Ltd. property are several large quarry pits that have filled with water over time. Trout were secretly stocked by locals in the past and grew to large sizes, but failed to reproduce. The waters look very tempting, but recent observations indicate that there are no trout left in any of the ponds.

☐ Tent Mountain Lake (AB)

49°34'46"N 114°43'21"W

Cutthroat trout to 30 cm

Tent Mountain Lake is a small brush-fringed lake set at the head of Crowsnest Creek, immediately below Tent Mountain Pass. The lake is accessible from the Tent Mountain Collieries road, which branches south from Highway 3 between Island and Crowsnest Lakes. Although this shallow lake holds a few small cutthroat trout, it is likely that you will see more moose than trout. For keeners, fight through the underbrush and try the area close to the outlet creek.

◢ Phillipps Lake (AB-BC)
49°38'31"N 114°39'45"W
Cutthroat trout 50 cm (1.5 kg)
Phillipps Lake is a small, circular sinkhole lake located at the summit of Phillipps Pass, astride the provincial boundary and either a BC or Alberta license will do (regulations for Phillipps Lake are the same for both jurisdictions). A stiff 3 km hike up a rocky road leads from Crowsnest Provincial Park, just west of the BC-Alberta boundary to the lake. Phillipps holds plenty of nice cutthroat trout averaging 25–35 cm in length. Fish holding waters can be reached from virtually any location around the lake.

Phillipps Lake

Phillipps Lake cutthroat trout

■ Chinook Lake [aka Allison Reservoir] (AB)
49°40'19"N 114°36'07"W
Rainbow trout to 50 cm, Cutthroat trout to 50 cm
Brook trout to 40 cm
This popular fishing spot is situated west of Coleman and five km north of Highway 3 and is accessed by a good gravel road. Chinook Lake and its nearby campground are busy all summer long. Extensive flooding caused by the dam at the south end of the lake has left an abundance of sunken deadfall around the entire shoreline. Rainbow and cutthroat trout are stocked regularly and predominate, with the average fish being 20–30 cm in length. A few brook trout still inhabit the lake. Fly fishing from a boat or float tube is very effective on Chinook Lake, particularly in the evening. Patient anglers who work the shoreline all around the lake will do well. One section of shoreline (near the access road) serves as a beach for locals in the summertime. Don't expect a lot of solitude at Chinook Lake.

Chinook Lake

■ Window Mountain Lake (AB)
49°45'38"N 114°38'24"W
Rainbow trout to 45 cm
Window Mountain is an exquisite body of water tucked into the side of Mt. Ward and stands out as one of the Region's hidden treasures. To reach the lake, one must drive 15 km north on the Allison Creek Road and then follow a rough side road for another 2 km to the trailhead (much of the 2 km side road will be hiked, depending on how much grief you want to inflict on your vehicle). From the hiking trailhead, a short but steep 2 km hike leads to the lakeshore. The beautifully coloured waters of Window Mountain Lake contain plenty of rainbow trout, most averaging 25–35 cm in length. Although fly fishing is the most effective method of angling at Window Mountain, casting a fly is difficult from most locations around the lake. If a hatch is not on at Window Mountain Lake, fishing a lure or wet fly deep generally produces. And no, you cannot see the "window" in Window Mountain from the lake.

Window Mountain Lake

Window Mountain Lake rainbow trout

⬛ Coleman Fish and Game Pond (aka Hidden Lake) (AB)

49°39'20"N 114°33'35"W

Rainbow and Cutthroat trout to 50 cm (1.5 kg)

This small man-made pond is located northwest of Coleman and offers very good fishing for those who can find it. From the west end of Coleman, take the (signed) road that leads north to the Crowsnest gun range (bypassing the junction to the McGillivray Youth Camp). Opposite the entrance to the gun range, a rough half-kilometre long road leads down to the Coleman Fish and Game Pond. Insect life is prolific in the pond, and the fish grow rapidly, with most in the 30–35 cm range. Although many people fish from shore and are successful, a boat or float tube will dramatically increase your fish catching. Fly fishing and spin casting are both effective techniques on the Coleman Fish and Game Pond. An aerator on the lake in winter has resolved the pond's winterkill issues.

Coleman Fish and Game Pond

Tyler Ambrosi with Coleman Fish and Game Pond rainbow trout

Bellevue Sub-Region

The Bellevue Sub-Region extends east from Blairmore through the Frank Slide and past the communities of Bellevue and Hillcrest, and out to the neighbouring foothills. The Crowsnest River is the primary attraction, and is revered by many fly fishing enthusiasts. Lee Lake is the most significant still water in the Sub-Region and is very popular with local anglers.

⬛ Crowsnest River (Blairmore to Oldman Reservoir) (AB)

Rainbow trout to 60 cm (2.5 kg)
Bull trout to 70 cm (4.0 kg)
Brown trout to 65 cm (3.0 kg)
Cutthroat trout to 45 cm
Whitefish to 40 cm

The lower Crowsnest River, from Blairmore downstream to the Oldman River, is an excellent trout stream. Special regulations apply to season, limits and sizes to the Crowsnest River. Be sure to read the Sportfishing Regulations before heading out, as new catch-and-release regulations are in effect. Treated sewage effluent from the communities of the Crowsnest Pass enters the river downstream of Bellevue, enriching the waters. Plant, insect, and in turn trout life, flourishes. The Crowsnest River continues to receive, and is deserving of, worldwide attention from anglers. Therefore, fishing pressure is increasing annually, and there are few stretches of water where you won't run into other anglers during the summer. Reel-screaming rainbow trout are plentiful in the river, with most fish averaging 25–35 cm, while beauties over 50 cm in length are caught regularly. Above Lundbreck Falls, cutthroat and bull trout can also be caught. Below the falls in addition to rainbows, there are brown trout, some of which reach massive proportions (75+ cm) as well as big bulls. The Crowsnest River has excellent hatches of mayflies and caddis flies as well as big stoneflies, and the fly fishing can be spectacular at times. Highway 3 parallels the river for much of its course, although it often means a bit of a walk to actually reach the river. Do not cross any private property without prior permission. The waters downstream from Lundbreck Falls, particularly those near the base of the falls, are usually busy due to the proximity of the provincial campground.

Note: Whirling disease has been detected in the Crowsnest drainage.

Vic Bergman photo

Crowsnest River

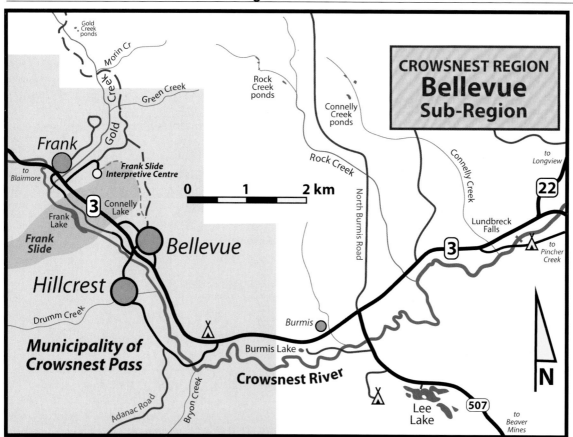

Local Knowledge

For fishing gear, up-to-date information on local waters, or even to book a guided trip, be sure to stop by The Crowsnest Angler, just off Highway 3 in Bellevue Owner Vic Bergman will set you up with the proper equipment and flies. Vic knows the lakes, rivers and streams in southern Alberta and southeast BC and will have current info on what places are hot (or not). His specialty is the Crowsnest River, located only a few hundred metres from the shop. Check out the website at *crowsnestangler.com*.

Crowsnest River brown trout

Curtis Hall photo

■ Frank Lake (AB)

49°35'17"N 114°23'52"W
Rainbow trout to 55 cm (2.0 kg)
Cutthroat trout to 45 cm
Whitefish to 40 cm

Frank Lake is little more than a widening of the Crowsnest River, caused by the multitude of boulders of the 1903 Frank Slide. Stream flow is slowed somewhat, and this stretch of the river does take on some lake-like characteristics. The downstream side of the enormous boulders that are strewn about form potential hiding spots for fish. Mud flats are a problem later in the season after runoff, as the flats extend far out from the shore in many places, leaving the fish-holding waters beyond the reach of a cast. Rainbow trout average 20–30 cm in length, with larger ones taken regularly. Plenty of whitefish can be caught in the fall. Techniques that are effective on the Crowsnest River proper are equally effective in Frank Lake.

Crowsnest River rainbow trout

Vic Bergman photo

Frank Lake (Crowsnest River)

Gold Creek (AB)

Rainbow trout to 30 cm
Brook trout to 30 cm
Cutthroat trout to 30 cm
Whitefish to 30 cm

Gold Creek is a major tributary of the Crowsnest River joining at the town of Frank. Gold Creek is an idyllic trout stream, with wonderful pools and riffles over its entire length. The section immediately above the town of Frank is the least accessible, as Gold Creek has carved a deep canyon. Above the canyon, a rough 2WD road crosses Gold Creek twice, and is passable as far as the former townsite of Lille. Rainbow, cutthroat and brook trout can all be caught in Gold Creek. There's plenty of fish, but few whoppers. For those who have had their fill of the Crowsnest River crowds, Gold Creek is a great getaway.

Gold Creek

Morin Creek, Green Creek (AB)

Rainbow trout to 25 cm
Cutthroat trout to 25 cm

Green and Morin Creeks are both tributaries of Gold Creek. They contain small rainbow and cutthroat trout in their lower sections, within a few hundred metres of their confluence with Gold Creek.

Gold Creek ponds (AB)

49°38'35"N 114°23'21"W
Brook trout to 25 cm

These hard-to-find ponds are located downstream from the second crossing of Gold Creek on the Lille road. The main pond is shallow and the fish can be seen easily. This very small population of brook trout is self-perpetuating and cannot even stand up to a minimal harvest. Please release all of the trout you catch.

Connelly Lake (AB)

49°35'28"N 114°22'17"W
Status: Devoid of fish

This small pond is located just west of Bellevue on the edge of the Frank Slide. It has never been stocked and contains no fish.

Connelly Creek ponds, Rock Creek ponds (AB)

Cutthroat trout to 35 cm

Both Connelly Creek and Rock Creek can be accessed from the North Burmis Road, which leads north from Highway 3 at the Highway 507 junction at Burmis. Both creeks have numerous beaver dam complexes, and many hold small cutthroat trout. In the right pond, a 40 cm beast is not out of the question. Access to most of the ponds requires permission from private land owners.

Burmis Lake (AB)

49°33'13"N 114°17'59"W
Rainbow and Cutthroat trout to 35 cm

This small lake is located between Highway 3 and the Crowsnest River just west of Burmis and is reached by following a dirt road that leads east from Highway 507 just before the Crowsnest River bridge. Burmis Lake is very shallow, and so is susceptible to winterkill. Food is plentiful in the lake and the fish grow rapidly. Fingerlings stocked in the spring can reach 30 cm by the fall. Fish that manage to overwinter can be very respectable in size in their second year. The lake itself is so small that proficient spin casters can generally fling a lure from one side of the lake to the other. *Note: Whirling disease has been detected in Burmis and Lee Lakes.*

Burmis Lake

Lee Lake (aka Lees Lake) (AB)

49°32'31"N 114°14'46"W
Rainbow and Cutthroat trout to 50 cm (1.5 kg)

Lee Lake is located alongside Highway 507, approximately three kilometres south of Highway 3. Formerly enclosed by private property, Lee Lake has had public access for many years now. The lake is very popular with locals, and it is rare not to see anglers at Lee Lake. Bait fishers tend to keep to the shore, while fly fishers take to the water. Lee Lake is stocked annually with fingerlings. The fish are easy to catch and most will be in the 15–25 cm range. In general, the lake is shallow, but it does have a few deep holes accessible to those with a boat. The boundary areas between the shallow and deep water are always productive. Fish also feed in the shallower waters, especially in the evenings in the summer, where major mayfly hatches can inspire nightly feeding frenzies.

Vic Bergman photo
Lee Lake

Lee Lake rainbow trout

FERNIE REGION

The Elk River is the focal point of the Fernie Region in terms of geography and angling. Changes in the 1990s to fishing regulations on the Elk River transformed it into a world-class cutthroat fishery. The quality fishing opportunities on the Elk River far exceed all other waters in the Region. Grave Lake, near Sparwood, is the only lake of major size. Small backcountry lakes dot the region and do provide alternate angling experiences. The Fernie Region splits into three Sub-Regions, two of them around the communities of Fernie and Sparwood, and a third around the former townsite of Corbin and the former Coal Mountain mine at the head of Michel Creek.

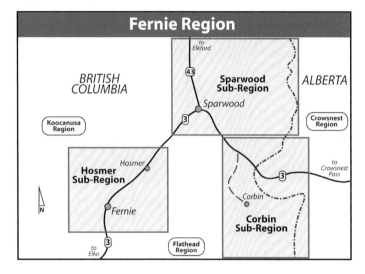

Elk River Regulations

Several decades ago, the Elk River was regarded as nice stream where you could catch a few cutthroat trout. Then catch-and-release regulations were instituted on the Elk River, and it wasn't long before it became a "world class" cutthroat river. Special designation for the Elk River as Class II waters establishes limits to guided and non-guided angling, reflects priority for local residents and requires special classified water licences. The success of these regulations has been incredible. Other waters, such as Elk tributaries, the Bull and Wigwam rivers, along with the upper Kootenay, St. Mary and White rivers and Skookumchuk Creek have in recent years been afforded similar Class II status. The quality of angling has improved dramatically in all of these waters. A special booking system for non-resident anglers is now in place on the Wigwam River, Skookumchuk Creek and Michel Creek, where non-resident, non-guided angler use had exceeded targets and created overcrowding on the river and extra pressure on fish populations.

Hosmer Sub-Region

Highway 3 runs lengthwise through the Hosmer Sub-Region, affording access from east and west. The Fernie area is very spartan in terms of fishing opportunities. Other than the Elk River, which is outstanding, only two small lakes – Island and Hartley – will even attract the eye of potential anglers.

◼ Elk River (Hosmer to Elko) (BC)
Cutthroat trout to 55 cm (1.5 kg)
Bull trout to 80 cm (6.0 kg)
Whitefish to 40 cm

The Elk River flows south down the Elk Valley on its way to Lake Koocanusa. The section between the hamlet of Hosmer and the city of Fernie has become very popular for fly fishers in drift boats. Hosmer is located at a bridged highway crossing of the Elk River and has a good put-in site for drift boats. Similarly, Highway 3 crosses the Elk River again at Fernie, where there are good take-out sites. The river is wide and strong, with long stretches of riffles and deep pools. Runoff occurs in late spring and continues into early summer, muddying the river significantly. By mid-summer, the river clears magnificently, and fishing is at its prime. Cutthroat trout are plentiful and are of particular delight to dry fly enthusiasts. Cutthroat average 30–40 cm in length, with beauties of 50 cm and over available in good numbers. Bull trout and whitefish are also present in the river. Read your fishing regulations and be aware of all of the special restrictions in force on the river, including which sections of the river are catch-and-release only.

Elk River float

Elk River cutthroat trout

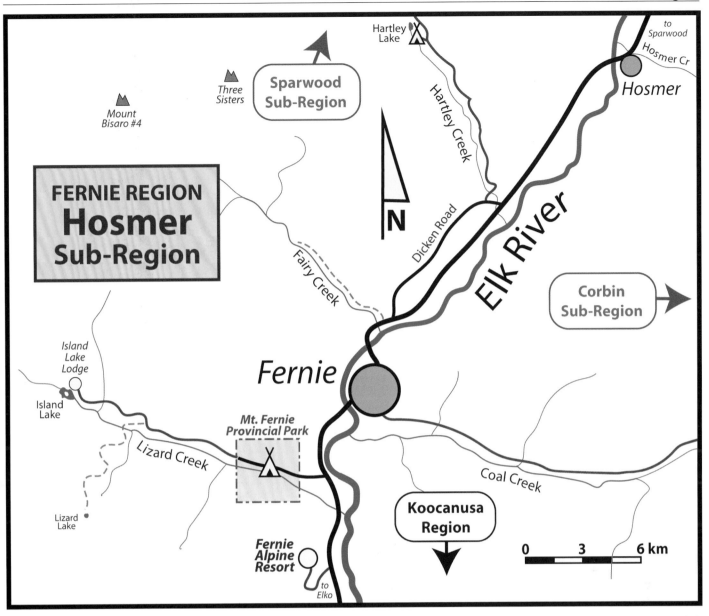

FERNIE REGION
Hosmer
Sub-Region

■ **Coal Creek, Fairy Creek, Lizard Creek, Hartley Creek, Hosmer Creek (BC)**

Cutthroat trout to 35 cm

The Elk Valley in this Sub-Region is very deep and steep-sided. As a result, minor tributaries to the Elk River tend to be very turbulent much beyond their confluence with the main river. Cutthroat trout in the 15–25 cm range can be taken from these creeks. Of more significance, fishing is generally very good where these creeks empty into the Elk River, particularly when the tributaries are clear and the main river is dirty. Note that special restrictions apply to part of Coal Creek. Check the regulations.

□ **Island Lake (BC)**

49°30'26"N 115°10'41"W

Cutthroat trout to 35 cm

Island Lake is located west of Fernie, and can be reached by taking the dirt road that continues past the Mt. Fernie Provincial Park campground. Signs on the access road indicate that Island Lake Lodge is private and accessible only to those staying at Island Lake Lodge. The public can access the road, but it is best to check with the lodge before travelling on the road. Island Lake itself is very pretty, with many bays and tree-studded islands. Below the lodge, a point of land juts out into the lake and most anglers can cast to fish from the point. Cutthroat trout have been stocked in Island Lake in the past but have had trouble maintaining strong populations. However, there are always a few trout out and about, most in the 15–25 cm range.

Island Lake

■Lizard Lake (BC)

49°28'39"N 115°08'32"W

Status: Devoid of fish

Lizard Lake is a teeny-tiny, snow-bound, avalanche-swept pond high up on Lizard Ridge that is free of ice for only a few brief weeks each year. It has never been stocked and contains no fish.

Lizard Lake

■ Hartley Lake (BC)

49°36'32"N 114°03'17"W

Cutthroat trout to 35 cm

Diminutive Hartley Lake is located approximately 8 km west of Highway 3 on the Hartley Pass road. The lake is very shallow and is strewn with deadfall, much of it old logs from a former logging operation in the area. Heavy brush surrounds much of the lake, making it difficult to cast to the fish-holding waters. Cutthroat trout in Hartley Lake are plentiful, but are small, with most being in the 20–25 cm range. Fly fishing is very limited for those on shore. Spin casting is much more likely to get positive results.

Hartley Lake

Elk River float trips

If you are looking for one of the premier angling experiences in the Canadian Rockies, try a float trip on the Elk River with the top-notch guides at Fernie Wilderness Adventures. You will soon be on the river and hooked up with superb cutthroat and bull trout in an adventure you will never forget. Ask for Curtis. Check out the website at *fwaflyfishing.com*.

Sparwood Sub-Region

The Sparwood Sub-Region has the Elk River as its core as it flows south to Fernie. Highway 3 is the major transportation link east and west. Highway 43 branches north from Sparwood to connect with Elkford and provides access to a number of lakes. Grave Lake, northeast of Sparwood, is accessible by vehicle and is popular with locals. Most of the rest of the limited fishing opportunities in this Sub-Region are smaller creeks or secluded alpine lakes, including Harriet, Wilimena, Big, Josephine, Mite and Barren.

■ Elk River (Fording River to Hosmer) (BC)

Cutthroat trout to 60 cm (2.0 kg)

Bull trout to 80 cm (6.0 kg)

Whitefish to 40 cm

This section of the Elk River, which flows south from its confluence with Fording River to the small community of Hosmer, offers superb angling for cutthroat trout. The confluence with the Fording River is the northernmost point to put in watercraft and be able to drift without problems. Above its confluence with Fording River, the Elk River is very shallow in spots and sweepers can extend far into the river, causing navigation problems. Below Fording River, the Elk River is generally wide and deep enough to permit a good drift, although the water flow drops significantly into the fall. Access to the put-in point below Fording River is on the paved road that leads to Line Creek coal mine. The Elk River is paralleled by Highway 3 below Sparwood and Highway 43 above. This allows for good access for those fishing from shore, although a rough walk through a tangle of forest is often required. Cutthroat trout in the 25–35 cm range are found in every good hole along the river, with some big fellas usually lurking about. Dry fly fishing is preferred by most anglers, although a nymph fished deep can be dynamite. Be aware that the Elk River is subject to special angling regulations.

Elk River

Curtis Hall photo

Elk River cutthroat trout

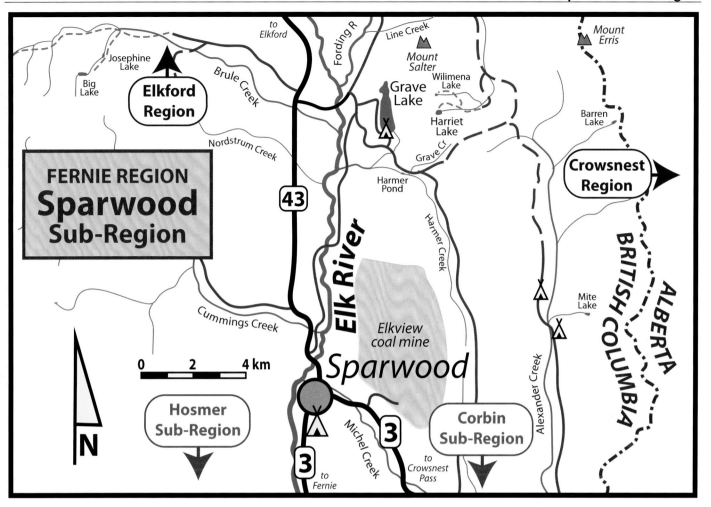

⊗ Line Creek (BC)

Status: Closed to angling

Line Creek, one of the major tributaries to Fording River, is closed to fishing.

▪ Brule Creek, Cummings Creek, Grave Creek, Harmer Creek, Nordstrum Creek (BC)

Cutthroat trout to 35 cm

These tributaries of the Elk River generally hold small cutthroat trout. The best fishing is in the lower sections of the creeks, close to their confluence with the Elk. Trout tend to be small, with most in the 15–25 cm range.

▪ Josephine Lake (BC)

49°52'58"N 115°02'32"W

▪ Big Lake (BC)

49°52'48"N 115°03'11"W

Cutthroat trout to 40 cm

These two remote, subalpine lakes are located high in a secluded basin off upper Brule Creek near Hornaday Pass. A well-defined trail leads up Brule Creek and over Hornaday Pass, but the route into Big and Josephine Lake is a little more rugged. Josephine is the smaller of the two lakes and is set lower in the basin. Both Big and Josephine have stocked populations of cutthroat trout. Fish in the two lakes average 20–30 cm in length.

▪ Grave Lake (aka Emerald Lake) (BC)

49°51'46"N 114°50'04"W

Rainbow trout to 55 cm (1.5 kg)

Cutthroat trout to 50 cm

Brook trout to 45 cm

Kokanee to 35 cm

Grave Lake is located on the east side of the Elk River, approximately 15 km north of Sparwood. Access to the lake is over gravel roads from Highway 43 (at Line Creek) or from the Lower Elk Valley Road. A nice campground maintained by the Sparwood Fish and Game Association is situated at the south end of the lake. Private property and recreational homes are found along much of the lake's western shore. Grave Lake is a lovely green body of water almost three kilometres in length, with a dramatic mountain background on its east side. A boat is essential for angling on Grave Lake, and trolling is the most effective tactic. Fly fishing is usually restricted to the extensive shallows at the south end. The lake's fish population is made up of rainbow, cutthroat and brook trout, as well as a substantial kokanee population. Trout taken will average 30–40 cm in length with kokanee slightly smaller. Kokanee are taken by those trolling with lures such as Wedding Bands and Kokanee Killers behind a gang troll. Depth finders and down-riggers are common among the regulars on Grave Lake.

Grave Lake

☐ Harmer Pond (BC)

49°49'49"N 114°48'56"W

Cutthroat trout to 30 cm

This small man-made pond on Harmer Creek is located approximately 4 km by road southeast of Grave Lake. Cutthroat trout inhabit the lake, but their numbers are limited. Flashy lures worked from the shore tend to attract trout. Due to the limited population of fish, it is recommended that anglers practice catch-and-release at Harmer Pond.

Harmer Pond

◩ Harriet Lake (BC)

49°51'46"N 114°47'46"W

Cutthroat trout to 45 cm

This stunning lake is set in a picturesque subalpine basin on the east side of Sheep Mountain, due west of Grave Lake. Access to the lake requires driving a rough 2WD road and then a hike on a short but steep 3 km trail. The trail climbs to the crest of a rocky ridge, before dropping down to the shores of Harriet Lake. Several primitive campsites are found along the lakeshore. Harriet Lake holds plenty of cutthroat trout in its emerald waters, with most trout taken ranging from 25–35 cm in length. Heavy forest cover clings to half of the shoreline. The remainder is scree and grass-covered slopes that offer ample casting room. Fly fishers using a wet line and a nymph will do well. Dry fly fishing tends to improve in the evening. Although many anglers will be frustrated with fish jumping just beyond the reach of their longest cast, those who are patient at Harriet Lake will be successful.

Harriet Lake

◻ Wilimena Lake (BC)

49°52'13"N 114°47'55"W

Cutthroat trout to 35 cm

Wilimena Lake is situated in the basin immediately north of its neighbour, Harriet Lake. The trailhead for Wilimena Lake is the same as Harriet, although the trail into Wilimena is much less defined. Be prepared for a little scrambling and stumbling before you reach the shore at Wilimena. Cutthroat trout are bountiful in Wilimena, but their size is not impressive. Most trout caught will be in the 15–25 cm range. The best fishing is off of the open slopes on the lake's south side.

◻ Barren Lake (BC)

49°49'32"N 114°41'23"W

Cutthroat trout to 35 cm

"Barren" aptly describes this tiny lake and the desolate, rockbound basin in which it is set. Barren Lake is located at the head of a tributary of upper Alexander Creek, and can be reached on a combination of 2WD and 4WD roads, seismic cut lines and poor trails. The lake contains cutthroat trout that average 20–30 cm in length. The lack of vegetation around the lake allows plenty of backcasting room for fly fishers.

◻ Mite Lake (BC)

49°49'23"N 114°39'14"W

Cutthroat trout to 35 cm

Pint-size Mite Lake is situated in a stark basin beneath the peaks of the Continental Divide, due west of Mt. Ward. Mite's outlet creek is a tributary of Alexander Creek. Some route finding will be required to reach the lake from logging roads along Alexander Creek. Cutthroat trout are present in Mite Lake, with the average fish being 20–30 cm in length. It's doubtful that you will meet up with other anglers at Mite.

Corbin Sub-Region

The Corbin Sub-Region is set amid the rugged peaks on the western (BC) side of the Continental Divide gap at Crowsnest Pass and offers some good stream and lake fishing for cutthroat and rainbow trout. The main east-west transportation connection is Highway 3. The Byron Creek mine road and the Flathead River Forest Service Road offer vehicular access south from Highway 3 to the upper Michel Creek environs. The former mining community of Corbin and the Coal Mountain mining operations are the geographical centre of the Sub-Region. Summit Lake, alongside Highway 3 just west of the BC-Alberta boundary, is a popular angling location. Michel Creek and its tributaries are great cutthroat trout streams once the high water has passed.

Winterkill

Winterkill occurs in lakes when fish suffocate from the lack of dissolved oxygen. When snow covers the ice on a lake, it limits the sunlight reaching aquatic plants. The plants then cut back on the amount of oxygen they produce, and if the lack of sunlight goes on long enough, the vegetation dies. The plants then start to decompose, which uses oxygen dissolved in the water. When oxygen depletion becomes severe enough, the fish in the lake will die. Winterkill happens in the Rockies in winters with heavy snowfall. The lack of oxygen in a lake can be mitigated by the installation of an aeration system, which adds oxygen directly by agitating the water and by diffusion through open water. Summit Lake is a prime example of a lake that is prone to winterkill. At least three times in the last 25 years the lake has suffered catastrophic fish losses during harsh winters with excessive snowfall.

Late season ice at Summit Lake

⬛ Summit Lake (BC)
49°38'31"N 114°41'50"W
Cutthroat trout to 55 cm (1.5 kg)
Rainbow trout to 55 cm (1.5 kg)
Summit Lake is situated in a narrow valley below Highway 3 on the BC side of Crowsnest Pass. Fine rainbow trout in Summit Lake were a big attraction until a severe winterkill in the mid-1990s. Cutthroat trout were then planted in the lake and flourished, but then also succumbed to winterkill. Gerrard-strain rainbow trout were then successfully replanted and grew to good sizes. Unfortunately, the long winter of 2017-18 resulted in another winterkill, eliminating most of Summit's fish population. Westslope cutthroat trout were stocked in 2018 and 2019 and

hopefully they will succeed in the manner of previous plantings. Fishing from shore is practical at Summit, and fish can be taken from most places along the railway tracks. Those with a boat will have access to more fish-holding waters and will likely have a little more success. Very heavy weed growth in the summer months will inhibit some tactics such as trolling. Chironomid fishing is very popular at Summit Lake in the early season. Due to the amount of pollutants that have seeped into the lake over time from the nearby CPR operations, it is strongly suggested that you return your catch to the water and not take any home for supper.

Summit Lake

Tyler Ambrosi with Summit Lake rainbow

⬛ Michel Creek (BC)
Cutthroat trout to 35 cm
Bull trout to 50 cm (1.5 kg)
Whitefish to 30 cm
Michel Creek boasts some excellent waters as it flows from headwaters near Flathead Pass to its confluence with the Elk River at Sparwood. Cutthroat trout in the 20–30 cm range can be taken from virtually every pool on the creek. Some of the best waters are below the confluence of Alexander Creek with Michel Creek. There are special rules in effect for fishing Michel Creek. Check the regulations.

Michel Creek

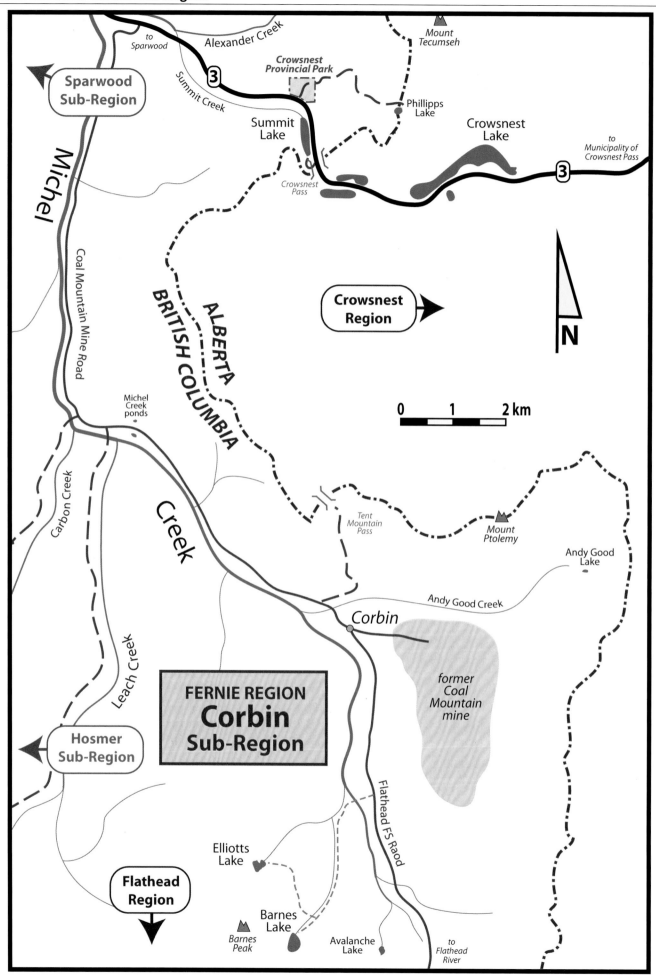

Michel Creek cutthroat trout

Curtis Hall photo

Barnes Lake

▢ Alexander Creek (BC)

Cutthroat trout to 30 cm

A major tributary of Michel Creek, Alexander Creek is accessed from the Transportation Department weigh scales, 3 km west of the BC-Alberta boundary. Alexander Creek holds plenty of small cutthroat trout along its entire length.

☐ Summit Creek (BC)

Rainbow trout to 35 cm

From the outlet at Summit Lake to its confluence with Alexander Creek, Summit Creek holds rainbow trout and possibly a few cutthroat trout. The waters immediately below Summit Lake that include some overgrown ponds hold the best potential.

▢ Leach Creek, Wheeler Creek, Carbon Creek, Andy Good Creek (BC)

Cutthroat trout to 25 cm

These tributaries of Michel Creek all hold small cutthroat trout.

☐ Michel Creek ponds (BC)

49°34'55"N 114°47'21"W

Brook trout to 30 cm

This series of very small interconnected ponds alongside the Coal Mountain road hold a population of skittish brook trout. The trout can easily be seen in the ponds, but tend to flee at the slightest hint of shadow or movement. Sometimes frustrating, but a lot of fun. Catch-and-release is the only option to maintain this fragile population.

▢ Barnes Lake (BC)

49°26'44"N 114°42'15"W

Cutthroat trout to 35 cm

Barnes Lake is reached via a 6 km hike on old roads from the Flathead FS Road. Hunters in the fall and snowmobilers in the winter will visit this area a lot more than anglers in the summer. A primitive campsite is located on the shore. Barnes Lake is surrounded by forest and is set in a steep-walled basin. Avalanche paths sweep down onto the lake at several locations. The thick forest cover will restrict most attempts at fly fishing. Cutthroat trout are present in Barnes Lake, with the average being 20–30 cm in length.

▢ Elliotts Lake (BC)

49°27'49"N 114°42'49"W

Status: Doubtful

This beautiful lake is located in a subalpine basin approximately 3 km south of Barnes Lake. An abandoned mining road leads to within 400 m of the lake. Simply following the outlet stream up from the road will lead to the lakeshore. The lake looks as though it has the potential to hold trout, but it has never been stocked. Even if you don't catch any fish, the scenery at the lake makes a trip worthwhile.

Elliotts Lake

▢ Avalanche Lake (BC)

49°26'47"N 114°40'42"W

Status: Devoid of fish

To reach Avalanche Lake requires a wicked 3 km bushwhack from the Flathead Road. There are no trails here. The lake is at the base of a major avalanche path and each winter the lake is buried by snow slides. This means ice-out is much later than would normally happen and winterkill is probable. Although the lake was stocked with cutthroat trout in the past, examination indicates that none remain.

▢ Andy Good Lake (BC)

49°32'24"N 114°34'51"W

Status: Devoid of fish

Diminutive Andy Good Lake at the head of Andy Good Creek has never been stocked and holds no fish.

SKOOKUMCHUCK REGION

Fine lake fishing for rainbow trout is the main fare of the Skookumchuck Region, which divides into two Sub-Regions. The main access is along north-south Highway 93/95. The southern Sub-Region includes the popular summer destination of Wasa Lake Provincial Park and surrounding fishing lakes. The northern Sub-Region includes the hamlet of Skookumchuck and centres on Premier Lake Provincial Park.

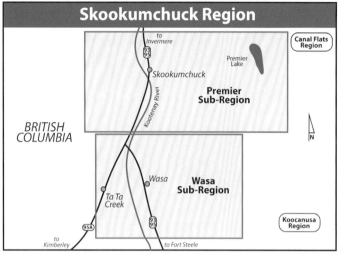

Wasa Sub-Region

The Kootenay River and Wasa Lake are the major water features of this Sub-Region, but are not the major angling attractions. Skookumchuck Creek, a tributary of the Kootenay, is highly regarded as an excellent cutthroat trout stream. Several lakes in the Sub-Region, including Tamarack, Larchwood, Lazy, Sowerby and HaHas contain fine rainbow trout and are undoubtedly the area's prime angling attractions.

■ Kootenay River (BC) (Skookumchuck to Wasa)
Cutthroat trout to 55 cm (1.5 kg)
Bull trout to 80 cm (6.0 kg)
Whitefish to 45 cm
This section of the Kootenay River flows from Skookumchuck to Wasa, paralleling Highway 93/95. Fishing improves after spring runoff, although anglers tend to prefer local lakes to the Kootenay River. Cutthroat trout predominate in the river, with specimens regularly exceeding 45 cm in length. As the river is murky much of the fishing season, anglers using bright lures often have the best success.

Kootenay River

■ Wasa Lake (BC)
49°46'49"N 115°44'05"W
Largemouth bass to 60 cm (2.5 kg)
Yellow perch to 35 cm
Wasa Lake is much more popular with the beach crowd than it is with anglers. Wasa is promoted as the "warmest lake in the Kootenays" for good reason. The nearby provincial park is packed each summer with families who partake in sun, sand and water fun. Fishing at Wasa Lake is focused on the lake's population of largemouth bass and yellow perch. A variety of lures, spinners and buzz baits will attract the attention of the bass, most of which will average 25–35 cm in length. Some quite large bass have been taken from the lake in the past. Try around the boat docks for the big ones. The perch are smaller but more numerous and are fun to catch. A bubble and worm or fly will drum up some perch action.

Wasa Lake

☐ Lewis Slough (BC)
49°45'47"N 115°43'46"W
Largemouth bass to 55 cm (2.0 kg)
Yellow perch to 30 cm
This large slough extends south from Wasa Lake and contains largemouth bass and yellow perch. It is seldom fished, as it is difficult to reach the fish-holding waters due to the swampy shoreline.

■ Lazy Lake (aka Rock Lake, Stevens Lake) (BC)
49°49'34"N 115°37'16"W
Rainbow trout to 60 cm (2.5 kg)
This pretty lake is located approximately 15 km east of Wasa Lake in the upper Lewis Creek valley. A campground is located at the north end of the lake. Access is via good gravel road that begins on the south side of Wasa Lake. Lazy Lake is hemmed in large part by significant cliff formations and is very deep. Fishing from a boat is the only viable option at Lazy Lake. Rainbow trout caught in Lazy Lake will average 30–40 cm in length, although larger trout are caught regularly. Gang trolls and flatfish are the standard angling technique at Lazy Lake.

Lazy Lake rainbow trout

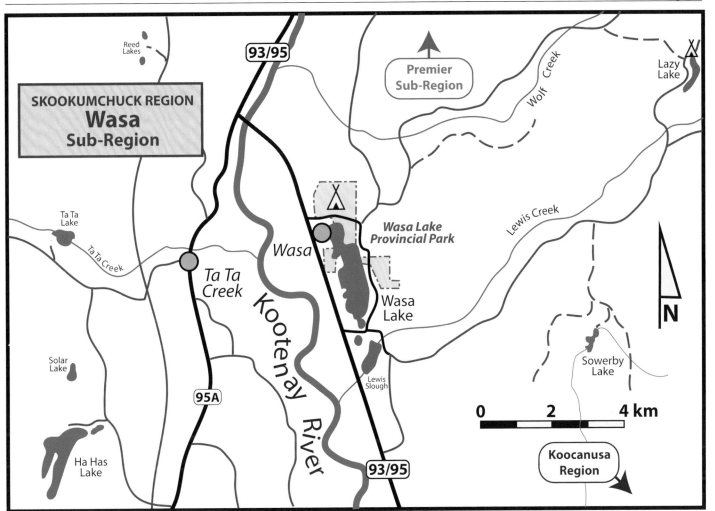

SKOOKUMCHUCK REGION
Wasa
Sub-Region

Reed Lakes

93/95

Premier Sub-Region

Wolf Creek

Lazy Lake

Ta Ta Lake

Ta Ta Creek

Wasa

Wasa Lake Provincial Park

Lewis Creek

Ta Ta Creek

Kootenay River

Wasa Lake

Solar Lake

N

95A

Lewis Slough

Sowerby Lake

0 2 4 km

Ha Has Lake

93/95

Koocanusa Region

Lazy Lake

◼ Sowerby Lake (aka Grundy Lake) (BC)
49°45′59″N 115°39′38″W
Rainbow trout to 60 cm (2.5 kg)
Sowerby Lake is located south of the Wasa-Lazy Lake Road and is protected by a maze of logging roads and a final one kilometre section of ugly, potholed 4WD road. Fishing is best in the deeper waters at the far end of the lake, opposite the access road. The lake can be fished from shore, but a boat, canoe or float tube is much preferable. Most fish taken will be in the 30–40 cm range. Fly fishing is generally excellent at Sowerby. If the fish are rising, use a dry fly. If all seems quiet on the surface, a wet line and nymph will bring on some action. Chironomid fishing works well in the springtime at Sowerby.

◼ Wolf Creek (BC)
Rainbow trout to 35 cm
Cutthroat trout to 35 cm
Wolf Creek flows west to the Kootenay River and is accessed by a good gravel road that leads northeast from Wasa Lake. Wolf Creek has many good sections as it flows through open meadows and farmland. Rainbow and cutthroat in small sizes predominate, and a few brook trout may be present as well. Be sure to gain permission before entering private land.

◼ Ha Has Lake (aka Stony Lake) (BC)
49°44′49″N 115°49′30″W
Rainbow trout to 60 cm (3.0 kg)
Kokanee to 35 cm
Ha Has Lake is located southwest of the hamlet of Ta Ta Creek and is accessible from Lost Dog Creek Forest Service Road. The lake has had problems with alkalinity in the past, particularly when water levels have been low. With normal or high water levels, the fertility of the lake is outstanding, and the rainbow trout grow very quickly. An average trout from Ha Has Lake will generally be in the 40 cm+ range. Large trout, weighing 2–3 kg, are caught regularly. Kokanee have also been planted in Ha Has. The lake is very shallow with extensive weedbeds. Fishing a chironomid pattern over the weedbeds is usually very effective. Dry fly enthusiasts will enjoy the evening hatches at Ha Has.

◻ Solar Lake (Little Ha Has Lake, Stony Pothole Lake) (BC)

49°45'38"N 115°49'17"W
Rainbow trout to 55 cm (1.5 kg)

Tiny Solar Lake is located less than a kilometre north of Ha Has, and is accessed by a rough 4WD road. Solar Lake has experienced the same alkalinity problems as nearby Ha Has Lake during times of low water. The rainbow trout in Solar also grow quickly on the abundant feed. Expect fat rainbows in the 30–40 cm range.

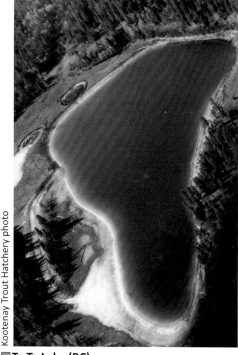

Solar Lake

◻ Ta Ta Lake (BC)

49°45'38"N 115°49'17"W
Brook trout to 40 cm
Cutthroat trout to 40 cm

Ta Ta Lake is situated on Ta Ta Creek, approximately 4 km by road west of Highway 95A. On first appearance, Ta Ta Lake seems little more than a large marsh with a few patches of open water. Casting to the open water is difficult from shore due to the vast reed growth around the lake. The lake holds brook and the odd cutthroat trout that average 25–35 cm in length.

Ta Ta Lake

◼ Reed Lakes (BC)

49°49'16"N 115°47'57"W
Status: Devoid of fish

The two tiny Reed Lakes can be accessed from Ta Ta Lake on very rough roads. Reed Lakes have never been stocked and hold no fish.

Premier Sub-Region

Premier Lake Provincial Park is the focal point for this Sub-Region. The park can be accessed by a paved and gravel road that leads west from Highway 93/95 just north of the community of Skookumchuck. Premier Lake is renowned, along with Whitetail and Whiteswan lakes, as a trophy rainbow lake. Virtually all of the Sub-Region's fishing pressure is directed at Premier Lake. Quartz, McNair, Echo, Tamarack, Larchwood and Johnson Lakes all receive steady business during the summer and fall. Other lakes in the Sub-Region are accessed by foot and receive little attention from anglers.

◮ Premier Lake (BC)

49°56'23"N 115°39'17"W
Rainbow trout to 70 cm (4.0 kg)
Brook trout to 60 cm (3.0 kg)

If you are after huge rainbow trout, then Premier Lake stands out as, indeed, one of the "premier" fishing lakes in the East Kootenays. This fact is attested to by the large numbers of anglers who annually make their way to this beautiful body of water set in wooded hills 15 km east of Highway 93/95 at Skookumchuck. A major campground with boat launch facilities is located at the south end of the lake in Premier Lake Provincial Park. Rainbow trout in excess of 15 kg have been taken from Premier in the past, although average catches today tend to be in the 35–45 cm range, with trout in the 2–3 kg category taken frequently. A few chunky brook trout also inhabit Premier. A boat is essential for fishing on Premier and trolling is a most effective technique. Although gang trolls and flatfish predominate among fishing gear on Premier, anglers slowly trolling a wet fly behind a boat can expect good results. A productive area is along the rockbluff approximately halfway down the lake. Dry fly fishing can be excellent in the evening in the shallows at either end of the lake.

Premier Lake

Premier Lake rainbow trout

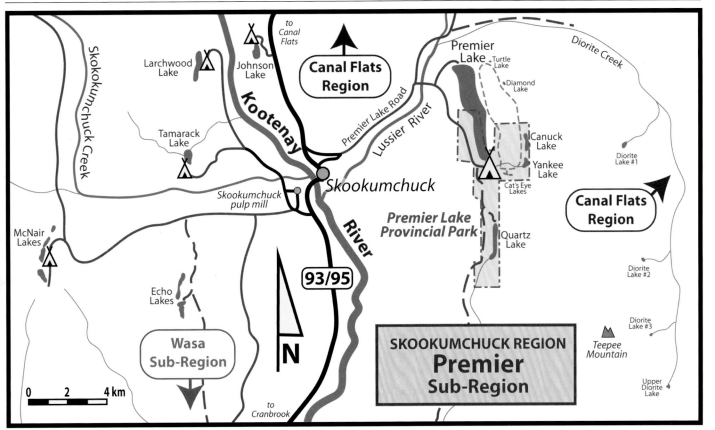

Quartz Lake (aka Rockbluff Lake) (BC)

49°53'37"N 115°38'32"W
Rainbow trout to 60 cm (2.5 kg)
Kokanee to 35 cm

Quartz Lake is located less than 3 km south of Premier Lake. The easiest access is by road from Premier Lake Provincial Park. There is also a rough road up Wolf Creek from Wasa Lake. From Premier Lake, a campsite and boat launch is reached in short order. Quartz holds hard-fighting rainbow trout in the 30–40 cm range, with plenty of larger ones in the lake. Tactics for Premier Lake apply equally well to Quartz. The drop-off between the shallow and deep water is highly visible in Quartz Lake and should not be overlooked by anglers. Kokanee have been stocked in Quartz in recent years and are targeted by many anglers.

Quartz Lake

Cat's Eye Lakes (aka Bear Paw Lakes) (BC)

49°54'49"N 115°38'04"W
Rainbow trout to 30 cm

The two Cat's Eye Lakes are the first of a series of lakes that can be reached via an excellent hiking trail from the campground at the south end of Premier Lake. Cat's Eyes are small and shallow and although the water is clear, it has a distinctive green-yellow hue. Rainbow trout have been stocked in the lakes, but their numbers are limited.

Yankee Lake (aka Twin Lake) (BC)

49°55'04"N 115°37'33"W
Rainbow trout to 55 cm (1.5 kg)

Yankee Lake is the next stop on the hiking trail from the Premier Lake campground. Yankee's pretty green waters hold plenty of rainbow trout that are not subject to heavy fishing pressure. As such, fishing tends to be decent at Yankee for trout that average 30–40 cm in length. Fishing from shore is practical from many locations, although an energetic soul who brings a float tube to the lake will be rewarded handsomely. If fly fishing from shore, expect to put your roll casting technique to good use.

Yankee Lake

■ Canuck Lake (aka Twin Lake) (BC)

49°55'31"N 115°37'30"W

Rainbow trout to 55 (1.5 kg)

Canuck Lake is located a short distance by trail beyond Yankee Lake and is similar in size and character, hence the name Twin Lakes is used by some people to describe the two. The rainbow trout in Canuck Lake tend to be similar in size to those in Yankee Lake, most in the 30–40 cm range, with a few exceeding 45 cm in length. Lily pads and shallows are a bit more of a problem at Canuck but a short search along the shoreline and one will locate good casting spots. Lures and flies will both be effective at Canuck Lake.

South Echo Lake

■ McNair Lakes (BC)

49°52'52"N 115°52'57"W

Cutthroat trout to 45 cm

Rainbow trout to 45 cm

The McNair Lakes are located in heavy forest at the height of land between Skookumchuck Creek and Lost Dog Creek, approximately 13 km west of Highway 93/95 at Skookumchuck on the McNair FS Road. Logging roads from Skookumchuck pass close by the lakes. The level of water in the lakes fluctuates significantly from season to season. During most of the fishing season there is a wide gravel beach surrounding the lakes. McNair North is usually stocked with rainbow and McNair South with cutthroat. Trout close to shore are spooked easily, making long casts or patience necessary to take fish. Trout from the lakes will average 25–35 cm in length.

Canuck Lake

■ Diamond Lake (BC)

49°57'04"N 115°38'37"W

Rainbow trout to 35 cm

Diamond Lake is the last of the fishable waters along the trail around the eastern side of Premier Lake. Being at the end of the chain, Diamond receives the least fishing pressure of the four lakes. Rainbow trout inhabit the lake in good numbers, and average 20–30 cm in length.

■ Turtle Lake (BC)

49°58'03"N 115°38'42"W

Status: Devoid of fish

Tiny Turtle Lake, at the northeastern end of Premier Lake, is home to plenty of western painted turtles, but nothing in the way of game fish.

■ Echo Lakes (aka North and South Echo Lakes, Echoes Lakes) (BC)

49°52'17"N 115°48'31"W

Rainbow trout to 60 cm (2.5 kg)

The two Echo Lakes, less than 50 metres apart, are set on a pleasant forested and meadowed bench west of Skookumchuck. Access is on rough roads that lead south from the McNair FS Road. The lakes have extended shallows, but there are numerous places along the lakeshore from which to fish. Fly fishing from a boat or float tube will be the most effective in catching the lakes' rainbow trout but spin casters will have luck as well. The rainbows in the Echo Lakes grow fast and many are caught that exceed 50 cm in length, although the average will likely be in the 25–35 cm range. Spring and fall are normally the best times of year to take trout from Echo Lakes.

North McNair Lake

■ Skookumchuck Creek (aka Skookumchuck River) (BC)

Cutthroat trout to 50 cm (1.5 kg)

Bull trout to 70 cm (5.0 kg)

Whitefish to 45 cm

Skookumchuck Creek is a major tributary to the Kootenay River in this Region. The upper Skookumchuck offers outstanding cutthroat trout fishing. The best access to the upper creek is not from roads leading west from near the confluence of the Skookumchuck and the Kootenay as one would expect, but rather from the Findlay Creek Road, northwest of Canal Flats. Skookumchuck Creek has innumerable fine holes that are home to beautifully coloured cutthroat trout averaging 30–40 cm in length and fly fishing is great for beginner and expert alike. Special restrictions apply to Skookumchuck Creek. Check the regulations.

◼ Tamarack Lake (BC)

49°55'14"N 115°48'17"W

Rainbow trout to 55 cm (1.5 kg)

Tamarack Lake sits amid forested surroundings 5 km by gravel road west of the Skookumchuck pulp mill. Rainbows averaging 30–40 cm in length are the average catch from Tamarack. A boat or float tube is strongly suggested at Tamarack as fish tend to keep to the deeper waters for most of the day. Slowly trolling a wet fly behind the boat will produce positive results.

Tamarack Lake

◪ Larchwood Lake (BC)

49°57'01"N 115°47'47"W

Rainbow trout to 55 cm (1.5 kg)

Larchwood Lake was rehabilitated in the early 1990s and has proved to be an excellent lake since the restocking program began. Rainbow trout are plentiful in the lake, with most trout in the 25–35 cm range. Fly fishers do well in Larchwood, especially in the extensive shallows or in the margin between the shallows and the deeper water. Trolling is also popular at Larchwood. The lake is long and narrow, and fishing from shore is possible from many locations. The campground at Larchwood Lake is very popular throughout the summer months.

Larchwood Lake

◼ Johnson Lake (BC)

49°57'22"N 115°45'51"W

Rainbow trout to 50 cm

Brook trout to 40 cm

Johnson Lake is set in a wooded hollow west of Highway 93/95, approximately 4 km north of Skookumchuck. Access is good on a gravel road from the highway to one of the two recreation sites at the lake. Johnson Lake itself is fairly shallow and nutrient rich. Stocked rainbow trout grow well in this habitat, and most fish caught will be in the 25–35 cm range. A few brook trout may be present as well. There are a number of spots to fish from shore, but long casts will be required to get out past the shallow water. A boat or float tube is recommended.

Johnson Lake

◼ Lussier River (Diorite Creek to Kootenay River) (BC)

Cutthroat trout to 45 cm

Bull trout to 70 cm (4.0 kg)

Whitefish to 40 cm

The lower section of the Lussier River, from the Diorite Creek junction to the Lussier's confluence with the Kootenay River, is a good cutthroat trout fishery. Private land and the lack of access to the creek are the main problems. The main access points outside the private lands (near bridges, etc.) tend to be overfished. For those who receive permission from landowners to fish the river, cutthroat trout in the 25–35 cm range will be in good supply.

◼ Diorite Creek (BC)

Cutthroat trout to 35 cm

The sparkling waters of Diorite Creek constitute a major tributary of the lower Lussier River. There has been little or no human activity in much of the Diorite Creek valley, and access is generally difficult. The creek holds small cutthroat trout that are very willing to rise to a fly.

◼ Diorite Lakes #1, #2, #3 (BC)

(#2) 49°53'51"N 115°34'34"W

Cutthroat trout to 40 cm

All of the larger lakes in the Diorite Creek drainage have been stocked in the past with cutthroat trout, which now reproduce naturally. The valley is for explorers only, as there are few trails of any significance. For those who have the energy and willpower to search out the Diorite Lakes, the prize will be feisty cutthroat trout in the 25–35 cm range.

Diorite Lake #2

Kootenay Trout Hatchery photo

◼ Upper Diorite Lake (BC)

49°50'34"N 115°32'58"W

Cutthroat trout to 45 cm

Upper Diorite Lake is situated in a pristine basin at the head of Diorite Creek. Reaching the lake will be very difficult, with a good option being a continuation of the Mt. Fisher hike down into upper Diorite Creek valley. Take note that this area is for explorers only. Upper Diorite Lake's population of stocked cutthroat trout has done well, and they are in the lake in good numbers. Expect an average trout to be 30–40 cm in length.

ELKFORD REGION

The Elkford Region covers the upper Elk River Valley, from the town of Elkford north to, and including, Elk Lakes Provincial Park. Highway 43 connects Elkford south to Sparwood and Highway 3. The Elk River Forest Service Road extends north for 70 km from Elkford to Elk Lakes Provincial Park. Most fishing opportunities in the Region are of a backcountry nature, with many fine cutthroat trout lakes. The area around the town of Elkford constitutes the Fording Sub-Region, with the glacier-mantled peaks and high country of Elk Lakes Provincial Park serving as a second Sub-Region.

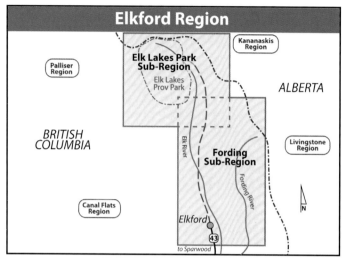

Elkford Region

Palliser Region

Elk Lakes Park Sub-Region

Elk Lakes Prov Park

Kananaskis Region

ALBERTA

BRITISH COLUMBIA

Elk River

Fording Sub-Region

Fording River

Livingstone Region

Canal Flats Region

Elkford

43

to Sparwood

N

Fording Sub-Region

The coal-mining community of Elkford is the self-proclaimed "Wilderness Capital of BC." Unarguably the most isolated town in the Rockies, Elkford is indeed the gateway to the rugged tracts of land of the upper Elk River Valley. The rise in prominence of the Elk River and its cutthroat fishery have raised the profile of Elkford in recent years, but there are a lot of people who have enjoyed the upper Elk Valley for many years, whether for fishing, hunting or camping. The Elk River dominates angling opportunities in and around Elkford. Other fishing locales are rather limited, with Lost Lake being one of the few bright spots

■ Elk River (Weary Creek to Fording River) (BC)
Cutthroat trout to 55 cm (1.5 kg)
Bull trout to 80 cm (6.0 kg)
Whitefish to 45 cm
The Elk River passes through the town of Elkford on its journey from Weary Creek downstream to Line Creek. This section of the river is an outstanding cutthroat trout fishery. Although it is technically possible to take a canoe on the Elk River below Elkford to Line Creek, superior canoeing skills are strongly suggested, as there are numerous obstacles. The Elk River Forest Service Road parallels the river above Elkford, although it will always require some nasty bushwhacking to actually reach the river. Below Elkford, Highway 43 serves as general access, with bushwhacking also required here. Once the river clears up in mid-summer, fly fishing for cutthroat trout is excellent. Many people consider the Elk River to be the best cutthroat trout stream in the Rockies. Cutthroat trout taken are normally 25–35 cm in length, as well as being very fat and healthy. Larger trout in the 50 cm range are not uncommon. Whitefish can also be taken from the river, and

most large pools will have their resident bull trout. Special Class II Waters regulations apply to the Elk River.

Elk River

■ Fording River (BC)
Cutthroat trout to 40 cm
Bull trout to 65 cm (3.0 kg)
Whitefish to 35 cm
The Fording River, downstream from Josephine Falls to its junction with the Elk River near the Line Creek coal mine, possesses many kilometres of fine stream fishing. Cutthroat trout in the 25–35 cm in range will be the normal catch from the river. Whitefish are plentiful in the fall and big bull trout can be found in the deep pools. ⊗ The Fording River is closed to fishing above Josephine Falls.

Josephine Falls on Fording River

■ Boivin Creek, Crossing Creek, Bingay Creek, Forsyth Creek, Aldridge Creek, Bleasdell Creek (BC)
Cutthroat trout to 40 cm
Bull trout to 65 cm (3.0 kg)
All of the major tributaries of this segment of the Elk River hold cutthroat trout in good numbers. Active and abandoned logging and mining roads lead up most tributary valleys, allowing some form of access. Trout in these creeks will tend to average 15–25 cm in length. ⊗ The 3 km section of Forsyth Creek below Connor Lakes is permanently closed to angling.

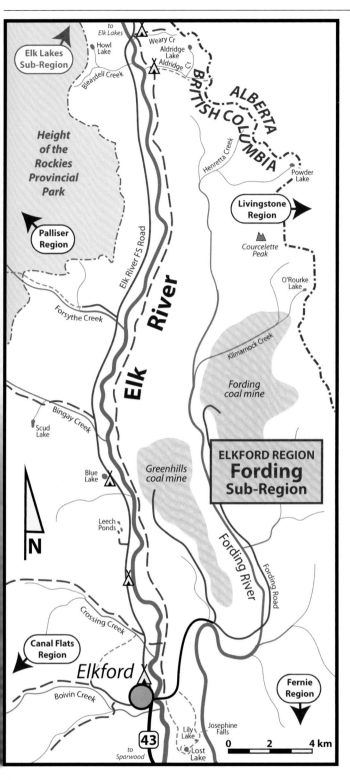

preferred locations. The lake is stocked regularly with rainbow that average 25–35 cm in length. Brook trout are present as well. Spin casting with lures is usually effective at Lost Lake.

Lost Lake

■ Lily Lake (BC)

50°00'09"N 114°53'34"W

Status: Devoid of fish

Diminutive Lily Lake is located 1 km beyond Lost Lake on the Forest, Falls and Lakes circuit. There are no fish in Lily Lake, but there's plenty of waterfowl if you're into birdwatching.

Lily Lake

■ Blue Lake (BC)

50°00'09"N 114°53'34"W

Status: Doubtful

Blue Lake and its campground are located just west of the Elk River Forest Service Road approximately 20 km north of Elkford. The lake was stocked in the past, and fish populations were dependent on regular stockings. Water levels in Blue Lake fluctuate significantly over the course of the year, rising with the snow melt and then receding during the summer and fall. Trout, if there are any in the lake, are very limited in number.

■ Leech Ponds (BC)

50°07'15"N 114°56'49"W

Cutthroat trout to 35 cm

Brook trout to 35 cm

These small ponds are located a few hundred metres west of the Elk River Forest Service Road. Heavy reed growth and extensive shallows make shore fishing difficult. The ponds were stocked in the past with brook trout and more recently with cutthroat trout. Trout caught will average 20–30 cm in length.

■ Lost Lake (BC)

50°00'09"N 114°53'34"W

Rainbow trout to 40 cm

Brook trout to 40 cm

Lost Lake is one of the primary destinations for hikers on Elkford's popular Forest, Falls and Lakes Interpretive Hiking Trail. The trail to Lost Lake is a pleasant 2.5 km walk from the trailhead on the Greenhills Mine Road. An alternate access involves driving rough roads from the Line Creek bridge over the Elk River, followed by a short 1 km hike. Heavy forest cover that makes casting quite difficult in places surrounds Lost Lake. Two wooden docks have been built at the lake, and anglers are usually present from these

Leech Ponds

Kootenay Trout Hatchery photo

◼ Scud Lake (BC)
50°10'02"N 115°03'54"W
Cutthroat trout to 40 cm
Scud Lake is a tiny body of water situated in the upper Bingay Creek watershed. Rough roads lead up the Bingay Creek valley from the Elk River Forest Service Road, and an even rougher trail leads into the basin holding Scud Lake. The lake is seldom visited, and reports indicate that there still are cutthroat trout present. Expect trout in the 25–35 cm range.

⍰ O'Rourke Lake (BC)
50°10'34"N 114°45'10"W
Cutthroat trout
O'Rourke Lake is located in a stark basin at the head of Kilmarnock Creek. An abandoned road leads up Kilmarnock Creek from the Greenhills Mine Road, but the final few kilometres to the lake are for route finders only. O'Rourke Lake was stocked in the past with cutthroat trout, but few reliable reports are available as to their current status.

⍰ Powder Lake (BC)
50°13'32"N 114°46'04"W
Cutthroat trout
Abandoned logging and seismic roads lead from the Elk River into the Henretta Creek valley and eventually to McQuarrie Creek and Powder Lake. The lake is in a high, alpine basin that sees few humans. Cutthroat trout have been stocked in Powder Lake in the past, but their reproductive success is unknown. Trout in other lakes of similar character tend to be 25–35 cm in length.

⍰ Aldridge Lakes (BC)
50°22'30"N 115°00'06"W
Status: Unknown
There are several fine lakes located at the source of Aldridge Creek in the rocky basin northwest of Fording River Pass. These lakes have never been stocked, but it is possible that trout may have entered from Aldridge Creek over time. The lakes are worth a look, scenically at least, if you are in the Fording River Pass environs.

◼ Howl Lake (BC)
50°22'30"N 115°00'06"W
Cutthroat trout to 40 cm
Howl Lake is isolated high up in the Bleasdell Creek drainage, west of the Elk River. Access is for explorers only. Howl Lake was stocked in the past with cutthroat, which are reportedly still present in good numbers and average 25–35 cm in length.

Elk Lakes Park Sub-Region

The rugged beauty of Elk Lakes Provincial Park attracts numerous hikers each summer despite the lengthy 70 km drive on gravel and dirt roads from Elkford to reach the core area of the park. An alternate route of access along a 10 km long hiking trail leads to the Elk Lakes from Peter Lougheed Provincial Park in Alberta. Both the Upper and Lower Elk lakes are very much of interest to anglers, as are Cadorna, Abruzzi and Wolverine lakes in the Cadorna Creek watershed.

◼ Upper Elk Lake (BC)
50°33'02"N 115°06'43"W
◭ Lower Elk Lake (BC)
50°33'02"N 115°06'43"W
Cutthroat trout to 50 cm (1.5 kg)
Bull trout to 60 cm (2.5 kg)
Whitefish to 40 cm
The Elk Lakes are set amid the spectacular glaciated peaks of the French Military Group and are an increasingly popular destination for hikers. The Elk River Forest Service Road is a 70 km long road that it usually in decent shape and leads to the parking area below Lower Elk Lake. From the trailhead, it is an easy 2 km hike to Lower Elk Lake. Upper Elk Lake is another kilometre above Lower Elk Lake. Fishing is slow much of the summer in both the larger Upper and smaller Lower Elk lakes due to heavy silting. In the late summer, as the lakes begin to clear, the fishing generally picks up, and cutthroat trout averaging 25–35 cm in length can be taken in fair numbers. Bull trout and whitefish can also be caught. The Upper Lake has a massive log jam at its outlet, in which the trout tend to hide, and is definitely worth a look. The outlet of the Lower Lake is very productive in the fall.

Upper Elk Lake

Lower Elk Lake

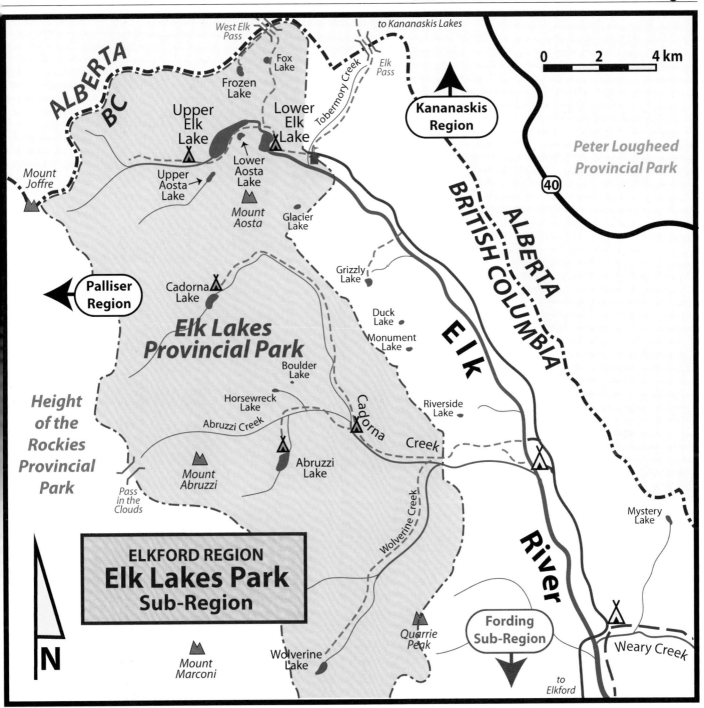

0 2 4 km

Height of the Rockies Provincial Park

ELKFORD REGION
Elk Lakes Park
Sub-Region

N

■ **Upper Aosta Lake (BC)**
50°32'20"N 115°06'46"W
■ **Lower Aosta Lake (BC)**
50°33'06"N 115°06'09"W
Cutthroat trout to 50 cm (1.5 kg)

The Aosta Lakes are set on a low bench just above the southern shoreline of Upper Elk Lakes. Lower Aosta can be reached via a short but steep 200 m trail from the Upper Elk Lake shoreline trail, approximately one-third of the way down Upper Elk Lake. Upper Aosta is a little more difficult to find. It is hidden in heavy forest approximately half a kilometre southwest of the west end of Upper Elk Lake. Both Upper and Lower Aosta Lakes are stocked regularly with cutthroat trout. Trout caught in both lakes will average 25–35 cm in length, with larger ones present in good numbers.

Lower Aosta Lake

■ Fox Lake (BC)

50°34'33"N 115°05'21"W
Status: Devoid of fish
Fox Lake is a small lake located less than a kilometre west of Elk Pass and 3 km above Upper Elk Lake. Fox Lake was rumored in the past to contain both cutthroat and bull trout. However, this seems unlikely, as Fox Lake annually dries up to the point of being incapable of holding fish.

■ Frozen Lake (BC)

50°34'32"N 115°06'09"W
Cutthroat trout to 40 cm
Frozen Lake is a particularly stunning body of water set precariously on a lip high on Mount Fox. Frozen Lake is popular among day hikers from both the Elk Lakes and Peter Lougheed provincial parks. The final approach to the lake is most easily accomplished by following the provincial boundary, where the semblance of a trail exists. As its name suggests, Frozen Lake is very sheltered and generally remains icebound well into July. The lake holds plenty of cutthroat trout, with most in the 20–30 cm range. The lake's crystal-clear waters allow for sight fishing.

Frozen Lake

■ Elk River (Elk Lakes to Weary Creek) (BC)

Cutthroat trout to 50 cm (1.5 kg)
Bull trout to 80 cm (5.0 kg)
Whitefish to 45 cm
The Elk River, which eventually flows into Lake Koocanusa, some 200 km distant, has its humble beginnings in the glaciers of Elk Lakes Provincial Park. The Elk River Forest Service Road, north of Elkford, follows the course of the river and provides vehicle access. A tough bushwhack through thick forest will often be required to reach the water. As it drains Lower Elk Lake, the Elk River flows at a gentle gradient, with plenty of wide sweeping corners and undercut banks. Fishing quality in this section of the river, extending for 25 km below Elk Lakes, is limited due to the high amount of silt carried by the river. Cutthroat trout are in the river, but their size and numbers are not as bountiful as in the lower Elk River. Trout caught between Elk Lakes and Weary Creek will average 15–25 cm in length. As the Elk River picks up tributary streams and begins to increase in size, the quality of fishing increases. Be aware of the special Class II Waters regulations in effect on the Elk River.

Elk River cutthroat trout

■ Glacier Lake (BC)

50°31'47"N 115°04'26"W
Cutthroat trout to 40 cm
Glacier Lake is the northern most of a series of lakes in a line of hanging valleys on the eastern side of the Elk River Valley that begins approximately 5 km south of Lower Elk Lake. A rough trail leads up to Glacier Lake from the valley bottom. The cutthroat trout in Glacier Lake have done well, with the average fish being 25–35 cm in length.

■ Grizzly Lake (BC)

50°30'20"N 115°02'11"W
Cutthroat trout to 40 cm
Grizzly Lake is the largest of the small lakes on the eastern side of the upper Elk River Valley. A well-defined trail with a difficult to find trailhead, following a ford of the Elk River, leads steeply up for 4 km into the secluded valley holding Grizzly Lake. Cutthroat trout, which average 20–30 cm length, are plentiful in the lake.

Grizzly Lake

Frank Slide Interpretive Centre photo

■ Duck Lake (BC)

50°29'53"N 115°01'44"W
Cutthroat trout to 40 cm
Duck Lake is found in the next side valley south from Grizzly Lake. Duck is a high subalpine lake in a small basin at substantial elevation above the Elk River Valley, very similar to Grizzly. A rough, ill-defined trail leads to Duck. Duck holds cutthroat trout that average 20–30 cm in length.

■ Monument Lake (BC)

50°29'34"N 115°01'09"W
Status: Doubtful

Kootenay Trout Hatchery photo

Monument Lake

Monument is the next lake south in the Grizzly-Duck-Monument chain. Monument was stocked several times with cutthroat trout, but recent reports indicate that no trout remain in the lake.

■ Cadorna Creek, Weary Creek, Tobermory Creek (BC)

Cutthroat trout to 45 cm
These tributaries of the upper Elk River all offer good fishing for cutthroat trout. All three creeks are accessed by trail and are fished lightly. Cutthroat caught from these creeks average 25–35 cm in length. Larger trout are regularly caught in the meadow section of Cadorna Creek, along the Abruzzi and Cadorna lake trails.

Note: Flooding and logjams have created a good-sized body of water just a few kilometres up the Cadorna/Abruzzi trail. Locally known as "Frank Lake," it has inconvenienced hikers who must now find higher ground to skirt the lake.

Cadorna Creek

◾Cadorna Lake (BC)

50°30'00"N 115°07'00"W
Cutthroat trout to 50 cm (1.5 kg)

Lovely Cadorna Lake is situated in a grand basin at the head of Cadorna Creek. The 15 km access trail makes this hike an overnighter. The lake holds plenty of cutthroat trout averaging 25–35 cm in length. Fish can be taken from most locations around the lake, although the outlet and its accompanying log jam provide the best opportunities. Take note that all of the valleys in the Cadorna Creek drainage (Cadorna, Abruzzi, Wolverine) are prime grizzly bear habitat.

Cadorna Lake

◭Abruzzi Lake (BC)

50°26'58"N 115°04'50"W
Cutthroat trout to 55 cm (1.5 kg)

Abruzzi Lake is reached by following a well-defined, 11 km long horse trail up from the Elk River. Abruzzi Lake is a stunningly beautiful body of water, and the quality of angling equals its scenic splendour. The lake holds plenty of cutthroat trout, with fish in the 30–40 cm range being the normal catch. The area around the log jam at the outlet invariably holds fish, but anglers shouldn't confine their efforts to the outlet. Fish can be caught from almost anywhere around the lake. Watch for fish cruising slowly along the shoreline, often within a few metres of shore. A well-placed Royal Coachman in front of a cruising trout will bring on some frantic action.

Abruzzi Lake

Abruzzi Lake cutthroat trout

◾Wolverine Lake (BC)

50°22'58"N 115°03'43"W
Cutthroat trout to 50 cm

Wolverine is the most southerly of the three lakes that make up the Cadorna Creek trio, Abruzzi and Cadorna lakes being the northern counterparts. Wolverine is reached by a 9 km trail from the Elk River. Wolverine holds cutthroat trout in good numbers, with an average catch being 25–35 cm in length.

Wolverine Lake

Fiore Olivieri photo

◾Horsewreck Lake (BC)

50°28'17"N 115°05'08"W

☐Boulder Lake (BC)

50°28'28"N 115°04'52"W
Cutthroat trout to 35 cm

These two small tarns are located in a rocky basin north of Abruzzi Creek, opposite the Abruzzi Lake outlet. Access is by bushwhacking up from the valley bottom. Horsewreck and Boulder lakes both contain cutthroat trout which average 25–35 cm in length. In the past, Horsewreck has offered better angling than Boulder.

☐Riverside Lake (BC)

50°28'16"N 114°59'55"W
Cutthroat trout to 40 cm

This small lake is located in a hidden valley north of Cadorna Creek on the east face of Riverside Mountain. It was stocked in the past with cutthroat trout, and it likely that they are present in small numbers. Expect to catch trout in the 20–30 cm range.

LIVINGSTONE REGION

The Livingstone Region consists of two major river basin watersheds – the Oldman and the Highwood. Vehicle access is via Highways 3, 22, and 541 and the Forestry Trunk Road. The Region divides naturally on geographical boundaries into the Oldman and the Highwood Sub-Regions. Fishing opportunities in the south are generally stream-oriented. In the Highwood Valley to the north, backcountry lakes are the primary destination for anglers.

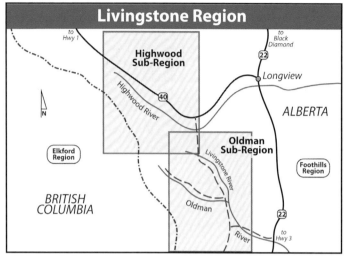

Oldman River in The Gap

Oldman Sub-Region

The Oldman Sub-Region extends from the headwaters of the Oldman River, high among the peaks of the Continental Divide, to the Oldman Reservoir on the prairies north of Cowley. Above the reservoir, the Oldman River is a regarded as a stellar trout stream, particularly in its more inaccessible spots. The Livingstone River, protected by catch-and-release regulations, affords excellent angling. The upper Oldman River basin is the source for many tributary streams, including Dutch, Hidden and Racehorse creeks, which have fine cutthroat trout fisheries.

Patrick Shandrowsky with Oldman River cutthroat trout

▲Oldman River (Oldman Falls to Oldman Reservoir) (AB)
Cutthroat trout to 55 cm (2.0 kg)
Rainbow trout to 55 cm (2.0 kg)
Bull trout to 70 cm (4.0 kg)
Brown trout to 55 cm (2.0 kg)
Whitefish to 40 cm
This section of the Oldman River flows from Oldman Falls downstream to the Oldman Reservoir north of Cowley. Primary vehicular access is via Highways 22 and 517, and the Forestry Trunk Road. This section of the river has many kilometres of fishable water, including the canyon, known as The Gap, which cuts through the Livingstone Range. As it is more difficult to access the river in The Gap, fishing pressure is less and in turn the area provides better fishing than other sections. From The Gap downstream to the reservoir, you are more likely to catch a rainbow trout, although cutthroat trout and even a few brown trout are present. Much of this section is catch-and-release. Above The Gap cutthroat and bull trout predominate, with rainbow still present. Most fish taken from this stretch of river will be in the 25–35 cm range. Anglers should note that the Oldman is usually very turbulent and dirty until at least mid-July when runoff is complete.

Oldman River bull trout
Note: Whirling disease has been detected in the Oldman drainage.

■Oldman River (Upstream from Oldman Falls) (AB)
Cutthroat trout to 50 cm (1.5 kg)
Rainbow trout to 40 cm
Bull trout to 60 cm (3.0 kg)
Whitefish to 35 cm
The extreme upper reaches of the Oldman River, above splendid Oldman Falls, are reached from logging roads that branch west of the Forestry Trunk Road. The falls serve as a natural barrier, preventing stocked fish from the lower river from travelling upstream. Above the falls, there are native cutthroat and bull trout in good numbers and good sizes.

Jonathan Shandrowsky with upper Oldman River bull trout

Patrick Shandrowsky photo

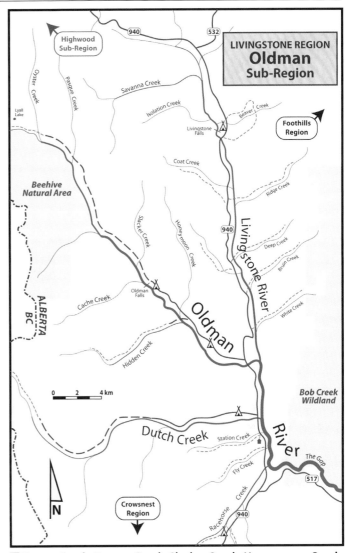

▪ Racehorse Creek (AB)

Cutthroat trout to 50 cm

Racehorse Creek, including both North and South Racehorse creeks, is a major tributary of the Oldman River, connecting just west of The Gap. Lower Racehorse Creek is accessible from the Forestry Trunk Road and from trails that lead west from the Racehorse Creek campground. The upper sections of North and South Racehorse creeks can be reached from the Atlas (Allison Creek) Road, which joins Highway 3 west of Coleman. Virtually the entire Racehorse watershed is fishable, with cutthroat trout in the 20–30 cm range being the normal fare. Much larger fish are present in good numbers.

▪ Vicary Creek, Daisy Creek (AB)

Cutthroat trout to 35 cm

Bull trout to 40 cm

Tributaries to Racehorse Creek, Vicary and Daisy Creeks are both tributaries to Racehorse Creek. Abandoned logging roads up both creeks offer easy access to anglers. They have been favourites of local anglers for many years, particularly the lower section of Daisy Creek. Both creeks contain healthy populations of small cutthroat trout averaging 15–25 cm in length.

▪ Fly Creek, Station Creek (AB)

Cutthroat trout to 25 cm

These two minor tributaries of the Oldman River join the big river just north of The Gap. Station and Fly Creek hold cutthroat trout in small sizes, few exceeding 20 cm in length. Both creeks have rough trails that lead up from the Forestry Trunk Road.

▪ Dutch Creek (AB)

Cutthroat trout to 40 cm

Bull trout to 55 cm (1.5 kg)

Whitefish to 35 cm

Dutch Creek is a major tributary of the Oldman River and offers excellent stream fishing for small cutthroat trout over its entire length. Lower Dutch Creek can be reached from logging roads branching west from the Forestry Trunk Road, while upper Dutch Creek can be accessed from logging roads on Racehorse Creek. Cutthroat trout averaging 20–30 cm in length are the norm in Dutch Creek. Walking up or downstream from any of the main access points will increase fishing potential.

▪ Oyster Creek, Pasque Creek, Slacker Creek, Honeymoon Creek, Hidden Creek (AB)

Cutthroat trout to 30 cm

Bull trout to 35 cm

These tributaries of the upper Oldman River are seldom fished, but contain small cutthroat trout. All can be accessed from logging roads radiating out from logging roads on the upper Oldman River. Trout in the creeks but small, most in the 15–25 cm range.

Chris Mouriopoulos photo

Karl Peters fishing on Hidden Creek

◼Lyall Lake (AB)
49°50'06"N 114°41'59"W
Status: Devoid of fish
This pretty lake in the extreme headwaters of the upper Oldman River watershed holds no fish.

🅰Livingstone River (AB)
Cutthroat trout to 45 cm
Bull trout to 60 cm (2.5 kg)
Whitefish to 40 cm
The Livingstone River is a major tributary of the Oldman River and flows south from its headwaters on Plateau Mountain to its junction with the Oldman north of The Gap. The Livingstone River is paralleled for much of its length by the Forestry Trunk Road, which offers ready access to anglers. The cutthroat trout fishery in the Livingstone has boomed since the institution of catch-and-release regulations on the river. Cutthroat trout are found in virtually every pool and average 20–30 cm in length. Bull trout are present in limited numbers, and there are large runs of whitefish in the Livingstone each fall. Cutthroat trout can be taken almost anywhere along the river, although the stretch around Livingstone Falls is particularly promising. Expect company if fishing anywhere near Livingstone Falls, due to the proximity of the large forestry campground.

Livingstone Falls

Livingstone River cutthroat trout

◼Savanna Creek, Isolation Creek, Coat Creek, Spears Creek, Beaver Creek, Ridge Creek, White Creek, Deep Creek, Bruin Creek (AB)
Cutthroat trout to 30 cm
Bull trout to 40 cm
All of the tributaries of the Livingstone River contain populations of small cutthroat trout. Although the trout are small, with few specimens larger than 25 cm in length, they are plentiful, and even the most inexperienced angler should catch fish. The best waters are those nearest the Livingstone River, especially when the tributaries are clearer than the main river.

Highwood Sub-Region

The Highwood River serves as the backbone of this Sub-Region, situated directly north of the Oldman River watershed. The area's main thoroughfare is Highway 40 (Kananaskis Trail), which runs north-south between Peter Lougheed Provincial Park and Highwood Junction. The Forestry Trunk Road connects Highway 40/Highway 541 with the Oldman River and eventually the Crowsnest Pass. A gas station, with a selection of fishing supplies, is located at Highwood Junction at the merger of Highways 40 and 541 and the Forestry Trunk Road. The Highwood River is popular with anglers, but it is the Highwood's backcountry lakes that are the real magnets. The majority of the region's fine lakes, including Carnarvon, Loomis and Lake of the Horns, are located high among the peaks of the Continental Divide and require substantial effort by foot to reach. *Note: Highway 40 is closed from December 1 through June 14 each year to protect sensitive wildlife habitat.*

◼ Highwood River (AB)
Rainbow trout to 50 cm
Brook trout to 40 cm
Cutthroat trout to 40 cm
Bull trout to 70 cm (3.5 kg)
Whitefish to 35 cm
The Highwood River begins as a tiny stream below Highwood Pass and then flows south and east, eventually joining the Bow River as a major tributary east of Calgary. The upper Highwood, bracketed by the Elk Range to the west and the Highwood Range to the east, is readily accessible to anglers from Highways 40 and 541, which parallel the river. Rainbow trout are in the majority in the Highwood River, with trout most averaging 25–35 cm in length. The river has repetitive sequence of pools and riffles over its course, and the fishing is generally good after the river clears in mid-summer.

◼ Highwood River ponds (AB)
Brook trout to 35 cm
The wide, forested Highwood River valley provides excellent habitat for the local beaver population, a fact attested to by the area's seemingly endless chain of beaver ponds. Many of the ponds contain small brook trout. Some of the ponds are subject to winterkill and only personal inspection will determine which ponds hold trout and which don't. Two of the better systems are the ponds immediately west of Highwood Junction, and those at the Trout Ponds Day Use Site, just south of the confluence of Picklejar Creek and the Highwood River. Trout taken from the ponds will average 15–25 cm in length.

◼ Mist Creek, Odlum Creek, Loomis Creek, McPhail Creek, Carnarvon Creek, Picklejar Creek, Lantern Creek, Lineham Creek, Stony Creek, Cat Creek, Strawberry Creek, Fitzsimmons Creek, Baril Creek, Etherington Creek (AB)
Rainbow trout to 30 cm
Cutthroat trout to 30 cm
Brook trout to 30 cm
Bull trout to 35 cm
These tributaries to the upper Highwood River contain small trout. The lower portions of the creeks, near their junction with the Highwood, usually hold rainbow and brook trout, while the

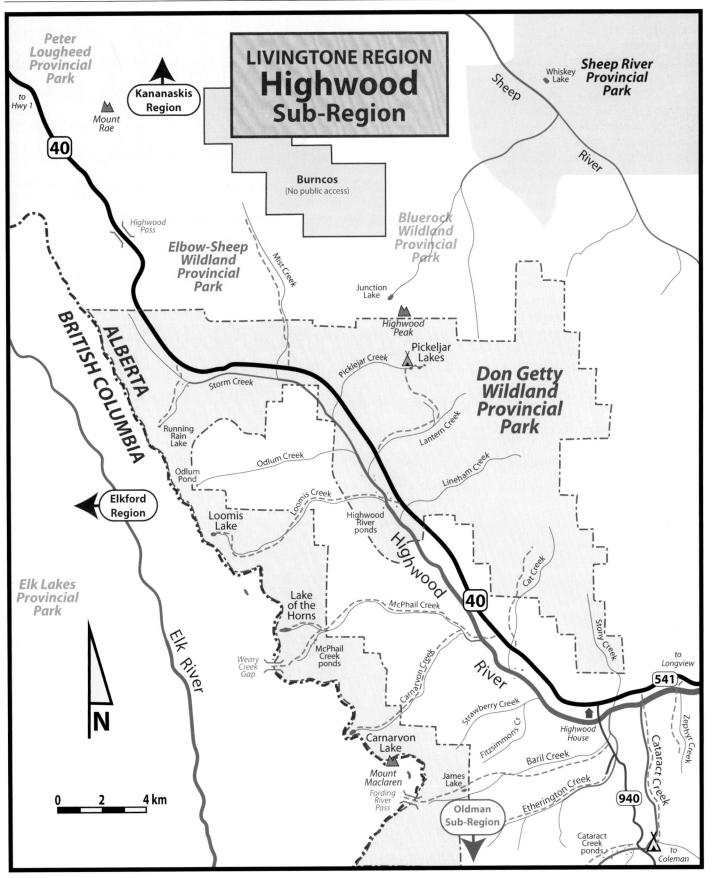

upper reaches are more likely to hold cutthroat and the odd bull trout. Regardless of species, don't expect many trout larger than 25 cm in length.

⊗ Storm Creek (AB)

Status: Closed to angling

Storm Creek, which joins with Mist Creek to form the Highwood River, is closed to angling to protect spawning bull trout.

▲ Picklejar Lakes (AB)

(4th lake) 50°31'09"N 114°07'01"W

Cutthroat trout to 40 cm

The chain of four Picklejar Lakes is set in a spectacular subalpine basin. The lakes are very popular with hikers in the summer, so expect a little company. Picklejar Lakes can be reached by a 4 km trail from Highway 40 at Lineham Creek (not from Picklejar Creek, as one would normally expect). Each of the four Picklejar Lakes is unique in its setting and quality of angling. The upper (first) lake holds the least potential, although a few trout do make it in each summer via the outlet creek. The second lake is the deepest of the four lakes, and its shoreline is largely made up of scree slopes. The best potential in the third lake lies near the inlet stream. The third lake is very shallow but always seems to have a few schools of skittish but slightly larger trout cruising about. The lowest (fourth) lake is generally regarded as the best fishing. Fish can be taken from almost any location around the lake, although the area near the outlet is invariably full of fish. Fly fishers will have a heyday at the fourth lake. Cutthroat trout in the lakes are plentiful but are not large. Most fish caught will be in the 15–25 cm range. It's interesting to note that the Picklejar Lakes have never been stocked and maintain their population through natural propagation.

Picklejar Lake #4

Picklejar Lakes cutthroat trout - "Like fishing in a picklejar!"

■ Running Rain Lake (aka Storm Lake) (AB)

50°30'19"N 114°56'40"W

Status: Doubtful

Tiny Running Rain Lake is nestled in a small basin immediately beneath the continental divide. From Highway 40, a rough 3 km trail leads up the north side of the outlet creek to the lake. The lake once held a limited population of cutthroat trout. Flooding in 2013 destroyed the outlet dam, significantly lowering the water levels. Recent reports indicate there are no fish remaining in the lake.

Running Rain Lake (before 2013 flood)

□ Odlum Pond (AB)

50°28'24"N 114°54'45"W

Cutthroat trout to 35 cm

Odlum Pond is the small tarn at the head of Odlum Creek, and is reached by a 12 km trail, which includes a ford of the Highwood River. Cutthroat trout in Odlum Pond are small, averaging 15–25 cm in length.

■ Loomis Lake (AB)

50°27'12"N 114°54'14"W

Cutthroat trout to 55 cm (1.5 kg)

Access to the pleasing blue waters of Loomis Lake is difficult, and includes a 12 km hike, a ford of the Highwood River and a steep headwall. Despite its lengthy and problematic access, Loomis is popular with backcountry anglers due to the number and size of its cutthroat trout. Trout caught from Loomis will average 30–40 cm in length. Much of the lake has a scree-covered shoreline, and the bottom drops away quickly. Lures or flies fished deep tend to produce results.

Loomis Lake

Loomis Lake cutthroat trout

■ Lake of the Horns [aka McPhail Lake] (AB)

50°24'50"N 114°51'25"W

Cutthroat trout to 55cm (1.5 kg)

Lake of the Horns is nestled in a rocky amphitheatre high on the flank of Mt. McPhail. Superb cutthroat trout fishing is the reward for those completing the 12 km trek to reach its shores. A ford of the Highwood River and a tricky ascent of a cliff band loom as major hazards on this hike. The lake itself is above treeline, and there is plenty of casting room, although wind will likely be a significant factor. The cutthroat trout in Lake of the Horns average 25–35 cm in length, with fish exceeding 50 cm taken on occasion. As it is a very deep lake, and the bottom drops off quickly, a wet fly line fished deep is generally a successful technique.

Lake of the Horns

☐ McPhail Creek ponds (AB)

50°24'54"N 114°50'02"W
Cutthroat trout to 35 cm

The interconnected series of beaver ponds on McPhail Creek directly below the Lake of the Horns hold small cutthroat trout. Flooding in 2013 severely damaged some of the larger dams. It is likely that beaver have started to fix up some of the dams. Any trout in the ponds and creek tend to be wary and challenging to catch. Trout caught in the ponds will average 15-25 cm in length.

◬ Carnarvon Lake (AB)

50°22'22"N 114°48'52"W
Cutthroat trout to 55 cm (1.5 kg)

Carnarvon Lake is similar in character to other lakes in the area. It is located in an enclosed basin high on Mt. Strachan, immediately east of the Continental Divide. Reaching the lake requires a ford of the Highwood River, and later, a short climb up exposed rock which is very dangerous in foul weather. Despite its protective barriers, Carnarvon Lake is popular with hikers and anglers. Set amid stark, rocky surroundings, Carnarvon's exquisite blue waters hold plenty of cutthroat trout, mostly of which will be in the 30–40 cm range. The lake drops off quickly around most of the shore, but a shelf exists on the west end of the lake near the primitive campsite. Hungry trout continually cruise the shallows and if the wind conditions are tolerable, sight fishing is possible. A dry fly in the shallows is sure to attract attention. If fishing in the deep water wet fly line and nymph or a lure fished deep is the best option.

Carnarvon Lake

■ James Lake (AB)

50°19'52"N 114°44'17"W
Status: Devoid of fish

This pleasant pond is located alongside the Fording River Pass trail up Baril Creek. The lake has never been stocked and most likely does not contain any fish. James Lake is a nice spot for a break on the way to Fording River Pass.

■ Cataract Creek (AB)

Brook trout to 40 cm
Cutthroat trout to 40 cm
Rainbow trout to 40 cm
Bull trout to 60 cm (3.0 kg)
Whitefish to 35 cm

Cataract Creek, as its name suggests, contains many splendid waterfalls along its length. Cataract Creek joins the Highwood just east of the junction of the Forestry Trunk Road, Highway 40 and Highway 541 and possesses several stretches of fine fishing with numerous falls and deep pools in the lower section. However, a difficult ford of the Highwood River is required to reach lower Cataract Creek. Above the Cataract Creek Forest Service campground, there are numerous beaver ponds where the creek flows through a wide, flat valley. Fishing in the creek and the beaver ponds is excellent for small brook trout. Most of the trout taken will be in the 15–25 cm range, but they are very plentiful. In the upper reaches of Cataract Creek, more cutthroat trout will be present.

Cataract Creek

Lost Creek, Cummings Creek, Wilkinson Creek (AB)
Brook trout to 30 cm
Cutthroat trout to 30 cm
Lost, Cummings and Wilkinson creeks are tributaries of Cataract Creek and they all contain small brook. A few cutthroat trout may be present as well. Trout caught from these creeks will be small, with the average in the 15–25 cm range. The Forestry Trunk Road parallels Wilkinson Creek and provides easy access. Cummings and Lost Creek are reached by logging roads that branch off the Forestry Trunk Road.

Whiskey Lake (AB)
50°36'22"N 114°44'51"W
Status: Devoid of fish
This small lake is located just west of the Bluerock Campground at the terminus of the Sheep River Trail (Highway 546). Whiskey Lake has never been stocked and likely does not contain any fish.

Junction Lake (AB)
50°32'59"N 114°47'18"W
Status: Devoid of fish
Junction Lake is located in a high basin at the head of a tributary of Junction Creek. Nine kilometres of hiking are required to reach the lake. There is no record of fish plantings in Junction Lake and the lake dries up each fall to the point of being unable to hold fish.

Curtis Hall photo

FOOTHILLS REGION

This scenic Region stretches west and south of Calgary amid the foothills of the spectacular Rocky Mountains. Highway 22 is main north-south transportation route and passes through the Chain Lakes Sub-Region. Highways 66 and 68 provide direct links to the Lower Elbow and Sibbald Sub-Regions, respectively. The area is popular with Calgarians, due to the proximity to the city. Most of the lakes are man-made, including Chain Lakes Reservoir, the Region's largest body of water. The majority of lakes hold rainbow trout in smaller sizes. Angling on the many streams in the Region is very popular, with the Elbow River and its tributaries being prime objectives.

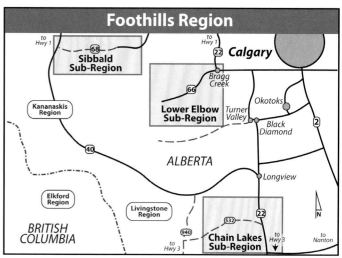

Chain Lakes Sub-Region

Chain Lakes Reservoir and Provincial Park is the focal point of the Sub-Region and is located alongside Highway 22 approximately 25 km south of Longview. Highway 22 is the main transportation link north and south, with Secondary Roads 532 and 533 offering alternate access. Chain Lakes Reservoir provides good fishing for rainbow trout throughout the season. West of Chain Lakes, along Secondary Road 532, Bear Pond and Big Iron Lake are unique in having arctic grayling populations that winterkilled in 2017-18 and were restocked with rainbow trout. The rest of the Sub-Region's fishing opportunities are found in the many small streams that flow west and hold a variety of trout.

Chain Lakes Reservoir (AB)
50°14'08"N 114°12'30"W
Rainbow trout to 50 cm
Bull trout to 60 cm (2.5 kg)
The elongated form of Chain Lakes Reservoir (three smaller lakes prior to the dam) sits between two long, low hills on the western side of Highway 22 between the junctions of Highways 532 and 533, approximately 25 km south of Longview. A major provincial campground is located at the south end of the lake. Rainbow trout can be taken in good numbers throughout the year, most averaging 25–35 cm in length, with larger ones caught regularly. Bull trout have been stocked in the lake, but their numbers are limited. Bait fishing from shore is the most popular method for catching rainbow trout, but not necessarily the most productive technique. Bait fishers tend to catch a lot of suckers along with the rainbows. Fly fishing or trolling from a boat tends to reduce the number of suckers caught.

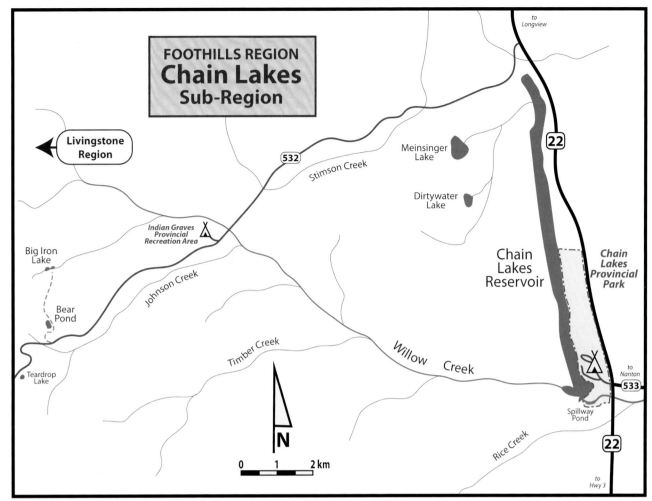

Chain Lakes Reservoir

▪ Chain Lakes Reservoir Spillway Pond (AB)

50°11'50"N 114°11'13"W

Rainbow trout to 35 cm

The section of Willow Creek that flows below the Chain Lakes Reservoir spillway generally holds trout that have been swept over the dam. This stretch is worthwhile if there is water flowing over the spillway. Rainbow trout can be very plentiful at times and will average 20–30 cm in length. Watch for signs prohibiting fishing immediately below the spillway.

Chain Lakes Reservoir Spillway Pond

▪ Willow Creek (AB)

Rainbow trout to 25 cm
Brook trout to 25 cm
Bull trout to 35 cm
Brown trout to 35 cm

The upper reaches of Willow Creek, which can be accessed from Highway 532 west of Chain Lakes, hold rainbow, bull, brown and brook trout in small sizes, with few larger than 25 cm. Some of the best waters are in the vicinity of the Indian Graves campground on Highway 532, where Willow Creek is characterized by long stretches of fishable water.

Willow Creek

Rice Creek (AB)
Rainbow trout to 25 cm
Brook trout to 25 cm
Rice Creek is a tributary of Willow Creek and joins downstream from the outlet at Chain Lakes Reservoir. Rice Creek holds small rainbows and brookies.

Timber Creek, Johnson Creek (AB)
Rainbow trout to 25 cm
Brook trout to 20 cm
Cutthroat trout to 20 cm
Bull trout to 30 cm
Timber and Johnson creeks are the two major tributaries of upper Willow Creek. Both creeks hold rainbow and brook trout in small sizes, as well as the odd cutthroat and bull trout. Johnson Creek runs alongside 532, while Timber Creek can be reached via a rough track downstream from Willow Creek at Indian Graves campground.

Bear Pond (AB)
50°13'07"N 114°25'48"W
Rainbow trout to 40 cm
Arctic grayling: doubtful
The trail to Bear Pond begins at a signed parking area on Secondary Road 532 approximately 18 km west of Highway 22. From the trailhead, a short but steep 1 km hike leads to the shore of man-made Bear Pond, a small, dark body of water. Bear Pond recently held plenty of stocked arctic grayling. Grayling, with their large dorsal fin and unique colouration, are beautiful fish and are particularly susceptible to a well-presented dry fly. Winterkill has been a problem in the past at both Bear Pond and nearby Big Iron Lake. It has been reported that virtually all of the grayling in Bear Pond died in the winter of 2017-18. Rainbow trout were restocked in Bear Pond in 2020.

Bear Pond

Bear Pond arctic grayling

Big Iron Lake (AB)
50°14'01"N 114°25'50"W
Rainbow trout to 40 cm
Arctic grayling: doubtful
Big Iron Lake is a small reed-fringed pond that is located 2 km by trail north of Bear Pond. As with neighbouring Bear Pond, Big Iron Lake in the past offered angling for arctic grayling in the 20–30 cm range. The winter of 2017-18 was devastating to Big Iron Lake and the grayling in the lake were decimated. In 2020, rainbow trout were stocked in Big Iron lake.

Big Iron Lake

Teardrop Lake (AB)
50°12'06"N 114°26'43"W
Status: Devoid of fish
Teardrop Lake is a small, circular pond alongside Secondary Road 532 west of the Bear Pond parking area. The lake holds no fish.

Meinsinger Lake (AB)
50°15'58"N 114°15'03"W
Dirtywater Lake (AB)
50°15'08"N 114°14'46"W
Status: Doubtful
These two shallow bodies of water, located south of 532 and west of Chain Lakes Reservoir, have never been stocked and are likely devoid of fish.

Stimson Creek (AB)
Rainbow trout to 20 cm
Cutthroat trout to 20 cm
The placid upper reaches of Stimson Creek, which is paralleled by Highway 532 west of Chain Lakes Reservoir, hold limited numbers of small rainbow and cutthroat trout.

Stimson Creek

Lower Elbow Sub-Region

The Lower Elbow Sub-Region is centered on the Elbow River and Elbow Falls Trail (Highway 66) in Kananaskis Country west of Bragg Creek, and is characterized by good brook and rainbow trout fishing at a number of man-made ponds and beaver pond complexes. McLean and Forgetmenot ponds and their accompanying picnic areas are busy spring through fall. When stocked, both ponds are excellent for novices and are accessible to handicapped persons. The Elbow River and its tributaries provide decent stream fishing.

Elbow River (AB)

Brook trout to 35 cm
Rainbow trout to 40 cm
Brown trout to 55 cm (1.5 kg)
Cutthroat trout to 35 cm
Bull trout to 60 cm (2.0 kg)
Whitefish to 30 cm
The Elbow River, paralleled by Highway 66 (Elbow Falls Trail) offers good fishing for brown, rainbow and brook trout averaging 20-30 cm in length. Bull and cutthroat can also be taken from the Elbow, with good angling for whitefish in the fall. The river's numerous pools are never more than a short stroll from the highway. Cobble Flats has gained renown as one of the Elbow's better stretches of fishable water. Walking a short distance upstream or downstream from one of the Sub-Region's many day-use sites along the river will generally bring an angler to an undisturbed hole. ⊗ The section between Elbow Falls and Canyon Creek is closed to angling.

Elbow Falls

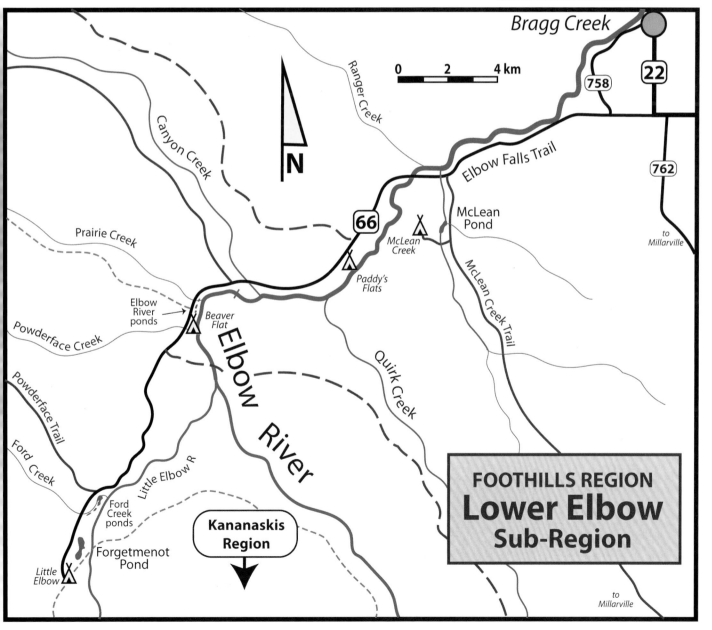

Elbow River

2013 Flood

In mid-June, 2013 record rainfall in the headwaters of the Bow, Elbow, Highwood and Sheep rivers triggered calamitous flooding downstream beginning on June 19. Weather stations confirmed that over 30 cm of rainfall fell in a 48-hour period at some locations. This torrential rainfall, combined with quickly-melting snowpacks, created floodwaters that ravaged everything in their path. Communities downstream, including High River, Canmore, Black Diamond, Turner Valley, Cochrane and Calgary were devastated and states of emergency were declared across southern Alberta. In the headwaters, bridges were lost, roads wiped out, streambeds torn apart and landscapes were changed forever. The effect on fish populations was traumatic and many streams are still recovering from the flood of 2013.

Flood damage along Elbow River

■ Allen Bill Pond (AB) (former site)

50°54'03"N 114°41'23"W
Status: Pond no longer exists
Allen Bill Pond was a small man-made lake located on the south side of Elbow River Trail 1 km west of the Elbow River Ranger Station. The massive 2013 flood took out the dam holding water in Allen Bill Pond. The pond and large parts of the picnic area no longer exist. The Elbow River does flow by where the pond used to be, so there may be the odd trout around. No word on whether the dam will ever be rebuilt.

■ Elbow River ponds (AB)

50°51'46"N 114°47'33"W
Brook trout to 30 cm
This series of small beaver ponds is easily accessed from Elbow Falls Trail at Beaver Flat campground and Beaverlodge picnic area. The ponds are situated between the highway and the Elbow River, and contain brook trout in the 15–25 cm range. As with most beaver ponds, the fish are generally very spooky, and fly casting room is inhibited by thick brush.

Elbow River ponds

■ Ford Creek ponds (AB)

50°48'13"N 114°50'33"W
Brook trout to 30 cm
Rainbow trout to 30 cm
This beaver pond complex is located at the junction of Elbow Falls Trail and Powderface Trail, where Ford Creek joins the Elbow River. The Ford Creek ponds hold brook trout in small sizes, most less than 25 cm in length. A few rainbows, as well as the odd cutthroat or bull trout, may also be present. Fly casting room is limited at the ponds.

Ford Creek ponds

■ Forgetmenot Pond (AB)

50°47'52"N 114°50'49"W
Rainbow trout to 40 cm
Man-made Forgetmenot Pond is situated at Little Elbow campground and picnic area. This pretty blue body of water is stocked annually and holds rainbow and brook trout in small sizes, averaging 20–25 cm in length. As with most easily accessed lakes, heavy early season fishing pressure reduces existing stocks rapidly, and after mid-summer the quality of fishing declines significantly. The addition of some dead trees into Forgetmenot's waters to provide cover has enhanced the habitat for the trout.

Forgetmenot Pond

Forgetmenot Pond rainbow trout

■ McLean Pond (AB)

50°53'15"N 114°40'10"W

Rainbow trout to 35 cm

McLean Pond was formed by damming McLean Creek and is located just over 1 km south of Elbow Falls Trail on McLean Creek Trail. Readily accessible from McLean Creek campground, the usually murky waters of McLean Pond hold stocked rainbow trout in the 15–25 cm range. Much of the shoreline is covered with heavy brush, making fly casting difficult. Lures, bait and flies are all effective at McLean Pond. Although it is stocked regularly, McLean Pond suffers from the annual early season rush of anglers.

McLean Pond

■ Little Elbow River (AB)

Brook trout to 30 cm

Bull trout to 35 cm

Rainbow trout to 30 cm

Cutthroat trout to 30 cm

Whitefish to 25 cm

The Little Elbow River is reached via hiking and equestrian trails from Little Elbow campground. The Little Elbow River offers good fishing for small brook trout in the 15–25 cm range, although a wide variety of fish can be taken. The quality of fishing generally improves as one travels upstream.

■ Quirk Creek, Ranger Creek, Canyon Creek, Prairie Creek, Ford Creek (AB)

Brook trout to 25 cm

Bull trout to 35 cm

Cutthroat trout to 25 cm

These tributaries of the Elbow River contain brook trout throughout, with some cutthroat and bull trout in their upper reaches. Roads or trails branching off Elbow Falls Trail provide access to the creeks.

Sibbald Sub-Region

The Sibbald Sub-Region is located in the extreme northeast corner of Kananaskis Country, centered on Highway 68 (Sibbald Creek Trail), which connects the Trans-Canada Highway to Highway 40. Angling opportunities are characterized by stream and beaver pond fishing for small brook and rainbow trout. Sibbald Lake and its campground, located 0.5 km east of the junction of Highway 68 and Powderface Trail, is the Sub-Region's most popular attraction. Jumpingpound and Sibbald creeks and their accompanying beaver pond complexes also attract anglers each season.

■ Sibbald Lake (AB)

51°02'55"N 114°52'00"W

Rainbow trout to 35 cm

Although Sibbald Lake is the largest body of water in the region, it rates as little more than an overgrown pond. Only 5 m deep at its deepest, Sibbald Lake is subject to regular winterkill. Fish populations are maintained by plantings and rainbow trout are stocked regularly. Trout taken from the lake will average 15–25 cm in length. Water levels in the lake fluctuate during the season, to a low point in the late fall. Bait fishing is the preferred method at Sibbald Lake. However, fly casting room is adequate, although the better fish-holding waters may be beyond the reach of novices. With a nice campground located at Sibbald Lake, anglers are present in force throughout the fishing season.

Sibbald Lake

Sibbald Lake rainbow trout

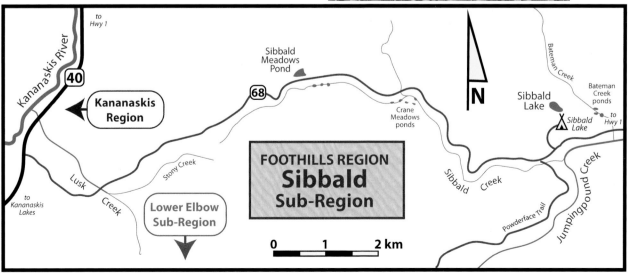

■ Jumpingpound Creek (AB)

Rainbow trout to 25 cm
Brook trout to 25 cm
Cutthroat trout to 25 cm
Bull trout to 35 cm
Whitefish to 25 cm

Jumpingpound Creek is the region's main waterway and in its upper reaches is accessed from the Powderface Trail, off Highway 68. Jumpingpound was noted for its good fishing in the past and it not surprisingly succumbed to heavy fishing pressure. Small rainbows in the 15–20 cm range are in the majority, although cutthroat, brook and bull trout as well as whitefish can all be taken. Jumpingpound Creek has a virtually unending series of fine pools, and prospective anglers are advised to keep moving either up or downstream, continually testing new holes.

Jumpingpound Creek

■ Sibbald Creek (AB)

Rainbow trout to 25 cm
Brook trout to 25 cm
Cutthroat trout to 25 cm
Bull trout to 30 cm

Sibbald Creek cuts through the heart of the Sub-Region and is the major tributary of Jumpingpound Creek. Sibbald Creek is paralleled by Highway 68 for much of its length. The numerous beaver ponds found along the course of Sibbald Creek generally hold more trout than the free-flowing waters. Small rainbow and brook trout are the usual catch, with small cutthroat and bull trout caught on occasion. Although casting distance is not usually a major factor when fishing on Sibbald Creek, wet feet are a certainty and heavy brush cover will deter many anglers.

Sibbald Creek

▲ Sibbald Meadows Pond (AB)

50°03'18"N 114°56'40"W
Rainbow trout to 35 cm
Brook trout

This small pond is located on the north side of Highway 68 approximately 7 km west of the junction with Powderface Trail. Sibbald Meadows Pond is a popular destination, with plenty of rainbow trout in the 15–25 cm range. A few brook trout may be in the pond as well. Fly casting room is available from many spots. Expect lots of company, as the picnic area at the pond is busy with families throughout the summer.

Sibbald Meadows Pond

Sibbald Meadows Pond rainbow trout

■ Crane Meadows Ponds (AB)

50°03'05"N 114°54'44"W
Rainbow trout to 25 cm
Brook trout to 25 cm

This series of interconnected beaver ponds is found on Sibbald Creek, on the south side of Highway 68 at Crane Meadows, 6 km west of Sibbald Lake. The ponds hold rainbow and brook trout in small sizes. The ponds are heavily overgrown with bush and fly casting is a virtual impossibility. Reaching some of the better ponds will require a good amount of dexterity and patience or will result in wet feet.

■ Bateman Creek Ponds (AB)

50°02'49"N 114°50'39"W
Rainbow trout to 25 cm
Brook trout to 25 cm

Bateman Creek is crossed by Highway 68 just east of Sibbald Lake. There is an extensive set of beaver ponds that hold rainbow and brook trout in the 15–20 cm range. The odd cutthroat or bull trout can be taken on occasion. Upstream from Highway 68, prospective anglers can work successive ponds, with better fishing the further upstream one goes.

■ Stony Creek, Lusk Creek (AB)

Cutthroat trout to 25 cm
Bull trout to 35 cm
Rainbow trout to 25 cm

Lusk Creek is a minor tributary of the Kananaskis River, and Stony Creek is a tributary of Lusk Creek. They can be accessed from Highway 40 or Highway 68. A variety of small trout can be taken from both creeks.

KANANASKIS REGION

Kananaskis Country is touted as Calgary's playground, and offers virtually every kind of outdoor experience. The main access to the Region is on Highway 40, which branches south from the Trans-Canada Highway. Anglers have a wide variety of streams and lakes to choose from. Accessible roadside lakes and hidden backcountry gems abound. The Region divides into three Sub-Regions: the Peter Lougheed Provincial Park Sub-Region around the Kananaskis Lakes; the Upper Elbow River Sub-Region; and the Barrier Sub-Region along the lower Kananaskis River extending from Fortress Junction to Barrier Lake.

Lougheed Park Sub-Region

The magnificent Kananaskis Lakes are the centrepiece of the immensely popular Peter Lougheed Provincial Park. The park is accessed from Highway 40 and the Smith-Dorrien Spray Lakes Trail and has several major campgrounds in the immediate vicinity of the lakes. From Upper Kananaskis Lake a series of trails radiate out into the surrounding backcountry. Anglers can make their way to numerous excellent cutthroat trout lakes, including Rawson, Aster, Three Isle and Maude.

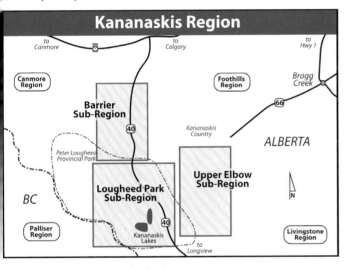

Upper Kananaskis Lake (AB)

50°37'13"N 115°09'18"W
Cutthroat trout to 55 cm (1.5 kg)
Rainbow trout to 55 cm (1.5 kg)
Bull trout to 70 cm (5.0 kg)
The Kananaskis Lakes, with their impressive mountain background to the west, attract hordes of anglers and sight-seers alike each summer. On the Upper Lake, the mouth of the Upper Kananaskis River is usually productive as are the waters around the lake's several islands. Shorebound anglers tend to congregate along the numerous bays on the easily accessible northeast side, and although this area often produces well, other less-fished areas of the Upper Lake are definitely worth a look. The Upper Lake has never fulfilled its potential as a trophy lake due to the annual fluctuations in water levels caused by the hydroelectric dam on the lake. The Upper Lake is stocked regularly with large numbers of trout. Cutthroat and rainbow trout taken from the lake will average 30–40 cm in length. Large bull trout are also present in the upper lake. Due to the size of the lake, trolling is the most popular fishing technique.

Upper Kananaskis Lake

Upper Kananaskis Lake cutthroat trout

Lower Kananaskis Lake (AB)

50°38'40"N 115°08'06"W
Cutthroat trout to 60 cm (2.0 kg)
Rainbow trout to 60 cm (2. kg)
Bull trout to 80 cm (6.0 kg)
Lower Kananaskis Lake has a history of producing very large bull and cutthroat trout, but as with the Upper Lake, fluctuations in water levels due to the power dam have prevented the creation of a true trophy fishery. In recent years, bull trout stocks in the Lower Lake have stabilized, in large part due to protection in the regulations. Bull trout in the 40–70 cm range are caught regularly along with cutthroat and rainbow trout averaging 30–40 cm. On long, narrow Lower Lake, anglers tend to have the most success at the south end in the area around the penstock, and at the far north end in the bay by Canyon Dam. Trolling lures, flies or gang trolls is very effective on Lower Kananaskis Lake.⊗ The northwest bay is closed to angling.

Lower Kananaskis Lake

Hidden Lake (AB)

50°36'34"N 115°11'15"W
Status: Devoid of fish
Hidden Lake is a silted body of water situated in heavy forest on the west side of Upper Kananaskis Lake. Hidden Lake dries up each fall to the point of being incapable of holding fish. Attempts in the past to stock the lake have always failed.

Aster Lake (AB)

50°34'45"N 115°12'37"W
Cutthroat trout to 35 cm
Aster Lake is an oversized glacial tarn in a hidden valley, 10 km by trail above Upper Kananaskis Lake. Aster Lake has been stocked with cutthroat trout that now reproduce naturally. Cutthroat trout caught in Aster will average 20–30 cm in length. Flies work well, and fly casting room is available around the entire lake, due to its distinct alpine setting.

Aster Lake

Kananaskis Lake and reached by a 5 km trail. In the past, Rawson Lake was closed to angling and its healthy cutthroat trout population was used as brood stock by Alberta Fish and Wildlife. Today, Rawson Lake's cutthroat trout attract plenty of anglers and trout taken from Rawson average 25–35 cm in length, with much larger trout taken regularly.

🅰 Rawson Lake (AB)

50°35'28"N 115°09'17"W

Cutthroat trout to 55 cm (1.5 kg)

Rawson Lake is tucked away in a wooded valley south of Upper

Rawson Lake

Jim Rennels photo

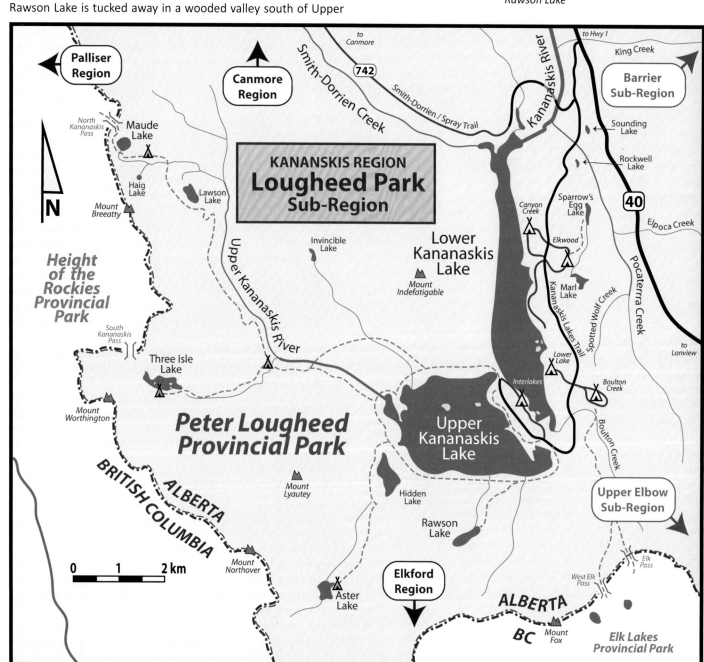

◼ Marl Lake (AB)
50°39'22"N 115°06'30"W
◼ Rockwall Lake (AB)
50°41'06"N 115°06'35"W
◼ Sounding Lake (AB)
50°41'36"N 115°06'21"W
Status: Devoid of fish
This series of shallow ponds and interconnecting beaver dams in the lower Pocaterra Creek drainage may have held fish at various times in the past, but it is unlikely that any remain. Would-be anglers will be deterred by the marshy access.

◻ Pocaterra Creek (AB)
◻ Elpoca Creek (AB)
◻ Spotted Wolf Creek (AB)
Cutthroat trout to 25 cm
Rainbow trout to 25 cm
Brook trout to 25 cm
Bull trout to 30 cm
Pocaterra, Elpoca and Spotted Wolf creeks hold a variety of trout in small sizes and are more productive than nearby lakes.

◻ Sparrows-Egg Lake (AB)
50°40'25"N 115°06'21"W
Rainbow trout to 60 cm (2.5 kg)
Cutthroat trout to 55 cm (2.0 kg)
Sparrows-Egg Lake is located in the marshy valley bottom, 2 km by trail from Elkwood Campground. Rainbow and cutthroat trout have both been stocked in Sparrows-Egg with great success. The fertility of the lake allows the trout to grow very quickly. The hard-fighting trout caught from the lake will average 35–45 cm in length. Fishing from shore is possible from many locations, but most anglers prefer to haul their belly boats to the lake. The downside to Sparrows-Egg is that the fish do not reproduce and the lake is prone to winterkill. Special regulations apply at Sparrows-Egg Lake.

◻ Spillway Lake (AB)
50°41'50"N 115°08'01"W
Rainbow trout to 35 cm
Cutthroat trout to 35 cm
Spillway Lake is located alongside the Smith-Dorrien/Spray Trail at the north end of Lower Kananaskis Lake. Its shallow waters generally hold a few schools of rainbow or cutthroat trout that have made their way in from Lower Kananaskis Lake and are unable to return. Spillway's trout are highly visible and are very spooky and difficult to catch. Watch for cars on your back cast if you're fly fishing.

◻ Boulton Creek
Rainbow trout to 30 cm
Brook trout to 25 cm
Cutthroat trout to 25 cm
Whitefish to 25 cm
Boulton Creek flows into the southern end of Lower Kananaskis Lake. There is a large campground on Boulton Creek. Fishing is generally poor for small rainbow trout, with cutthroat, brookies and whitefish present as well.

◮ Three Isle Lake (AB)
50°37'48"N 115°16'40"W
Cutthroat trout to 45 cm
Three Isle Lake is a beautifully coloured body of water set less than a kilometer below South Kananaskis Pass. Three Isle Lake has long been a favourite of backcountry anglers who take the 12 km hike up from Upper Kananaskis Lake. Cutthroat trout averaging 25–35 cm in length are present in good numbers and can be taken from most locations around the lake. Flies and lures will both work well at Three Isle. Water levels in the lake fluctuate dramatically from spring to autumn, continuing to drop as the year progresses. Initial starting levels after ice-off in early summer are largely determined by winter snowfalls and springtime precipitation.

Three Isle Lake

Three Isle Lake cutthroat trout

◼ Lawson Lake (AB)
50°40'38"N 115°15'57"W
Status: Devoid of fish
Lawson Lake is a picturesque tarn on the North Kananaskis Pass trail. Lawson was stocked in the early 1970s, but the trout failed to reproduce. At present there are no fish in Lawson.

◮ Maude Lake (AB)
50°41'22"N 115°17'36"W
Cutthroat trout to 45 cm
Maude Lake is set in the distinctly alpine environs of North Kananaskis Pass and offers anglers the twin jewels of superb scenery and excellent fishing. A tiring 17 km hike-in from Upper Kananaskis Lake is required to reach Maude Lake. An abundance of cutthroat trout in the 25–35 cm range inhabit the lake's clear waters, and can they be caught from most locations around the shoreline. Larger fish tend to keep to the deeper waters off the north and west corners of the lake, where steep terrain will generally limit fly casting. On calm evenings with insects hatching, a dry fly can be particularly effective.

Maude Lake

*Maude Lake
cutthroat trout*

■ **Haig Lake (aka South Maude Lake) (AB)**
50°40'52"N 115°17'14"W
Status: Devoid of fish
Haig Lake is the small tarn located less than a kilometre south of Maude Lake. Haig Lake has never been stocked and contains no fish.

■ **Invincible Lake (AB)**
50°39'44"N 115°12'58"W
Cutthroat trout to 40 cm
This small alpine lake on the west flank of Mt. Invincible holds stocked cutthroat trout in the 20–30 cm range. Trails are sketchy at best, leading 16 km from the north side of Upper Kananaskis Lake.

Invincible Lake

Jason Godkin photo

*Invincible Lake
cutthroat trout*

Jason Godkin photo

Upper Elbow Sub-Region

This Sub-Region is centered on Elbow Pass and the headwaters of the Elbow River and sits amid the rugged peaks east of Highway 40 at Highwood Pass. All angling prospects require hiking, with the shortest and most popular being the steep 1 km walk from Highway 40 to Elbow Lake. The Elbow River begins in Elbow Lake and flows east, before eventually emptying into the Bow River at Calgary. The Elbow River offers fair stream fishing in its upper reaches. Other lake fishing opportunities in the region require day hikes at a minimum and include Lower Tombstone, Talus, and Burns lakes, all of which contain cutthroat trout.

Elbow Sheep Wildland – Burncos

There is a parcel of private land smack dab in the middle of the Elbow-Sheep Wildland that belongs to P. Burns Resources and P. Burns Mines Ltd, collectively referred to as the Burncos. For a century, the public was granted right-of-way access across the Burncos property that connected the Sheep and Elbow valleys and provided access to Rickert's Pass, Burns Lake and a number of great mountain scrambles. The Sheep River Valley has been part of Kananaskis Country for almost 40 years. Burncos has now closed their property to recreational use, which leaves few options for public use. It is hoped that the government can negotiate a settlement with Burncos that will satisfy both sides and allow the public to pass through the property. Parks has put up signs at appropriate trailheads advising hikers of the situation.

■ **Elbow Lake (AB)**
50°38'21"N 115°00'31"W
Brook trout to 35 cm
Cutthroat trout to 35 cm
Elbow Lake is situated at the summit of Elbow Pass, and is a steep 1 km by trail from Highway 40. The pretty blue waters of Elbow Lake attract numerous visitors every summer, so don't expect solitude. Brook trout predominate, with most fish taken from the lake averaging 20–25 cm in length. Several projects have been undertaken in recent years to enhance the lake's habitat, which hopefully will result in larger trout. Forest cover and extended shallows around much of the lake will deter many fly fishers. However, fish can be taken very close to shore in many spots, particularly in the deeper waters off the scree slopes along the north side.

Elbow Lake

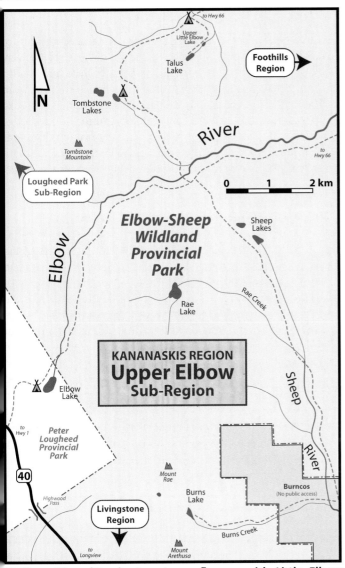

sides by forest, contains plenty of small cutthroat trout averaging 20–25 cm in length. ■ Dramatically set beneath the towering east face of Tombstone Mountain, the shallow Upper Lake has never been stocked and contains no fish.

Lower Tombstone Lake

■ Rae Lake (AB)

50°39'19"N 115°58'22"W

Status: Doubtful

The dark waters of Rae Lake lie tucked into the side of Mt. Rae's eastern outlier. The lake is approximately 10 km by trail from Highway 40, and it receives minimal attention from anglers. Rae Lake at one time held a good population of cutthroat trout. However, winterkill is a potential problem at Rae Lake. Recent reports indicate that there are no fish remaining in Rae Lake.

Rae Lake

■ Burns Lake (AB)

50°36'15"N 115°56'36"W

Cutthroat trout to 40 cm

Burns Lake is located in a rocky basin at the head of a minor tributary of the upper Sheep River. The lake is a distant 15 km by trail from Elbow Lake or 16 km by trail from Highway 546 (Sheep River Trail). There is shorter 5 km scramble up and over a steep headwall that begins at Ptarmigan Cirque on Highway 40. The difficulty of this route protects Burns Lake from all but the most enterprising day hikers. Those who do reach the lake, from whatever route they choose, will be rewarded by plentiful cutthroat trout averaging 25–35 cm in length.

■ Elbow River (Headwaters to confluence with Little Elbow River) (AB)

Brown trout to 55 cm (1.5 kg)
Brook trout to 35 cm
Rainbow trout to 40 cm
Cutthroat trout to 40 cm
Bull trout to 60 cm (2.0 kg)
Whitefish to 30 cm

The upper reaches of the Elbow River flow northeast from its source at Elbow Lake. Access is along a hiking trail that parallels the river between the Elbow Pass region and Highway 66 (Elbow Falls Trail) at Little Elbow Campground. Cutthroat, brook and bull trout are all present in this upper section, which near Elbow Lake is little more than a small creek. Brown and rainbow trout become more prevalent in the overfished lower reaches of the Elbow River which is accessible via Elbow Falls Trail (Highway 66) from Bragg Creek.

▲ Tombstone Lakes (AB)

(Lower) 50°41'19"N 115°59'22"W

Cutthroat trout to 35 cm (Lower Lake only)

Despite their ominous name, the Tombstone Lakes are set in a delightful basin. They are located 10 km by trail from Highway 40 via Elbow Lake. There is a small backcountry campground at Lower Tombstone. The tiny Lower Lake, surrounded on three

Burns Lake

Jason Godkin photo

101

◻ Sheep River (Headwaters to Junction Creek) (AB)

Rainbow trout to 50 cm
Brook trout to 35 cm
Cutthroat trout to 35 cm
Bull trout to 60 cm (3.0 kg)
Whitefish to 35 cm

The upper Sheep River is accessed by trails from Bluerock Campground at the end of the Sheep River Trail (Highway 546). Although there is a good variety of fish, angling is regarded only as fair in the upper Sheep River. Expect to catch rainbow, cutthroat or brook trout in the 15–25 cm range.

◻ Cougar Creek (AB)

Cutthroat trout to 30 cm
Bull trout to 35 cm

This tributary of the Sheep River holds small cutthroat and bull trout.

◻ Sheep Lakes (aka Sheep Lake and Cougar Lake) (AB)

50°39'59"N 115°57'16"W
Status: Doubtful

These two shallow lakes are located at the headwaters of the Sheep River. It is doubtful that fish could overwinter in the lakes.

◻ Talus Lake (AB)

50°43'20"N 115°58'43"W
Cutthroat trout to 40 cm

Talus Lake is located at the head of a minor tributary stream that enters the Little Elbow River approximately 10 km upstream from Little Elbow Campground. Ill-defined trails lead south along Talus Lake's outlet creek from the main hiking trail along the Little Elbow River to the shores of this appropriately named body of water. Talus (scree) slopes make up the shore of virtually the entire lake. Cutthroat trout in the 25–35 cm range are the normal catch from Talus Lake, and fly fishing is the most effective technique.

Talus Lake

◻ Upper Little Elbow Lake (AB)

50°43'30"N 115°58'31"W
Status: Doubtful

Little Upper Elbow Lake is the small pond located below the Talus Lake headwall. It has never been stocked and likely contains no fish.

Barrier Sub-Region

Highway 40 (Kananaskis Trail) runs through the core of the Sub-Region, from the Trans-Canada Highway to Peter Lougheed Provincial Park in the south. Limited supplies are available at Fortress Junction and Ribbon Creek Alpine Village. The area has several major frontcountry campgrounds as well as a Travel Alberta Information Centre at Barrier Lake. Winding its way north to the Bow River, the beautiful Kananaskis River and its multitude of accompanying beaver ponds are within easy walking distance of Highway 40 for most anglers. Barrier Lake, formed by a dam on the Kananaskis River, is one of only a handful of lakes in the Canadian Rockies that contain brown trout, and for this reason it attracts many anglers. Travelling south along Highway 40 you pass the Mt. Lorette Ponds and Wedge Pond, both of which offer good roadside fishing and are stocked annually. The Ribbon Creek-Galatea Creek loop presents a challenging hike with some fine backcountry fishing en route in Ribbon, Galatea and Lillian lakes.

◻ Barrier Lake (AB)

51°01'44"N 115°03'25"W
Brown trout to 60 cm (2.5 kg)
Brook trout to 55 cm (1.5 kg)
Rainbow trout to 55 cm (1.5 kg)
Whitefish to 40 cm

The Barrier Dam on the Kananaskis River creates Barrier Lake, a beautiful green-coloured body of water. The level of the water in the lake fluctuates with the seasons and with the use of the dam. Late in the fall and early in the spring, the area around the inlet of the Kananaskis River becomes one large mud flat intersected by the river winding back and forth. As the dam fills with meltwater, the mudflats disappear and the lake gains almost 2 km in length. Barrier Lake holds plenty of brown trout and whitefish in the 25–35 cm range as well as a few brook and rainbow. Fishing is best from a boat, although there are a few locations where shore-bound anglers do well. A number of points that jut out into the lake hold good possibilities, as does the area around the inlet and the main bay near Barrier Dam.

Barrier Lake

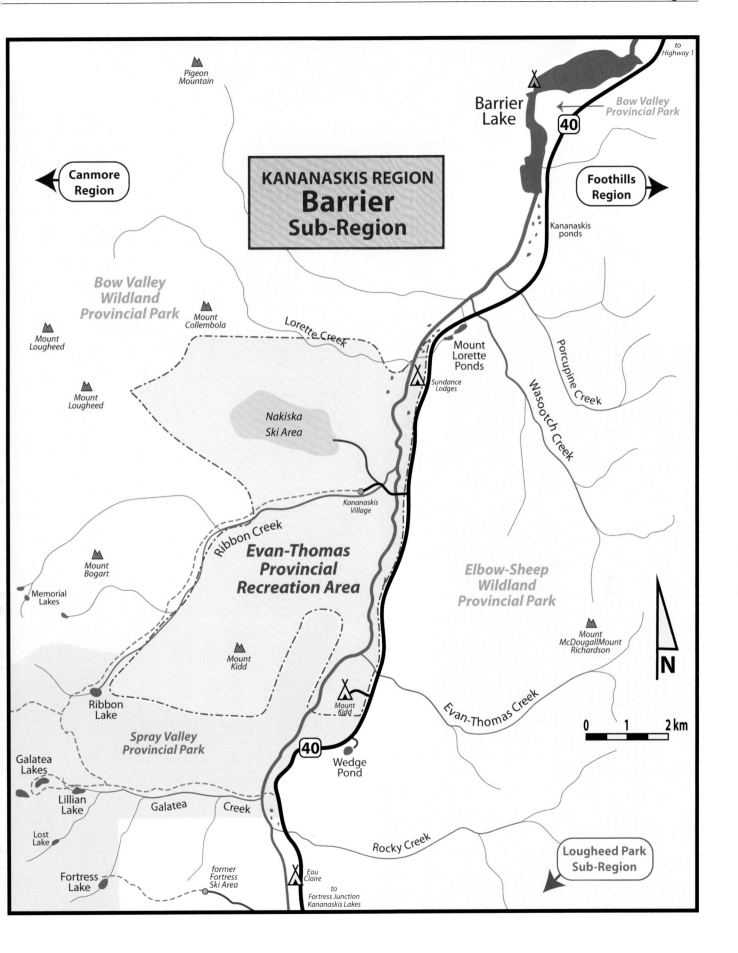

Pigeon Mountain

Barrier Lake

to Highway 1

Bow Valley Provincial Park

40

KANANASKIS REGION
Barrier
Sub-Region

◄ Canmore Region

Foothills Region ►

Bow Valley Wildland Provincial Park

Mount Collembola

Lorette Creek

Kananaskis ponds

Mount Lorette Ponds

Mount Lougheed

Sundance Lodges

Mount Lougheed

Nakiska Ski Area

Porcupine Creek

Wasootch Creek

Kananaskis Village

Ribbon Creek

Evan-Thomas Provincial Recreation Area

Mount Bogart

Memorial Lakes

Elbow-Sheep Wildland Provincial Park

Mount McDougall Mount Richardson

N

Mount Kidd

Mount Kidd

Evan-Thomas Creek

Ribbon Lake

0   1   2 km

Spray Valley Provincial Park

Galatea Lakes

40

Wedge Pond

Lillian Lake

Galatea Creek

Lost Lake

Rocky Creek

Lougheed Park Sub-Region

Fortress Lake

former Fortress Ski Area

Eau Claire

to Fortress Junction Kananaskis Lakes

103

■ Kananaskis River (AB)
Brook trout to 40 cm
Rainbow trout to 40 cm
Cutthroat trout to 40 cm
Brown trout to 55 cm (1.5 kg)
Whitefish to 40 cm
Bull trout to 60 cm (2.5 kg)

The Kananaskis River flows from the Kananaskis Lakes to the Bow River and is paralleled by Highway 40 for much of its length. The Kananaskis River has many deep pools and nice riffle sections but does not have a good reputation for angling. The river holds a variety of fish, with brook trout predominating, although cutthroat, rainbow and brown are taken on occasion. Be aware that the release of water from the dam on Lower Kananaskis Lake can cause changes in water levels over a few hours that in addition to being hazardous, usually disrupts fishing. The changing water levels results in a poor habitat and affects the overall quality of the fishery.

Kananaskis River

■ Kananaskis ponds (AB)
50°59'40"N 115°04'32"W
Brook trout to 30 cm

There is a seemingly endless maze of beaver ponds that parallel the Kananaskis River between Barrier Lake and Ribbon Creek. Although some are subject to winterkill, most hold small brook trout averaging 15–25 cm in length. The ponds closest to the highway are generally overfished and reaching the more productive ponds usually means working through a tangle of brush and deadfall. Wet feet are a sure bet. Major clusters of ponds are found along the river south of Barrier Lake, including Beaver Ponds Picnic Area, and near the junction of the Kananaskis River with Porcupine, Wasootch and Rocky creeks.

Kananaskis ponds

■ Mount Lorette Ponds (AB)
50°58'10"N 115°06'28"W
Rainbow trout to 35 cm

The Mount Lorette Ponds consist of a series of small man-made lakes built to provide handicapped and elderly persons the opportunity to fish. A network of paved trails leads from the parking lot past a picnic area to all the ponds where stocked rainbow in the 20–30 cm range are the normal catch. The ponds are stocked annually and are usually fished out by mid-summer unless supplemented by fall plantings.

Mount Lorette Ponds

■ Wedge Pond (AB)
50°52'22"N 115°08'07"W
Arctic grayling to 35 cm

Wedge Pond is a man-made lake situated alongside Highway 40. Winterkill of the stocked trout population was a problem in the past, and Wedge Lake has been re-stocked with arctic grayling, which appear to be thriving. The arctic grayling taken from the pond average 20–30 cm in length. For those who are fly fishing, there is plenty of backcasting room around the entire lake. Grayling can be taken with flies or small lures and spinners.

Wedge Pond

■ Evan-Thomas Creek (AB)
Brook trout to 25 cm
Brown trout to 30 cm
Rainbow trout to 25 cm
Cutthroat trout to 25 cm
Whitefish to 25 cm

Evan-Thomas Creek, a major tributary of the Kananaskis River, has fair angling in its lower sections. Brook trout in small sizes predominate, with a variety of other trout and whitefish also available.

■ Ribbon Creek (AB)

Cutthroat trout to 25 cm
Brook trout to 25 cm
Bull trout to 30 cm

The lower reaches of Ribbon Creek hold a few small cutthroat trout and may also hold the odd brook or bull trout. Fishing is best restricted to the waters within a kilometre of the Kananaskis River. This section also includes a number of beaver ponds.

■ Ribbon Lake (AB)

50°53'11"N 115°14'36"W
Cutthroat trout to 45 cm

Ribbon Lake is an exquisite body of water set on a lip above Ribbon Falls. The lake is guarded by cliffs, making access very difficult. The first 11 km of the 13 km trail are a straightforward hike up Ribbon Creek at a very moderate grade to the delightful Ribbon Falls. Once past the falls, the trail rises steeply, soon coming to a series of exposed ledges and cliff faces to which chains have been attached to aid climbing. Even so, it is still a dangerous section, particularly in wet weather, and the faint-of-heart are strongly advised to pass on this lake or to use the longer Guinn's Pass or Buller Pass access routes. Ribbon Lake holds cutthroat averaging 25–35 cm in length. Casting a fly is difficult around much of the shoreline due to heavy brush, although there are enough suitable locations to keep fly fishers happy. A distinctive drop-off can be seen around the entire lake, and fishing this zone where the shallow meets the deep is usually very productive.

Ribbon Lake

■ Memorial Lakes (aka Bogart Lakes) (AB)

50°55'35"N 115°14'33"W
Cutthroat trout to 30 cm

The three Memorial Lakes are located in a secluded basin at the head of the North Fork of Ribbon Creek. Access to the lakes is on a 10 km trail that begins at Ribbon Creek. The Memorial Lakes hold cutthroat trout that average 20–30 cm in length. The lower lake has by far the best potential for anglers. The upper lake drains dry each fall.

Memorial Lakes

Jim Rennels photo

▲ Lillian Lake (AB)

50°51'49"N 115°15'02"W
Cutthroat trout to 45 cm

Lillian Lake is a very popular backcountry destination, and is crowded with hikers throughout the summer. Located 6 km by trail from Highway 40, the shallow, olive-coloured waters hold cutthroat averaging 20–30 cm in length. Due to water clarity, fish can be seen far out into the lake and casting ahead of cruising fish will produce positive results even though heavy forest cover around much of the shore will inhibit fly casting. Under low light conditions, fish can very often be taken within a few metres of shore by keen-eyed anglers.

Lillian Lake

■ Galatea Lakes (AB)

(Lower) 51°51'57"N 115°15'53"W
Cutthroat trout to 45 cm

Little more than a kilometre by ill-defined trail above the Lillian Lake campsite lie the twin gems of Lower and Upper Galatea Lakes. Both of these turquoise bodies of waters hold cutthroat in the 20–30 cm range. Lower Galatea Lake offers much better angling than its upper sibling. The lakes are set in rockbound basins at tree line, and there is plenty of fly casting room is available around the lakes. Both lakes are very clear and drop off quickly, and a wet fly fished deep generally gets strikes.

Upper Galatea Lake

Lower Galatea Lake

◼ Galatea Creek (AB)

Cutthroat trout to 25 cm

Bull trout to 30 cm

Brook trout to 25 cm

The lower two kilometres of Galatea Creek contains a few small cutthroat, bull and brook trout.

◼ Lost Lake (South Galatea Lake) (AB)

50°51'07"N 115°15'30"W

Status: Doubtful

This small lake is situated at the headwaters of Galatea Creek. The lake has never been stocked, but trout may have made their way in from the creek.

◼ Fortress Lake (AB)

50°50'05"N 115°14'08"W

Cutthroat trout to 45 cm

Beautiful Fortress Lake is set beneath the imposing north wall of The Fortress, and is reached by a 4 km hike from the former Fortress Ski Area. Fortress Lake holds cutthroat trout averaging 25–35 cm in length. Scree slopes from The Fortress make up of half of the lake's shore, with the rest a mixture of forest and meadow, allowing for reasonable fly casting opportunities. Due to the proximity of its mountain backdrop, Fortress Lake is often in shadow and usually is not ice-free until July.

Fortress Lake

Fortress Lake cutthroat trout

CANAL FLATS REGION

Columbia Lake, the headwaters of the Columbia River, is physically the centerpiece of this Region. The community of Canal Flats situated at the south end of Columbia Lake and is the service centre for the immediate area. Bisecting the region is Highway 93/95, which leads south to Cranbrook and north to Invermere. Whitetail and Whiteswan lakes are the two most popular angling destinations in the Region and each is the focal point of its own Sub-Region.

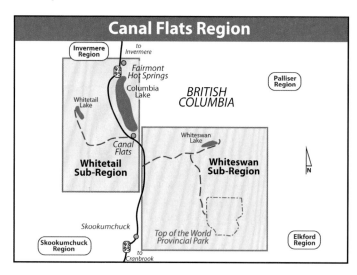

Whitetail Sub-Region

Columbia Lake has never been renowned for great fishing, although very large bull trout are taken on occasion. The Kootenay River is the main waterway, and the quality of fishing is generally determined by the clarity of the water. Dutch Creek, a tributary of the Columbia, and Findlay Creek, a tributary of the Kootenay, both offer good river fishing. Whitetail Lake, 26 km by gravel road from Highway 93/95, is the Sub-Region's angling masterpiece, with large rainbow trout plentiful in this Rockies' classic.

◼ Columbia Lake (BC)

50°14'45"N 115°51'34"W

Bull trout to 90 cm (10.0 kg)

Rainbow trout to 55 cm (1.5 kg)

Cutthroat trout to 55 cm (1.5 kg)

Whitefish to 40 cm

Kokanee to 35 cm

The pretty, aquamarine waters of Columbia Lake serve as the source of the mighty Columbia River, which eventually flows into the Pacific Ocean at Astoria, Oregon. Although Columbia Lake's fishing is generally regarded as substandard due to the coarse fish population, anglers are occasionally rewarded with huge bull trout often weighing 7 kg or more. Rainbow trout are stocked in large numbers annually in the lake. The waters where Dutch Creek empties into the north end of Columbia Lake tend to be the most productive, although cutthroat and rainbow trout can be taken from many locations on the lake. Trolling will be the most effective angling technique.

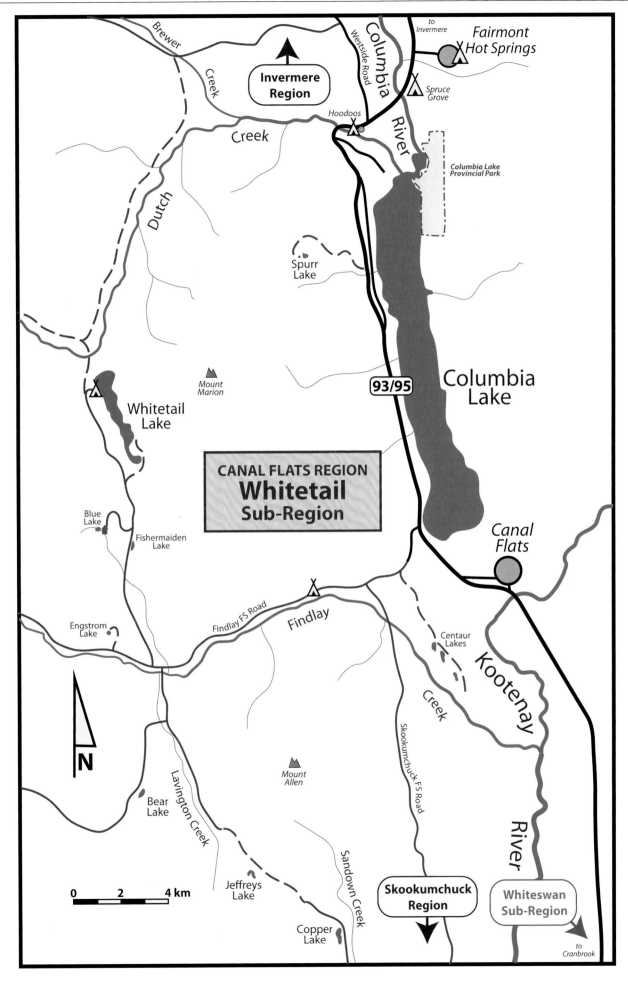

Brewer

Creek

to Invermere

Fairmont
Hot Springs

Westside Road

Columbia

Invermere
Region

Spruce
Grove

Hoodoos

River

Creek

Columbia Lake
Provincial Park

Dutch

Spurr
Lake

93/95

Columbia
Lake

Mount
Marion

Whitetail
Lake

CANAL FLATS REGION
Whitetail
Sub-Region

Blue
Lake

Fishermaiden
Lake

Canal
Flats

Findlay FS Road

Findlay

Centaur
Lakes

Engstrom
Lake

Creek

Kootenay

N

Skookumchuck FS Road

Mount
Allen

River

Bear
Lake

Lavington Creek

Sandown Creek

0   2   4 km

Jeffreys
Lake

Skookumchuck
Region

Whiteswan
Sub-Region

Copper
Lake

to
Cranbrook

Columbia Lake

■ Kootenay River (BC) (Kootenay National Park to Canal Flats)

Cutthroat trout to 50 cm
Bull trout to 75 cm (5.0 kg)
Whitefish to 40 cm
Kokanee to 35 cm

The Kootenay River flows out of the Kootenay Valley into the Rocky Mountain Trench at Canal Flats. The Kootenay River continues to flow south and by a quirk of geography misses Columbia Lake by less than two kilometres. The two river systems eventually reconnect at Castlegar after each river has travelled hundreds of kilometres. The Kootenay is a relatively large river as it flows south to Canal Flats, and it receives heavy runoff in the spring. The river is often muddy until mid-summer, after which cutthroat and bull trout can be taken in increasing numbers as the river clears. Fall is the best time for whitefish and kokanee.

Kootenay River

■ Dutch Creek (BC)

Cutthroat to 50 cm
Bull trout to 75 cm (5.0 kg)
Whitefish to 40 cm
Kokanee to 35 cm

Dutch Creek is regarded by locals as the "true source" of the Columbia River as it is the main tributary flowing into Columbia Lake. Dutch Creek has gained a reputation over time as a fine trout stream. Cutthroat in the 25–35 cm range can be taken from the many pools along the entire length of the creek, while bull trout exceeding 60 cm in length are found in some of the larger holes. The lower reaches of Dutch Creek in the vicinity of Highway 93/95 tend to get overfished. The upper river, which is accessed by logging roads branching from the Westside Road, sees lesser numbers of anglers and holds the promise of better fishing. Water clarity is stunning in the late summer and fall and Dutch Creek's cutthroat are always eager to rise to a well-presented dry fly.

■ Brewer Creek (BC)

Cutthroat trout to 40 cm
Bull trout to 60 cm (2.5 kg)
Whitefish to 35 cm

Brewer Creek is a major tributary of Dutch Creek and can be reached from logging roads connecting with the Westside Road. Cutthroat averaging 20–30 cm in length are the dominant species with a few bull trout and whitefish present as well.

◭ Spurr Lake (aka Spur Lake, Brady Lake) (BC)

50°15'58"N 115°55'06"W
Rainbow trout to 55 cm (1.5 kg)

This small forest-encircled lake is located approximately 6 km by rough road from Highway 93/95. Spurr Lake holds an abundance of rainbow trout, most in the 25–35 cm range. Although fish can generally be taken fairly close to shore, fishing from a boat or float tube is preferable. Lures and flies will do equally well in Spurr Lake.

Spurr Lake

◭ Whitetail Lake [aka Deer Lake] (BC)

50°12'44"N 116°01'33"W
Rainbow trout to 70 cm (4.0 kg)
Brook trout to 55 cm (2.0 kg)

Whitetail Lake is steadily gaining a superb reputation as one of the best fishing lakes in the entire Rockies. The lake is set in a valley between the Dutch and Findlay Creek drainages. Access to the campground at the north end of the lake is via a good 26 km gravel road from Highway 93/95 at Thunder Hill, above the south end of Columbia Lake. Whitetail Lake has been designated as a trophy lake, and consequently special limits on number and size of trout kept are in effect, as well as restrictions on bait and type of hook. Rainbow trout upwards of 50 cm in length are taken with amazing regularity, and trophy fish of 60 cm or more are not uncommon. Fly fishing enthusiasts love Whitetail's extended shallows and crystal-clear water, where large rainbows cruise constantly. Chironomid fishing in the early season is simply out-of-this-world! A boat or float tube is essential to fish Whitetail effectively. ⊗ All inlet and outlet streams of Whitetail Lake are closed to angling.

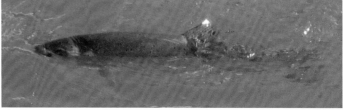
Whitetail Lake rainbow trout

Whitetail Lake

☐ Blue Lake (BC)

50°10'17"N 115°01'27"W

Rainbow trout to 35 cm

Blue Lake is a small but colourful lake located 26 km from Highway 93/95 (2 km southwest of Whitetail Lake). The lake contains rainbow trout averaging 25–35 cm in length. The Columbia Outdoor School at the Blue Lake Centre is busy throughout the summer, and Blue Lake is usually a hive of canoeing, swimming and fishing activity.

Blue Lake

☐ Fisher Maiden Lake (BC)

50°10'03"N 116°00'51"W

Rainbow trout to 35 cm

Tiny Fisher Maiden Lake is located alongside the Whitetail Lake road and fishing for its stocked rainbow trout is restricted to youngsters and senior citizens only. Casting room is limited around this small pond. The rainbow trout in Fisher Maiden Lake with average 15–25 cm in length.

Fishermaiden Lake

☐ Findlay Creek (BC)

Cutthroat trout to 50 cm

Bull trout to 70 cm (4.0 kg)

Whitefish to 40 cm

Findlay Creek is a major tributary of the Kootenay River, and joins the Kootenay approximately 5 km south of Canal Flats. A gravel road beginning at Thunder Hill off Highway 93/95, above the south end of Columbia Lake, leads up the Findlay Creek drainage. Although several kilometres of Findlay Creek are virtually impossible to access due to a deep canyon, there are many stretches of fishable water. Cutthroat trout averaging 20–30 cm in length predominate, with bull trout and whitefish present in fair numbers as well.

Findlay Creek

☐ Engstrom Pond (aka Burks Pond) (BC)

50°08'01"N 116°02'17"W

Rainbow trout to 35 cm

Brook trout to 35 cm

Tiny Engstrom Pond is reached via some rough dirt roads that lead off the Findlay Creek Forest Service Road. The almost perfectly circular pond is crystal clear, and fish can easily be seen cruising along the seam between the shallows and deeper water. Rainbow and brook trout inhabit Engstrom Pond in relatively equal numbers, and the size of the fish will average 15–25 cm in length. For those fly fishing, roll casting will be essential, as the forest cover hugs the lake in the areas where the shallows are least extensive. Lures and bait are also effective.

Engstrom Pond

☐ Bear Lake (aka Shallow Lake) (BC)

50°04'47"N 116°00'40"W

Brook trout to 40 cm

Bear Lake is located in Lavington Creek drainage and can be reached on logging roads. As its alternate name suggests, the lake is not very deep, and shallow water extends far out from the shoreline. Brook trout are present in the lake in the 20–30 cm range.

Bear Lake

■ Lavington Creek (BC)
Cutthroat trout to 35 cm
Lavington Creek is a tributary of Findlay Creek and can be reached by following logging roads that branch south off of the main Findlay Creek Road. Lavington Creek holds small cutthroat trout, few larger than 25 cm in length.

■ Jeffreys Lake (BC)
50°03'06"N 115°56'56"W
Cutthroat trout to 45
Jeffreys Lake is located at the height of land separating Lavington and Sandown Creek, and can only be reached through private property after receiving permission from the owner. The lake's colouration is particularly stunning, with the dark blues of the depths contrasted against the light greens of the shallows. The margin separating the deep and shallow waters is productive for cutthroat trout that average 25–35 cm in length.

■ Copper Lake (BC)
50°01'52"N 115°54'04"W
Cutthroat trout to 35 cm
Copper Lake is situated at the head of Sandown Creek, and can be reached by a rough road that leads north up Sandown Creek. Copper Lake is not heavily fished and does hold cutthroat trout in the 20–30 cm range.

☐ Centaur Lakes (BC)
50°07'40"N 115°50'32"W
Brook trout to 40 cm
The Centaur Lakes consist of a series of shallow, interconnected lakes situated on the benches above the southwest corner of Columbia Lake. Access is on poorly maintained roads off the main Findlay Creek Road. Extensive shallows around the lakes makes fishing awkward in many places. Brook trout were stocked in the past, but it is likely that numbers of trout in the lake are limited at best.

Northern Centaur Lake

Whiteswan Sub-Region

Whiteswan Provincial Park is located southeast of Canal Flats and is the core of this Sub-Region. The Park is reached by following the 24 km gravel access road that branches east from Highway 93/95, approximately 5 km south of Canal Flats. Note that the access road passes through the Lussier River canyon and may cause palpitations for those not used to narrow mountain roads overlooking deep canyons. Whiteswan Lake itself receives heavy fishing pressure all season long. Nearby Alces Lake is popular with fly fishers. Top of the World Provincial Park, located in rugged backcountry south of Whiteswan, attracts hikers and anglers to appropriately named Fish Lake. The White River, and its numerous tributaries, are found to the north of Whiteswan, and offer some outstanding stream fishing for cutthroat trout.

A Nice Warm Feeling

The Canadian Rockies possesses a number of wonderful hot springs. Most, such as Banff, Radium, Fairmont and Miette, are highly developed. There is no better thing to do at the end of a day of fishing, especially in the cool days of spring or fall, than to take a dip in a hot spring. Lussier Hot Springs, located within Whiteswan Lake Provincial Park, is a particularly ideal post-fishing take-a-dip location. Lussier Hot Springs are semi-developed (parking area, change booth, no charge, nice rock pools) and are very popular with non-anglers as well. If in the area, don't miss the opportunity to take a plunge in Lussier Hot Springs. For those with a bit more adventurous spirit, Ram River Hot Springs are located not so far from Lussier Hot Springs but must be accessed from the Premier Lake area.

Lussier Hot Springs

■ Whiteswan Lake (BC)
50°08'43"N 115°28'21"W
Rainbow trout to 75 cm (4.0 kg)
Whiteswan Lake and its provincial park are enormously popular the summer, and the campgrounds are invariably filled to overflowing every weekend. Whiteswan is a long, narrow lake sandwiched between the rugged peaks of the Hughes and Van Nostrand Ranges. Whiteswan's deep, dark waters hold rainbow trout averaging 30–40 cm in length, with much larger individuals present in good numbers. Gang trolls and flatfish predominate among fishing equipment on Whiteswan Lake, although fly fishing has become much more popular in recent years. There are some excellent chironomid fishing opportunities at Whiteswan in the spring. Simply trolling a wet fly behind a boat at a slow speed is usually productive, or in the late evening, if wind conditions are

favourable, there is superb dry fly fishing in the shallow waters at both ends of the lake. Wind can be a problem at Whiteswan as it generally picks up in intensity by mid-day and remains strong throughout much of the afternoon. ⊗ All of Whiteswan's inlet and outlet creeks are closed to angling. Check regulations, as there are special limits on trout taken from the lake. Be aware of logging and ore trucks on the main access road from Highway 93/95.

Whiteswan Lake rainbow trout

Whiteswan Lake

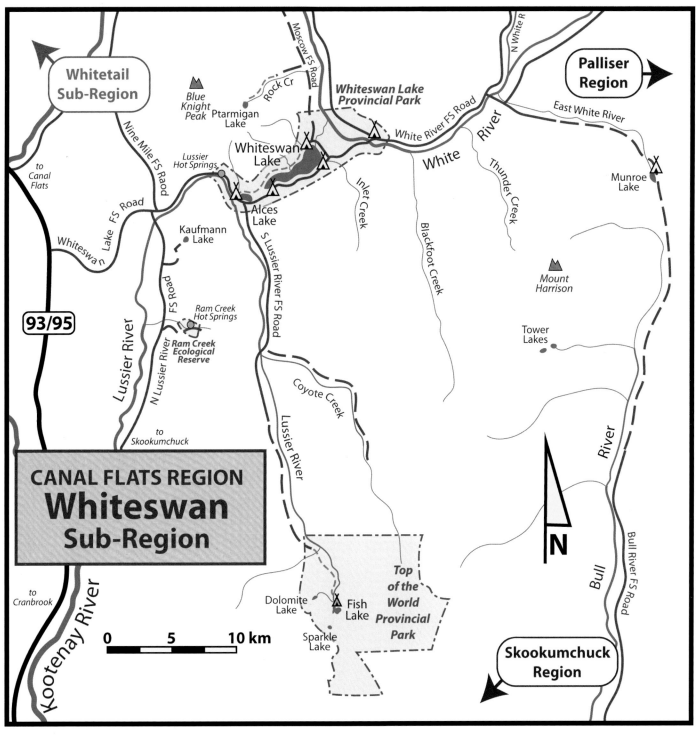

⬛ Alces Lake (aka Moose Lake) (BC)

50°07'12"N 115°32'14"W

Rainbow trout to 60 cm (2.5 kg.)

Alces Lake is situated alongside the main Whiteswan Provincial Park access road, 2 km before reaching Whiteswan Lake. Alces Lake is no longer restricted to fly fishing only, which has increased its popularity in recent years. Alces' pleasing blue-green waters hold plenty of rainbow trout averaging 30–40 cm in length. Trolling a fly along the margin that separates the shallows from the deeper water is generally an effective technique. Chironomid fishing on a dry line with a strike indicator over the lake's weed beds is very popular and successful in the early season.

Alces Lake

Alces Lake rainbow trout

⬛ Kaufmann Lake (BC)

50°06'33"N 115°37'02"W

Brook trout to 35 cm

Cutthroat trout to 35 cm

Rainbow trout to 35 cm

Kaufmann Lake is hidden in a small side valley above the Lussier River and can be reached by following a confusing series of logging roads that lead south and east off of the Whiteswan Lake access road. A very steep hill is encountered just before the lake, and it is best to walk the hill rather than drive it. Kaufmann Lake is a secluded gem of emerald green water, encircled by a pleasant mixed forest. Fly fishing is difficult from shore due to the forest cover, but those spin casting with lures or bait will do well. Brook trout were originally stocked in Kaufmann, and although cutthroat and rainbow have been introduced more recently, the brook trout are definitely found in greater numbers. Fish caught tend to be small but plentiful, with the average in the 20–25 cm range.

Kaufmann Lake

Arek Nyor with Kaufmann Lake brook trout

⬛ Ptarmigan Lake (BC)

50°10'53"N 115°32'29"W

Cutthroat trout to 35 cm

Ptarmigan Lake is set in an alpine basin north of Whiteswan Lake and is reached by following a 6 km trail, half of which is an abandoned logging road. Ptarmigan was stocked in the past with cutthroat trout, which are doing well. The trout average 25–35 cm in length and can be taken from most locations around the lake. Forest, meadow, brush and avalanche slope make up the shoreline, and there are numerous locations from which to fish.

Ptarmigan Lake

⬛ White River (BC)

Cutthroat trout to 50 cm

Rainbow trout to 50 cm

Bull trout to 70 cm (4.0 kg)

Whitefish to 40 cm

The White River is the major flowing water of the Sub-Region, rushing south and west from headwaters along the continental divide before swinging north to join the Kootenay River. Logging roads from the Kootenay River and from Whiteswan Lake make their way up all the branches of the White River. The upper portions of the White offer outstanding fishing for cutthroat trout and are far removed from heavy fishing pressure. Cutthroat trout from the White will average 25–35 cm in length. Whitefish are also found along the river's entire length, with rainbow trout populating the area below the White River's confluence with Whiteswan Lake's outlet creek. Large bull trout, protected by regulations, enter the White River system each fall. Just seeing one of these 5 kg monsters in one of the smaller tributaries is a heart-stopping event.

White River

North White River (BC)
Cutthroat trout to 50 cm
Bull trout to 70 cm (4.0 kg)
Whitefish to 40 cm
The North White River possesses the characteristics of the upper White River and is accessed from logging roads branching off the White. Cutthroat trout averaging 20–30 cm are plentiful with bull trout and whitefish also present in fair numbers.

East White River (BC)
Status: Closed to angling
The East White River is major tributary of the White River and flows northwest from its source at Monroe Lake to join the White River. The East White has been closed to angling to protect the bull trout population.

East White River bull trout

Munroe Lake (BC)
50°08'03"N 115°06'11"W
Cutthroat trout to 45 cm
Munroe Lake is a small, placid body of water at the head of the East White River. Munroe's stunning blue-green waters receive little fishing pressure each season due to the lengthy access. The plentiful cutthroat trout in Munroe Lake will average 25–35 cm in length. A boat or float tube is essential for any angling success at Munroe Lake. Fish can be taken equally effectively with lures or flies.

Munroe Lake

Munroe Lake cutthroat trout

Tower Lakes (BC)
50°01'07"N 115°13'16"W
Cutthroat trout to 35 cm
The diminutive Tower Lakes are located in the shadow of Mt. Harrison, the highest mountain in the Region. The lakes are reached after bushwhacking from logging roads in the extreme upper Bull River drainage. Map, compass and wilderness experience are prerequisites for anyone planning to fish Tower Lakes. The lakes have been stocked in the past with cutthroat trout, which are now reproducing naturally. Fish caught from the two Tower Lakes (individually named as Tower #1 and Tower #2) will average 20–30 cm in length.

Lussier River (BC) (Headwaters to Diorite Creek)
Cutthroat trout to 40 cm
Bull trout to 60 cm (2.5 kg)
Whitefish to 35 cm
The Lussier River flows from headwaters in Top of the World Provincial Park and eventually joins the Kootenay River. The upper section, above the junction with Diorite Creek, offers fine streamside angling over much of its course. The canyon section, which is paralleled by the Whiteswan Lake road, is virtually impossible to access. Above the canyon, the Lussier River can be reached by following the Top of the World Provincial Park road. The upper Lussier is criss-crossed with logging roads and is readily accessible. Cutthroat trout predominate in the Lussier, with average specimens running in the 25–35 cm range.

Lussier River

Coyote Creek (BC)
Cutthroat trout to 35 cm
Bull trout to 55 cm (2.0 kg)
Whitefish to 30 cm
Coyote Creek is a major tributary of the upper Lussier River and can be reached from logging roads that branch off of the Top of the World Provincial Park road. Coyote Creek has many fine pools, and cutthroat trout of 20–30 cm in length will be the average fare.

◢ Fish Lake (BC)

49°50'47"N 115°26'34"W

Cutthroat trout to 45 cm
Bull trout to 70 cm (4.0 kg)

Fish Lake is a very popular backcountry hiking destination, located in the heart of Top of the World Provincial Park. Fish Lake is reached via a 6 km trail after a 55 km drive on a gravel road from Highway 93/95. There is a backcountry campground at the lake, as well as a BC Parks cabin, which is available for a minimal fee on a first-come, first-served basis. Fishing is usually top-notch, as cutthroat trout in the 20–35 cm range abound in the lake's sparkling green. Large bull trout are also present in small numbers. Fishing from shore is limited in many locations due to the heavy forest cover, which rings the lake. Spin casters will be able to cover more water than fly fishers. Despite the seemingly remote location, Top of the World Provincial Park, and Fish Lake in particular, are busy throughout the summer months.

Wayne Pierce photo

Fish Lake

Aaron Pierce with Fish Lake cutthroat trout

■ Dolomite Lake (BC)

49°51'11"N 115°27'59"W

Cutthroat trout to 50 cm

Dolomite Lake is set in a narrow basin north of Fish Lake. The lake is reached by hiking a heart-pounding two kilometre trail up to the crest of Wild Horse Ridge, and then descending steeply down the other side of the ridge. Those anglers who reach Dolomite Lake are rewarded with chunky cutthroat trout ranging from 30–40 cm in length. The bottom drops off quickly all around the lake, and there are several good spots from which to cast a fly and reach the fish-holding waters. Be forewarned that the hike to Dolomite Lake, although not particularly long, is very strenuous.

■ Sparkle Lake (BC)

49°50'03"N 115°26'57"W

Status: Devoid of fish

Sparkle Lake is set in a windswept basin high above the inlet to Fish Lake and is very popular as a half-day hike from the Fish Lake campground. Sparkle Lake has never been stocked and contains no fish.

Backcountry buddy

PALLISER REGION

This is one of the most rugged and unspoiled Regions of the Rockies and includes two of British Columbia's most spectacular provincial parks: Mount Assiniboine and Height of the Rockies. Access into the Region is by hiking trails only. There are numerous excellent cutthroat trout lakes, rivers and streams in the Region. Connor Lakes in the south, and the lakes in the core area of Mount Assiniboine Park in the north are truly outstanding. Anyone planning to fish this corner of the Rockies can expect to do a significant amount of legwork prior to the reward of great fishing.

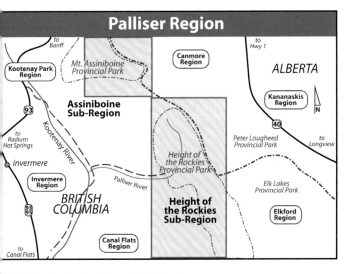

Height of the Rockies Sub-Region

The Height of the Rockies (HOTR) Provincial Park sits amid some of the most striking mountain scenery on the continent. The park runs from Palliser Pass and Banff National Park in the north to Connor Lakes in the south, taking in peaks, valleys, lakes and rivers on the British Columbia side of the Continental Divide. All of the fishing opportunities in this Sub-Region are remote, and virtually all will require a hike of some magnitude. Cutthroat trout are the predominant species in the area's rivers and lakes.

Palliser River (BC)
Cutthroat trout to 50 cm
Bull trout to 75 cm (5.0 kg)
Whitefish to 35 cm
The Palliser River is a major tributary of the Kootenay Riverand joins the Kootenay approximately 20 km south of Kootenay National Park. The primary road access up Palliser River watershed is from Settlers Road in Kootenay National Park. The Palliser Forest Service Road branches east from Settlers Road and ascends the Palliser River drainage to the provincial park boundary near Joffre Creek. Although the river is very fast in sections, there are many excellent pools that hold sizeable cutthroat trout. Trout in the Palliser River will average 25–35 cm in length. Large bull trout up to 5 kg can be found in the large pools.

Albert River (BC)
Cutthroat trout to 40 cm
Bull trout to 60 cm (2.5 kg)
Whitefish to 35 cm
The Albert River, a major tributary of the Palliser, is accessible from a Forest Service road that branches off the Palliser Forest Service Road. The Albert is fast flowing, much like the Palliser, and it likewise holds cutthroat and the occasional bull trout in its many pools. Cutthroat caught in the Albert River will average 20–30 cm in length. From roads on the upper reaches of the Albert, a short but ill-defined trail leads to Leman Lake and the upper Spray River.

Albert River

Fenwick Lake (BC)
50°29'18"N 115°3715"W
Rainbow trout to 35 cm
Cutthroat trout to 35 cm
Fenwick Lake is located 6 km west of the Kootenay Forest Service Road along a rough but passable track. Set in marshy surroundings, Fenwick Lake contains good numbers of rainbow trout averaging 20–25 cm in length. There may be a few cutthroat, remnants of past plantings, still in the lake. Fish can be taken from the shoreline of this narrow lake, although using a boat will increase angling prospects. Fenwick is relatively shallow and subject to winterkill on occasion.

Fenwick Lake

Fenwick Lake rainbow trout

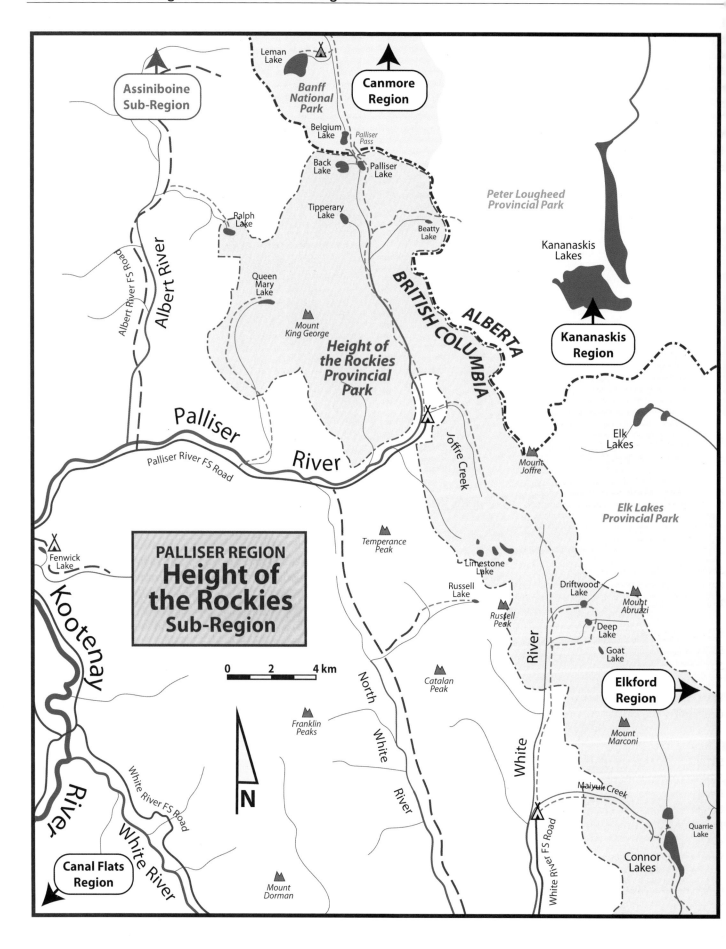

Assiniboine Sub-Region

Canmore Region

Leman Lake

Banff National Park

Belgium Lake

Palliser Pass

Back Lake

Palliser Lake

Ralph Lake

Tipperary Lake

Beatty Lake

Peter Lougheed Provincial Park

Kananaskis Lakes

Albert River FS Road

Albert River

Queen Mary Lake

Mount King George

Height of the Rockies Provincial Park

ALBERTA

BRITISH COLUMBIA

Kananaskis Region

Elk Lakes

Palliser

River

Palliser River FS Road

Joffre Creek

Mount Joffre

Elk Lakes Provincial Park

Temperance Peak

Limestone Lake

Driftwood Lake

Mount Abruzzi

PALLISER REGION
Height of the Rockies Sub-Region

Fenwick Lake

Russell Lake

Russell Peak

Deep Lake

Goat Lake

Elkford Region

0   2   4 km

Kootenay

Catalan Peak

White River

Mount Marconi

N

White River FS Road

Franklin Peaks

North White River

River

Maiyuk Creek

White River FS Road

Quarrie Lake

River

White River

Canal Flats Region

Mount Dorman

Connor Lakes

☐ Belgium Lake (NP)

50°42'48"N 115°23'19"W

Cutthroat trout to 35 cm

Belgium Lake is set in the alpine environs of Palliser Pass at the extreme southern end of Banff National Park. Access is via trail south from the Spray River or north from the Palliser River. This shallow lake has a small population of cutthroat trout that face the annual threat of winterkill. Fish from Belgium Lake will average 20–30 cm in length. The lake's pristine alpine surroundings provide ample room for fly casting.

Belgium Lake

■ Palliser Lake (BC)

50°42'09"N 115°22'58"W

Status: Devoid of fish

Palliser Lake is an appealing body of water on the BC side of Palliser Pass, but it has never been stocked and contains no fish.

■ Back Lake (BC)

50°42'12"N 115°23'32"W

Status: Devoid of fish

Back Lake is an algae-infested pond that sits in a rocky basin less than a kilometre above Palliser Lake.

■ Tipperary Lake (BC)

50°39'30"N 115°22'19"W

Status: Doubtful

Tipperary Lake is located in a basin west high above the Palliser River. The lake has never been stocked and it is unlikely that trout could enter the lake from the Palliser River.

■ Beatty Lake (BC)

50°39'16"N 115°18'04"W

Status: Devoid of fish

Beatty Lake is set in a forested basin on the western side of South Kananaskis Pass. The main trail access is from Three Isle Lake in Peter Lougheed Park in Alberta. There is no record of Beatty Lake ever being stocked, and it is not possible for fish to enter the lake from the Palliser drainage.

■ Queen Mary Lake (BC)

50°36'43"N 115°26'30"W

Cutthroat trout to 50 cm

Queen Mary Lake is set in the midst of the spectacular peaks of the Royal Group. The main access is via a rough horse trail that leads up Queen Mary Creek from the Palliser River. There are numerous creek crossings on this route. For those on foot, an alternate route into the lake is south from Ralph Lake. This requires a serious hike into Ralph Lake and then some good route-finding over to Queen Mary Lake. Reports indicate that the cutthroat trout fishing at Queen Mary Lake is good. Most trout taken from the lake will be in the 25–35 cm range, with larger fish present in good numbers.

■ Ralph Lake (BC)

50°39'01"N 115°28'37"W

Cutthroat trout to 45 cm

Ralph Lake is set high in an alpine basin above the Albert River. Access is on a very steep 5 km trail from the Albert River Forest Service Road. Much of the shoreline around Ralph Lake is treeless, and the lake affords itself well to fly casting. The cutthroat trout in the lake are numerous, with most averaging 25-35 cm in length. Be aware that the Ralph Lake basin is prime grizzly bear habitat.

Ralph Lake

Ralph Lake cutthroat trout

■ Limestone Lakes (BC)

50°28'35"N 115°14'22"W

Status: Doubtful

The Limestone Lakes are located on a barren plateau at the head of Joffre Creek. They are accessed via long and difficult trails either from Joffre Creek in the north, or from the White River in the south. The lakes have never been stocked, and it is doubtful if they hold any fish.

■ White River (BC) (Headwaters to HOTR park boundary)

Cutthroat trout to 40 cm

Bull trout to 60 cm (2.5 kg)

The extreme upper reaches of the White River, which are inside the Height of the Rockies Provincial Park, can only be accessed by trail. Fishing is excellent for cutthroat trout in any of the pools on the river. Most trout caught will be in the 20–30 cm range.

■ Maiyuk Creek (BC)

Cutthroat trout to 35 cm

Maiyuk Creek is a tributary of the upper White River. Logging roads off the White River branch up Maiyuk Creek as far as the Height of the Rockies boundary. From the end of the road, a 7 km trail leads up Maiyuk Creek to Connor Lakes. Maiyuk Creek holds cutthroat trout in small sizes.

△ Connor Lakes (BC)

(Lower Lake) 50°19'01"N 115°05'10"W

Cutthroat trout to 60 cm (2.5 kg)

The three Connor Lakes are the angling gems of the Sub-Region. Access is by trail only, either 7 km up Maiyuk Creek from the White River, or 10 km up Forsyth Creek from the Elk River. There are several primitive campsites on the lower lake, as well as a small BC Forest Service cabin that is available on a first-come, first-serve basis. For many years, Connor Lakes have been regarded as some of the finest cutthroat trout waters in the Rockies. The lower lake is the largest, extending over 3 km in length. The middle lake is small, little more than 200 m across. The upper lake is almost 1 km in length. Cutthroat trout in all three lakes grow to large sizes, with fish over 2 kg caught each season. Lures and flies are the standard fishing gear. Although a few intrepid hikers and some horse parties bring belly boats to Connor Lakes, most anglers are relegated to shore. Fishing from shore is not a major disadvantage as the fish can be taken in the crystal clear waters close to shore. For those uncomfortable fishing a very large lake from shore, the small middle lake is a good option.

Lower Connor Lake

Upper Connor Lake

Connor Lake cutthroat trout

■ Quarrie Lake (BC)

50°20'08"N 115°03'23"W

Cutthroat trout to 40 cm

Quarrie Lake is located in the Quarrie Creek valley, immediately west of the valley that holds Connor Lakes. Access is difficult, either along a rough trail up Quarrie Creek itself, or through a rocky gap from Connor Lakes. Quarrie Lake sees few angers each year. The lake reportedly holds cutthroat trout that average 20–30 cm in length.

■ Deep Lake (BC)

50°26'15"N 115°09'30"W

Cutthroat trout to 40 cm

Deep Lake is situated in the upper White River drainage and can be reached on trails from the White River. The lake can also be accessed by a rough trail from the Abruzzi Creek drainage through the Pass in the Clouds. As its name suggests, the lake has significant depth, as the bottom drops off quickly on all sides. Cutthroat trout in Deep Lake are numerous, averaging 25–35 cm in length.

Deep Lake

Deep Lake cutthroat trout

■ Driftwood Lake (BC)

50°26'48"N 115°09'45"W

Cutthroat trout to 55 cm (1.5 kg)

Driftwood Lake is located one small valley north of Deep Lake, and is accessed by the same trail from the White River. Avalanche slopes make their way down to Driftwood Lake, and each winter and spring debris is strewn out onto the ice-covered lake. In early summer the ice melts and the driftwood is deposited at the high water mark. As with neighbouring Deep Lake, the cutthroat trout in Driftwood Lake are numerous, but tend to be larger, with plenty of 40 cm + brutes.

Driftwood Lake

Fiore Olivieri with Driftwood Lake cutthroat trout

◻ Goat Lake (BC)
50°24'11"N 115°08'33"W
Status: Doubtful
Lovely Goat Lake is situated in an alpine meadow one valley to the south of Deep Lake. Unlikely that there are any fish in the lake.

Goat Lake

◻ Russell Lake (BC)
50°27'32"N 115°19'16"W
Status: Doubtful
Russell Lake is set in a basin at the head of the North White Riverand is accessed via a trail up the North White River. Russell Lake has never been stocked and it is doubtful if there are any fish in the lake.

Assiniboine Sub-Region

The Assiniboine area is one of the true gems in the Canadian Rockies and has been a favourite of backcountry travelers since the turn of the 20th century. Despite lengthy access routes, incredible scenery and good fishing ensure that the Assiniboine area will be crowded each summer. Lake Magog, set beneath the awe-inspiring summit of Mt. Assiniboine, represents the heart of the Sub-Region. The main campground is located on the bench above Magog's northwest shore, while Assiniboine Lodge (reservations only) and the government-run Naiset Cabins (also require reservations) are found on the lake's northeast corner. Sunburst, Cerulean, Elizabeth and Gog lakes are all within the Assiniboine core area, and Wedgwood and Og lakes are easy half-day trips from Lake Magog. Access to the Assiniboine core area is by trail, although helicopter access is becoming increasingly popular. The most common hiking route in is up Bryant Creek from the Mt. Shark trailhead and Spray Lakes Reservoir. Other routes include Sunshine Village and Ferro Pass. All routes into Assiniboine require a hike of at least 28 km.

◭ Magog Lake (BC)
50°54'07"N 115°37'52"W
Cutthroat trout to 60 cm (2.0 kg)
Magog Lake, at 2 km long, is the largest lake of the Assiniboine area. Its treeless shoreline offers ample room for fly casting, and its waters hold some fine cutthroat trout. Trout taken from the lake will average 30–40 cm in length. As with most lakes in the area, water clarity dictates that low light periods (early morning and late evening) will be the most productive as this is the time fish enter the shallower water to feed. High winds are often a problem for fly fishermen on Magog during the daytime. Magog has no outlet stream, but the areas around the several inlet creeks hold fish.

Magog Lake and Mount Assiniboine

Magog Lake cutthroat trout

119

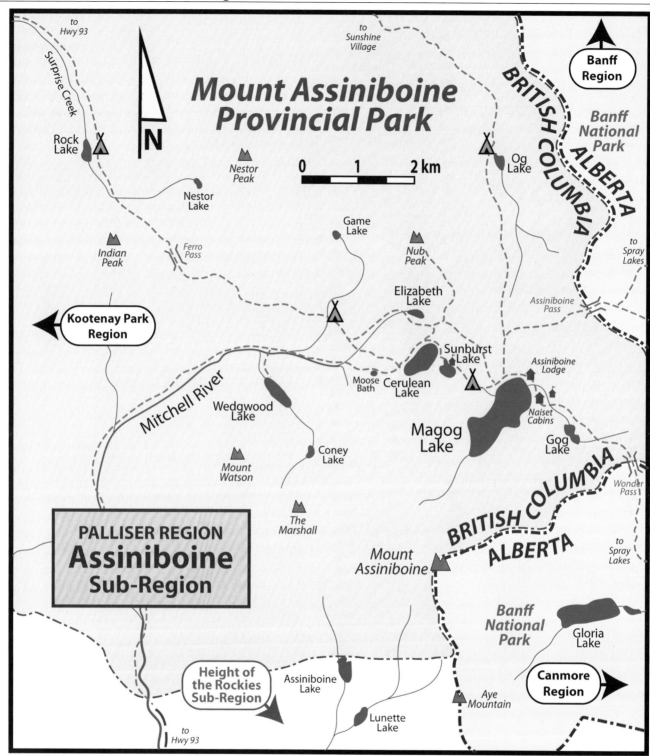

to
Hwy 93

Surprise Creek

to
Sunshine
Village

**Banff
Region**

BRITISH COLUMBIA
ALBERTA

**Mount Assiniboine
Provincial Park**

N

Rock
Lake

Nestor
Peak

*Banff
National
Park*

Og
Lake

0   1   2 km

Nestor
Lake

Ferro
Pass

Game
Lake

*Nub
Peak*

to
Spray
Lakes

Indian
Peak

Elizabeth
Lake

*Assiniboine
Pass*

**Kootenay Park
Region**

Sunburst
Lake

*Assiniboine
Lodge*

Mitchell River

Moose
Bath

Cerulean
Lake

*Naiset
Cabins*

Wedgwood
Lake

Magog
Lake

Gog
Lake

Coney
Lake

BRITISH COLUMBIA

*Wonder
Pass*

Mount
Watson

ALBERTA

to
Spray
Lakes

The
Marshall

**PALLISER REGION
Assiniboine
Sub-Region**

Mount
Assiniboine

*Banff
National
Park*

Gloria
Lake

**Height of
the Rockies
Sub-Region**

Assiniboine
Lake

**Canmore
Region**

to
Hwy 93

Lunette
Lake

Aye
Mountain

■ **Gog Lake (BC)**

50°53'54"N 115°36'38"W

Cutthroat trout to 40 cm

Gog Lake is located just over 1 km southeast of the Naiset Cabins in a quiet basin on the trail to Wonder Pass. Much of Gog's shoreline allows fly casting, and its sheltered setting usually protects it from the strong winds that prevail on other lakes in the area. The cutthroat trout in the lake average 25–35 cm, which is small by Assiniboine standards, but they are plentiful. Trout seem to be evenly distributed throughout the lake, but most anglers will choose to work from the accessible north and east shores despite the prospect of wet feet. The drop-off near the inlet creek tends to produce well.

Gog Lake

Og Lake (BC)

50°56'55"N 115°37'56"W

Status: Doubtful

Og Lake is located amid the near moonscape at the south end of the appropriately named Valley of the Rocks. The rockbound waters of Og Lake were stocked in the past with cutthroat trout, but it appears they were not able to reproduce in the lake. Recent survey indicates that few, if any, trout remain in Og Lake.

Og Lake

Sunburst Lake (BC)

50°54'34"N 115°38'53"W

Rainbow trout to 60 cm (2.0 kg)

Sunburst Lake is located just over 1 km west of Lake Magog by trail and was long regarded as one of the premier fly fishing lakes in the Rockies. The lake still has a good reputation and large rainbow trout (and a few rainbow-cutthroat hybrids) in the 2-3 kg range are taken regularly from Sunburst. Most fish taken from the lake will average 30–40 cm in length. Anglers' preference for casting locations range from the scree slopes on the south side of the lake to the wooded north and west shores. Lures can be as effective as fly fishing at most times. The lakeshore view of Sunburst, with Mount Assiniboine peeking over the southern skyline, is one of the most idyllic in all of the Rocky Mountains.

Sunburst Lake

Sunburst Lake rainbow trout

Big Wally

July 30, 1983. 7:00 p.m. Cerulean Lake. I was alone and fishing where the trail from Sunburst Lake meets Cerulean Lake. I was fly fishing with a sinking line with a big Doc Spratley on. I hooked bottom on one cast and it took a bit for the hook to come loose. On the next cast, I again let the line sink deep. I thought I hooked bottom a second time. Then the line started to move. This wasn't bottom, this was a fish and it was a big one. It took 25 minutes of hard fighting until I even could get a look at the fish. It was a monster, and if I lost it, nobody would ever believe my fish story. Another five minutes and I managed to land the fish. It was a legitimate 1 metre long cutthroat trout! I immediately went back to the Lake Magog campground (acting cool, like I catch fish like this all the time). Virtually everybody in the campground came to look at the fish. One fellow, who said he fished for salmon all the time, estimated it to be from 15 to 18 pounds (7-8 kg). I took the fish over to the warden's cabin on the other side of Magog Lake and the warden, upon seeing the fish, said, "You caught Big Wally! I've seen him in Cerulean for years!" I then went to the Assiniboine Lodge and asked when the next helicopter flight would be coming in and asked if the pilot could fly Wally out. Wally spent the next two days buried in a snowfield above Sunburst Lake and then was flown out by helicopter and taken to Banff, where I picked him up a couple of days later after I hiked the 30 km out from Assiniboine. Wally was taken to a taxidermist and mounted and currently resides on a wall at my mother's house in Invermere, BC.

Author (in younger days) with Big Wally

Cerulean Lake (BC)

50°54'40"N 115°39'19"W

Cutthroat trout to 60 cm (2.5 kg)

Cerulean Lake is located a short walk west of Sunburst Lake and in the past attracted many anglers because of its reputation for trophy-sized trout. Some extremely large cutthroat trout and rainbow-cutthroat hybrids still inhabit the lake's deep, blue-green waters. Fish exceeding 2 kg are caught each year. Special catch-and-release regulations are presently in effect in Cerulean. The shoreline offers a few opportunities for fly casting, the best being the shoreline near the junction to Sunburst Lake and the junction to Elizabeth Lake. Lures can be very effective in Cerulean at times. As Cerulean has no inlet creek and only a tiny outlet, fish in the lake tend to keep to the boundary separating the shallow water from the deep. At most locations around the shore this zone is within casting distance, and if wind and light conditions are right, the large fish can often be sighted from shore.

Cerulean Lake

Tyler Ambrosi with Cerulean Lake cutthroat trout

◼ Elizabeth Lake (BC)

50°55'12"N 115°39'27"W

Cutthroat trout to 35 cm

The remarkably clear waters of Elizabeth Lake, found in a small larch-filled basin less than 1 km north of Cerulean Lake, are home to a healthy population of cutthroat trout. Elizabeth is an outstanding lake for novice anglers, as small cutthroat in the 15–25 cm range can be caught from most spots along the lakeshore. Try off the top of the big rock on the opposite side of the lake.

Elizabeth Lake

◼ Moose Bath (BC)

50°54'33"N 115°40'12"W

Status: Devoid of fish

Moose Bath is a small, shallow pond below the western end of Cerulean Lake. Moose Bath has long been rumoured to contain trout. Despite the rumours, Moose Bath dries up in summer to the point of being incapable of holding trout.

☐ Wedgwood Lake (BC)

50°54'19"N 115°41'59"W

Cutthroat trout to 50 cm

Forest-enclosed Wedgwood Lake is located in a side valley south of the Mitchell River, some 4 km by trail below Cerulean Lake. Less heavily fished than other lakes in the Assiniboine area because of its location, Wedgwood holds uniquely patterned cutthroat trout averaging 25–35 cm in length. With the exception of a few isolated openings, casting a fly is difficult due to the proximity of the forest cover to the lakeshore. A very distinctive drop-off dividing the shallow water from the deep is visible from shore, this zone usually holding fish although both the outlet and inlet areas can also be very productive at times. The fish in Wedgwood tend to travel in schools and because of the clarity of the water, it is often more useful to walk along the shore keeping an eye on the water than to cast into an area where no fish can be seen.

Wedgwood Lake

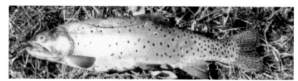

Wedgwood Lake cutthroat trout

◼ Coney Lake (BC)

50°53'39"N 115°41'20"W

Status: Doubtful

Coney Lake is situated in a rocky amphitheatre, half a kilometre upstream from the inlet of Wedgwood Lake. The lake is algae-infested and it is doubtful that it holds fish.

◼ Mitchell River (BC)

Cutthroat trout to 35 cm

Bull trout to 60 cm (3.0 kg)

Whitefish to 30 cm

The Mitchell River flows westward from the Assiniboine core area to its confluence with the Cross River and possesses numerous fine pools that hold fish. Access is along a horse trail that parallels the Mitchell River downstream of Wedgwood Lake, and eventually reaches logging and mining exploration roads at the provincial park boundary. Seldom fished, the Mitchell River is generally productive by mid-summer after the spring runoff is complete. Cutthroat trout in the 15–25 cm range are the normal catch.

Mitchell River

Mitchell River cutthroat trout

⚄ Game Lake (BC)
50°56'05"N 115°40'52"W
Status: Unknown

This small tarn at the head of Nestor Creek, a tributary of the Mitchell River, may contain small populations of cutthroat trout that have entered from Nestor Creek. No trails to the lake exist. Those interested in reaching the lake should simply follow Nestor Creek upstream from the Ferro Pass trail. Game Lake is set in an enclosed basin and remains frozen until mid-July.

⚄ Nestor Lake (BC)
50°56'21"N 115°43'46"W
Status: Unknown

Nestor Lake, the headwaters of Surprise Creek, receives few or no visitors each year. The lake is likely to hold a few cutthroat trout that have made their way in from Surprise Creek.

⚄ Rock Lake (BC)
50°56'58"N 115°45'29"W
Cutthroat trout to 30 cm

Rock Lake is situated halfway along the Ferro Pass trail access to Assiniboine and is popular as a stopover point. Rock Lake is a good spot for novice anglers, as it holds plenty of small cutthroat

in the 15–20 cm range. The shoreline is forgiving in terms of fly casting from most locations, although wet feet are likely on the east side of the lake. The rockslide on the western side allows casting without wet feet but be aware that rocks will claim the hooks of those fly fishers with sloppy back casts. Even though they are tiny, the eager trout in Rock Lake will give pleasure to beginners, as casting distance and technique are not important. Surprise Creek, which is the outlet for Rock Lake, holds trout for a kilometre or so downstream from the lake before becoming too steep and rapid on its descent to the Simpson River. The Verdant Creek Fire of 2017 burned much of the Simpson River valley and the Surprise Creek valley. Check with BC Parks regarding access. A new bridge over the Simpson River at the Surprise Creek cabin was completed in 2020.

Rock Lake

⚄ Assiniboine Lake (BC)
50°51'12"N 115°40'42"W
⚄ Lunette Lake (BC)
50°50'41"N 115°40'26"W
Status: Unknown

These two small, remote lakes are accessible by trail from logging roads on the Mitchell River. They have never been stocked, but may contain natural populations of cutthroat trout. An ill-defined trail leads east up Aurora Creek, a tributary of the Mitchell River, before turning north at Assiniboine Creek into the basin containing Assiniboine and Lunette Lakes. Be forewarned that this is very rugged and isolated country, and it is home to many a grizzly bear.

Backcountry buddy

INVERMERE REGION

This Region is set in the heart of the Rocky Mountain Trench, and Windermere Lake serves as its focal point. Invermere is the business centre of the valley, and offers numerous services including sporting goods stores. The main valley also harbours the small towns of Wilmer and Windermere, and is linked by Highway 95, north to Golden, Highway 93 east to Banff, and Highway 93/95 south to Cranbrook. Fifteen kilometre long Lake Windermere is more renowned for its warm waters, boardsailing and water skiing than for its fishery. The Columbia River, flowing downstream from Lake Windermere, holds plenty of whitefish and some large bull trout while nearby Toby and Horsethief creeks offer decent stream fishing. The Invermere Region is divided into two Sub-Regions: the Windermere Sub-Region, which encompasses the eastern side of Lake Windermere; and the Westside Sub-Region, which is west and north of Lake Windermere.

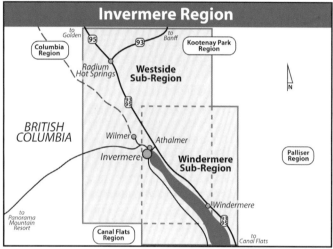

Windermere Sub-Region

This Sub-Region includes Windermere Lake and the area on the east side of the lake. The small community of Windermere is located just off Highway 93/95 and does offer basic tourist services. Other than Windermere Lake, fishing opportunities are limited to small creeks and a few small lakes in the Windermere Creek drainage.

The "Other" Fish

In addition to the game fish targeted by anglers in the waters of the Canadian Rockies, there also exists a myriad of other fish that are generally referred to as "coarse" or" non-game fish." Many are native and some are introduced. These non-game fish species include varieties of suckers, dace, minnows, shiners, chub and squawfish. Although they are not popular with anglers, they are an important part of the ecosystem and in many cases provide food for the game fish population.

◼ Lake Windermere (BC)
50°27'44"N 116°00'07"W
Rainbow trout to 55 cm (1.5 kg)
Cutthroat trout to 45 cm
Brook trout to 45 cm
Bull trout to 70 cm (4.0 kg)
Kokanee to 35 cm
Largemouth bass to 50 cm (1.5 kg)
Whitefish to 40 cm
Burbot to 60 cm (2.0 kg)

Lake Windermere has never gained a good reputation for fishing, despite the wide variety of game fish available. This is partly because the lake also has a large population of non-game fish, also known as "coarse" fish. Kokanee have been stocked in the lake, and their population has grown in recent years. This has increased the lake's angling popularity somewhat. Rainbow trout can usually be taken in the spring, in the weeks immediately after ice-out. During the summer, trolling in the areas around the lake's many inlet creeks such as Goldie Creek and Windermere Creek will often produce trout. Anglers can also catch the occasional largemouth bass, chub, or burbot. Winter sees the most angling activity on Lake Windermere.

Lake Windermere

◼ Columbia River (Lake Windermere to Radium) (BC)
Bull trout to 70 cm (4.0 kg)
Whitefish to 40 cm
Cutthroat trout to 45 cm
Rainbow trout to 45 cm
Brook trout to 45 cm

The Columbia River flows north from Lake Windermere and possesses numerous deep pools. It offers fair fishing for bull trout and whitefish. Cutthroat, rainbow and brook trout are also present. One of the best sections is just downstream of Windermere Lake where the river is still very clear. Also test the waters where major tributaries, such as Toby and Horsethief creeks, join the Columbia River. The Wilmer Sloughs, a series of large, shallow lakes approximately 5 km north of Lake Windermere, hold little in the way of fish and are best left to the ducks.

Columbia River

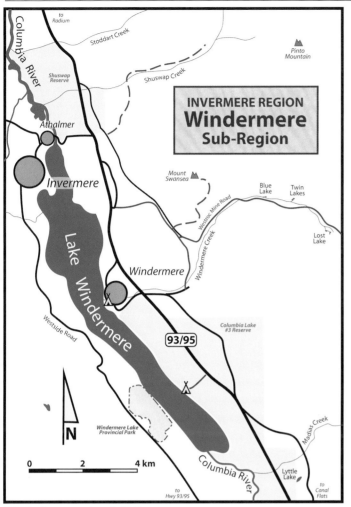

Windermere Sub-Region map showing INVERMERE REGION Windermere Sub-Region, Columbia River, to Radium, Stoddart Creek, Shuswap Creek, Pinto Mountain, Shuswap Reserve, Athalmer, Invermere, Mount Swansea, Blue Lake, Twin Lakes, Westroc Mine Road, Lost Lake, Windermere, Windermere Creek, Lake Windermere, Westside Road, 93/95, Columbia Lake #3 Reserve, Windermere Lake Provincial Park, Madias Creek, Columbia River, Lyttle Lake, to Hwy 93/95, to Canal Flats, N, 0 2 4 km

◼ Windermere Creek (BC)

Cutthroat trout to 35 cm

This small stream flows from headwaters above Twin and Lost Lakes to Windermere Lake. The upper portion of the creek can be accessed from the Westroc Mine Road. Windermere Creek is very popular with local youngsters and contains plenty of small cutthroat trout, most in the 15–25 cm range.

Windermere Creek

Note: To reach Blue Lake, Twin Lakes, Lost Lake, and upper Windermere Creek, the Westroc Mine Road, owned by Certainteed Gypsum Canada must be driven. During working hours, the road is very dangerous due to the many large trucks that haul gypsum. Check with the Certainteed Gypsum Canada mine office (250-342-9410) for hours of operation, and for procedure for driving the mine road.

◻ Blue Lake (BC)

50°29'41"N 115°54'12"W

Cutthroat trout to 30 cm

At one time, this small but incredibly deep lake was a most incredible shade of blue, due to its mineral content. In recent years, road construction and the unsightly realignment of Windermere Creek has ruined Blue Lake's natural beauty, and severe silting is rapidly filling up the lake. A small number of cutthroat trout still inhabit the lake.

Blue Lake

◮ Twin Lakes (BC)

50°29'38"N 115°53'17"W

Cutthroat trout to 35 cm

Twin Lakes, a half-kilometre hike, is a popular picnic spot and receives heavy fishing pressure during the summer. Cutthroat trout in the lakes average 15–20 cm in length, although bigger ones are often seen in the larger of the two lakes. The larger lake is an extremely deep body of water that is almost completely encircled by a high cliff. For those fly fishing, there are few locations to cast from, the most popular being the narrow channel between the two lakes.

Twin Lakes

Twin Lakes cutthroat trout

❓Lost Lake (BC)

50°28'55"N 115°52'04"W

Cutthroat trout

In a blatant display of industrial pollution, the gypsum mine above Lost Lake has virtually filled in the original Lost Lake with debris and totally destroyed what was at one time an excellent cutthroat fishery. Downstream from the former site of Lost Lake there are small beaver dams on Windermere Creek that may hold a few small cutthroat trout.

◼ Stoddart Creek (BC)

Cutthroat trout to 20 cm
Bull trout to 30 cm

Stoddart Creek is a small stream that flows west to join the Columbia River. Access is from abandoned logging roads that intersect with Highway 93/95. Stoddart Creek holds a few small cutthroat and bull trout.

◼ Shuswap Creek (BC)

Cutthroat trout to 20 cm
Bull trout to 30 cm

Old logging roads that extend high into the Shuswap Creek drainage offer access to prospective anglers. Small bull trout are present in the upper reaches with small cutthroat predominant downstream.

◼ Lyttle Lake (BC)

50°24'07"N 115°53'05"W

Status: Doubtful

Lyttle Lake is a shallow pond located east of Highway 93/95 just south of Fairmont. Private property restricts access to the lake. Lyttle Lake held some cutthroat trout in small sizes in the past.

Westside Sub-Region

◼ Toby Creek (BC)

Cutthroat trout to 40 cm
Bull trout to 70 cm (4.0 kg)
Whitefish to 35 cm
Kokanee to 30 cm

Toby Creek parallels the road to Panorama Mountain Resort. However, direct access to Toby Creek is difficult, as it flows through a deep canyon for much of its course. After runoff is complete, fishing is usually decent for cutthroat and bull trout. There is excellent angling for whitefish and kokanee in the fall.

Toby Creek whitefish

◭Lillian Lake (BC)

50°30'29"N 116°05'54"W

Rainbow trout to 55 cm (1.5 kg)
Brook trout to 40 cm

Lillian Lake is located just off the Panorama Mountain Resort road and is popular with locals, especially in the weeks after ice-out. Lillian's pretty blue-green waters hold plenty of rainbow trout in the 25–35 cm range, the zone dividing the deep water from the shallows usually holding the most fish. Brook trout in the same sizes can also be taken from Lillian. Trolling a fly through the deeper waters can be productive at times. During low light periods, many of the larger fish make their way into the shallow waters to feed. Chironomid fishing is popular in the spring. A boat is strongly advised, as fishing from shore at Lake Lillian is difficult because of access problems due to private land.

Lillian Lake

Lillian Lake rainbow trout

✖Barbour's Rock [aka Bluff Lake] (BC)

50°30'10"N 116°08'07"W

Status: Private property. Closed to angling

Brook trout

Barbour's Rock is located three kilometres beyond Lake Lillian and just to the north of the Panorama Mountain Resort road Barbour's Rock sits at the base of an impressive cliff face. Access is restricted due to private land around the entire lake. In the past, when there was public access, Barbour's Rock held small brook trout.

◼ Lake Eileen (BC)

50°31'20"N 116°05'57"W

Status: Devoid of fish

Shallow Eileen Lake is little more than an overgrown marsh located 1 km north of Lake Lillian and contains no fish.

◼ Munn Lake (aka Wilmer Lake) (BC)

50°32'49"N 116°04'53"W

Rainbow trout to 50 cm
Brook trout to 50 cm

The elongated form of Munn Lake is located less than a kilometre west of the townsite of Wilmer. The lake is best in the spring soon after ice-melt. Munn's dark waters hold stocked rainbow trout averaging 20–30 cm in length. There may also be a few brook trout present, remnants of past plantings. Although fishing is possible from many locations along the shore, a boat is recommended.

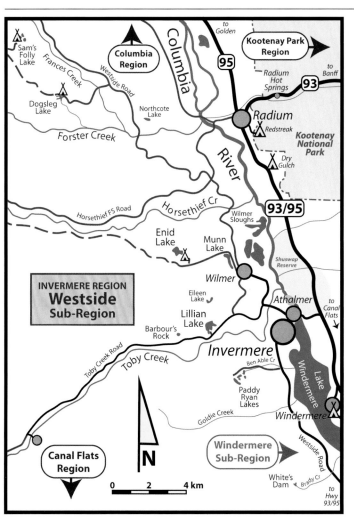

Enid Lake

Tyler Ambrosi with
Enid Lake
rainbow trout

Munn Lake

Enid Lake (BC)

50°32'54"N 116°07'27"W
Rainbow trout to 65 cm (3.0 kg)
Brook trout to 55 cm (2.0 kg)
Enid Lake is a popular camping and picnic spot situated 2 km beyond Munn Lake. Both rainbow and brook trout can be taken from Enid, with rainbows in the majority. Most fish caught will average 25–35 cm in length, although some very large rainbow trout have been taken from Enid in the past. As with nearby Lillian Lake, the margin between the deep and shallow waters is often productive, although many anglers prefer to troll the deep waters in search of lunkers.

Horsethief Creek (BC)

Cutthroat trout to 40 cm
Bull trout to 70 cm (4.0 kg)
Whitefish to 35 cm
Kokanee to 30 cm
Horsethief Creek is similar to all of the major creeks in the area that join the Columbia River from the west. It offers fair fishing in the late summer and early fall, particularly during whitefish runs. The lower portion of Horsethief Creek is reached by taking the Westside Road north from Wilmer The upper section is accessed by numerous logging roads that run through the upper Horsethief Drainage. Due to its glacial origins, Horsethief Creek is notorious for being silted later into the summer than other local creeks.

Forster Creek (aka Forester Creek, #2 Creek) (BC)

Cutthroat trout to 40 cm
Bull trout to 70 cm (4.0 kg)
Whitefish to 30 cm
Forster Creek is another of the many large creeks that enter the Columbia River from the west. It is accessed from the Westside Road and subsidiary logging roads. Forster Creek holds cutthroat trout that average 20–30 cm in length.

Northcote Lake (BC)

50°37'03"N 116°09'58"W
Status: Doubtful
This shallow lake is located east of the Westside Road. Although Northcote Lake has held brook and rainbow trout in the past, it is unlikely that there are any fish in the lake today.

◼ Dogsleg Lake (aka Dogleg Lake) (BC)

50°38'02"N 116°13'47"W
Rainbow trout to 60 cm (2.5 kg)

Dogsleg Lake is a promising body of water situated several kilometres west of the Wetside Road. The lake is very susceptible to winterkill, but the stocked trout tend to grow very quickly due to the tremendous amount of feed. Rainbow trout in Dogsleg will average 35–45 cm in length, with lots of fat specimens present. Stick to the edge of the shallows if you are fishing from in a boat. You will undoubtedly see some large shadows cruising through the shallows.

Dogsleg Lake

Dogsleg Lake
rainbow trout

◮ Sam's Folly Lake (BC)

50°39'59"N 116°15'45"W
Rainbow trout to 60 cm (2.5 kg)

Sam's Folly Lake is located approximately 5 km north of Dogsleg Lake and is reached by following a very rough and often confusing dirt road. Sam's Folly is in fact two interconnected lakes that are quite different in nature. The first lake is very shallow with extensive weed beds. The second lake is much deeper with less weed growth. Both lakes hold rainbows in the 25-40 cm range. The first lake is more suited to fly fishing, with lures more productive in the second lake. A boat or float tube is essential on the first lake; fishing from shore will work at the second lake.

Sam's Folly
first lake

Tyler Ambrosi
at Sam's Folly

Sam's Folly
rainbow trout

☐ Dorothy Lake (BC)

50°29'56"N 116°01'30"W
Rainbow trout to 35 cm
Brook trout to 35 cm

Dorothy Lake is located in Invermere next to Kinsmen Beach and Windermere Lake. The lake is open for angling for those aged 12 and under. Dorothy is stocked regularly with catchable-sized rainbow trout, and was stocked previously with brook trout. Trout caught in the lake will average 20–30 cm in length. Weeds extend out all around the lake, so the best fishing spot is the dock that juts out into the deeper water. On warm summer days, western painted turtles can be seen sunning themselves on logs around the lake.

Dorothy Lake

⊗ Paddy Ryan Lakes (BC)

(Fifth lake) 50°28'48"N 116°04'33"W
Status: Closed to angling

Being the source of Invermere's water supply, the Paddy Ryan Lakes are closed to angling and are fenced off.

◼ Ben Able Creek (BC)

Brook trout to 20 cm
Rainbow trout to 20 cm

Tiny Ben Abel Creek, the outlet creek for Paddy Ryan Lakes, contains small brook and rainbow trout and has long been a favourite of local youngsters.

◼ White's Dam (BC- Private Lake)

50°25'20"N 116°01'23"W
Cutthroat trout to 35 cm (catch & release only)

Reached by following a veritable maze of logging roads on the west side of Lake Windermere, White's Dam retains little of its past glory. Cutthroat trout exceeding 80 cm in length were taken from this overgrown beaver pond in years past, but overfishing led to a severe decline in both number and size of trout taken. At present it holds a small population of cutthroat averaging 20–30 cm in length. The lake itself and much of the access road is private property, owned by SRL-K2 Ranch. A sign near the lake indicates, "SRL. Private Property. No hunting. No shooting. No motorized vehicles. You are welcome to walk, bicycle or horseback ride on the property."

White's Dam

Johann Danielson
with White's Dam
cutthroat trout

COLUMBIA REGION

The Region to the west of the Columbia River and small towns of Brisco, Spillimacheen and Parson has many excellent trout lakes. The main route through the area is the Westside Road, a gravel and dirt road that can be accessed from Highway 95 at Brisco, Spillimacheen, Parson, Radium and Wilmer. Since virtually all of the lakes can be reached by vehicle, they are favourites of local anglers, and most spots are busy spring through fall. The most popular of the lakes include Cartwright, Jade, Cleland, Mitten, Wilbur and Nine Bay. The Region divides into two Sub-Regions: the southern half, which is west of Brisco; and the northern half, which is west of Parson.

Brisco Sub-Region

The lakes to the west of Brisco are known collectively as the Fish Lakes. Most can be accessed from short roads that branch off the Westside Road. The lakes in this Sub-Region are found in several clusters. Cleland, Jade, Topaz and Cub lakes form one cluster. Farther south, Dunbar, Twin and Botts lakes, form another group. Farther south still, Hall, Halgrave and Steamboat lakes are bunched together on the flank of Steamboat Mountain. Cartwright Lake is known for its great rainbow trout fishery, and receives the heaviest angling pressure of all lakes in the area.

☐ Hall Lakes (BC)
50°44'52"N 116°18'56"W
Brook trout to 35 cm
Cutthroat trout to 35 cm
These two shallow lakes are located 1 km east of the Westside Road. The Hall Lakes contain a few brook trout in small sizes, averaging 15–25 cm in length. Some cutthroat trout may still be in the lake as well. Most of the fish are concentrated in the larger lake and are very spooky due to their shallow habitat. Although fishing from shore is possible from a number of locations, a boat is recommended.

Hall Lake (main lake)

▲ Halgrave Lakes (BC)
(Upper) 50°44'00"N 116°16'50"W
Cutthroat trout to 45 cm
A good logging road that branches east off the Westside Road just before the crossing of Frances Creek leads to a campsite at Upper Halgrave Lake. Shallows around the entire lake make the use of a boat essential, although there is a point that juts out into the lake that offers hope for shorebound anglers. The shoreline mud can even make launching of a boat very difficult. Wet flies are particularly effective in taking the lake's cutthroat, which average 25–35 cm in length. Lower Halgrave Lake can be reached via a short side road approximately 1 km past Upper Halgrave on the road to Steamboat Lake. As with the Upper Lake, shallows extend far out from shore around Lower Halgrave. Fishing techniques that work on Upper Halgrave will work on Lower Halgrave and fish taken will be of similar size.

Upper Halgrave Lake

Upper Halgrave Lake cutthroat trout

■ Steamboat Lake (BC)
50°44'51"N 116°17'30"W
Rainbow trout to 55 cm (1.5 kg)
Steamboat Lake is nestled high on the side of Steamboat Mountain. The lake is reached by taking the Halgrave Lakes cut-off from the Westside Road. Although most of the rainbow trout in Steamboat Lake are in the 25–35 cm range, there are lots of big fish and they can be seen tantalizingly cruising the shallows. Both flies and lures are effective, but a boat is recommended for angling success.

Steamboat Lake rainbow trout

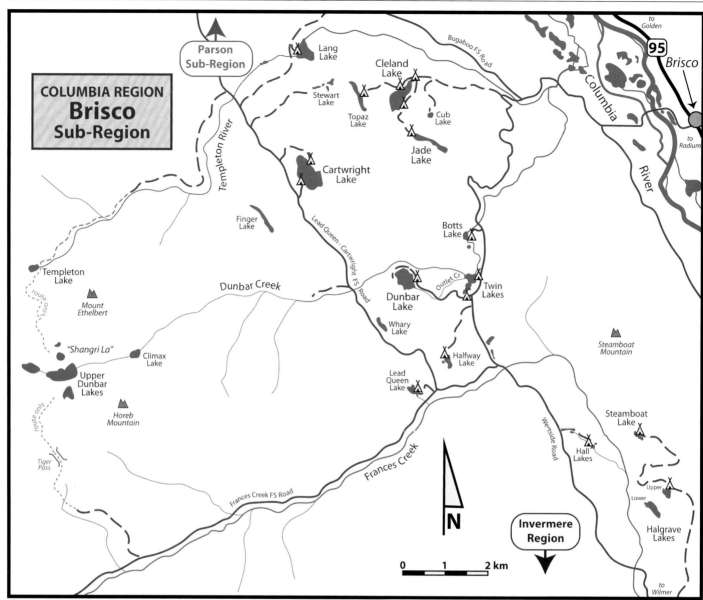

If fishing from shore, the best opportunities are found near the dam at the lake's outlet. From a boat, schools of fish can usually be seen in the main part of the lake. However, due to the shallow nature of the lake, the trout are very wary, and many anglers will no doubt be frustrated.

Steamboat Lake

Lead Queen Lake

Lead Queen Lake brook trout

◼ Lead Queen Lake (BC)

50°45'38"N 116°22'51"W

Brook trout to 40 cm

Lead Queen Lake is located north of Frances Creek, approximately 2 km off the Westside Road. Lead Queen is a very shallow lake bordered by marsh on its western side and is little more than a very large beaver pond. Lead Queen at one time contained a healthy population of cutthroat trout. Illegally stocked brook trout outcompeted the cutthroat and now are the only species in the lake. Fish caught will range from 25 to 35 cm in length.

■ Whary Lake (BC)

50°46'31"N 116°23'49"W

Status: Doubtful

Whary Lake is situated in a valley alongside the Frances-Cartwright FS Road, approximately 2 km past the turnoff to Lead Queen Lake. Looking down from the road, Whary looks promising. However, it has never been stocked and it is unlikely to have fish.

■ Frances Creek (BC)

Cutthroat trout to 30 cm

Frances Creek parallels the Westside Road for several kilometres. It is well-known among locals as an excellent trout stream. Cutthroat trout averaging 20–25 cm in length are abundant, especially in the numerous pools and log jams along the creek. A few brook trout may be present as well.

■ Halfway Lake (BC)

50°46'00"N 116°22'10"W

Rainbow trout to 40 cm

A rough road through a thick lodgepole pine forest leads west from the Westside Road into Halfway Lake. A boat is preferable for fishing at Halfway Lake, as there is substantial reed growth around most of the lake. Rainbow trout in the 25–35 cm size are plentiful. Trolling a fly behind a boat or canoe is usually very effective, especially for novices who haven't mastered all the intricacies of fly casting. Lures and spinners are also quite effective at Halfway Lake.

Halfway Lake

Halfway Lake rainbow trout

Introduction of Illegal Brook Trout

Twin, Dunbar, Botts, Hall and Lead Queen lakes at one time were excellent cutthroat trout fisheries. Illegal plantings of brook trout in these waters in the past decimated the existing native cutthroat trout populations. Brook trout, native to eastern Canada and waters with large predators, tend to reproduce in greater numbers than the native cutthroat. Their advantage in numbers then allows the brookies to outcompete the cutthroat, in turn driving down the number of cutthroat trout in the lakes. To try to reduce the number of brook trout in many of these lakes,

BC fishing regulations allow anglers to keep up to 20 brook trout per day in some lakes, while requiring to release of any cutthroat trout. Know your trout! Check regulations regarding specific lakes.

◬ Twin Lakes (BC)

(2nd lake) 50°47'07"N 116°21'40"W

Brook trout to 40 cm

Cutthroat trout to 40 cm

The Twin Lakes are oddly named, as they in fact actually consist of three lakes all joined by narrow channels. All three lakes hold brook and cutthroat trout in the 20–30 cm range, with brookies in the vast majority. The small, shallow first lake usually has a few trout that congregate around one of several natural springs. The second lake is the deepest and holds the most fish. The third lake is the largest, but is very shallow. Its best potential is in its northeast corner where Dunbar Creek flows through. The completion of a dam on the third lake stabilized water levels but caused a major drowning of trees around all three lakes. As the trees died and fell into the lakes, the fish habitat was improved, as the fish tend to seek the security of the deadfall. Although fishing from shore is possible, a boat is recommended for all of the lakes. Both dry and wet flies will work very well at Twin Lakes.

Twin Lakes (second lake)

Johann Danielson with Twin Lakes brook trout

■ Dunbar Lake (aka Big Fish Lake) (BC)

50°47'13"N 116°23'11"W

Rainbow trout to 55 cm (1.5 kg)

Brook trout to 40 cm

Cutthroat trout to 40 cm

Dunbar Lake was renowned in past years for its healthy population of large cutthroat, many topping the 2 kg mark. Years ago overharvest decimated Dunbar's cutthroat and the lake has never been able to fully recover. Illegal planting of brook trout accelerated the demise of the native cutthroat. More recently, rainbow trout have been stocked in Dunbar and they are beginning to take hold. Dunbar is a strikingly beautiful lake, and holds rainbow and brook trout that average 20–30 cm in length. The odd cutthroat may still exist in the lake. For those anglers without a boat, the best opportunities are found in the series of dams below the lake's outlet. The fish may be smaller, but they will plentiful. If you're fishing from a boat, trolling along the margin separating the shallow water from the deep holds the best potential.

Dunbar Lake

◼ Botts Lake (BC)
50°47'50"N 116°21'44"W
Brook trout to 40 cm
Cutthroat trout to 40 cm

Tiny, marsh rimmed Botts Lake is little more than a widening of Dunbar Creek. Botts Lake holds brook trout and the odd cutthroat trout in the 20–30 cm range and usually produces well throughout the summer and fall. Those fly fishing will need a boat to reach fish-holding. A small, deep pond located only a few hundred metres from the southwest corner of Botts Lake also holds trout in fair numbers. You will likely have to drag your boat through marshy ground to reach the back pond.

Botts Lake

◼ Dunbar Creek, Outlet Creek (aka South Salmon River) (BC)
Brook trout to 30 cm
Rainbow trout to 30 cm
Cutthroat trout to 30 cm

Outlet Creek connects Dunbar to Twin Lakes, where it joins Dunbar Creek. Dunbar Creek connects Twin and Botts Lakes. Dunbar Creek is never more than a short hike from the Westside Road. Both creeks have plenty of log jams and deep pools that hold small brook trout in the 15-25 cm range. A few remnant cutthroat may still be in the creeks. Rainbow will also be found closer to Dunbar Lake.

◼ Cleland Lake (BC)
50°49'56"N 116°23'25"W
Rainbow trout to 65 cm (2.5 kg)

Cleland Lake is the largest of the Cleland-Jade-Topaz-Cub cluster, and receives significant attention from anglers. All four of the lakes are reached by taking the rough road that branches northwest from the Westside Road just over 1 km above the Templeton River bridge. Cleland's translucent blue-green waters hold rainbow trout averaging 30–40 cm in length. Much larger fish are taken regularly. A boat is a must for fishing at Cleland Lake. During the day, most fish are taken from the deeper waters, but as daylight fades, many of the larger fish make their way into the shallow waters to feed, making evenings a prime time for dry fly enthusiasts.

Cleland Lake

Cleland Lake rainbow trout

◮ Jade Lake (BC)
50°49'17"N 116°22'23"W
Rainbow trout to 65 cm (2.5 kg)

Jade Lake is located approximately 2 km by rough road beyond the campsite on the eastern side of Cleland Lake. No longer restricted to fly fishing only, Jade Lake attracts many anglers each year. Jade's stunning green waters hold plenty of hard-fighting rainbows averaging 35–50 cm in length. From a boat, fish can generally be seen feeding in the shallows at both ends of the lake all during the day, with increased activity in the shallows during low light periods. Fly fishers patiently working the shallows with a chironomid pattern will usually produce positive results. In the deep middle section of the lake, trolling is the most effective technique.

Jade Lake

*Stefan Danielson
with Jade Lake
rainbow trout*

■ Topaz Lake (BC)

50°50'50"N 116°24'24"W

Rainbow trout to 40 cm

Topaz Lake is located at the end of a rough and often muddy 2 km access road from the campsite on the north side of Cleland Lake. Topaz Lake is very shallow and has been prone in the past to winterkill. Topaz is stocked regularly, and rainbow trout are still present in the lake, with most averaging 20–30 cm in length. Topaz is a long and narrow lake that is best fished from a boat, although fish can occasionally be taken from shore when they are feeding in the shallows.

■ Cub Lake (BC)

50°50'49"N 116°22'37"W

Rainbow trout to 40 cm

Cub Lake is a small, round, sinkhole lake ringed by marsh and does not overwhelm anyone with its beauty. Fishing from shore is a near impossibility due to extensive lily pads. Trolling or casting from a boat is necessary. Cub does hold small rainbows in good numbers, most averaging 20–30 cm in length.

Cub Lake

*Cub Lake
rainbow trout*

■ Cartwright Lake (BC)

50°48'43"N 116°25'29"W

Rainbow trout to 65 cm (2.5 kg)

Cartwright Lake is the most popular lake in the Brisco Sub-Region. The campground at Cartwright is busy with anglers from June through the end of October. Rainbow trout averaging 30–40 cm are taken in good numbers from the lake's deeper waters all during the season. Trolling is the most common fishing technique, and many anglers come prepared with fish finders and downriggers. Extended shallows around the entire lake make fishing from shore very inefficient, although patient fly fishers in a boat or float tube can take cruising trout.

Cartwright Lake

□ Stewart Lake (BC)

50°49'52"N 116°26'10"W

Rainbow trout to 30 cm

Stewart Lake is little more than an overgrown beaver pond located between Cartwright and Lang Lakes. Stewart Lake's waters are often murky, but hold small rainbow averaging 20–25 cm in length.

■ Lang Lake (aka Lang's Lake) (BC)

50°50'40"N 116°25'44"W

Cutthroat trout to 40 cm

Rainbow trout to 40 cm

Lang Lake is located north of Cartwright Lake and is accessed from the Bugaboo Forest Service Road. Lang Lake is very shallow and a boat is required to reach the fish-holding waters. Cutthroat and rainbow trout have both been stocked in Lang Lake in the past, and most caught will be in the 20–30 cm range. Lures and flies both work well at Lang Lake.

Lang Lake

◼ Templeton River (aka North Salmon River) (BC)

Cutthroat trout to 30 cm
Rainbow trout to 30 cm

The best fishing on the Templeton River is found in the area above Lang Lake where a seemingly infinite series of small beaver ponds exist. Cutthroat and rainbow in the 15–25 cm range can be taken at most spots along the river. The area on the Templeton River around the lower bridges on the Westside Road has some fine pools.

Templeton River

◼ Upper Dunbar Lakes (aka Horeb Lakes) (BC)

50°44'57"N 116°32'38"W
Cutthroat trout to 40 cm

The Upper Dunbar Lakes consist of series of pristine alpine tarns at the head of Dunbar Creek. The lakes are set in a magnificent basin appropriately named Shangri-La. Cutthroat trout have been stocked in some of the lakes in the past and are reported to be present in fair numbers. Not all of the lakes in the basin were stocked, but trout seem to have made their way into most of them. Anglers are advised to watch the waters for trout activity. The main access routes to the Upper Dunbar Lakes are difficult: one route is over Tiger Pass and Tiger Glacier from the Frances Creek drainage; the second is an alpine route with few trails from Templeton Lake, one drainage to the north. Both are for route-finders armed with map and compass. Helicopter access is becoming more popular for this area.

◼ Climax Lake (BC)

50°45'39"N 116°31'15"W
Cutthroat trout to 40 cm

Climax Lake is located on Dunbar Creek, approximately 2 km downstream from the Horeb Lakes, and has been stocked with cutthroat trout that have seldom been tested by anglers. Access to Climax Lake is the same as for Horeb, either down over Tiger Pass or up Dunbar Creek.

◼ Templeton Lake (BC)

50°47'20"N 116°34'30"W
Cutthroat trout to 40 cm

Templeton Lake is a seldom-visited lake that is the source of its namesake river. A rough 6 km trail to the lake begins from logging roads that head west from the Cartwright Lake road. Templeton Lake has been stocked in the past with cutthroat trout. Trout taken from the lake average 20–30 cm in length.

Templeton Lake

◼ Columbia River (BC) (Radium to Spillimacheen)

Bull trout to 80 cm (7.0 kg)
Rainbow trout to 40 cm
Cutthroat trout to 40cm
Whitefish to 35 cm
Kokanee to 35 cm

The slow-moving Columbia River runs muddy for much of the year. This section of the Columbia River has never had a good reputation for fishing, although it contains bull trout and whitefish, as well as the occasional rainbow or cutthroat trout.

Columbia River

Parson Sub-Region

The area to the west of the small community of Parson holds a number of lakes with excellent records as producers of large rainbow trout. Primary access is Highway 95, which leads from Golden in the north and Radium in the south. Logging roads that are rough in spots lead from Highway 95 and Parson to a majority of the lakes. Mitten, Nine Bay and Rocky Point are the most popular of the region's waters and hold some big trout. Other lakes include Loon in the north; Wilbur, Summit and Three Island in the central portion; and Bittern, Little Mitten and McClain to the south. Some excellent stream fishing opportunities exist in the Parson region, the most notable being the Spillimacheen River and Bobbie Burns, Bugaboo and Driftwood creeks.

◩ Wilbur Lake (BC)
51°00′33″N 116°40′46″W
Rainbow trout to 65 cm (2.5 kg)
Wilbur Lake is the closest of the west side lakes to Parson. It is located 10 km from Parson by logging road. Wilbur is stocked regularly and holds hard-fighting rainbow trout that average 30–40 cm in length. Wilbur fishes best from a boat, whether trolling or casting a fly. The small bay off the northeast end of the lake is fairly shallow, and fish can be seen cruising. Using a wet fly line and casting ahead of cruising trout with a nymph can be dynamite. Check regulations regarding size limits.

Wilbur Lake

Wilbur Lake rainbow trout

☐ Hobo Lake (BC)
51°01′52″N 116°40′32″W
Rainbow trout to 35 cm
Hobo Lake is a small lake located northeast of Wilbur Lake and is accessed by rough roads. Hobo Lake holds a small population of rainbow trout in the 20–30 cm range.

◼ Rocky Point Lake (BC)
51°00′55″N 116°46′12″W
Rainbow trout to 55 cm (1.5 kg)
The Rocky Point–Three Island-Summit complex is just under 30 km from Parson by logging road (Turn left at Km 21 on the Spillimacheen River Forest Service Road). Be forewarned that the last few kilometres of road into Rocky Point Lake are horrendous. The lake is named for a number of prominent rocky points jutting out along the lakeshore. Rocky Point holds good numbers of rainbow trout that average 25–35 cm in length, although much larger specimens are caught very frequently. A boat is necessary for fishing at Rocky Point.

Rocky Point Lake

Tyler Ambrosi with Rocky Point Lake rainbow trout

◼ Summit Lake (aka Bridal Lake) (BC)
51°01′25″N 116°48′25″W
Brook trout to 55 cm (1.5 kg)
Cutthroat trout to 35 cm
Summit Lake is situated just a few kilometres to the west of Rocky Point Lake at a height of land between Bobbie Burns Creek and the Spillimacheen River drainages. The shallow waters of Summit Lake hold brook trout, stocked regularly, as well as possible remnants of a cutthroat trout population. Although the brook trout only average 20–30 cm in length, they are plentiful. From a boat, trout can be taken from most locations around the lake.

Summit Lake

■ Three Island Lake (BC)

51°00'43"N 116°47'04"W

Rainbow trout to 60 cm (2.0 kg)

Three Island Lake is located in the forested basin immediately southwest of Rocky Point Lake. Three Island Lake holds good-sized rainbow trout in its numerous bays and around its three prominent islands. Trout average 25–35 cm in length, with larger ones taken regularly. A boat is recommended, although shorebound anglers may have some success from one of the points that jut into the lake, or in one of the many small inlets.

■ Loon Lake (BC)

51°03'21"N 116°48'14"W

Rainbow trout to 55 cm (1.5 kg)

Pretty Loon Lake is set alongside logging roads approximately 3 km beyond the Rocky Point Lake cut-off on the Spillimacheen River FS Road. The lake holds stocked rainbow trout in good numbers. The rainbow trout in Loon average 25–35 cm in length, with larger ones present. Trolling is the normal technique on Loon, although many anglers to head to the middle of the lake and simply fish off of the bottom of the lake with bait.

Three Island Lake

Loon Lake

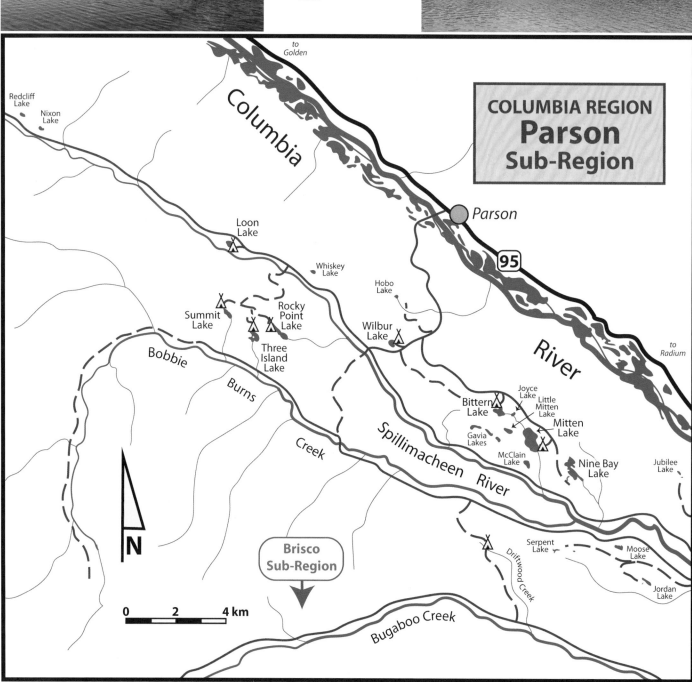

Whiskey Lake (BC)

51°02'58"N 116°46'20"W

Status: Doubtful

Whiskey Lake is located north of the Spillimacheen FS Road in an open clear-cut about 2 km east of Loon Lake. The lake once held some rainbow trout, but it is unlikely that any remain.

Nixon Lake (BC)

51°06'34"N 116°57'07"W

Rainbow trout to 40 cm

Nixon Lake is a small lake located approximately 35 km from Parson on the north side of the Spillimacheen River. No road goes to Nixon, so a short walk through the forest is required to reach the lake. Nixon holds good numbers of small rainbows, most in the 20–30 cm range.

Kootenay Trout Hatchery photo

Nixon Lake

Redcliff Lake (BC)

51°06'58"N 116°57'59"W

Rainbow trout to 40 cm

Intrepid anglers will find the quiet waters of Redcliff Lake 2 km beyond Nixon Lake off of the Spillimacheen River road. A short hike is needed to get to the lake. Redcliff Lake holds rainbow trout averaging 20–30 cm in length, which can generally be taken from shallows around the lake.

Spillimacheen River (BC)

Rainbow trout to 40 cm

Cutthroat trout to 40 cm

Bull trout to 60 cm (3.0 kg)

Whitefish to 35 cm

Kokanee to 35 cm

The Spillimacheen River enters the Columbia River at Spillimacheen. It possesses many kilometres of fine fishing and is easily accessed for its entire length from logging roads from Parson. Rainbow and cutthroat trout are the dominant species, and average 20–30 cm in length. Large bull trout are taken on occasion. In the fall, the Spillimacheen River is noted for its excellent angling for whitefish and kokanee.

Spillimacheen River

Mitten Lake (BC)

50°57'52"N 116°34'21"W

Rainbow trout to 70 cm (3.5 kg)

Mitten Lake is located approximately 15 km by logging road from Parson. Mitten Lake is one of the most popular angling spots in the region and has a large campground. Rainbow trout, which average 25–35 cm in length, are caught in good numbers throughout the season. Large trout, upwards of 3 kg, are taken regularly. Trolling is the standard fishing method on Mitten, although dry fly fishing enthusiasts using chironomid patterns usually do well in the spring in the lake's extended shallows.

Mitten Lake

Little Mitten Lake (BC)

50°58'06"N 116°35'23"W

Rainbow trout to 55 cm (1.5 kg)

Little Mitten Lake is located less than a kilometre northwest of Mitten Lake. Rough logging roads lead to within a few hundred metres of Little Mitten. The lake is stocked regularly with rainbow trout that see few anglers each season. Trout in the lake average 25–35 cm in length, with larger trout caught regularly.

Gavia Lakes (BC)

50°58'09"N 116°36'45"W

Rainbow trout to 40 cm

The string of three Gavia Lakes are found a little over a kilometre northwest of Mitten Lake and logging roads pass close to the lakes. Gavia #1 (most northerly) and Gavia #3 are stocked regularly with rainbow trout. Middle Gavia #2 is too shallow for trout to overwinter. Trout in Gavia #1 and #3 will average 25–35 cm in length.

Joyce Lake (BC)

50°58'32"N 116°35'11"W

Rainbow trout to 40 cm

Joyce Lake is actually a pair of deep potholes alongside the Mitten Lake road. Both of the lakes hold stocked rainbow trout that average 25–35 cm in length.

McClain Lake (BC)

50°57'09"N 116°34'30"W

Rainbow trout to 55 cm (1.5 kg)

McClain Lake is set in forested surroundings approximately half a kilometre southwest of Mitten Lake. If you can work your way on a maze of logging roads, you can get close to McClain's shore. Stocked rainbow trout are found in good numbers in lightly fished McClain Lake. Most fish caught will be 25–35 cm in length.

◼ Bittern Lake (BC)

50°58'38"N 116°35'55"W

Rainbow trout to 55 cm (1.5 kg)

Bittern Lake lies two kilometres by road northwest of Mitten Lake. Anglers hold Bittern in high regard and its campground is full through much of the season. Bittern holds rainbow trout that average 30–40 cm in length. Shallows around the lake require the use of a boat to reach fish-holding waters. The deeper waters on the western side of the lake hold the most potential, especially along the boundary of the deep and shallow waters.

Bittern Lake

◭ Nine Bay Lake (BC)

50°56'54"N 116°32'24"W

Rainbow trout to 70 cm (3.5 kg)

The Nine Bay Lake parking area (basically the side of the road) is situated two kilometres beyond the campground at Mitten Lake. To reach Nine Bay Lake, a short hike on a 250 m trail is required. The lake contains rainbow trout in good numbers and sizes. Rainbows in Nine Bay Lake average 30–40 cm in length, with beauties of over 2 kg taken frequently. Fly fishers love this lake and it usually has a little flotilla of watercraft covering each bay. Chironomid fishing is extremely popular in the springtime. Large rainbow trout love to feed on the extended shallows found around the entire lake.

Nine Bay Lake

Nine Bay Lake rainbow trout

◼ Hobo Creek (BC)

Rainbow trout to 25 cm

Hobo Creek connects Bittern Lake to Mitten Lake before emptying into the Spillimacheen River. Hobo Creek holds small rainbow trout.

◼ Moose Lake (BC)

50°54'48"N 116°29'46"W

Rainbow trout

Moose Lake is a seldom-fished lake located south of the Spillimacheen River, approximately 12 km west of the hamlet of Spillimacheen. Moose Lake reportedly contains small rainbow trout.

◼ Jordan Lake (BC)

50°53'50"N 116°28'59"W

Rainbow trout

Jordan Lake is located approximately 2 km southeast of Moose Lake. Jordan Lake was stocked in the past with rainbow trout. The lake's narrow width allows reasonable angling opportunities from shore.

◻ Serpent Lake (BC)

50°54'45"N 116°33'11"W

Status: Doubtful

Serpent Lake is located a little over 2 km southwest of the confluence of Bobbie Burns Creek with the Spillimacheen River. Serpent receives few visitors, and fishing reports are non-existent. It appears that Serpent Lake dries up to the point each year of not being able to hold fish.

◼ Jubilee Lake (BC)

50°57'08"N 116°28'28"W

Rainbow trout to 40 cm

Tiny Jubilee Lake is located on the forested bench on the west side of the Columbia River. Jubilee is stocked regularly with rainbow trout and they are present in the lake in good numbers. Most fish taken will average 25–35 cm in length.

Kootenay Trout Hatchery photo

Jubilee Lake

◼ Bobbie Burns Creek (BC)

Rainbow trout to 35 cm
Cutthroat trout to 35 cm
Bull trout to 70 cm (4.0 kg)
Whitefish to 30 cm
Kokanee to 30 cm

Bobbie Burns Creek is accessible from logging roads for most of its fishable length. Bobbie Burns Creek is a major tributary of the Spillimacheen River, and possesses the same variety of game fish. Rainbow and cutthroat trout can be taken from most locations, with the odd bull trout present as well. Whitefish and kokanee become more plentiful in the fall.

▪ Bugaboo Creek (BC)

Cutthroat trout to 35 cm
Bull trout to 60 cm (3.0 kg)
Whitefish to 30 cm

Bugaboo Creek is born high amid the glaciers of the spectacular Bugaboo Mountains. Bugaboo Creek flows east, eventually emptying into the Columbia River just south of Spillimacheen. Although it is silted much of the year due to its glacial origins, Bugaboo Creek generally clears up enough by late summer to offer fair stream fishing in its lower reaches. Cutthroat trout in the 20–30 cm range are the normal catch, with bull trout and whitefish present as well. Bugaboo Creek is paralleled by logging roads for its entire length.

Bugaboo Falls on Bugaboo Creek

▪ Driftwood Creek (BC)

Cutthroat trout to 35 cm

Driftwood Creek is a tributary of Bugaboo Creek. It is accessible by logging roads in the Bugaboo and Bobbie Burns Creek drainages. Driftwood Creek holds plenty of small cutthroat, few larger than 25 cm in length. This is an excellent creek to gain some fishing experience on.

▪ Columbia River (BC) (Spillimacheen to Parson)

Bull trout to 80 cm (7.0 kg)
Cutthroat trout to 40 cm
Rainbow trout to 40 cm
Whitefish to 35 cm

The slow-moving Columbia River is of little interest to most anglers as it continues north on its roll to the Pacific. Bull trout and whitefish are caught in the river, along with the occasional rainbow or cutthroat trout.

Fishing buddy

KOOTENAY PARK REGION

The upper Kootenay River and its main tributary, the Vermilion River, serve as the main arteries for this Region, which includes all of Kootenay National Park. Highway 93 (Banff-Windermere Highway) connects the Region north and east to the Trans-Canada Highway and Banff, and south to Radium and the Columbia Valley. Fishing opportunities in the Region are somewhat limited, with small lakes and large rivers being the main sites. Cutthroat trout are the predominant species. Sub-Regions are based on the drainages of the two main rivers: the Kootenay and the Vermilion.

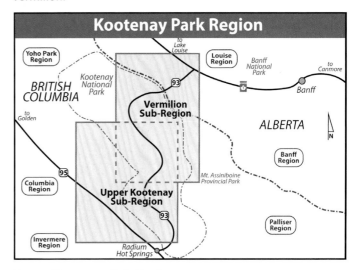

Upper Kootenay Sub-Region

The upper Kootenay River, from its headwaters through Kootenay National Park, is the main waterway through the Sub-Region. In Kootenay National Park, short side trails lead from Highway 93 to Dog and Cobb lakes, while pretty Olive Lake lies alongside the highway at the crest of Sinclair Pass. The upper Kootenay River valley, which is outside the national park, connects over a very low height of land with the Beaverfoot River. The upper Beaverfoot is accessible from roads that branch south off the Trans-Canada Highway east of Golden. There are a number of good fishing lakes in this area, including Dainard, Diana and Marion.

▪ Kootenay River (NP-BC) (Headwaters to national park boundary [south])

Cutthroat trout to 50 cm
Bull trout to 70 cm (4.0 kg)
Whitefish to 35 cm
Kokanee to 35 cm

The Kootenay River, which flows south from headwaters in the Vermilion Range, offers many kilometres of decent stream fishing. Cutthroat trout in the 25–35 cm range predominate, with both whitefish and bull trout also present in good numbers. North of the Kootenay Park boundary, the Kootenay River has a slow flow and frequent marshy areas. The river is still relatively small as it crosses the park boundary, but begins to drop in elevation and loses most of its marshy features. After joining the Vermilion River (which is larger than the Kootenay at their confluence), the Kootenay possesses enough volume to genuinely be given river status. Flowing back and forth across the wide Kootenay Valley,

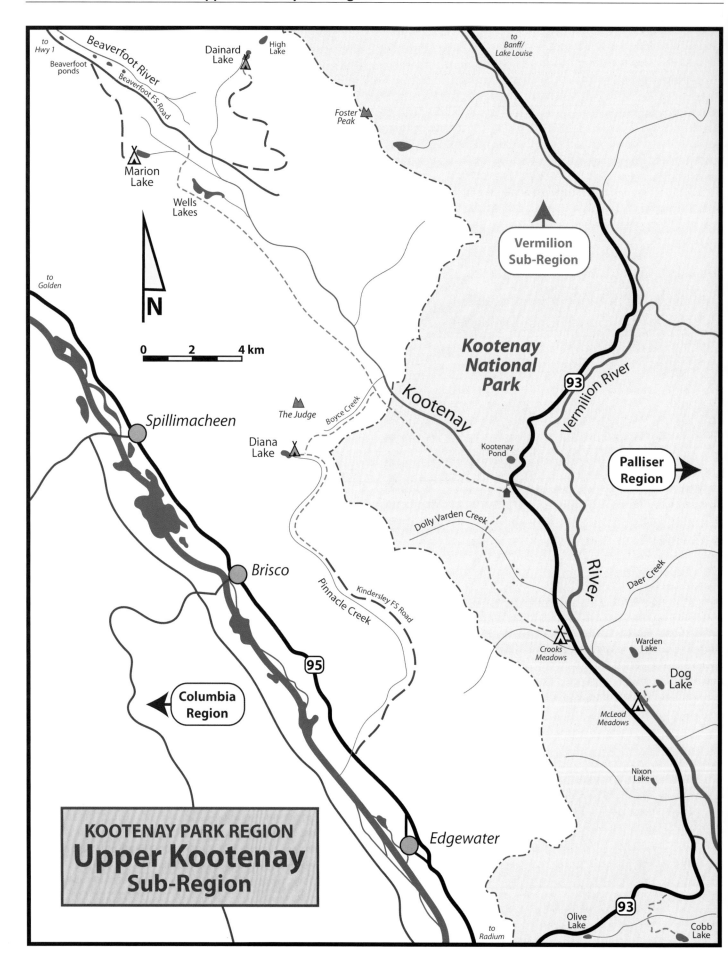

the river develops into a series of pools and riffles. The junctions of the Kootenay with minor tributaries are generally productive, especially when the main river is silted. Within Kootenay National Park these minor tributaries include Dolly Varden, Daer, Pitts, Swede and Rubie creeks.

Kootenay River

☐ Olive Lake (NP)

50°40'26"N 115°56'13"W

Brook trout to 25 cm

Olive Lake is a delightful little pond of a particularly pleasing shade of green. Olive Lake sits alongside Highway 93 at the summit of Sinclair Pass. Although it was stocked in the past with brook, rainbow and cutthroat trout, only brook trout are present today and most of the fish are small, few reaching 20 cm in length. The waters of Olive Lake are particularly unproductive, and studies have shown that the trout in Olive grow exceedingly slowly. Casting a fly is a difficult proposition around most of the shoreline due to the proximity of the forest cover. Olive is a very shallow and clear lake and fish can easily be seen swimming in and around the submerged deadfall and casting ahead of cruising fish with a fly or lure is generally effective.

Olive Lake

☐ Cobb Lake (NP)

50°39'38"N 115°52'34"W

Brook trout to 45 cm

Cobb Lake, located 3 km by trail from Highway 93, lies in a quiet opening in the forest. The boggy shoreline will ensure that most anglers end up with wet feet. Cobb's dark waters may still hold limited numbers of brook trout averaging 20–30 cm in length. Flies are very effective at Cobb Lake, but fly casting is difficult with the exception of the few locations where forest cover opens up slightly. As the lake's bottom drops off quickly, lures and spinners are more effective.

Cobb Lake

■ Dog Lake (NP)

50°46'52"N 115°55'44"W

Brook trout to 40 cm

Rainbow trout to 35 cm

Lovely Dog Lake, which is located 3 km by trail from the McLeod Meadows campground, is one of the Sub-Region's more popular hiking destinations. It is also popular with anglers as it holds a healthy population of brook trout in the 25-35 cm range. The odd rainbow trout is still present in the lake as well. Lures are effective and fish can be taken close to shore in many locations. On a calm day, fish can easily be seen swimming about in Dog Lake's pretty green waters.

Dog Lake

Dog Lake rainbow trout

141

◻ Warden Lake (NP)
50°47'45"N 115°56'58"W
Status: Doubtful
Tiny Warden Lake is located amid heavy forest cover on the west side of the Kootenay River north of Dog Lake. Access is on the West Kootenay Fire Road, which connects to the Macleod Meadows Campground. Although Warden Lake looks promising, it has never been stocked, and likely contains no fish.

◼ Nixon Lake (NP)
50°44'20"N 115°55'58"W
Status: Devoid of fish
This small, shallow pond located less than a kilometre west of Highway 93 by trail has never been stocked and contains no fish.

◻ Dolly Varden Creek and Ponds (NP)
Cutthroat trout to 25 cm
Bull trout to 35 cm
Despite its name, Dolly Varden Creek holds far more cutthroat trout than bull trout (formerly known as Dolly Varden). Several kilometres upstream from the Kootenay lies a series of small beaver dams where cutthroat in the 15–25 cm range are plentiful. Fishable waters can be reached by either following the creek upstream through very thick brush, or by following the fire road that connects Kootenay Crossing with Crook's Meadow.

◻ Daer Creek, Pitts Creek, Swede Creek, Rubie Creek (NP)
Cutthroat trout to 25 cm
Bull trout to 25 cm
These tributaries of the Kootenay River hold small cutthroat trout in pools along their length.

◼ Kootenay Pond (NP)
50°53'33"N 115°02'31"W
Status: Devoid of fish
Kootenay Pond was a popular angling location in the past, but required regular plantings as the trout did not reproduce. No trout exist in the lake today.

Kootenay Pond

◻ Beaverfoot River (BC)
Cutthroat trout to 40 cm
Rainbow trout to 40 cm
Bull trout to 60 cm (3.0 kg)
Whitefish to 35 cm
The Beaverfoot is a major tributary of the Kicking Horse River and forms the southwestern boundary of Yoho National Park. Access to fishable waters in the upper reaches is via the Beaverfoot Forest Service Road, which heads south from the Trans-Canada Highway just west of the park gates at the western entrance to the park. The river holds cutthroat and rainbow, with a few good-sized bull trout lurking about. Fine meadows and great pools characterize the upper Beaverfoot.

Beaverfoot River

◻ Beaverfoot Ponds (BC)
51°08'29"N 116°32'35"W
Rainbow trout to 35 cm
Cutthroat trout to 35 cm
There is an extended series of beaver ponds attached to the upper Beaverfoot River that can be accessed from the Beaverfoot FS Road. The ponds hold both rainbow and cutthroat trout in the 15–25 cm range.

◮ Diana Lake (BC)
50°53'45"N 116°14'09"W
Cutthroat trout to 45 cm
Spectacular Diana Lake is set high in the Brisco Range and is generally overlooked by anglers because of awkward access. The most common access is via logging roads up Pinnacle Creek east of the town of Edgewater in the Columbia Valley. At the end of the road, a 4 km hike up Diana's outlet creek is required to reach the lake. An alternate route, which requires good route-finding skills, leads up from Boyce Creek, just outside the Kootenay Park boundary north of Kootenay Crossing. Diana Lake is seldom ice-free until early July due to its sheltered location. The lake holds plenty of finicky cutthroat trout averaging 25–35 cm in length. Fly fishing is effective, and fly casting is possible from numerous locations around the lake, with a few large boulders being the preferred locations. Hordes of horseflies are unwanted summer companions at Diana.

Diana Lake cutthroat trout

Diana Lake

Dainard Lake

◼ Marion Lake (BC)
51°02'51"N 115°21'30"W
Rainbow trout to 55 cm (1.5 kg)
Cutthroat trout to 55 cm (1.5 kg)
Marion Lake is reached after a long drive on the Beaverfoot Forest Service Road from the Trans-Canada Highway just outside the west entrance to Yoho National Park. The lake is surrounded by a combination of marsh and logged-out and burned-out forest. Marion holds plenty of rainbow and cutthroat trout in the 25–35 cm range. A boat is required, as shallows extend well out from the shoreline. Trolling up and down the deeper waters generally produces positive results.

◼ High Lake (BC)
51°06'20"N 115°15'22"W
Status: Doubtful
Appropriately named, High Lake is set in a rocky pocket very high on the mountain above Dainard Lake. It is very unlikely that there are any fish in High Lake.

◻ Wells Lakes (BC)
51°01'51"N 115°18'40"W
Cutthroat trout to 35 cm
The Wells Lakes are a series of small, interconnected shallow lakes just off the upper Kootenay River. Access is via a long 20 km trail from Kootenay Crossing in Kootenay National Park, or by a longer 50 km drive up the Beaverfoot River and down the upper Kootenay River. Small cutthroat trout in the 20–25 cm range are reported to be present in the lakes in limited numbers.

Vermilion Sub-Region

The Vermilion Sub-Region encompasses the northern half of Kootenay National Park and holds limited possibilities for anglers. The Vermilion River, which parallels Highway 93 (Banff-Windermere Highway), is silted for much of the year and has never been noted for good fishing. Trying some of the Vermilion's small tributaries, or taking a short hike up the Simpson River, represent much more worthwhile ventures in terms of stream fishing potential. The most popular backcountry destinations in the area are Kaufmann Lake and Floe Lake, both of which are more noted for their splendid scenery than their fishing.

Marion Lake

◭ Dainard Lake (BC)
51°05'49"N 115°16'16"W
Cutthroat trout to 40 cm
Dainard Lake, hidden high in the Vermilion Range near the headwaters of the Kootenay River, receives little attention from anglers despite the prospect of very good fishing. Access is via logging roads up the Beaverfoot River from the Kicking Horse River, followed by a short 1 km trail. Dainard Lake is located just outside the western boundary of Kootenay National Park on the opposite side of the mountains from the famed Rockwall area. Dainard contains cutthroat trout averaging 25–35 cm in length. Fish are numerous and can be taken from almost any spot around the lake.

◭ Kaufmann Lake (NP)
51°16'14"N 116°14'14"W
Brook trout to 40 cm
Kaufmann Lake is located 14 km by unmaintained trail from the popular attraction of Marble Canyon on Highway 93. Kaufmann Lake lies tucked away in a hanging valley beneath the towering peaks of the Continental Divide. The lake was at one time popular with backpackers. Kaufmann is a long, narrow lake that contains brook trout ranging from 15–25 cm in length, which can be taken from most locations around the lakeshore. The area around the inlet creek at the far end of the lake usually holds fish and offers plenty of backcasting room for those who are fly fishing. Flies and lures will work well at Kaufmann Lake.

Dainard Lake cutthroat trout

Kaufmann Lake

*Kaufmann Lake
brook trout*

☐ Tokumm Creek (NP)

Cutthroat trout to 30 cm
Bull trout to 40 cm

Tokumm Creek parallels the Kaufmann Lake trail for almost its entire distance, and at a glance appears to have plenty of potential as a trout stream. Unfortunately, fish cannot make it upstream past the falls in Marble Canyon, so the only fishing in Tokumm Creek is in the last half kilometre before it joins the Vermilion River.

◼ Vermilion River (NP)

Bull trout to 70 cm (3.0 kg)
Cutthroat trout to 35 cm
Whitefish to 35 cm

The Vermilion River is relatively accessible as it flows alongside Highway 93 (Banff-Windermere Highway). However, the river remains very silted for much of the year, due to its glacial origins. The Vermilion does possess some fine holes, and for a few brief weeks each autumn it clears enough to allow the prospect of fair fishing. Bull and cutthroat trout and whitefish in the 20–30 cm range can be taken, with large bull trout to 60 cm also caught on occasion. The best fishing spots tend to be where one of the tributary streams joins the Vermilion River, particularly if the side creeks are clearer than the main river. The junction of the Vermilion and Simpson Rivers in particular is a prime fishing location.

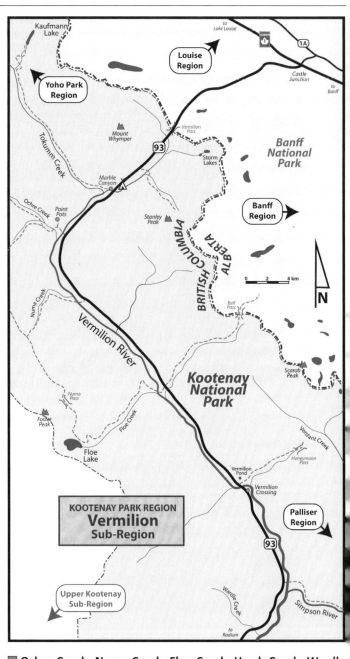

◼ Ochre Creek, Numa Creek, Floe Creek, Hawk Creek, Wardle Creek (NP)

Bull trout to 25 cm
Cutthroat trout to 20 cm

Once their waters have cleared after runoff, all of the major tributaries of the Vermilion River contain small cutthroat and bull trout in their lower reaches within a kilometre of their confluence with the river.

☐ Vermilion Pond (NP)

50°01'47"N 115°59'22"W
Cutthroat trout to 20 cm

Tiny Vermilion Pond is located just off Highway 93, about 1 km north of Vermilion Crossing amid the 2013 burn. The pond, amazingly, always seems to hold a few small cutthroat trout in its shallow waters. Most of the fish tend to keep to the middle of the pond beyond the reach of all but the most expert angler.

Floe Lake (NP)
1°03'10"N 116°08'30"W
Status: Devoid of fish
Floe Lake is one of the most beautiful spots in all the mountain parks. The magnificent Rockwall towers above stunning blue waters dotted with ice floes. Floe Lake and its surrounding alpine meadows are reached by a 10 km trail from Highway 93, and the area is popular with hikers throughout the summer. Floe Lake was stocked many years ago with cutthroat that grew to good sizes but were unable to reproduce. No trout remain in Floe Lake.

Simpson River

Verdant Creek (NP-BC)
Cutthroat trout to 25 cm
Bull trout to 40 cm
Verdant Creek is a major tributary of the Simpson River and can be reached by trails on the upper Simpson River or by the Honeymoon Pass trail, north of Vermilion Crossing. The many pools on Verdant Creek are home to cutthroat and bull trout that average 20-25 cm in length. The Verdant Creek fire of 2017 destroyed forests up the Simpson River, Verdant Creek and Simpson River drainages. Check with Parks Canada and BC Parks regarding access.

Floe Lake

Storm Lakes (NP)
50°12'50"N 116°01'35"W
Status: Devoid of fish
The two tiny Storm Lakes are located at the head of the Vermilion River beneath the western face of Storm mountain. Bushwhacking through the deadfall of the massive fire of 1968 is required to reach the lakes. The Storm Lakes have never been stocked, and it is unlikely that they hold any fish.

Simpson River (NP-BC)
Cutthroat trout to 40 cm
Bull trout to 75 cm (4.0 kg)
Whitefish to 30 cm
The Simpson River, which flows from the Golden Valley in Mount Assiniboine Provincial Park to the Vermilion River in Kootenay Park, has long stretches of fishable waters. The 8 km stretch above its confluence with the Vermilion River is within the boundaries of Kootenay National Park and contains many large pools home to cutthroat and whitefish, and usually a large bull trout or two. Expect to catch cutthroat trout averaging 25–35 cm in length. Above the 8 km mark on the trail (signs mark the boundary), the Simpson River flows inside Mount Assiniboine Provincial Park and a BC license is required. This stretch of river is characterized by faster waters and fewer pools. Because no glaciers feed the Simpson River, it is generally very clear and the spring runoff usually short-lived.

Be ready for some BIG trout action in the Canadian Rockies!

145

CANMORE REGION

The bustling community of Canmore serves as the centre of the Region and offers complete tourist facilities including sporting goods stores. The Trans-Canada Highway, leading east to Calgary and west to Banff, is the main transportation artery. The 1-A Highway and the Smith-Dorrien/Spray Trail provide access to areas off the Trans-Canada Highway. The Bow River and the Spray Lakes Reservoir are the most significant water features in the Region. Angling opportunities in the Region are good, and range from river to stream to lake. Access varies from highway to gravel road to trail. The Region is divided into three Sub-Regions: the Three Sisters Sub-Region around Canmore; the Smith-Dorrien Creek drainage; the backcountry surrounding Marvel Lake in Banff National Park.

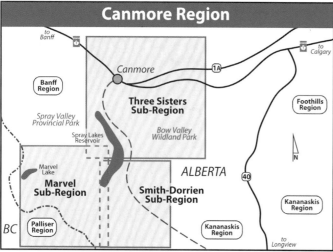

Three Sisters Sub-Region

The Three Sisters Sub-Region extends from the Spray Lakes Reservoir to Canmore, and then east along the Bow River valley as far as Chief Hector Lake. Vehicular access is on the Trans-Canada Highway, the 1-A Highway and the Smith-Dorrien/Spray Trail. The Bow River, which flows through Canmore, receives heavy fishing pressure. From Canmore, the graveled Smith-Dorrien/Spray Trail heads directly west through Whiteman Gap into Spray Valley Provincial Park. The road leads past Whiteman Pond in short order to Goat Pond and the Spray Lakes Reservoir. Spray Lakes Reservoir is a very popular spot with anglers and is busy all season long. Gap Lake, Grotto Mountain Pond, Canmore beaver ponds and the Steele Brothers' Ponds are all located east of Canmore and are accessed from the 1-A Highway. Continuing east on the 1-A, one reaches Chief Hector Lake and its monster rainbow trout.

Clean, Drain, Dry

To protect waters of the Canadian Rockies against invasive species, all anglers need to adopt the principles of Clean, Drain, Dry as soon their boat or watercraft is removed from the water:
1. **CLEAN** off all plant parts, animals, and mud from boat and equipment (e.g. boots, waders, fishing gear). Use a power wash station if available.
2. **DRAIN** onto land all items that can hold water (e.g. buckets, wells, bilge, and ballast).
3. **DRY** all items completely before launching into another body of water.

Local Knowledge

When fishing any region in the Canadian Rockies, it is always an advantage to have local knowledge, whether looking for information on lakes or tips on what to use. If in Canmore, be sure to drop in at Wapiti Sports and speak with Nick Schlacter or one of his knowledgeable staff. Outstanding float trips on the Bow River can be arranged through Wapiti Sports along with other guided trips to local waters (including ice fishing).

■ Spray Lakes Reservoir (AB)
50°54'34"N 115°20'29"W
Lake trout to 85 cm (8.0 kg)
Cutthroat trout to 60 cm (2.0 kg)
Whitefish to 45 cm
The Spray Lakes Reservoir, which measures over 20 km in length, is located southwest of Canmore in a deep valley between the Goat and Kananaskis Ranges in the heart of the Spray Valley Provincial Park. The Reservoir is accessed by the Smith-Dorrien/Spray Trail that connects Canmore with the Kananaskis Lakes. Due to the lake's size, a boat is recommended for fishing, but boaters should be aware that very strong winds are common and often keep all crafts off the water for days at a time. Huge lake trout inhabit the lake, with whitefish also present in good numbers, as well as a few cutthroat trout. Most lake trout caught will be in the 40–50 cm range. Early spring and late fall are generally the best time for lake trout. Winter also sees significant angling activity at Spray Lakes Reservoir. Bait and lures are generally effective for lake trout. For shorebound anglers, areas around the many inlet creeks hold trout.

Spray Lakes Reservoir

Spray Lakes Reservoir lake trout

Nick and Marla Schlacter photo

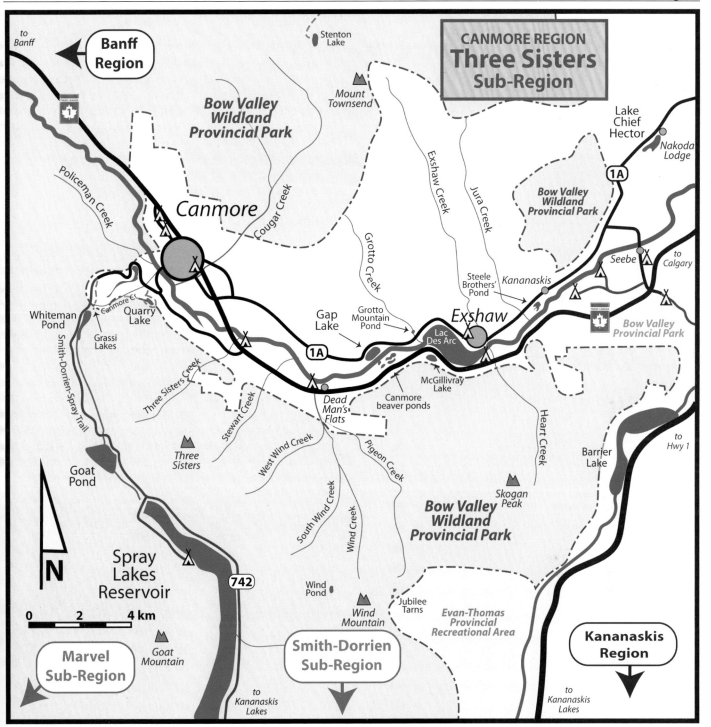

Goat Pond (AB)

51°00'57"N 115°24'07"W

Lake trout to 60 cm (2.0 kg)

Brook trout to 40 cm

Cutthroat trout to 40 cm

Whitefish to 35 cm

Goat Pond is a man-made lake 2 km northwest and downstream of Spray Lakes Reservoir. It is part of the reservoir/power complex and sits alongside the Smith-Dorrien/Spray Trail. Most of the shoreline and lake is cluttered with deadfall and although lake trout and whitefish are there for the catching, most anglers will catch more snags than fish. Cutthroat and brook trout may be present in small numbers as well.

Whiteman Pond (aka Whitemans Pond) (AB)

51°04'09"N 115°24'44"W

Brook trout to 35 cm

Lake trout to 55 cm (1.5 kg)

Whitefish to 40 cm

Whiteman Pond is a very narrow stretch of water alongside the Smith-Dorrien/Spray Trail at Whiteman Gap. It holds brook and lake trout as well as the odd whitefish. Angling is possible only from the road side of the pond.

Grassi Lakes (AB)

51°04'21"N 115°24'24"W

Brook trout to 25 cm

These two tiny charming lakes of exquisite color are set in the basin immediately beneath Whiteman Gap. The lakes are a very popular hiking destination for locals. Both Grassi Lakes contain a very limited number of brook trout in the 15–20 cm range.

Lower Grassi Lake

■ Quarry Lake (aka Canmore Mines No. 3) (AB)

51°04′29″N 115°22′22″W

Arctic grayling to 35 cm

Quarry Lake, as one might expect, is a water-filled abandoned rock quarry. It is located in a pleasant meadow approximately 1 km south of the Smith-Dorrien/Spray Trail just west of Canmore and is very popular with locals for strolling or walking the dog. The lake was stocked at one time with rainbow trout, which failed to reproduce. Quarry Lake is now stocked with arctic grayling, which average 20–30 cm in length. Although grayling can be taken by a number of methods, they seem particularly susceptible to the fly, and fly casting room is available around the entire lake. Watch your backcast for innocent bystanders.

Quarry Lake

■ Canmore Creek (AB)

Cutthroat trout to 30 cm

Brook trout to 30 cm

Brown trout to 30 cm

Whitefish to 30 cm

The waters of Canmore Creek begin at the bottom of the power complex below Whiteman Gap and flow for a few short kilometres before joining the Bow River. Alberta Fish and Wildlife is attempting to reintroduce cutthroat trout to the creek. In addition to the stocked cutthroat, there are brook and brown trout present in the creek. Most trout caught will be in the 15–25 cm range. Check your regulations as special restrictions apply on Canmore Creek.

■ Policeman Creek (AB)

Brown trout to 30 cm

Brook trout to 30 cm

Whitefish to 25 cm

Policeman Creek flows within Canmore and is very popular with local youngsters, in particular the area around the bridge that leads to downtown Canmore. Brown and brook trout averaging 15–25 cm in length are caught in the creek.

■ Bow River (AB) (Downstream from Banff Park east boundary)

Brown trout to 75 cm (4.0 kg)

Rainbow trout to 65 cm (3.0 kg)

Brook trout to 50 cm (1.5 kg)

Bull trout to 75 cm (4.0 kg)

Whitefish to 55 cm (1.5 kg)

The stretch of the Bow River downstream from the Banff National Park boundary is a high-quality fishery, and is steadily gaining more attention from anglers. Although this section of the Bow is accessible on foot from the Trans-Canada and 1-A Highways, guided drift boats have become very popular. The Bow River provides some excellent river fishing for brown trout, with large individuals in the 2–3 kg range taken regularly. Whitefish can be taken in good numbers in the fall. The area around the Trans-Canada Highway bridge east of Canmore and the old CPR bridges seem inordinately popular and are heavily overfished, even though other excellent pools are waiting just around the bend both upstream and downstream. Fishing slows dramatically during run-off, which lasts from June through mid-July. Early season fishing from mid-April to late-May is usually very productive, the action picking up again in August through October.

Nick and Marla Schlacter photo
Bow River float trip

Nick and Marla Schlacter photo
Nick Schlacter with Bow River brown trout

Canmore Beaver Ponds (AB)

50°02'58"N 115°13'39"W
Rainbow trout to 35 cm
Brown trout to 35 cm

The Canmore beaver ponds are interconnected with various channels of the Bow River and are located alongside the 1-A Highway 4 km east of Canmore. The ponds contain rainbow trout along with a few brown trout. Trout caught in the ponds will average 15–25 cm in length.

☐ Pigeon Creek, Wind Creek, South Wind Creek, West Wind Creek, Stewart Creek, Three Sisters Creek (AB)

Brook trout to 30 cm
Rainbow trout to 30 cm
Brown trout to 30 cm
Whitefish to 30 cm

These small tributaries of the Bow River are located south of Canmore. They hold small numbers of brook, rainbow and/or brown trout, and the occasional whitefish.

■ Wind Pond (AB)

50°58'22"N 115°15'08"W

■ Jubilee Tarns (AB)

50°58'08"N 115°12'58"W
Status: Devoid of fish

Wind Pond and the Jubilee Tarns are very small lakes located high in the Wind and West Wind Creek drainages. They have never been stocked and contain no fish.

Gap Lake (AB)

51°03'16"N 115°14'02"W
Brook trout to 40 cm
Brown trout to 60 cm (2.0 kg)
Whitefish to 50 cm

Gap Lake is sandwiched between the 1-A Highway and the C.P.R. mainline, 8 km east of Canmore. Brown and brook trout in the 25–35 cm range predominate, with large whitefish present in fair numbers as well. A boat is recommended for those fishing Gap Lake.

Gap Lake

Gap Lake brown trout

▲ Grotto Mountain Pond (AB)

50°03'57"N 115°12'08"W
Rainbow trout to 35 cm
Whitefish to 25 cm

Grotto Mountain Pond and its nearby popular picnic area are situated on the north side of 1-A Highway just west of Lac Des Arc. The pond is stocked regularly with rainbow trout. Trout caught in the pond are not large, averaging 15–25 cm in length, but are plentiful. A few whitefish may also be present in the pond. Grotto Mountain Pond is a pleasant location, and always seems busy with families.

Grotto Mountain Pond

☐ Lac Des Arc (AB)

50°03'13"N 115°10'57"W
Brown trout to 55 cm (1.5 kg)
Whitefish to 50 cm

Lac Des Arc is merely an overflow basin for the Bow River during high water, and is no more than 1–2 m deep. The lake itself almost dries up completely on occasion. Accordingly, any fish population will tend to keep near the river on the north side, although whitefish and brown trout might be taken from a boat in the shallow waters that make up the main part of the lake.

■ McGillivray Pond

50°03'13"N 115°11'49"W
Status: Doubtful

McGillivray Pond is the small body of water that sits on the south side of the Trans-Canada Highway at the west end of Lac Des Arc. McGillivray Pond has never been stocked and likely holds no fish.

☐ Steele Brothers' Ponds (AB)

50°04'30"N 115°07'45"W
Brook trout to 40 cm
Rainbow trout to 40 cm
Brown trout to 55 cm (2.0 kg)
Whitefish to 30 cm

This series of large, interconnected beaver ponds is located immediately east of the Steele Brothers' lime plant on the 1-A Highway. The ponds contain good numbers of brook trout, with browns, rainbows and the occasional whitefish present as well. As with most beaver dams, the surrounding vegetation growth is heavy. Finding a spot to cast from effectively may prove difficult, and wet feet are likely.

🅰 **Chief Hector Lake (aka Hector Lake)**
(Private lake, fee required to fish)
50°08'06"N 115°03'19"W
Rainbow trout to 75 cm (4.0 kg)
Chief Hector Lake is located on the Morley First Nations Reserve, and is accessed from the 1-A Highway at Nakoda Lodge. As the lake is on a First Nations reserve it is beyond federal or provincial jurisdiction for angling licences. A licence is therefore not required, but a fee must be paid for angling at Chief Hector Lake. The lake is catch-and-release only. Chief Hector Lake is relatively shallow and an aeration system prevents winterkill. It is possible to fish from shore, but a watercraft is a superior option. The rainbow trout in the lake are huge, with average trout being around 50 cm in length and 2 kg+ in weight. Most fish are very wary, as they have been caught several times. However, an angler who shows a bit of patience will be rewarded. Fly fishing is the most effective method of angling at Chief Hector Lake. Be prepared for some screaming reels!

Chief Lake Hector

Don Shandrowsky with Chief Lake Hector rainbow trout

■ **Stenton Lake (aka South Ghost Lake) (AB)**
50°10'33"N 115°17'01"W
Cutthroat trout to 45 cm
Stenton Lake is located at the headwaters of South Ghost River, and is accessed by a 10 km trail up the South Ghost River. Although the lake is situated almost due north of Canmore, road access to the trail is via the Forestry Trunk Road west of Cochrane. Stenton Lake contains a good population of cutthroat trout that average 25–35 cm in length.

Smith-Dorrien Sub-Region

The Smith-Dorrien/Spray Trail is a gravel road connecting Canmore and Peter Lougheed Provincial Park, and it provides access to this rugged area noted for its outstanding day and half-day hikes. Mud Lake and the Hogarth Lakes are located in the wide valley at the head of the Smuts and Smith-Dorrien watersheds. Spur valleys to the west of the Smith-Dorrien valley hold Commonwealth Lake and the Burstall Lakes, while to the east, consecutive side valleys hold Rummel, Chester and Headwall lakes.

■ **Warspite Lake (AB)**
50°42'18"N 115°13'21"W
Status: Devoid of fish
Warspite Lake is located on the west side of the Smith-Dorrien valley approximately 5 km west of Lower Kananaskis Lake. A 2 km trail leads from the Mt. Black Prince Day Use area to Warspite Lake. Warspite Lake almost dries up completely each year and holds no fish.

■ **Black Prince Lakes (aka Construction Lake) (AB)**
50°41'27"N 115°13'56"W
Status: Devoid of fish
The Black Prince Lakes are set in a high basin above Warspite Lake. The lakes have never been stocked and contain no fish.

■ **Headwall Lakes (aka Ranger Lakes) (AB)**
50°48'27"N 115°14'44"W
Cutthroat trout to 40 cm
The Headwall Lakes are located 7 km by trail from the Chester Lake parking area. The lakes are set in rocky, windswept basins with a general lack of vegetation around the shoreline. Both the lower and upper lakes hold plenty of cutthroat trout averaging 20–30 cm in length. The trout tend to keep to the area around the distinctive drop-off zone. Flies and lures both work well in Headwall Lakes.

Lower Headwall Lake

■ **Chester Lake (AB)**
50°48'42"N 115°16'26"W
Northern Dolly Varden to 55 cm (1.5 kg)
Cutthroat trout to 45 cm
Chester Lake and its appealing larch-filled valley are reached by a 6 km walk-in from the Smith-Dorrien/Spray Trail. The lake attracts numerous day hikers and anglers throughout the summer. Chester Lake was stocked in 1974 with Northern Dolly

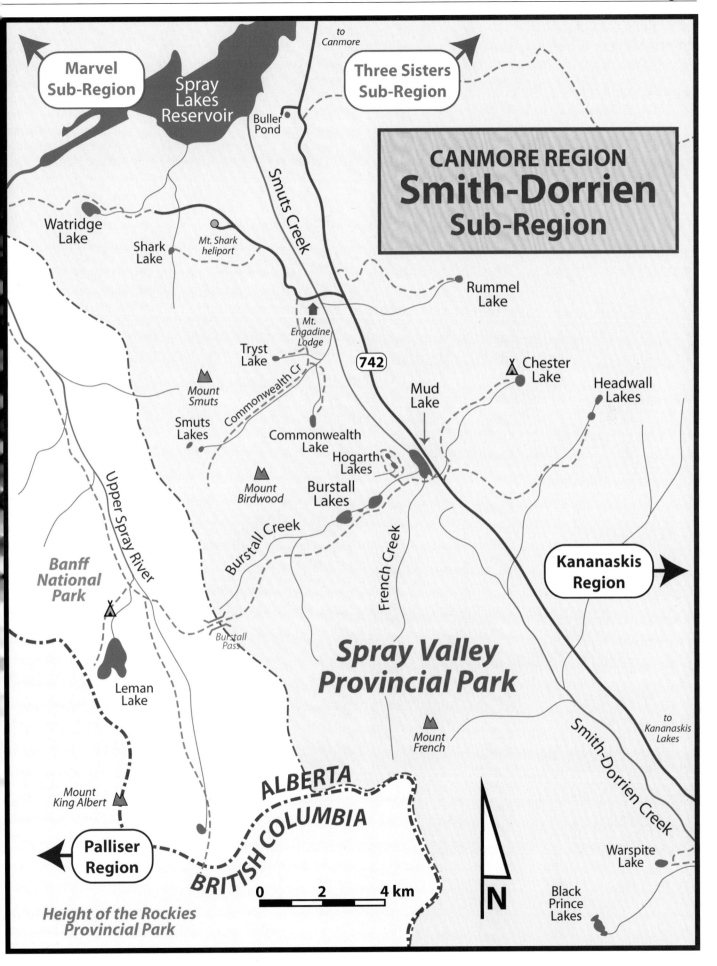

Marvel Sub-Region

Spray Lakes Reservoir

Three Sisters Sub-Region

to Canmore

Buller Pond

Smuts Creek

CANMORE REGION
Smith-Dorrien
Sub-Region

Watridge Lake

Shark Lake

Mt. Shark heliport

Rummel Lake

Mt. Engadine Lodge

Tryst Lake

Commonwealth Cr

742

Mud Lake

Chester Lake

Headwall Lakes

Mount Smuts

Smuts Lakes

Commonwealth Lake

Hogarth Lakes

Mount Birdwood

Burstall Lakes

Burstall Creek

French Creek

Kananaskis Region

Upper Spray River

Banff National Park

Burstall Pass

Spray Valley Provincial Park

Leman Lake

Mount French

Smith-Dorrien Creek

to Kananaskis Lakes

Mount King Albert

ALBERTA

BRITISH COLUMBIA

Palliser Region

0   2   4 km

N

Warspite Lake

Black Prince Lakes

Height of the Rockies Provincial Park

Varden, a close relative of the bull trout, which are now reproducing naturally. Cutthroat trout have also been stocked in Chester Lake, and are doing well. Northern Dolly Varden from Chester will average 30–40 cm in length, with the cutthroat trout averaging 25–35 cm in length. Fly fishing is effective for both the dollies and the cutthroat. Check your regulations, as special restrictions are in effect at Chester Lake.

Chester Lake

Chester Lake Northern Dolly Varden

Jason Godkin photo

🅰 Rummel Lake (aka West Galatea Lake) (AB)
50°50'03"N 115°17'45"W
Cutthroat trout to 45 cm
Rummel Lake is reached by following a 5 km trail from the Smith-Dorrien/Spray Trail opposite Mt. Engadine Lodge. Alternate access involves bushwhacking south from the Chester Lake trail. Rummel Lake is set in a charming basin, and its clear waters hold cutthroat trout in good numbers in the 25–35 cm range. Open shoreline of meadow and scree offer ample room for fly casting.

Rummel Lake

✖ Smith-Dorrien Creek (AB)
Status: Closed to angling
Smith-Dorrien Creek has been recognized as the primary spawning location for bull trout from Lower Kananaskis Lake. As such, it has been permanently closed to angling.

■ Mud Lake (AB)
50°47'39"N 115°18'34"W
Cutthroat trout to 35 cm
Bull trout to 55 cm (1.5 kg)
Northern Dolly Varden to 45 cm.
Whitefish to 30 cm
Mud Lake is fed by the meltwaters of Robertson Glacier, and true to its name, remains chocolate-coloured for most of the year. Accordingly, fishing is usually slow for cutthroat, bull trout and whitefish that inhabit Mud's roadside waters. It has been reported that Northern Dolly Varden have made their way down Chester Creek and now inhabit Mud Lake as well.

■ Burstall Lakes (AB)
50°47'07"N 115°19'33"W
Cutthroat trout to 35 cm
Northern Dolly Varden to 35 cm
This series of fine lakes sits in a meadowed valley 2 km west of Mud Lake on the Burstall Pass trail. The lakes contain cutthroat trout in the 20–30 cm range, and may also contain a few Northern Dolly Varden that have migrated from Chester Creek and Mud Lake. Burstall Creek, which flows from Burstall Lake to Mud Lake, contains a few small trout. The lake level drops significantly in dry years, which may affect the lakes' ability to hold trout at times.

Upper Burstall Lake

■ Hogarth Lakes (AB)
50°47'42"N 115°19'18"W
Cutthroat trout to 40 cm
These two emerald-green bodies of water are located 2 km by trail from the Mud Lake Parking area. The lakes receive surprisingly little attention from anglers despite their proximity to the Smith-Dorrien/Spray Trail. The lakes contain a population of native cutthroat trout averaging 20–30 cm in length, and extreme water clarity allows the angler to see fish cruising about. Flies are effective. Casting room is adequate around the larger lake.

■ Commonwealth Lake (Lost Lake) (AB)
50°48'23"N 115°20'45"W
Cutthroat trout to 40 cm
Commonwealth Lake is situated in a secluded side valley off Commonwealth Creek and can be reached along abandoned logging roads from the Smith-Dorrien/Spray Trail. The lake receives few visits from anglers each season because of a lack of defined trails. Commonwealth Lake holds cutthroat in the 20–30 cm range and is encircled by forest, making fly casting difficult from most locations. Nearby Commonwealth Creek contains small cutthroat trout.

Tryst Lake (AB)
50°49'00"N 115°21'36"W
Status: Doubtful

Tryst Lake is a small tarn set in a hanging valley to the north of Commonwealth Creek and Lake. A 2 km trail leads to the lake from the Smith-Dorrien/Spray Trail. The lake has never been stocked and likely contains no fish.

Smuts Creek (AB)
Cutthroat trout to 25 cm
Bull trout to 40 cm
Whitefish to 25 cm
Northern Dolly Varden to 30 cm

Smuts Creek flows alongside the Smith-Dorrien/Spray Trail from Mud Lake to the Spray Lakes Reservoir and offers a few stretches of decent stream fishing. Cutthroat trout in small sizes predominate, with the odd bull trout or whitefish also present. Northern Dolly Varden, originally planted in Chester, have been reported in Smuts Creek.

Smuts Creek

Smuts Lake (aka Birdwood Lakes) (AB)
(Lower lake) 50°47'48"N 115°23'19"W
Cutthroat trout to 40 cm

These two small lakes are located at the head of Commonwealth Creek and are reached by a poorly defined 7 km trail. Both lakes are set in distinctive alpine cirques with little vegetation. The upper lake has better-quality angling, although cutthroat trout average 20–30 cm in length can be taken from both lakes. Flies and lures are both very effective in the Smuts Lakes.

Upper Smuts Lake

Smuts Lake cutthroat trout

Watridge Lake (AB)
50°51'02"N 115°25'41"W
Cutthroat trout to 55 cm (1.5 kg)

Watridge Lake is situated just outside the boundary of Banff National Park in Kananaskis Country. Access to the lake is on a 2 km long trail from the Mt. Shark trailhead. Watridge Lake is popular with local anglers who fish its clear, green waters for fine cutthroat trout averaging 25–35 cm in length. Fishing pressure is steady throughout the season. For those who will be fly fishing, a belly boat is a good option for Watridge, as fly casting room is limited around much of the lake.

Watridge Lake

Watridge Lake cutthroat trout
Jason Godkin photo

Shark Lake (aka Marushka Lake) (AB)
50°50'28"N 115°23'53"W
Cutthroat trout to 35 cm

Shark Lake is a diminutive forest-enclosed lake set beneath the northeast face of Mt. Shark. The lake is accessible from the Watridge Lake trail by following a 3.5 km route along Shark Lake's outlet stream. Shark Lake holds cutthroat trout in the 20–30 cm range.

Shark Lake
Jason Godkin photo

Buller Pond (AB)
50°52'04"N 115°21'11"W
Rainbow trout to 35 cm

This small pond and its picnic site are located alongside the Smith-Dorrien/Spray Trail on the south end of the Spray Lakes. Rainbow trout are stocked in Buller Pond, and they average 20–30 cm in length.

Buller Pond

Marvel Sub-Region

The Marvel Sub-Region is always close to the peaks of the Continental Divide and possesses some incredible scenery. The main access into Marvel Lake is via a hiking trail that begins at the Mt. Shark trailhead at the south end of Spray lakes Reservoir. Stunning Marvel Lake, with its beautiful translucent blue-green waters, is the dominant feature to the north. To the south are the upper Spray River and Leman Lake. Large cutthroat trout are present in several lakes in the Sub-Region, including Marvel, and Leman Lakes.

▲ Marvel Lake (NP)
50°52′43″N 115°33′15″W
Cutthroat trout to 60 cm (3.0 kg)
Marvel Lake is set in a long, narrow valley, 15 km by trail from the Mt. Shark trailhead. The lake is over 4 km in length and 75 m in depth. Marvel Lake holds some immense cutthroat trout, upwards of 3 kg. Most trout taken from the lake, however, will average 25–40 cm in length. Due to the lake's size, fishing from shore is often a frustrating proposition. Anglers generally have the most success at the western end of the lake where the main streams enter the lake. This location can be reached by hiking the Wonder Pass route along the north side of the lake. Where the trail begins its steep climb up to the pass, branch left and down to the end of the lake. Luckily, fish can be taken from most spots around the lake. Fly fishing is very productive at Marvel Lake and packing in a float tube is a very worthwhile venture. Those with lures will have success as well, especially in the lake's deeper waters. ⊗ Marvel Lake is closed to angling at its east end, and markers are in place to indicate the no angling zone. The outlet creek is closed from Marvel Lake to its junction with Bryant Creek.

Marvel Lake

Marvel Lake cutthroat trout

■ Terrapin Lake (NP)
50°51′53″N 115°35′32″W
Cutthroat trout to 40 cm
Terrapin Lake is sandwiched between Marvel Lake to the east and Lake Gloria to the west. It is reached via a short spur trail off the Marvel Pass trail. The silty blue waters of Lake Terrapin hold cutthroat trout in the 20–30 cm range, for which the angling is generally poor. The tall grass and reeds along the shoreline makes angling very difficult.

Terrapin Lake

■ Gloria Lake (NP)
50°51′53″N 115°36′10″W
Cutthroat trout to 50 cm (1.5 kg)
Gloria Lake is one of the most exquisitely coloured lakes in the Canadian Rockies. Gloria's rich blue waters hold some fine cutthroat trout, but few anglers make it to the lake each year. Cutthroat trout in the lake average 25–35 cm in length. Fish will tend to keep near shore because of the silted nature of the water. Fishing near one of the many inlet streams can be particularly effective. The quality of trails diminishes rapidly beyond the area of the outlet stream and those anglers travelling along the shoreline will encounter heavy brush.

Gloria Lake

■ Marvel Pass lakes (NP-BC)
50°50′48″N 115°34′32″W
Status: Devoid of fish
These promising looking waters situated in the alpine meadows of Marvel Pass have never been stocked and contain no trout.

■ Cabin Lake (NP)
50°50′17″N 115°34′12″W
Status: Devoid of fish
Cabin Lake is the largest of the Marvel Pass lakes and lies just inside the boundary of Banff National Park. Cabin Lake has never been stocked and contains no trout.

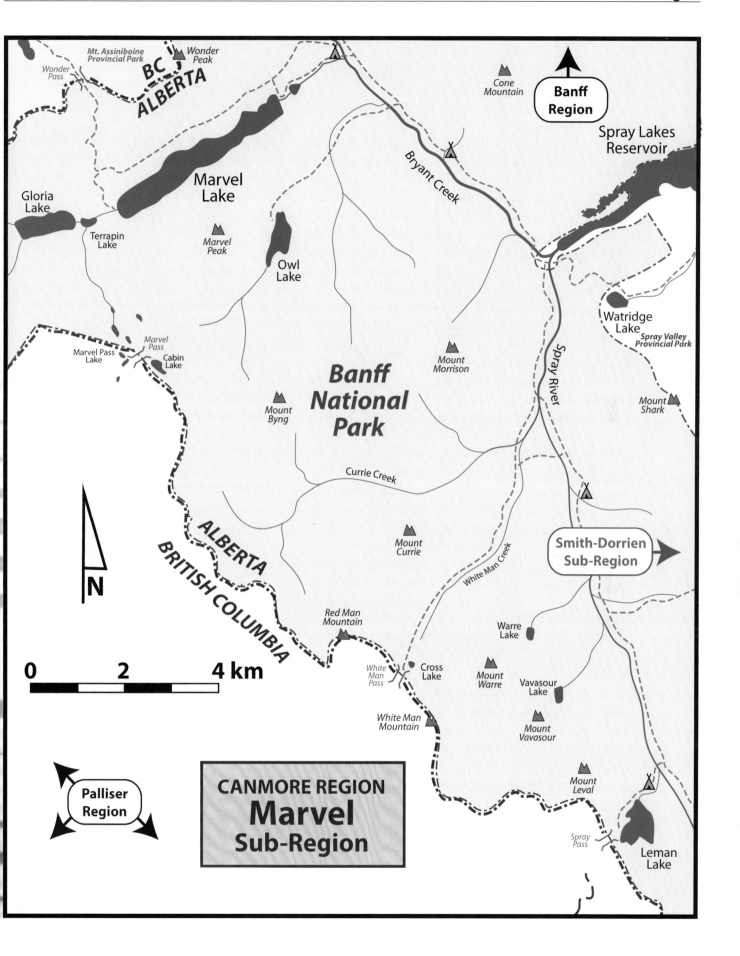

■ Owl Lake (NP)
50°51'44"N 115°31'56"W
Brook trout to 60 cm (2.0 kg)
Owl Lake is located in a side valley west of Bryant Creek. Access is via a 15 km hike from the Mt. Shark trailhead. Water levels in Owl fluctuate dramatically both seasonally and annually. Brook trout inhabit the lake, and they average 25–35 cm in length, although larger fish are present in good numbers.

Owl Lake

Owl Lake brook trout

■ Bryant Creek (NP)
Cutthroat trout to 35 cm
Bull trout to 60 cm (2.5 kg)
Whitefish to 35 cm
Bryant Creek is a noisy companion to hikers travelling to either Marvel Lake or Mt. Assiniboine Provincial Park. Bryant Creek's sparkling waters hold small cutthroat trout, most in the 20–30 cm range. The creek is very popular in its lower reaches, within a kilometre or two of the Spray Lakes Reservoir, where bull trout and whitefish can also be taken. In the meadow section upstream from the Bryant Creek Warden Cabin, there are several kilometres of slow, fishable water as well as numerous beaver ponds.

Bryant Creek

⊗ Spray River (upper) (NP)
Status: Closed to angling
Cutthroat trout
The upper Spray River, which flows from the Palliser Pass region down to the Spray Lakes Reservoir, is closed to angling.

■ Cross Lake (NP)
50°46'51"N 115°29'29"W
Status: Devoid of fish
Cross Lake is located in a meadow just below the summit of White Man Pass. Cross Lake has never been stocked and contains no fish.

■ Warre Lake (NP)
50°47'02"N 115°26'59"W
■ Vavasour Lake (NP)
50°46'32"N 115°26'41"W
Status: Devoid of fish
These two high lakes are located in hanging valleys north of Leman Lake on the west side of the Spray River valley. Neither lake has been stocked and they hold no fish.

☐ Leman Lake (NP)
50°45'04"N 115°25'12"W
Cutthroat trout to 55 cm (1.5 kg)
Leman Lake is located on the western side of the upper Spray River valley, near the summit of Spray Pass. Standard access to Leman Lake is either via the 14 km trail from the Spray Lakes Reservoir or the 13 km Burstall Pass trail. A seldom used 2 km access route begins on the BC side from logging roads on the upper Albert River, and alternates between game trails and bushwhacking. A topographic map is strongly recommended for this route. Leman Lake was very popular in the past due to its large trout in the 3 kg+ range, and it subsequently suffered badly through a period of over harvest. With the dramatic decline in the quality of fishing, the number of anglers also declined. Legislation protecting cutthroat trout in Banff National Park will hopefully restore Leman Lake to its past glory. There are also some concerns about the reproductive success of trout in Leman Lake. It seems that the lake still does hold some very large cutthroat trout in its striking waters, although limited in number. Fishing the obvious divide between the shallow and deep waters is the best strategy. Lures and flies will have both been effective in the past.

Leman Lake cutthroat trout   *Leman Lake*

BANFF REGION

This Region is centered on the world-renowned tourist town of Banff. Services of all types can be obtained in the Banff townsite, including the sale of fishing tackle. Access is on the Trans-Canada Highway, which continues east to Calgary and west to Lake Louise. Lake Minnewanka is a favourite of anglers who come in search of its huge lake trout. The Bow River also attracts plenty of attention. Backcountry lakes make up the much of the rest of the region's angling opportunities. The Region is divided into four Sub-Regions. The first is in the immediate vicinity of Banff and includes Lake Minnewanka. The other three Sub-Regions are largely backcountry and have many popular day hiking and overnight destinations. These Sub-Regions include the Cascade River drainage and the area north of Banff; the Sunshine Village area; and the Egypt Lake environs.

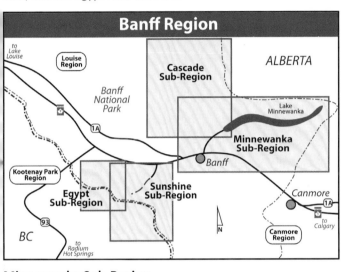

Minnewanka Sub-Region

The Banff townsite is the hub of the Sub-Region. Dining, bars and shopping take precedence over angling among visitors. The Trans-Canada Highway provides Banff's link to the outside world. Lake Minnewanka is the primary fishing destination for most anglers. Two Jack Lake, just off the Lake Minnewanka Road, is also active during the summer. The Bow River is readily accessible near the townsite and is always usually alive with canoeists and anglers.

■ Lake Minnewanka (NP)
51°16'22"N 115°24'35"W
Lake trout to 1.2 m (15.0 kg)
Bull trout to 80 cm (6.0 kg)
Rainbow trout to 65 cm (2.5 kg)
Whitefish to 45 cm

Lake Minnewanka, at 20 km in length, is one of the largest lakes in the Canadian Rockies. The lake is reached by taking the paved road that branches north from the Trans-Canada Highway at the western entrance to Banff. Lake Minnewanka's depths hold lake trout of immense proportions that each year tempt innumerable anglers to test their skills against these monsters. The first weeks after ice-out are generally the most productive, as the lake trout move into shallower water (still up to 20 m deep) and begin to feed actively. Trolling or jigging in the areas around inlet creeks at this time of year can be very productive. As summer progresses,

the lake trout tend to move out to deeper waters and fishing slows noticeably. Although lake trout in the 15 kg range have been taken on occasion, most will average 50–60 cm in length and 2–3 kg in weight. Aside from lake trout, Minnewanka holds rainbow trout, bull trout and whitefish in good numbers. Boats are available for rent at Lake Minnewanka. There are a number of guiding operations on Minnewanka, including renowned Banff Fishing Unlimited. Due to the size and location of the lake, boaters should be very aware of changing weather conditions, and of the strong winds that can appear suddenly.

Lake Minnewanka

Lake Minnewanka lake trout

■ Ghost Lakes (NP)
51°15'50"N 115°14'27"W
Lake trout to 75 cm (5.0 kg)
Bull trout to 70 cm (4.0 kg)
Rainbow trout to 60 cm (2.0 kg)
Whitefish to 40 cm

The Ghost Lakes are simply an extension of the extreme eastern end of Lake Minnewanka. The actual Ghost Lakes vary in size and number with fluctuating water levels. The variety of fish in Ghost Lakes is identical to those in Minnewanka, although generally in slightly smaller sizes. Reaching the Ghost Lakes requires either a long boat trip down the entire length of Minnewanka, or an 8 km hike-in from the Ghost River Road. If fishing from shore, the best areas tend to be those where the lakes are at their narrowest point.

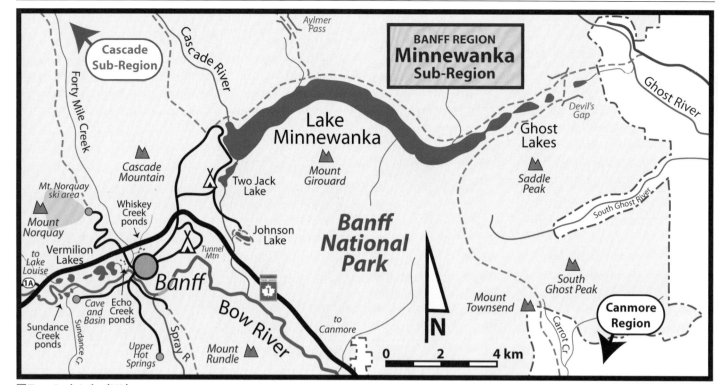

Two Jack Lake (NP)

51°13'53"N 115°29'34"W
Rainbow trout to 55 cm (1.5 kg)
Lake trout to 70 cm (4.0 kg)

Two Jack Lake is located less than 1 km south of Lake Minnewanka, and offers a pleasant respite for those fishermen overwhelmed by the size of Minnewanka. Rainbow trout predominate and average 25–35 cm in length. Lake trout are also present in fair numbers. The nearby campground ensures that Two Jack's shores will be busy all summer long.

Two Jack Lake

Whirling Disease

Whirling disease affects trout, salmon and whitefish and is caused by a parasite called *Myxobolus cerebralis*, which produces spores. The spores are eaten by Tubifex worms found in aquatic environments, which in turn infect fish that ingest the worms. The parasite affects cartilage near the spine, leading to deformities of the spine, causing the fish to whirl in circles, leading to the name "whirling disease." The spores can be transmitted from water body to water body in mud on equipment used for boating and fishing. Whirling disease is not harmful to humans. The first occurrence of whirling disease in Canada was confirmed

at Johnson Lake in Banff National Park in August, 2016. Within one month, there were confirmed cases of whirling disease in several nearby rivers and creeks, including the Bow River, Cascade River, Spray River, Carrot Creek and Healy Creek. In an attempt to control the spread of whirling disease, Parks Canada has removed all of the trout from Johnson Lake. Unfortunately, whirling disease has now been confirmed in Alberta in the Bow, North Saskatchewan, Red Deer and Oldman River watersheds.

⊗ Johnson Lake (NP)

51°11'46"N 115°28'49"W
Status: Closed to angling

Johnson Lake is located two kilometres south of Two Jack Lake and was the site of the first confirmed case of whirling disease in the Rocky Mountains in August, 2016.

Vermilion Lakes (NP)

51°10'30"N 115°37'49"W
Brook trout to 45 cm
Rainbow trout to 45 cm
Bull trout to 60 cm (2.0 kg)
Whitefish to 40 cm

These three shallow lakes located west of Banff alongside the Bow River have gained a reputation over the years for poor fishing. The two most easterly lakes have extended shallows and are of little value to fishermen relegated to shore. From a boat, fishing is fair, at best, in the deeper water that is accentuated by its darker colouration. The most westerly lake is the deepest of the three, but still not deep by normal standards being seldom more than a few metres in depth. Fishing is possible from a number of shoreline locations although getting there will require getting a little soggy. The best location is near the road where spring-fed creeks empty into the western end of Third Lake near a series of beaver houses. Brook trout in the 25–35 cm range is the normal catch, although rainbow and bull trout, as well as whitefish, are taken on occasion.

First Vermilion Lake

Bow River (NP) (Redearth Creek to Banff Park east boundary)

Bull trout to 70 cm (4.0 kg)
Brown trout to 55 cm (1.5 kg)
Rainbow trout to 50
Brook trout to 50
Cutthroat trout to 50 cm
Whitefish to 35 cm

This section of the Bow flows from Redearth Creek to the east park boundary. It includes the townsite of Banff and is characterized by slower water and deep pools. Canoeists frequent the river throughout the summer and anglers can always be seen working the shoreline for a wide variety of trout, including rainbow, brook, cutthroat and bull, most in the 25–35 cm range. Downstream from Bow Falls, brown trout can be caught in good numbers. Brown trout from this section of the Bow River will average 30–40 cm in length. The pool at the confluence of the Spray River with the Bow has lots of potential.

Bow River

Echo Creek ponds (NP)

51°11'04"N 115°35'15"W
Brook trout to 25 cm
Rainbow trout to 25 cm
Bull trout to 35 cm

The network of beaver ponds on Echo Creek that connects the Vermilion Lakes with the Bow River holds the promise of solitude due to difficult access and the guarantee of wet feet. Small brook and rainbow trout predominate, although bull trout are also present.

Whiskey Creek ponds (NP)

51°11'16"N 115°33'59"W
Brook trout to 25 cm
Rainbow trout to 25 cm

The maze of beaver ponds on Whiskey Creek is located between Banff townsite and the Trans-Canada Highway. Despite their proximity to the townsite, they see few anglers each season. The ponds hold small brook and rainbow trout.

Forty Mile Creek (NP)

Brook trout to 25 cm
Cutthroat trout to 25 cm
Rainbow trout to 25
Bull trout to 30 cm

Forty Mile Creek joins the Whiskey Creek pond complex north of Banff, after crossing under the Trans-Canada Highway just west of the Buffalo Paddock. Forty Mile Creek holds brook, cutthroat and bull trout, as well as the odd rainbow trout. ⊗ Be aware that the creek is closed to angling in the vicinity of the Banff townsite water intake. Check regulations.

Sundance Creek ponds (NP)

51°10'04"N 115°37'44"W
Brook trout to 25 cm
Cutthroat trout to 25 cm
Rainbow to 25 cm

This series of beaver dams extends for 3 km along Sundance Creek above its confluence with the Bow. The ponds are readily accessible from the Cave and Basin road. Small brook trout predominate with cutthroat and rainbow present as well.

Spray River (NP) (Downstream from Spray Lakes Reservoir)

Brook trout to 40
Brown trout to 45 cm
Rainbow trout to 40 cm
Cutthroat trout to 40 cm
Bull trout to 60 cm (3.0 kg)

The lower Spray River is a major tributary of the Bow River. It flows from the Spray Lakes Reservoir and joins the Bow just west of Banff. The river can be accessed for virtually its entire length from the Spray River Fire Road, which is closed to vehicle traffic. The lower Spray offers good fishing for cutthroat trout in its upper reaches. Further downstream, brook, rainbow and brown trout in the 25–35 cm range are the normal catch. Large bull trout can be taken on occasion along all stretches of the river.

Carrot Creek (NP)

Brown trout to 25 cm
Bull trout to 30 cm
Rainbow trout to 25 cm

Carrot Creek joins the Bow River 3 km west of the Banff Park Boundary. In its lower reaches, it holds bull, brown and rainbow trout in small sizes.

Cascade Sub-Region

The Cascade River and its accompanying fire road run directly through the heart of the Front Ranges. The southern end of the fire road meets the Lake Minnewanka Road approximately 1 km west of the lake itself and 5 km east of the Trans-Canada Highway overpass. Although the upper Cascade is very popular with outfitters, the area receives relatively few hikers each year because of the huge distances involved. Everyone entering the area should be aware that the Cascade Valley contains one of the highest concentrations of grizzly bears anywhere in the Rocky Mountains. All of the lakes in this Sub-Region require a significant hiking effort to be reached. What were most popular of the fisheries, including Elk, Mystic and Sawback lakes, are now closed to angling to protect native fish stocks.

■ Cascade River (NP)

Cutthroat trout to 35 cm
Brook trout to 35 cm
Rainbow trout to 30 cm
Bull trout to 60 cm (2.5 kg)
Whitefish to 30 cm

The Cascade River flows for over 35 km from headwaters before emptying into Lake Minnewanka. The Cascade River has innumerable excellent pools, and offers good fishing along its entire length. Cutthroat and brook trout in the 20–30 cm range will be the normal catch. The Cascade Fire Road, which is closed to vehicular travel, parallels the river for much of the distance and offers direct access. The lower sections of the river receive some fishing pressure, while the headwaters area is visited only by outfitters and seasoned backpackers.

Cascade River

☐ Stenton Pond (NP)

51°16'41"N 115°31'15"W
Brook trout to 20 cm

Stenton Pond is actually several small, shallow interconnected beaver ponds located alongside the Cascade Fire Road just over 2 km from the road's southern terminus on the Lake Minnewanka Road. The ponds hold small brook trout, few larger than 15 cm in length. Due to the shallow water, the fish are very wary and an abundance of shoreline vegetation and deadfall make fly fishing a difficult but interesting proposition.

■ Stony Creek (NP)

Cutthroat trout to 20 cm
Bull trout to 25 cm

Stony Creek is a major tributary of the Cascade River, and enters the Cascade approximately 15 km upstream from Lake Minnewanka. Fast-flowing Stony Creek holds both cutthroat and bull trout in small sizes and numbers.

☐ Stony Creek ponds (NP)

Brook trout to 25 cm

The Stony Creek ponds are located just over 2 km north of the bridge over Stony Creek on the Cascade Fire Road. Set in somewhat marshy surroundings between the fire road and the Cascade River, these beaver ponds at one time held a fair number of small brook trout. Reaching the ponds without getting wet will take some skill, as will casting to the easily spooked trout. Several of the ponds were damaged or destroyed by recent major flooding.

⊗ Cuthead Creek (NP)

Status: Closed to angling

Cuthead Creek enters the Cascade River approximately 20 km upstream from Lake Minnewanka. The creek is closed to angling.

■ Cuthead Lake (NP)

51°26'58"N 115°45'11"W
Cutthroat trout to 40 cm
Bull trout to 60 cm (2.0 kg)

Cuthead Lake lies in a secluded basin, far from civilization. The route to Cuthead Lake leaves the Cascade Fire Road 45 km north of Lake Minnewanka and ascends the Cuthead Creek drainage. From the fire road, the 4 km route to Cuthead Lake alternates between bushwhacking and game trail. Cuthead Lake's silted waters hold cutthroat trout averaging 25–30 cm in length as well as a few bull trout. Sparsely treed meadows around the lake offer ample room for fly casting.

Cuthead Lake

■ Bighorn Lake (NP)

51°27'53"N 115°38'35"W
Brook trout to 30 cm

Bighorn Lake is located in a barren cirque 4 km east of Cuthead Creek along an ill-defined trail. The route begins from the Cascade Fire Road, opposite Cuthead Lake valley. The trail winds its way through heavy timber, eventually emerging above treeline. The route then works its way steeply alongside Bighorn's tiny outlet creek, finally reaching the small basin holding the lake. The brook trout in Bighorn are reported to be small, most in the 20–25 cm range.

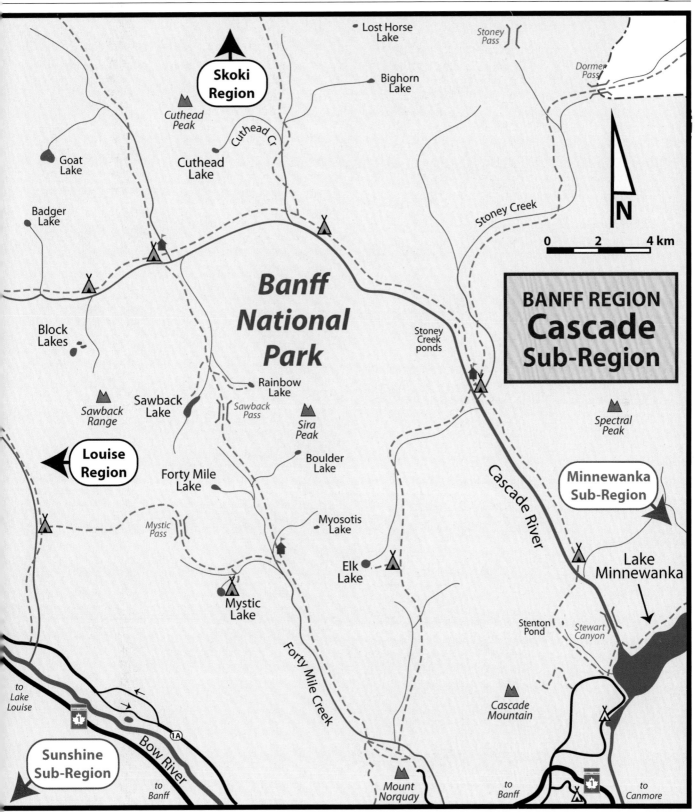

Block Lakes (NP)

(Upper lake) 51°22'15"N 115°50'35"W

Cutthroat trout to 40 cm

Quebec Red trout to 40 cm

The Block Lakes are located near the headwaters of the Cascade River and are set in a basin gouged high into the side of Block Mountain. The lakes are guarded by a 150 m–high cliff face and are only accessible to skilled climbers who register with the warden service before attempting the climb. A second ill-defined route, without a cliff, ascends from Johnston Creek above the Ink Pots. For explorers only. At one time, when Parks was dropping fish in every likely–looking body of water, the Block Lakes were stocked with exotic Quebec Red Trout. The Quebec Red Trout were able to reproduce and now populate the two lower lakes in the 20–30 cm range. Cutthroat trout averaging 25–35 cm are found in good numbers in the larger, upper Block Lake.

Badger Lake (NP)

51°24'14"N 115°51'37"W

Brook trout to 30 cm

Three kilometres of bushwhacking in a northerly direction from the upper Cascade River/Block Lakes campsite leads to isolated Badger Lake. The final half kilometre into Badger's rockbound surroundings requires negotiating a 150 m cliff. Registration with the warden service is mandatory. Difficult and dangerous access, along with recent reports indicating that few trout remain in Badger Lake will keep it off most anglers' "must-visit" list.

Cutthroat Trout Recovery Project

Native cutthroat trout are a threatened species in the mountain parks. Cutthroat populations have been decimated over the past 100 years by the introduction of non-native species including rainbow and brook trout. In some waters cutthroat have interbred with rainbow trout to produce hybrid cut-bows. The severe decline in numbers of the purebred, native cutthroat trout population resulted in Parks Canada making significant changes in policy and in regulations to protect the native species. A number of cutthroat-bearing lakes have been closed to angling. Regulations in Banff, Kootenay and Yoho National Parks have introduced zero possession limits for all species of fish (other than lake trout in Lake Minnewanka). In 2015, Parks Canada undertook a special project to reintroduce cutthroat to Rainbow Lake in Banff National Park. Rainbow trout in the lake were removed. Parks Canada then invited a dozen lucky Trout Unlimited volunteers to helicopter into Sawback Lake to catch cutthroat trout that would then be airlifted into Rainbow Lake. The project was deemed a success and native cutthroat trout now inhabit Rainbow Lake.

⊗ Sawback Lake (NP)

51°21'01"N 115°46'06"W

Status: Closed to angling

Cutthroat trout

Sawback Lake was known for many years for its fine cutthroat trout fishery. To ensure the health of the native cutthroat trout, Sawback Lake and its outlet creek have been closed to angling.

Sawback Lake

⊗ Rainbow Lake (NP)

51°21'28"N 115°43'46"W

Status: Closed to angling

Cutthroat trout

Rainbow Lake sits in a prominent bowl a little over a kilometre north and east of Forty Mile Summit. As its name suggests, the lake held rainbow trout at one time. The rainbow trout were removed from the lake and it was restocked with cutthroat trout from nearby Sawback Lake in a unique project in 2015. Rainbow Lake is closed to angling.

Rainbow Lake

Forty Mile Creek (NP) (Headwaters to Mt. Norquay)

Cutthroat trout to 25 cm

Brook trout to 25 cm

Whitefish to 25 cm

Bull trout to 30 cm

The upper sections of Forty Mile Creek flowing between Forty Mile Summit (Sawback Pass) and Mt. Norquay hold cutthroat trout in small sizes and may hold brook and bull trout and whitefish as well. Hiking trails parallel Forty Mile Creek for its entire length and offer easy access to the numerous pools.

Forty Mile Creek

Boulder Lake (NP)

51°21'06"N 115°42'36"W

Status: Doubtful

Diminutive Boulder Lake sits in a desolate cirque at an elevation of nearly 2400 metres and can be reached by following game trails along its outlet creek from the south side of Forty Mile Summit. The cutthroat trout once stocked in the lake either no longer exist or are present in very small numbers.

Forty Mile Lake (NP)

51°19'04"N 115°45'07"W

Brook trout to 30 cm

Forty Mile Lake is nestled in a high sub-alpine valley west of the main Forty Mile Creek valley. The lake sees very few human visitors each year. The most direct access is via ill-defined and often non-existent game trails that work up the small outlet creek, which enters Forty Mile Creek approximately 3 km above the Mystic Pass trail junction. The lake itself contains a small population of brook trout, few larger than 25 cm in length.

◼ Myosotis Lake (NP)

51°19'13"N 115°39'59"W

Status: Doubtful

Tiny Myosotis Lake is set in a barren cirque 2 km east of the upper Forty Mile Creek valley. The lake was stocked a number of years ago with rainbow trout and a few may have survived through natural propagation. Access is for route finders armed with map and compass.

⊗ Mystic Lake (NP)

51°16'42"N 115°44'58"W

Status: Closed to angling

Cutthroat trout

Bull trout

Mystic Lake is located 17 km from Johnston Canyon and 19 km from Mt. Norquay, near the midway point on the Mystic Pass trail. The lake is set in a sheltered basin 3 km below Mystic Pass. In the past, numerous hikers and horse parties made their way to Mystic Lake each year for the outstanding fishing. In an effort to protect native species, Mystic Lake and its outlet creek are closed to angling.

Mystic Lake

⊗ Elk Lake (NP)

51°17'17"N 115°39'21"W

Status: Closed to angling

Cutthroat trout

The impressive east face of Mt. Brewster towers over the pretty larch-filled basin containing Elk Lake. Elk Lake is located 14 km by trail from the Mt. Norquay parking area and was a favourite with Banff anglers for many years. As part of the master plan to safeguard native cutthroat trout, angling is not permitted in Elk Lake.

Elk Lake

Sunshine Sub-Region

The Sunshine Village ski area and its flower-filled meadows are the hub of the Sub-Region. Sunshine Village is accessed from the Bourgeau parking area via a gondola. If the gondola is not operating, it is a steep 6 km road walk to reach Sunshine Village. Most day hikers make their way through the Sunshine Meadows to nearby Rock Isle, Larix and Grizzly lakes, although return trips to Howard Douglas and Citadel lakes are well within a day's limit for most hikers. Sunshine Village is also the trailhead for the Citadel Pass route to Mount Assiniboine, with the Lake Magog campground 27 km distant.

☐ Bourgeau Lake (NP)

51°08'07"N 115°47'27"W

Brook trout to 40 cm

Bourgeau Lake is set in a deep, rocky amphitheatre just over 7 km by trail from the Trans-Canada Highway. In the past, numerous large trout were taken from Bourgeau, and the lake became very popular with anglers, which inevitably led to a decline in the quality of fishing. Today, most brook trout will only average 20–30 cm in length and are in very limited supply. Flies and lures are both productive at Bourgeau Lake. Fly casting room is adequate along much of the shoreline, although rocks will take the point off the hook of many a disgruntled fly fisher with poor back casting skills.

Bourgeau Lake

◼ Wolverine Creek (NP)

Status: Doubtful

Wolverine Creek is the outlet stream for Bourgeau Lake. It normally does dries up in the upper sections and does not connect to the lake itself. It's unlikely there are any fish in the upper sections, but there may be some trout in the extreme lower section near where it enters the Bow River.

◼ Harvey Lake (NP)

51°07'59"N 115°48'13"W

Status: Devoid of fish

Harvey Lake is the tiny body of water set in a high pass above Bourgeau Lake. It can be reached by rough trails that lead up the steep valley from Bourgeau Lake. Harvey Lake contains no fish.

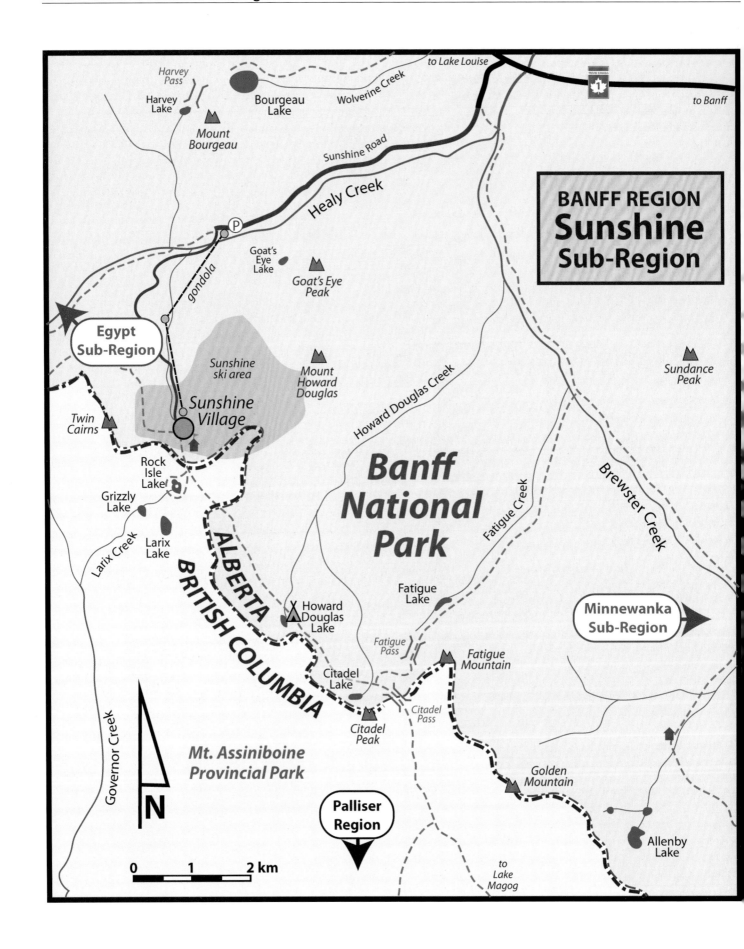

? Goat's Eye Lake (NP)

51°06'21"N 115°45'13"W

Status: Unknown

Goat's Eye Lake is a small tarn hidden high on the flank of Goat's Eye Peak. The lake was stocked in the past with rainbow trout. Few people make their way to the lake, and no reliable reports exist as to whether or not trout are still present in the lake. A difficult scramble up the side of Goat's Eye Peak generally deters most anglers.

✪ Rock Isle Lake (BC)

51°03'45"N 115°46'59"W

Status: Closed to angling

Brook trout

Picturesque Rock Isle Lake is located in the beautiful Sunshine Meadows just over a kilometre from Sunshine Village. The lake is closed to angling due to its use as water supply for the Village.

Rock Isle Lake

✪ Larix Lake (BC)

51°03'16"N 115°47'11"W

Status: Closed to angling

Brook trout

Larix Lake lies in a quiet, meadowed basin less than a kilometre below Rock Isle Lake. Larix Lake is closed to angling.

✪ Grizzly Lake (BC)

51°03'29"N 115°47'40"W

Status: Closed to angling

Brook trout

Grizzly Lake is a small, round body of water that is reached by following the outlet stream of Rock Isle Lake. Grizzly Lake is closed to angling.

⛺ Howard Douglas Lake (NP)

51°02'09"N 115°44'48"W

Brook trout to 40 cm

Howard Douglas Lake is located on the Citadel Pass trail 6 km from Sunshine Village. Howard Douglas is often overlooked by anglers on their way to the more renowned fishing waters of Mount Assiniboine Provincial Park. The waters of Howard Douglas hold a good number of small brook trout, most ranging from 15–25 cm, although trout reaching 40 cm are caught on occasion. The fish are equally distributed throughout the lake and can be taken from virtually any location.

Howard Douglas Lake

Howard Douglas Lake brook trout

⛺ Citadel Lake (aka Sunset Lake) (NP)

51°01'12"N 115°43'23"W

Rainbow trout to 55 cm (1.5 kg)

Citadel Lake lies less than half a kilometre south of the Citadel Pass trail and is hidden by a small knoll. Citadel Lake is seldom seen, much less visited by most hikers. The lake is set in a small basin with half its shoreline comprised of scree and half of meadow, the latter offering an abundance of fly casting spots. Heavily-spotted rainbow trout in the lake average 30–35 cm in length.

Citadel Lake

Citadel Lake rainbow trout

Jason Godkin photo

165

■ **Brewster Creek (NP)**
Bull trout to 30 cm
Cutthroat trout to 25 cm
Brewster Creek is paralleled by horse trails for its entire length, and possesses many kilometres of fishable waters. Small bull and cutthroat trout can be taken from most stretches, with brook and rainbow trout also taken occasionally in the lower reaches.

■ **Fatigue Lake (NP)**
51°02'22"N 115°41'38"W
Status: Devoid of fish
Fatigue Lake is set in an alpine basin beneath Fatigue Peak. The lake is reached by following ill-defined game trails up a tributary branching west off the Fatigue Pass trail. Rarely visited due to its isolated location, Fatigue Lake was once stocked with rainbow trout, but it is reported they no longer exist in the lake.

■ **Allenby Lake (NP)**
50°59'30"N 115°37'49"W
Rainbow trout to 35 cm
Allenby Lake is set in a hanging valley, 2 km west of the Brewster Creek-Allenby Pass trail to Mt. Assiniboine Provincial Park and is overlooked by most hikers. Rumours persist that Allenby Lake holds good numbers of rainbow trout in the 20–30 cm range.

Egypt Lake Sub-Region

Egypt Lake is located at the core of one of Banff National Park's most popular backpacking destinations. The Egypt Lake vicinity is crowded with hikers from mid-June through the end of September. The main access into this superb area begins at the Bourgeau Parking Lot and follows the 13 km trail over Healy Pass to Egypt Lake. Lakes within the immediate Egypt Lake complex include Egypt, Scarab, Mummy, Pharaoh, Black Rock and Sphinx. Shadow Lake at the northern end of the Egypt Lake area is accessed by a 14 km trail that begins at Redearth parking lot on the Trans-Canada Highway and which also serves as longer access to the Egypt Lake complex.

■ **Egypt Lake (NP)**
51°05'54"N 115°54'14"W
Brook trout to 40 cm
Cutthroat trout to 40 cm
Egypt Lake is located less than 1 km from the shelter and campground and is the most heavily fished lake of the area. Its deep, clear waters hold a good number of brook and cutthroat, most in the 25–35 cm range. The deep waters off the rockslide along the north shore generally hold the larger trout. Brook trout are in the majority, but both cutthroat and brookies can be taken from most spots, particularly around the area of the inlet creek that falls from Scarab Lake. The outlet pond and the outlet stream usually hold a few trout that can be spotted from shore, but due to their shallow habitat, the fish are very wary. Flies work well, but fly casting room is at a premium, so roll casting will be the order of the day from many locations. Lures are very effective in Egypt Lake, especially in the deep waters.

Tyler Ambrosi at Egypt Lake

■ **Scarab Lake (NP)**
51°05'57"N 115°55'02"W
Cutthroat trout to 40 cm
Scarab Lake is situated in a large basin above Egypt Lake, and is reached by following the steep trail that winds its way up the cliff band above Egypt's northwest corner. Silt from snowmelt accounts for Scarab's striking turquoise colour. The lake does not hold a large number of cutthroat trout, but they will average 25–35 cm in length. Scarab Lake's location near treeline ensures ample fly casting room. Due to the lake's high elevation and shaded position beneath Haiduk Peak, Scarab is often ice-covered well into July and spawning often occurs in late July.

Scarab Lake

□ **Mummy Lake (NP)**
51°05'21"N 115°54'49"W
Cutthroat trout to 50 cm
Mummy Lake can be reached either by the ill-defined and rocky trail from nearby Scarab Lake, or by a route which crosses the low pass northwest of Natalko Lake. Mummy Lake is long and narrow, and is set in a rocky, windswept valley located a few hundred metres above Scarab Lake. Its high elevation and absence of vegetation allow for fly casting around most of the shoreline. The lake is usually ice-covered until mid-July and spawning can occur as late as early August. The cutthroat trout in Mummy Lake are very limited in number, and average 30–35 cm in length.

Mummy Lake

◼ Pharaoh Creek (NP)
Brook trout to 25 cm
Cutthroat trout to 30 cm
The upper waters of Pharaoh Creek hold a fair number of trout downstream of the Egypt Lake outlet. For several kilometres Pharaoh Creek winds its way back and forth across open meadows. Brook trout in the 15–20 cm range are caught, as well as a few cutthroat trout.

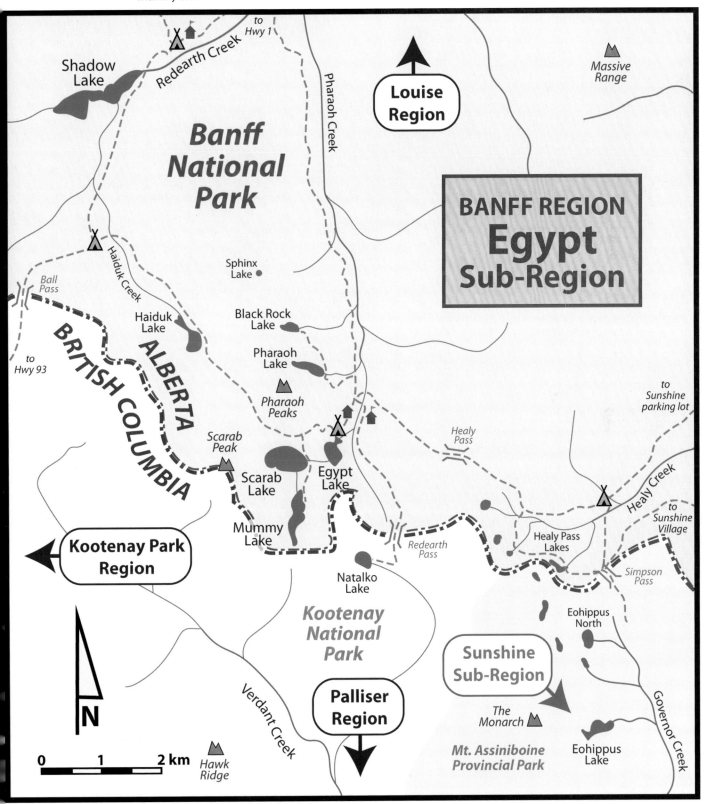

Shadow Lake

to Hwy 1

Redearth Creek

Pharaoh Creek

Louise Region

Massive Range

Banff National Park

BANFF REGION **Egypt Sub-Region**

Ball Pass

Haiduk Creek

Sphinx Lake

ALBERTA

BRITISH COLUMBIA

to Hwy 93

Haiduk Lake

Black Rock Lake

Pharaoh Lake

Pharaoh Peaks

Healy Pass

to Sunshine parking lot

Scarab Peak

Scarab Lake

Egypt Lake

Healy Creek

to Sunshine Village

Kootenay Park Region

Mummy Lake

Redearth Pass

Healy Pass Lakes

Simpson Pass

Natalko Lake

Kootenay National Park

Eohippus North

Sunshine Sub-Region

Governor Creek

N

0   1   2 km

Hawk Ridge

Verdant Creek

Palliser Region

The Monarch

Eohippus Lake

Mt. Assiniboine Provincial Park

☐ Pharaoh Lake (NP)

51°06'48"N 115°54'34"W

Cutthroat trout to 45 cm

Pharaoh, Black Rock and Sphinx lakes are located in successive side valleys north of Egypt Lake. The trail winds its way up the flank of Pharaoh Peak for just over a kilometre to the notch containing the deep, dark waters of Pharaoh Lake. The lake is set beneath the sheer cliffs of the Pharaoh Peaks. Scree slopes make up much of the shoreline, but there are a few spots that will permit a reasonable back cast for fly fishing. Cutthroat trout in the 30–35 cm range are present in limited numbers.

Pharaoh Lake

◢ Black Rock Lake (NP)

51°07'14"N 115°54'55"W

Cutthroat trout to 35 cm

Black Rock Lake lies one kilometre beyond Pharaoh Lake, and is set in a very similar basin as its neighbour. It is named for the dark cliffs above the west end of the lake. It holds good numbers of cutthroat trout averaging 20–25 cm in length. Trout can be seen well out into the lake due to the clarity of the water. Fly casting room is adequate along much of the shoreline. A few large boulders in the shallows along the north shore may tempt a few anglers to wade out in search of a better casting position.

Black Rock Lake cutthroat trout

Black Rock Lake

■ Sphinx Lake (NP)

51°07'47"N 115°55'30"W

Status: Devoid of fish

Tiny Sphinx Lake is situated in a small basin 2 km beyond Black

Rock Lake. Sphinx Lake at one time had a breeding population of cutthroat trout, but examination tends to indicate that no trout presently exist. A very poor and ill-defined trail leads past Black Rock Lake for those hardy souls wishing to check the lake out for themselves.

■ Natalko Lake (aka Talc Lake) (NP)

51°04'55"N 115°53'45"W

Brook trout to 35 cm

Natalko Lake is reached by following a 4 km trail south from the Egypt Lake. The lake itself is situated just within the boundary of Kootenay National Park. Natalko's waters are incredibly clear, even for a mountain lake, and as a result fish are easily spooked. Meadows form much of the shoreline, which allows plenty of room for fly casting. Although the lake holds plenty of brook trout averaging 25–30 cm, the wariness of the fish will surely test most angler's patience.

Natalko Lake

Jim Rennels photo

■ Healy Lakes (includes Square Lake) (NP)

51°05'27"N 115°51'46"W

Cutthroat trout to 25 cm

This series of interconnected ponds and small lakes is set in the beautiful meadows beneath the Monarch Ramparts southwest of Healy Pass. Access is by trail from the Bourgeau parking lot. The Healy Lakes contain small cutthroat trout. The size and number of trout varies with each lake, but few fish are larger than 15 cm in length. The marshy nature of the shoreline around most of the lakes will result in wet feet for most anglers.

Healy Pass Lakes from Healy Pass

■ Eohippus Lake (BC)

51°03'14"N 115°49'51"W

Rainbow trout to 40 cm

Eohippus Lake is a seldom-visited body of water nestled beneath the prominent east face of The Monarch. The most straightforward access involves hiking the crest of the Ramparts south from Healy Pass and dropping down to the lake from above. However, be aware that lingering snowpacks and dangerous cornices on the Ramparts prevent the use of this route until mid-summer. The lake is named for its outline's striking resemblance to a prehistoric species of horse. Rainbow trout are present in good numbers, and average 25–35 cm in length.

◼ Eohippus North (BC)

51°04'07"N 115°50'02"W
Rainbow trout to 35 cm
This unnamed lake a little over a kilometre north of Eohippus Lake holds a good population of small rainbow trout. The lake can be reached from either Eohippus Lake or from the Healy Pass Lakes.

◣ Haiduk Lake (NP)

51°07'07"N 115°56'29"W
Cutthroat trout to 50 cm
Secluded Haiduk Lake is situated 4 km northwest of Scarab Lake through Whistling Pass. It is also accessible by trail from Shadow Lake and Ball Pass. Haiduk Lake contains some fine cutthroat trout, with average fish being in the 25–35 cm range. Fishing is best along the scree slopes on the western side of the lake. The areas around the lake's several inlet creeks are also productive. Haiduk Lake is shaded much of the day by the high wall to the west and remains frozen into early July, with access trails remaining snowbound.

Haiduk Lake

Haiduk Lake cutthroat trout

◼ Shadow Lake (NP)

51°09'36"N 115°57'59"W
Cutthroat trout to 45 cm
Brook trout to 45 cm
Rainbow trout to 45 cm
Shadow Lake is a strikingly beautiful body of water, set in a forested valley beneath the east face of Mt. Ball. Shadow Lake is reached via the 14 km trail from Redearth Creek trailhead on the Trans-Canada Highway. Although it is the largest of the lakes in the Egypt/Sunshine complex, and in turn holds some good-sized trout, Shadow Lake has never gained a reputation for outstanding fishing. Trout in the lake will average 25–35 cm in length. Cutthroat and brook trout are caught with more regularity than rainbow, with the areas around inlet creeks being some of the better waters. The outlet bay also holds fish, particularly during the low light periods of early morning and late evening when fish enter the shallower waters to feed.

Shadow Lake

Jason Godkin photo

Shadow Lake brook trout

◼ Redearth Creek (NP)

Cutthroat trout to 25 cm
Brook trout to 25 cm
Rainbow trout to 25 cm
Redearth Creek flows from Shadow Lake to the Bow River. The creek holds cutthroat, brook and rainbow trout, although small in size and limited in number. Best fishing opportunities exist in the few kilometres of slow water below Shadow Lake and in the last half kilometre before Redearth Creek flows into the Bow River.

LOUISE REGION

This Region encompasses the heart of Banff National Park. Primary access is on the Trans-Canada Highway. The small village at Lake Louise provides limited tourist services. Hiking is required to reach most of the fishable waters in the Region. Three Sub-Regions make up the Louise Region. To the south is Castle Junction Sub-Region, which is highlighted by Taylor, Arnica and Twin lakes. North of Castle Junction is the Temple Sub-Region, which is centred on Lake Louise and Moraine Lake. To the north of Lake Louise is the Hector Sub-Region, which includes Hector and Bow lakes.

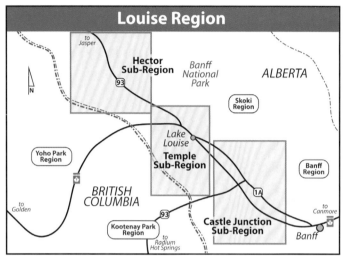

Castle Junction Sub-Region

The Castle Junction Sub-Region is centered on the impressive form of Castle Mountain and the junction of Highway 93 with the Trans-Canada Highway. This area has many fishing spots within easy hiking distance of major highways. Vista, Boom, Arnica and Twin lakes can all be reached by trails originating from Highway 93 (Banff-Windermere Highway). The Taylor Lake trail is accessed from the Trans-Canada Highway. Rockbound and Tower lakes have their trailheads on the Bow Valley Parkway. Luellen Lake is the only major backpacking destination in the Castle Junction Sub-Region, and its trail begins at Johnston Canyon on the Bow Valley Parkway.

◢ Taylor Lake (NP)

51°17'47"N 116°05'49"W
Cutthroat trout to 50 cm
Beautifully-coloured Taylor Lake is nestled in a high side valley 6 km by trail from the Trans-Canada Highway. Taylor Lake is a popular destination for day hikers throughout the summer months. The lake's icy waters hold plentiful cutthroat generally ranging from 25–35 cm in length. The area around the outlet is the most popular with anglers. For those willing to make the effort, the waters off the scree slopes on the south side of the lake are usually productive.

Taylor Lake cutthroat trout

Taylor Lake

◼ O'Brien Lake (aka Larch Lake) (NP)

51°17'12"N 116°04'56"W
Cutthroat trout to 50 cm
O'Brien Lake is located 2 km by trail from the outlet of Taylor Lake but is overlooked by most hikers visiting the area. O'Brien Lake holds feisty cutthroat trout in good numbers that average 30–40 cm in length. Great fishing and pleasant surroundings make O'Brien one of the gems of the entire Sub-Region. Flies work well at O'Brien, and sparse forest cover around much of the lake allows plenty of room for fly casting. Fish can be taken from most spots around the lake, although larger ones seem to prefer the deeper water off the scree slopes along the west shore. Much of the shoreline in the vicinity of the outlet creek is marshy, causing most dry-foot enthusiasts to avoid the area.

O'Brien Lake

O'Brien Lake cutthroat trout

◼ Boom Lake (NP)

51°15'48"N 116°05'54"W
Cutthroat trout to 50 cm
Cutthroat-rainbow hybrids to 50 cm
Boom Lake is a large body of water set beneath the impressive cliffs of Boom Mountain. The lake is reached on a 5 km hiking trail from Highway 93. Boom Lake holds cutthroat and cutthroat-rainbow hybrids averaging 25–35 cm in length. Patient anglers willing to work the shoreline will usually be rewarded with fish. During low light periods trout can often be seen feeding among the logs in the shallow waters around the outlet.

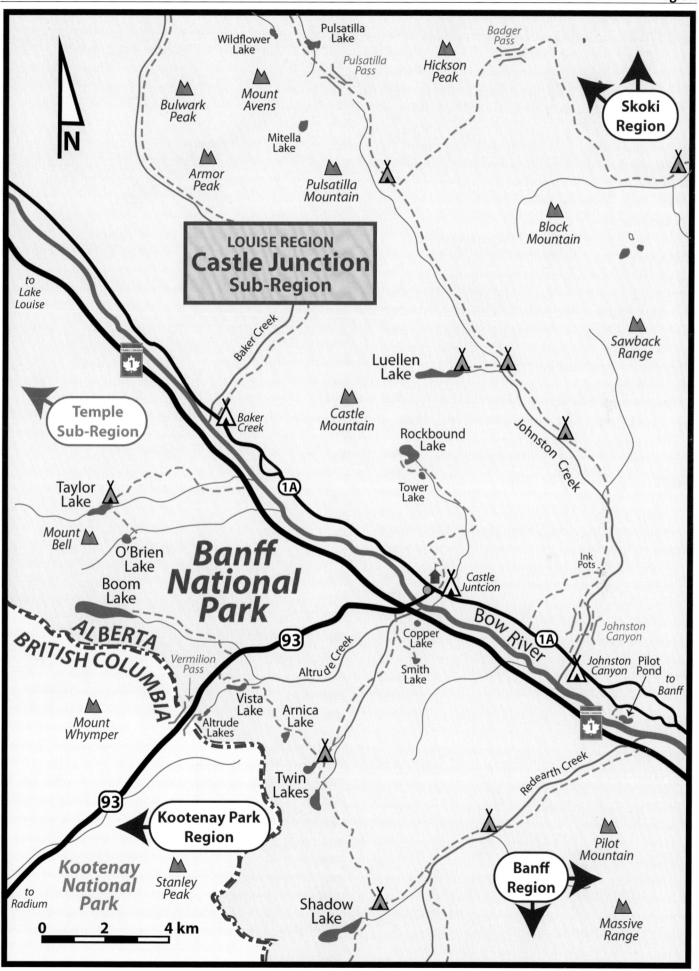

N

Wildflower Lake

Pulsatilla Lake

Pulsatilla Pass

Badger Pass

Hickson Peak

Skoki Region

Bulwark Peak

Mount Avens

Mitella Lake

Armor Peak

Pulsatilla Mountain

Block Mountain

LOUISE REGION
Castle Junction
Sub-Region

Baker Creek

Sawback Range

Luellen Lake

Johnston Creek

to Lake Louise

TRANS CANADA 1

Temple Sub-Region

Baker Creek

Castle Mountain

Rockbound Lake

Tower Lake

Taylor Lake

1A

Ink Pots

Mount Bell

O'Brien Lake

Boom Lake

Banff National Park

Castle Junction

Johnston Canyon

ALBERTA

BRITISH COLUMBIA

93

Vermilion Pass

Altrude Creek

Copper Lake

Smith Lake

Bow River

1A

Johnston Canyon

Pilot Pond

to Banff

Mount Whymper

Vista Lake

Arnica Lake

Altrude Lakes

TRANS CANADA 1

Redearth Creek

93

Kootenay Park Region

Twin Lakes

Pilot Mountain

Kootenay National Park

Stanley Peak

Banff Region

to Radium

Shadow Lake

Massive Range

0   2   4 km

Author with
Boom Lake
cutthroat

Boom Lake

Wayne Pierce photo (far left)

■ Boom Creek (NP)
Cutthroat trout to 35 cm
Boom Creek, between Boom Lake
and Highway 93, contains good
numbers of small cutthroat trout.

Boom Creek
cutthroat trout

□ Altrude Lakes (NP)
51°14'00"N 116°02'33"W
Cutthroat trout to 35 cm
The Altrude Lakes are passed daily by hundreds of vehicles on
nearby Highway 93. However, very few visitors stop and make
the short hike down to the lakes. The upper lake, which is visible
from the highway, likely no longer holds any trout. The lower
lake, located a few hundred metres beyond the upper lake, offers
relatively poor fishing for limited numbers of cutthroat averaging
20–30 cm in length. The best potential is in the area along the
distinctive drop-off zone.

■ Vista Lake (NP)
51°14'20"N 116°01'22"W
Brook trout to 40 cm
Cutthroat trout to 40 cm
Vista Lake sits at the bottom of a deep valley south of Highway
93. It is reached by a short, steep 1.5 km trail. Brook trout are
the dominant species in the lake, although cutthroat trout are
present as well. Looking down at the lake from the trailhead at
the highway, you will notice Vista's two-toned colouration. Those
anglers who make the trek down to the lake's shore are advised
to fish the zone along the obvious drop-off. Flies and lures both
work well in Vista Lake. Extensive submerged deadfall around
the shore offers good cover for trout.

■ Altrude Creek (NP)
Brook trout to 25 cm
Cutthroat trout to 25 cm
Bull trout to 35 cm
Altrude Creek, which flows from the Altrude Lakes through Vista
Lake before entering the Bow River, contains brook, cutthroat
and bull trout in small sizes. Fish can be taken along the entire
course of the creek. The best potential is in the lower reaches,
near the confluence with the Bow River.

▲ Arnica Lake (NP)
51°13'22"N 115°59'54"W
Cutthroat trout to 45 cm
Arnica Lake is set beneath the ominous cliffs of Storm Mountain's

north shoulder. It is reached by a 5 km trail from Highway 93.
Anglers heading for nearby Twin Lakes often overlook tiny
Arnica Lake. Despite the lake's small size, some fine cutthroat
trout inhabit Arnica's blue waters. Most trout taken will average
25–35 cm in length. Fly casting is a problem around much of
the shoreline because of trees. Arnica Lake is usually frozen into
early July because of its sheltered location.

Arnica Lake

■ Twin Lakes (NP)
(Upper) 51°12'42"N 115°59'09"W
(Lower) 51°12'06"N 115°58'53"W
Cutthroat trout to 40 cm
The striking east face of Storm Mountain rises above Twin
Lakes, and keeps the area in shadow much of the time. As a
result, the lakes thaw later in the year and area trails are usually
snowbound well into July. Access is via two 8 km-long hiking
trails beginning at the Vista Lake trailhead on Highway 93 or from
the Altrude Creek picnic site near Castle Junction. Both lakes
contain cutthroat trout in good numbers averaging 20–30 cm in
length. The Lower (south) Lake holds better potential for fly fishers as it
offers more backcasting room along its shoreline than the Upper Lake.

Upper Twin Lake

Lower Twin Lake

■ Copper Lake (NP)
51°15'37"N 115°55'22"W
Status: Devoid of fish
Copper Lake is a small lake set in a sinkhole, less than a hundred
metres from the busy Trans-Canada Highway. Despite its
proximity to the highway, Copper Lake saw little angling activity
in the past. A short trail leads from the Altrude picnic area to
Copper Lake. Rainbow trout once inhabited the lake, but failed
to reproduce.

◼ Smith Lake (NP)

51°14'59"N 115°55'32"W

Cutthroat trout to 35 cm
Brook trout to 35 cm

Tranquil Smith Lake is located less than 2 km by trail from the Altrude Creek picnic site. Smith Lake sits amid forested surroundings which will be a source of consternation for most fly fishers, as heavy tree cover makes its way down to the water's edge around much of the lake. The marshy nature of the lakeshore presents an additional barrier when trying to cast to the fish-holding waters. Cutthroat trout predominate, and average 20–30 cm in length. The occasional brook trout may also be present.

Smith Lake

☐ Tower Lake (NP)

51°18'27"N 115°55'30"W

Cutthroat trout to 30 cm

Tower Lake is located 8 km by steep trail from the Eisenhower Warden Station on the Bow Valley Parkway. It lies hidden behind the massive turrets of Castle Mountain. Tower Lake holds a very small population of cutthroat trout. Trout caught will average 20–25 cm in length. Although the trout can generally be seen from shore, they will be wary because of shallow waters and will be spooked by most casts. The terrain is favourable for fly casting, and the best tactic here is to cast a fly well ahead of fish as they cruise the shoreline for food.

Tower Lake

◼ Rockbound Lake (NP)

51°18'54"N 115°55'56"W

Brook trout to 45 cm
Cutthroat trout to 35 cm

Rockbound Lake sits in a rugged amphitheatre, less than 1 km above Tower Lake. Brook trout far outnumber cutthroat trout, with most fish taken averaging 20–30 cm. Fish can be seen from many locations along the shore in Rockbound's crystal-clear waters. Flies work well, and there is plenty of back casting room available.

Rockbound Lake

◮ Luellen Lake (NP)

51°20'26"N 115°54'55"W

Cutthroat trout to 55 cm (1.5 kg)

Luellen Lake is set in a long narrow valley 18 km by trail from Johnston Canyon. Luellen has been popular with backcountry fishermen for many years, on account of its plentiful supply of good-sized cutthroat. Most fish taken from the lake will average 30–40 cm in length. The lake is ringed by forest so roll casting will be the order of the day for those fly fishing. Anglers working up either the north or south side of the lake can generally sight schools of fish from shore. Due to less fishing pressure, the far end of the lake offers better prospects. ⊗ Luellen Lake below the markers and the outlet stream to the confluence with Johnston Creek is closed to angling.

Luellen Lake

Luellen Lake
cutthroat trout

Jason Godkin photo

173

■ **Pulsatilla Lake (NP)**
51°25'31"N 115°58'30"W
■ **Mitella Lake (NP)**
51°24'33"N 115°58'40"W
■ **Wildflower Lake (NP)**
51°25'41"N 115°59'34"W
Status: Devoid of fish
These three lakes located in the Pulsatilla Pass region are scenically spectacular but hold no angling potential. None of the three have ever been stocked and they contain no fish.

■ **Johnston Creek (NP)**
Cutthroat trout to 20 cm
Bull trout to 30 cm
Small cutthroat trout are plentiful in the upper Johnston Creek, above Johnston Canyon. The many fine pools are easily reached from the Luellen Lake/Pulsatilla Pass trail, which parallels Johnston Creek for its entire length. In the lower reaches of the creek, between Johnston Canyon and the Bow River, bull trout predominate.

■ **Ink Pots (NP)**
Status: Devoid of fish
The minuscule Ink Pots are a series of tiny, spring-fed pools that are found above Johnston Canyon and are accessed by a popular hiking trail. The Ink Pots contain no fish.

■ **Pilot Pond (aka Lizard Lake) (NP)**
51°13'44"N 115°48'48"W
Status: Devoid of fish
Pilot Ponds sits in a quiet, forest-encircled basin half a kilometre below the Bow Valley Parkway. The trailhead for Pilot Pond is at the viewpoint 1 km along the eastbound one-way section of the Bow Valley Parkway. Pilot Pond's clear waters at one time held plenty of solid rainbow and brook trout averaging 30–40 cm in length. Parks Canada's stocking policies changed in the late 1980s, and there have been no fish planted in Pilot Pond since then. Fish in Pilot Pond were unable to reproduce naturally, and it is very unlikely that any fish survive in the lake today.

Pilot Pond

■ **Bow River (NP) (Baker Creek to Redearth Creek)**
Cutthroat trout to 40 cm
Brook trout to 40 cm
Rainbow trout to 40 cm
Bull trout to 70 cm (5.0 kg)
Whitefish to 35 cm
The section of the Bow River flowing between Baker Creek and

Redearth Creek holds many kilometres of fishable waters, with its numerous deep pools. Cutthroat trout are usually taken in greater numbers by fly fishers than other species. Brook, rainbow and bull trout and whitefish are also present. Although this section of the river looks like it has enormous potential, it does not match the quality of the Bow River downstream from Canmore.

Temple Sub-Region

Fishing amid some of the most exquisite settings anywhere in the mountain world will tend to distract many anglers. Although more renowned for its scenery than for its fishing, this Region does possess a small number of good fishing spots. The Trans-Canada Highway heading west to Field and southeast to Banff is the area's main thoroughfare. As for fishing, the ever-popular Bow River can be reached from many locations along both highways. Despite the relatively poor angling offered by the twin jewels of Lake Louise and Moraine Lake, anglers are attracted to their shores each summer. Better fishing exists at lakes situated along the Bow Valley such as Mud, Lost, Kingfisher and Island, all accessible by short trails from the Trans-Canada Highway.

"If there is a lake, there needs to be fish in it."

Prior to 1900, over 90% of the nearly 1,500 lakes in the mountain parks were devoid of fish. Beginning in the 1920s, national park policy regarding the stocking of fish was altered and for the next 50 years fish were stocked in every likely looking body of water, which was virtually all of them. Unfortunately, native species that were already in some of these lakes were unable to compete with the introduced fish. Native species disappeared from many of their home ranges. Many different species of fish were introduced into park waters. Rivers and creeks connected to newly stocked lakes allowed the newly planted species to cover watersheds from end to end. In some lakes, native cutthroat and/or lake trout were stocked. In most other lakes, non-native rainbow or brook trout were the normal species stocked. However, many others, including Atlantic salmon, Quebec red trout, golden trout, splake (brook/lake trout hybrid), cisco, smallmouth bass and lake whitefish were introduced. Many plantings were not successful and the fish quickly died out. In many lakes, fish populations could only be maintained through regular plantings. In 1988, Parks Canada stopped its stocking program. Since then, many lakes have lost their fish populations entirely, as they were unable to reproduce in that particular environment. More recently, Parks Canada has initiated a policy of enhancing native fish stocks, in particular cutthroat trout and bull trout. Several successful projects in the past decade in the mountain parks have been geared towards this objective. New rules and regulations for angling in the mountain parks are designed to protect and preserve native populations.

■ **Lake Louise (NP)**
51°24'51"N 116°13'28"W
Whitefish to 35 cm
Bull trout to 70 cm (4.0 kg)
With Mts. Victoria and Lefroy providing a dazzling backdrop, Lake Louise's brilliant emerald-coloured waters have gained a world-wide reputation for scenic excellence. Unfortunately, Lake

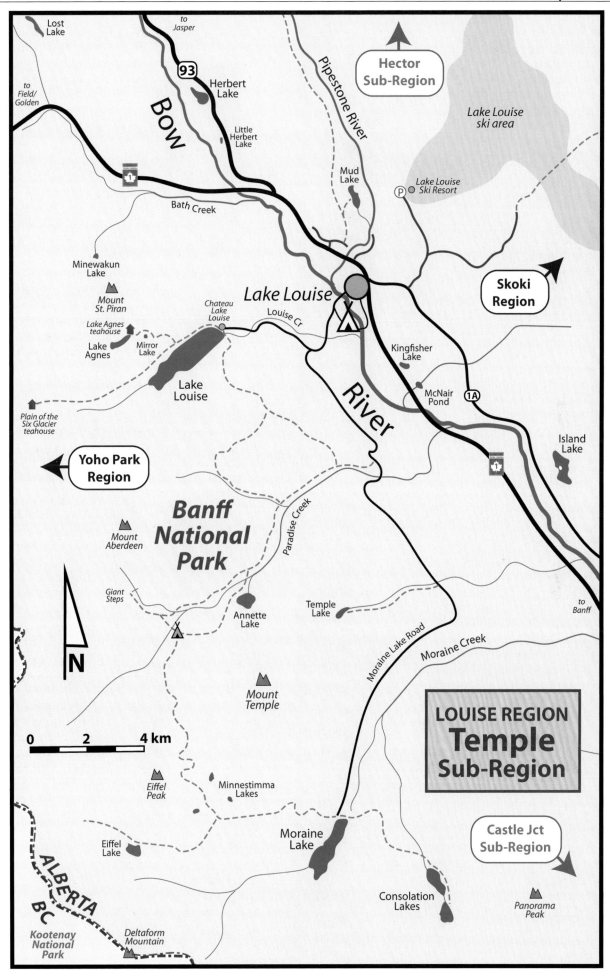

Louise's fishing is worthy of little acclaim. Whitefish in the 20–30 cm range and the occasional bull trout are all that are taken from Louise. It has been stocked in the past with splake, rainbow, cutthroat, and brook trout and it is possible, although unlikely, that very limited numbers of some of these species still exist. Canoes are available for rent during the summer.

Lake Louise

☐ Louise Creek (NP)
Cutthroat trout to 30 cm
Bull trout to 35 cm
This small creek flows from Lake Louise to the Bow River. Pools will hold a few trout in small sizes.

■ Mirror Lake (NP)
51°24'57"N 116°14'24"W
Status: Devoid of fish
This small lake along the trail from Lake Louise to Lake Agnes contains no fish and has never been stocked.

⊗ Lake Agnes (NP)
51°24'53"N 116°14'52"W
Status: Closed to angling
Brook trout/splake
Lake Agnes is nestled in a hanging valley behind the Beehives. It serves as the water supply for the Lake Agnes Teahouse and Chateau Lake Louise and is therefore closed to angling. The fish you see swimming in the lake are either brook trout or hybridized splake.

■ Minewakun Lake (NP)
51°25'49"N 116°15'19"W
Status: Devoid of fish
Tiny Minewakun Lake sits in a secluded basin beneath the north face of Mt. St. Piran, 2 km northwest of Lake Louise. The stocked brook trout stocked failed to reproduce and there are no fish in the lake

■ Moraine Lake (NP)
51°19'15"N 116°11'08"W
Bull trout to 70 cm (4.0 kg)
Cutthroat trout to 45
Moraine was widely recognized for many years as "the lake on the back of the Canadian twenty dollar bill." Today, it is one of the main tourist attractions in the region, rivaled only by Lake Louise itself. Fishing is very slow in Moraine Lake. There are small numbers of cutthroat in the 25–35 cm range and the occasional

bull trout of 50 cm or more in Moraine Lake's appealing turquoise waters. Canoes are available for rent at the lake during summer months.

Moraine Lake

■ Consolation Lakes (NP)
51°18'57"N 116°09'10"W
Brook trout to 40 cm
Cutthroat trout to 40 cm [lower lake only]
The beautiful Consolation Lakes are located 3 km by trail from the Moraine Lake parking lot. The lakes are set in a secluded subalpine valley beneath Mt. Babel. Both lakes contain brook trout averaging 20–30 cm in length, the lower lake also holds a few cutthroat trout in the same size range. The large boulders at the lower lake's outlet provide good casting platforms. Fish are found in the outlet creek in good numbers.

Lower Consolation Lake

Rachel Olson photo

Eiffel Lake

■ Eiffel Lake (NP)
51°19'16"N 116°14'38"W
Status: Devoid of fish
Eiffel Lake sits in the middle of barren Desolation Valley and is 6 km by trail from the Moraine Lake parking area. Eiffel Lake has never been stocked and contains no fish.

■ Minnestimma Lakes (NP)
51°20'03"N 116°13'16"W
Status: Devoid of fish
This series of shallow tarns in Larch Valley has never been stocked and is devoid of fish.

☐ Moraine Creek (NP)
Brook trout to 25 cm
Cutthroat trout to 25 cm
Bull trout to 30 cm

The outlet for Moraine Lake contains brook and cutthroat trout that are most plentiful in the vicinity of the confluence with Babel Creek. On the lower part of Moraine Creek, within a kilometre of the Bow River, limited numbers of small brook and cutthroat as well as bull trout can be taken.

⊗ Babel Creek (NP)
Status: Closed to angling
This small tributary of Moraine Creek is closed to angling.

◼ Temple Lake (NP)
51°21'52"N 116°10'54"W
Status: Doubtful
Diminutive Temple Lake is located on the eastern flank of magnificent Mt. Temple and is seldom visited by hikers or anglers. It is reached by following a rough trail on the banks of its outlet stream. The lake was stocked in the past with both rainbow and brook trout but it is unlikely that any fish remain in the lake.

◼ Lake Annette (NP)
51°22'00"N 116°12'34"W
Status: Devoid of fish
Lake Annette sits directly below the foreboding north face of Mt. Temple, in the heart of Paradise Valley. Its deep, dark waters at one time held a limited number of cutthroat and rainbow trout. Reproductive success in the lake was always suspect and no trout remain in the lake.

Lake Annette

◻ Paradise Creek (NP)
Cutthroat trout to 25 cm
Bull trout to 25 cm
Paradise Creek flows through the entire length of Paradise Valley. It contains small cutthroat in the middle section, between the Giant Steps and the Moraine Lake Road. It holds small cutthroat and bull trout in the lower reaches, near its confluence with the Bow River.

◼ Bow River (NP) (Pipestone River to Baker Creek)
Cutthroat trout to 40 cm
Brook trout to 40 cm
Rainbow trout to 40 cm
Bull trout to 70 cm (4.0 kg)
Whitefish to 35 cm
This section of the Bow River is accessible from both the Trans-Canada and the Bow Valley Parkway. The river contains some really fine-looking stretches of fishable water, although numbers

of trout are not high. Cutthroat and brook trout predominate in this section of the Bow River, although a variety of fish are present.

Bow River

◼ Island Lake (NP)
51°23'33"N 116°06'49"W
Status: Doubtful
Shallow Island Lake, located just east of the Bow Valley Parkway, has been stocked in the past with a variety of trout, none of which have been able to take hold. Most reports indicate that Island Lake is devoid of fish.

◻ McNair Pond (NP)
51°24'25"N 116°09'27"W
Cutthroat trout to 30 cm
Rainbow trout to 30 cm
Brook trout to 30 cm
McNair Pond is situated alongside the Bow Valley Parkway just east of the Trans-Canada/Parkway junction. The pond was formed during highway construction that resulted in the damming of a small creek. Much of McNair Pond's shoreline consists of dead trees that allow for very little fly casting room. Cutthroat and rainbow trout from 15–25 cm in length are likely present, with the occasional brook trout taken as well.

McNair Pond

☐ Kingfisher Lake (NP)
51°24'37"N 116°09'44"W
Brook trout to 35 cm
Rainbow trout to 35 cm

Kingfisher Lake is reached by a short 300 m trail from the Trans-Canada Highway. Brook trout averaging 20–30 cm in length are caught in greater number than rainbow trout in Kingfisher Lake. A wide margin of shallow water along with heavy forest cover around the shore makes Kingfisher unpopular with most fly fishing enthusiasts. However, casting distance is significantly reduced during low light conditions when trout enter the shallower waters to feed.

Kingfisher
Lake

◩ Mud Lake (NP)
51°26'28"N 116°10'36"W
Status: Doubtful

Mud Lake is located west of the Trans-Canada Highway in the Pipestone River drainage, and sits amid forested surroundings. Mud Lake was stocked at various times with cutthroat, rainbow and brook trout. Fish populations were dependent on regular plantings and it is doubtful that any fish remain in the lake.

◼ Pipestone River (NP)
Cutthroat trout to 35 cm
Bull trout to 55 cm (1.5 kg)
Whitefish to 30 cm

The Pipestone River flows southwest from its headwaters, in alpine meadows below Pipestone Pass, to Lake Louise where it joins the Bow River. It holds small cutthroat and the occasional bull trout over its entire length.

Pipestone
River

◼ Herbert Lake (NP)
51°27'36"N 116°13'21"W
Status: Devoid of fish

Herbert Lake is a popular roadside picnic spot along the Icefields Parkway. Herbert Lake's crystal-clear waters at one time held some nice brook trout. As with other nearby lakes, reproductive success was poor and no fish remain in the lake today.

Herbert Lake

⊗ Little Herbert Lake (NP)
51°27'05"N 116°12'59"W
Status: Closed to angling
Rainbow trout

Little Herbert Lake is little more than a roadside pond, located less than a kilometre south of Herbert Lake on the western side of the Icefields Parkway. Little Herbert Lake is closed to angling.

◼ Lost Lake (NP)
51°28'25"N 116°16'31"W
Status: Devoid of fish

Lost Lake is a seldom-visited body of water located on the north side of the Trans-Canada Highway, 2 km east of Kicking Horse Pass. It is a very shallow lake completely encircled by forest. Lost Lake was stocked in the past with cutthroat and brook trout, both of which failed to reproduce. As it has not been stocked in recent years, it is highly doubtful that any fish remain.

Hector Sub-Region

There are some excellent backcountry fishing opportunities in this Sub-Region, which is characterized by glaciers and rugged mountains. The Icefields Parkway runs through the middle of the Sub-Region paralleling the Bow River and passing close to popular Bow Lake. Farther south, a short spur trail leads from the Icefields Parkway down to Hector Lake. The Fish Lakes area, which includes nearby Moose and Pipestone lakes, is a favourite of backpackers. Another area popular with hikers is Dolomite Pass, which contains Helen, Katherine and Dolomite lakes.

◼ Bow Lake (NP)

51°40'27"N 116°27'36"W

Lake trout to 75 cm (5.0 kg)
Bull trout to 75 cm (5.0 kg)
Cutthroat trout to 55 cm (1.5 kg)
Rainbow trout to 55 cm (1.5 kg)
Whitefish to 40 cm

Bow Lake has been long-time favourite of anglers due to its roadside location and has consequently suffered a decline in the quality of fishing over the years. However, large lake and bull trout are still present in the lake and determined anglers can be rewarded with fish averaging 35–45 cm in length. Trolling is the standard angling method at Bow Lake. Areas around inlet creeks usually produce well as do the "narrows" where Bow Lake tapers down to Bow River width. Num-ti-jah Lodge, its bright red roof visible from the highway, provides lakeside accommodations and canoe rentals.

Bow Lake

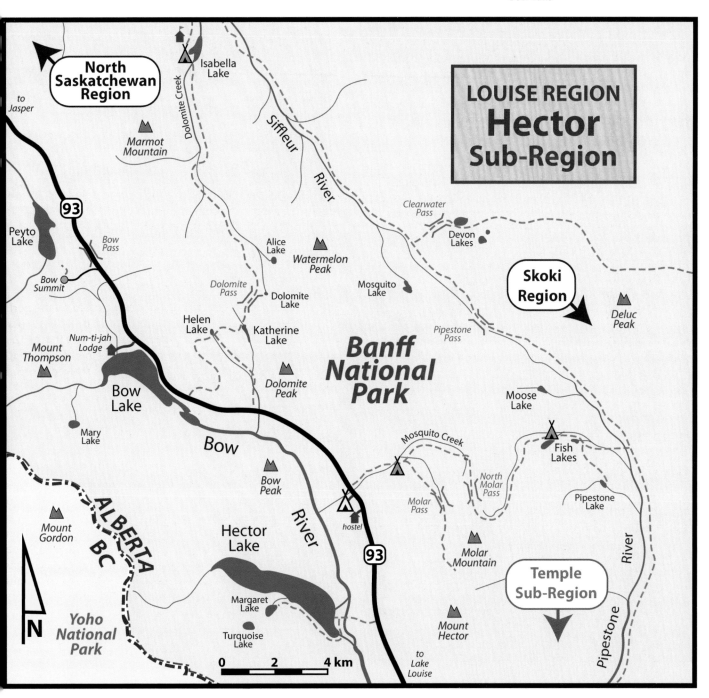

⊡ Mary Lake (NP)
51°34'47"N 116°22'31"W
Status: Unknown
Mary Lake is the small tarn hidden behind Crowfoot Mountain. It is 5 km distant from Bow Lake and remains a mystery to most anglers due to its isolated location. Mary Lake has been stocked in the past with both cutthroat and brook trout. The reproductive success of the trout in Mary Lake has never been determined, and reliable reports are not available.

⊗ Bow River (NP) (Bow Lake to Hector Lake)
Status: Closed to angling
▪ Bow River (NP) (Hector Lake to Pipestone River)
Cutthroat trout to 40 cm
Brook trout to 40 cm
Rainbow trout to 40 cm
Bull trout to 70 cm (4.0 kg)
Whitefish to 35 cm
The section of the Bow River flowing between Bow Lake and Hector Lake is closed to fishing. The Bow River from the outlet of Hector Lake downstream to the Pipestone River offers mediocre fishing at best. As the water clears and levels begin to drop in mid-summer, cutthroat, rainbow and brook trout in the 20-30 cm range can be taken. Although this stretch of the Bow possesses an abundance of fine pools, fish are less numerous than farther downstream and many anglers will be disappointed after working likely looking waters without positive results.

▪ Hector Lake (NP)
51°35'11"N 116°21'33"W
Lake trout to 75 cm (5.0 kg)
Bull trout to 75 cm (5.0 kg)
Cutthroat trout to 50 cm (1.5 kg)
Brook trout to 50 cm (1.5 kg)
Whitefish to 40 cm
Although it is only 2 km by trail from the Icefields Parkway, and noted for its splendid setting, Hector Lake receives relatively little pressure from visitors each summer. The trail to Hector Lake access includes a tricky ford of the Bow River. Hector Lake is a large lake by mountain standards, and is an imposing sight to those shorebound. Its silted waters hold a variety of fish, including large lake and bull trout. Areas around major inlet creeks and the lake's outlet hold the most potential for anglers.

Hector Lake

▪ Margaret Lake (NP)
51°39'01"N 116°30'12"W
Brook trout to 40
Cutthroat trout to 40 cm
Margaret Lake lies hidden in a quiet side valley south of Hector Lake. Access is difficult including two fords of the Bow River and a tedious hike along the south shore of Hector Lake. This keeps the number of anglers to a bare minimum each season. The lake's clear waters reportedly hold brook trout in the 25–35 cm range, with a few cutthroat trout present as well.

Margaret Lake (foreground) and Hector Lake (background)

⊡ Turquoise Lake (NP)
51°34'22"N 116°23'27"W
Status: Unknown
The beautifully coloured waters of Turquoise Lake are set in a rocky basin guarded by high cliffs, and are seldom seen by anglers. Intrepid individuals attempting to reach Turquoise from Lake Margaret are required to register out with the warden service, due to the exposed and dangerous nature of the climb. The lake was stocked in the past with splake, and although fish may still exist, very few accurate details concerning the lake are available.

▪ Mosquito Pond (NP)
51°39'34"N 116°15'20"W
Status: Devoid of fish
This small pond is located below North Molar Pass on the Fish Lakes trail. It generally serves as a watering hole for thirsty hikers. Mosquito Pond was stocked in the past with rainbow trout, of which none remain.

⊗ Fish Lakes (NP)
(Upper) 51°38'31"N 116°11'59"W
Status: Both lakes closed to angling
Cutthroat trout
The two Fish Lakes (Upper and Lower) are located 15 km by trail from the Icefields Parkway and are set in an open subalpine valley below North Molar Pass. The area is popular with backpackers who crowd the Fish Lakes campsite during summer months. The lakes are closed to angling to protect native cutthroat trout stock.

Lower Fish Lake

Moose Lake

■ Pipestone Lake (Deer Lake) (NP)

51°37'36"N 116°09'04"W

Cutthroat trout to 45 cm

Pipestone Lake is located 2 km southeast of Little Fish Lake along an ill-defined trail. It is an easy half-day excursion for anglers based at the Fish Lakes. Pipestone Lake holds plenty of cutthroat trout averaging 25–35 cm in length. Flies are very effective, and fly casting room is available at numerous locations around the lake.

Pipestone Lake

▲ Moose Lake (NP)

51°39'49"N 116°12'08"W

Cutthroat trout to 40 cm

Moose Lake is located on a bench amid mixed forest and meadow west of the Pipestone River. It can be reached by a 5 km trail from the Fish Lakes campground. Moose Lake's silty, green waters hold an abundance of cutthroat trout, mostly in the 20–30 cm range. Moose's cutthroat trout are easy to catch and offer good sport, especially for anglers who haven't yet fully mastered their casting skills. For those fly fishing, there is ample backcasting room around most of the lake.

Moose Lake cutthroat trout

⊗ Mosquito Lake (NP)

51°42'08"N 116°17'19"W

Status: Closed to angling

Mosquito Lake is set in alpine surroundings on the northwest side of Pipestone Pass, near the headwaters of the Siffleur River. A 2 km trek over open ground from the main Pipestone Pass trail leads to the lake, which usually remains frozen until mid-July. Mosquito Lake is part of the closure on all waters in the Siffleur and Clearwater River watersheds.

⊗ Siffleur River (NP) (Headwaters to national park boundary)

Status: Closed to angling

The Siffleur River flows northwest through a long, wide valley from the lofty heights of Pipestone Pass. The Siffleur River is closed to angling.

▲ Isabella Lake (NP)

51°51'47"N 116°25'23"W

Rainbow trout to 60 cm (2.0 kg)

Bull trout to 60 cm (2.0 kg)

Picturesque Isabella Lake, which has Dolomite Creek as both its inlet and outlet, stands out as the region's hidden treasure in terms of angling. As it is infrequently visited due to long approach routes, the quality of angling in Isabella Lake should remain high. The lake's silted waters hold plenty of rainbow trout in the 30–40 cm range. Larger trout are present in substantial numbers. Although rainbow trout can be taken from most spots around the lake, the area around the inlet usually proves to be the most productive. Flies and lures are both effective.

Isabella Lake rainbow trout

Isabella Lake

Jim Rennels photo

⊗ Dolomite Creek (NP)
Status: Closed to angling
Dolomite Creek, as a tributary of the Siffleur River, is closed to angling.

◼ Alice Lake (NP)
51°42'52"N 116°22'28"W
Status: Devoid of fish
Alice Lake is located in a stark, rocky basin above Dolomite Creek, and has never been stocked. The lake contains no fish.

◼ Dolomite Lake (NP)
51°41'42"N 116°22'41"W
Status: Devoid of fish
The striking blue waters of tiny Dolomite Lake are set in the flowered alpine meadows of Dolomite Pass. Few anglers ever make their way to Dolomite Lake. Although rainbow trout were stocked in the past, no fish remain in this tiny pond.

Dolomite Lake

◼ Katherine Lake (NP)
51°41'15"N 116°23'33"W
Cutthroat trout to 40 cm
The long, narrow form of Lake Katherine sits amid treeless surroundings just south of Dolomite Pass 8 km by trail from the Icefields Parkway. Due to its alpine environment, Lake Katherine is usually frozen into July. The lake's sparkling blue waters hold plenty of uniquely marked cutthroat trout in the 25–35 cm range. The waters in the vicinity of the several inlet creeks hold trout. Around most of the lake, the bottom drops off quickly, and a wet fly fished deep usually attracts some attention. With no tree cover, fly casting room is available from every location.

Katherine Lake

Katherine Lake cutthroat trout

◮ Helen Lake (NP)
51°41'08"N 116°24'48"W
Brook trout to 35 cm
Delicate Lake Helen is set in an appealing alpine meadow, 6 km by trail from the Icefields Parkway. Brook trout in the 20–30 cm range inhabit Helen's translucent green waters in fair numbers. Fish can generally be taken within a few metres of shore. If wind and light conditions are ideal, fish can be seen cruising about for food. Flies work well, and fly casting room is available around the entire lake.

Helen Lake

Helen Lake brook trout

⊗ Helen Creek (NP)
Status: Closed to angling
Helen Creek, which flows from Helen Lake to the Bow River, is closed to angling.

182

SKOKI REGION

The Region immediately east of Lake Louise is highlighted by some outstanding backcountry. Skoki Valley with its network of sparkling lakes and alpine meadows has been popular with hikers and anglers alike for almost 100 years. Beyond Skoki Valley is the remote Front Ranges area. This includes the drainages of the upper Red Deer, Clearwater and Panther rivers. Access to the Region is by trail only. Angling opportunities include Baker, Ptarmigan, Redoubt, Douglas and Red Deer lakes as the most promising locations.

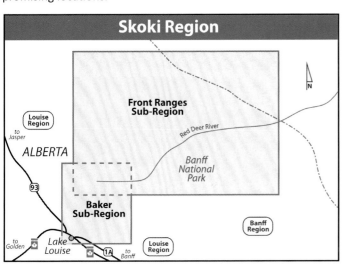

Baker Sub-Region

The main access into Skoki Valley begins at Lake Louise Ski Resort. It is a 15 km hike to Skoki Lodge, a historic backcountry chalet that is available by reservation only. Hidden, Ptarmigan, Redoubt, Baker, Skoki, Merlin, Castilleja and Red Deer lakes are all reached by short side trails en route to the lodge. Although cutthroat and rainbow are present in many lakes, most anglers come in pursuit of the large brook trout inhabiting Redoubt, Baker, Ptarmigan and Red Deer lakes. Longer trails radiate out from Skoki Valley, extending deep into the backcountry of Banff National Park along the Red Deer and Pipestone rivers and Baker Creek.

■ Baker Lake (NP)
51°29'31"N 116°02'26"W
Brook trout to 55 cm (1.5 kg)
Cutthroat trout to 45 cm
Baker Lake is the largest lake in the Skoki area. There is a backcountry campground at the eastern end of Baker Lake. The lake is set in a wide basin near treeline, and holds both cutthroat and brook trout ranging from 25–35 cm in length. Brook trout are caught more often than cutthroat, although both species inhabit all areas of the lake. The western end of the lake is usually productive, particularly near the inlet creek. Lures and wet flies fished deep tend to attract more brook trout, whereas cutthroat are more amenable to dry flies. Due to its high elevation and lack of tree cover around the shore, Baker is susceptible to strong winds.

Baker Lake

Baker Lake brook trout
Chaunce Olson photo

□ Little Baker Lake (NP)
51°29'06"N 116°01'48"W
Brook trout to 35 cm
Cutthroat trout to 35 cm
Little Baker Lake is located less than a kilometre from Baker Lake. Little Baker Lake holds small numbers of brook and cutthroat trout. Fly casting room is adequate along much of the shoreline, although fish-holding waters tend to be beyond the range of an average cast.

◪ Tilted Lake (NP)
51°29'04"N 116°01'29"W
Status: Doubtful
Tilted Lake is set in the same basin as Little Baker Lake. Recent reports suggest that Tilted Lake no longer holds fish.

■ Brachiopod Lake (NP)
51°28'48"N 116°01'36"W
Status: Devoid of fish
Despite rumours to the contrary, Brachiopod Lake contains no fish, and regularly dries up completely.

■ Baker Creek (NP)
Cutthroat trout to 25 cm
Brook trout to 25 cm
Bull trout to 30 cm
Whitefish to 25 cm
Baker Creek is best in its upper reaches, particularly in the meadows below Baker Lake. Baker Creek holds a variety of fish, with cutthroat and brook trout predominant in the upper sections, and bull trout more numerous downstream. Baker Creek is accessible from a trail that parallels the creek over its entire course.

Ptarmigan Lake (NP)

51°29'02"N 116°04'36"W
Brook trout to 50 cm
Cutthroat trout to 40 cm

Ptarmigan Lake is set in windswept Boulder Pass, 9 km from the trailhead at Lake Louise ski hill. The sparkling waters of Ptarmigan Lake hold both brook and cutthroat trout, averaging 25–30 cm in length. Brook trout are in the majority. Although fly casting room is available around the entire lake, this advantage is offset by frequent strong winds which make life miserable for most fly fishers. The area along the scree slopes and boulders on the south side tends to hold most of the fish.

Ptarmigan Lake

Ptarmigan Lake brook trout

Redoubt Lake (NP)

51°28'27"N 116°04'05"W
Brook trout to 55 cm (1.5 kg)
Cutthroat trout to 40 cm

Redoubt Lake is perched in a high, alpine basin less than a kilometre south of Ptarmigan Lake by rough trail. The lake is popular with backcountry anglers following ice-out, which generally occurs in early July. Redoubt Lake has earned a reputation for holding large brook trout. Brook trout taken from the lake will average 30–45 cm in length. A few cutthroat trout are still in the lake. Lures and flies both work well in Redoubt Lake. Redoubt's tundra-like setting allows for fly casting from all locations around the lake.

Redoubt Lake

Removing Brook Trout

In August of 2018, Parks Canada aquatic specialists dumped 1,700 litres of rotenone, a naturally occurring plant-based chemical, into Hidden Lake. The purpose was to kill all of the fish in Hidden Lake, which Parks Canada had determined to be a population of brook trout, a species planted many years ago. The brook trout outcompeted the native cutthroat trout and within ten years of their original planting had taken over the lake, eliminating all of the cutthroat. Since 2011, Parks Canada had attempted to eliminate the brook trout by electroshocking and netting, but was unable to completely eliminate the brook trout population. The rotenone introduced into Hidden Lake killed all fish in the lake, and after a period of time for the lake to rehabilitate, native cutthroat trout will be reintroduced into the lake.

Hidden Lake (NP)

51°29'06"N 116°06'32"W
Status: Closed
Will eventually be planted with cutthroat trout

Hidden Lake is set in a rocky amphitheatre, less than a kilometre along a side trail from Halfway Hut. Over time, Hidden Lake became overrun with brook trout, which destroyed the native cutthroat population. In 2018, Parks Canada removed all fish from Hidden Lake and will be introducing pure-strain cutthroat. Hidden Lake is currently closed to angling.

Hidden Lake

Corral Creek (NP)

Cutthroat trout to 25 cm
Brook trout to 25 cm

Corral Creek has a small population of brook and cutthroat trout in its upper reaches and also at its lower end near its confluence with the Bow River. The fast waters in the middle section hold very few fish.

Corral Creek

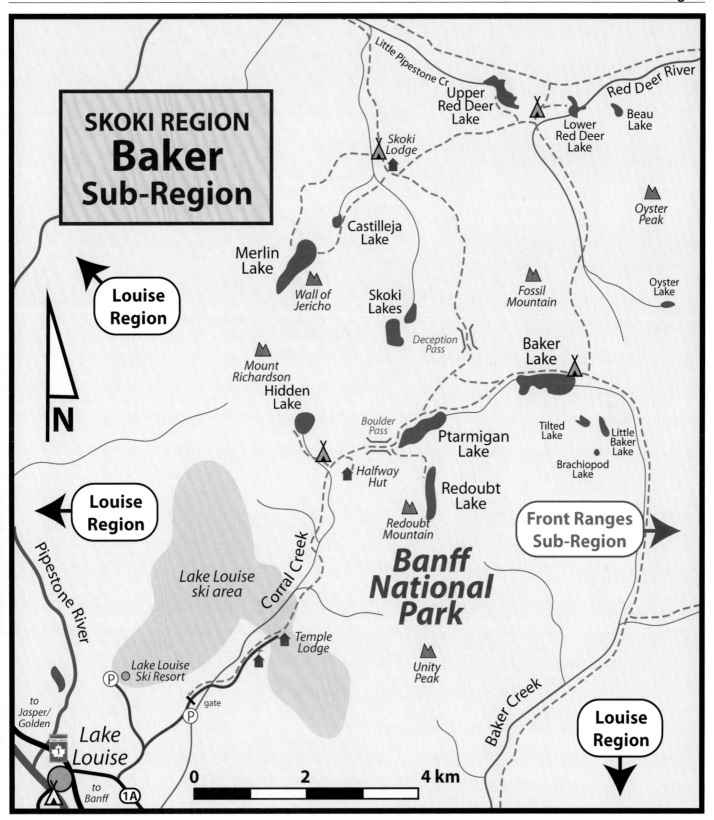

SKOKI REGION
Baker
Sub-Region

Louise Region

Louise Region

Louise Region

Front Ranges Sub-Region

Little Pipestone Cr

Red Deer River

Upper Red Deer Lake

Lower Red Deer Lake

Beau Lake

Skoki Lodge

Oyster Peak

Castilleja Lake

Oyster Lake

Merlin Lake

Fossil Mountain

Wall of Jericho

Skoki Lakes

Deception Pass

Baker Lake

Mount Richardson

Hidden Lake

Boulder Pass

Tilted Lake

Little Baker Lake

Ptarmigan Lake

Brachiopod Lake

Halfway Hut

Redoubt Lake

Redoubt Mountain

Banff National Park

Corral Creek

Lake Louise ski area

Unity Peak

Baker Creek

Pipestone River

Temple Lodge

Lake Louise Ski Resort

gate

to Jasper/Golden

Lake Louise

to Banff 1A

0   2   4 km

Skoki Lakes:

◼ **Zigadenus Lake (NP)**
51°30'03"N 116°05'03"W
Status: Devoid of fish

◻ **Myosotis Lake (NP)**
51°30'12"N 116°04'46"W
Status: Doubtful

The beautifully coloured Skoki Lakes (Zigadenus and Myosotis) are located high on the west side of Skoki Valley beneath the east face of Ptarmigan Peak. The lakes are visible to the west as you descend the north side of Deception Pass. They can be reached either by leaving the trail and working across the valley, or by following a rough trail that begins half a kilometre south of Skoki Lodge. Both lakes are heavily silted, which accounts for their striking green colour. Both lakes were stocked in the past with rainbow trout. Reports indicate that Zigadenus Lake is devoid of fish and it is doubtful that any trout remain in Myosotis Lake.

☐ Castilleja Lake (NP)

51°31'10"N 116°05'59"W

Status: Doubtful

Castilleja Lake is a small lake encountered on the trail to Merlin Lake from Skoki Lodge. Castilleja Lake was at one time stocked with brook and rainbow trout, but evidence indicates that the fish failed to take hold. There is a possibility some cutthroat may have entered the lake from the Pipestone River drainage.

Castilleja Lake

☐ Merlin Lake (NP)

51°30'46"N 116°06'36"W

Status: Doubtful

Picturesque Merlin Lake is set in a hanging valley above Castilleja Lake and is protected by a small cliff band requiring scrambling ability. Merlin Lake held a small population of rainbow and brook trout, but there are no records that the fish were able to reproduce. It is unlikely that any trout remain in Merlin Lake.

◪ Red Deer Lakes (NP)

(Upper) 51°32'27"N 116°03'11"W

Brook trout to 55 cm (1.5 kg)

Cutthroat trout to 50 cm

Rainbow trout to 50 cm

The two Red Deer Lakes are set in a wide, open valley 4 km by trail from Skoki Lodge. The upper lake, the larger of the two, lies west of the trail and contains good-sized cutthroat and brook trout. The lower lake, situated just east of the main trail, has brook trout and perhaps the odd rainbow. Both lakes offer lots of spots to take fish from. Fish from the lakes will average 25–35 cm in length. Flies and lures work well in both lakes. Although room for fly casting is available, the upper lake is very shallow for a fair distance out from shore, which makes it difficult for those fly fishing to reach deeper waters holding the fish. The best opportunities for fly fishing from shore are in the areas around the inlet and outlet streams. The marshy nature of the area almost ensures wet feet, and the abundance of reeds makes fly casting difficult at the lower lake. Several small streams wind back and forth across the marshy flats around the lower lake, and most hold a few trout.

Upper Red Deer Lake

Upper Red Deer Lake cutthroat trout

Lower Red Deer Lake

☐ Beau Lake (aka Hatchet Lake) (NP)

51°32'23"N 116°01'15"W

Brook trout to 30 cm

Rainbow trout to 30 cm

This small lake is located just east of lower Red Deer Lake (and is considered by some to be one of the Red Deer Lakes). Beau Lake holds both brook trout and maybe the odd rainbow trout in the 20–30 cm size range. Beau's swampy surroundings will provide ample opportunity to test waterproof boots.

Beau Lake

? Oyster Lake (NP)

51°30'19"N 116°00'26"W

Status: Unknown

Brook trout

Oyster Lake is a small body of water located in a hidden side valley on the south end of Oyster Peak. It was stocked many years ago with brook trout, which still may exist.

Oyster Lake

Front Ranges Sub-Region

The Front Ranges covers the watersheds of the upper Red Deer, Panther and Clearwater rivers. This Sub-Region lies deep within the Front Ranges of the Rocky Mountains in Banff National Park and is home to many grizzly bears. Visitors entering the Sub-Region are generally limited to horse parties and a few enterprising hikers, who should be aware that major river fords are to be expected on most trails in the Sub-Region and that there are no easy escape routes back to civilization. From the upper Red Deer River, which can be accessed from Skoki Valley, side trails branch to Douglas and Horseshoe lakes. The Cascade Fire Road, although lengthy, provides an alternate approach to the Sub-Region. Fishing opportunities are limited to remote backcountry lakes with small populations of trout. Almost all of the bodies of water (lakes, river and streams) in the Clearwater drainage are closed to angling.

⊗ Clearwater River (NP)
Status: Closed to angling
The Clearwater River flows eastwards from humble beginnings at the Devon Lakes at Clearwater Pass and eventually joins the North Saskatchewan River at Rocky Mountain House as a major tributary. The section of the Clearwater River within the boundaries of Banff National Park is closed to angling to protect the bull trout population.

⊗ Devon Lakes (NP)
51°43'43"N 116°15'14"W
Status: Closed to angling
The Devon Lakes are set in alpine surroundings, immediately east of Clearwater Pass. The Devon Lakes were for many years regarded as one of the Sub-Region's best fishing destinations, with large bull and lake trout. Parks Canada has begun a project in which lakes and rivers in the Clearwater and Siffleur drainage are being rehabilitated to be able to restore the area's bull trout.

⊗ Clearwater Lake (NP)
51°46'34"N 116°08'47"W
Status: Closed to angling
Clearwater Lake, merely a widening of the Clearwater River, is set in a wide valley, 10 km below Clearwater Pass on the Clearwater River. Clearwater Lake is closed to angling.

⊗ Trident Lake (NP)
51°47'53"N 116°07'04"W
Status: Closed to angling
Two kilometres downstream from Clearwater Lake the Clearwater River again widens, this time into the form of Trident Lake. Trident Lake is closed to angling.

⊗ Martin Lake (NP)
51°47'35"N 116°08'12"W
Status: Closed to angling
Martin Lake is located less than a kilometre above Trident Lake on Martin Creek. Martin Lake is closed to angling.

■ Red Deer River (NP) (Headwaters to national park boundary)
Brook trout to 35 cm
Cutthroat trout to 35 cm
Rainbow trout to 35 cm
Bull trout to 70 cm (4.0 kg)
Whitefish to 40 cm
The Red Deer River offers good river fishing as it flows east from its source at the Red Deer Lakes to the Banff National Park boundary. While the main river is often very silty until mid to late summer due to glacial runoff, many of the side channels and ponds provide excellent opportunities to catch trout at this time. The river is noticeably siltier downstream from the Drummond Glacier tributary. Brook trout predominate in the upper sections, with bull trout and whitefish becoming more plentiful downstream. In the vicinity of Red Deer Lakes, the occasional rainbow or cutthroat may also be caught. Horse trails along the upper Red Deer River connect with the Cascade Fire Road.

Red Deer River

◿ Douglas Lake (NP)
51°32'32"N 115°56'33"W
Cutthroat trout to 50 cm
This relatively large lake is set in a wide valley to the south of the main Red Deer River valley. Douglas Lake usually attracts a few eager anglers each season, despite a tricky ford of the Red Deer prior to reaching the Douglas Lake spur trail. Cutthroat trout averaging 30–40 cm in length inhabit the lake's silty waters in good numbers. Although brook trout were also stocked at one time in Douglas, reports indicate that few or none remain. The areas around the lake's inlet and outlet are generally the most productive, although cutthroat can be taken from most spots along the shore, the trout tending to keep fairly close to the shore in search of food due to silted waters. Lures work well in the silty water.

Douglas Lake

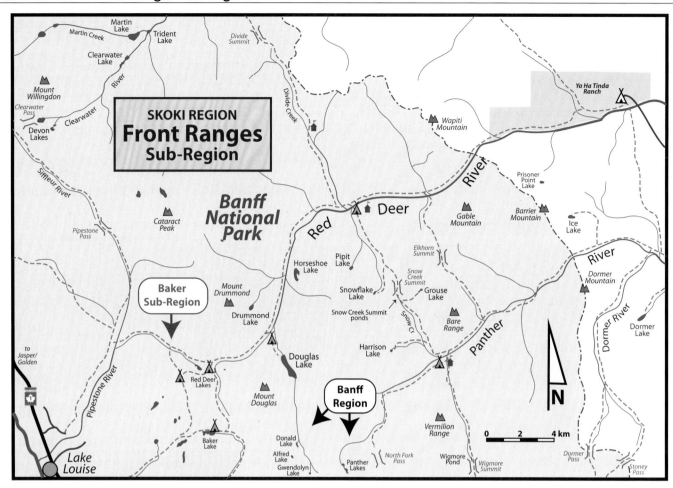

*Douglas Lake
cutthroat trout*

■ Donald Lake (NP)
51°29'00"N 115°55'51"W
■ Alfred Lake (NP)
51°28'25"N 115°56'14"W
■ Gwendolyn Lake (NP)
51°27'32"N 116°54'41"W
Status: Devoid of fish

These three remote lakes are located in the Valley of the Hidden Lakes, which is south of Douglas Lake. The lakes have never been stocked and contain no fish.

■ Horseshoe Lake [aka Skeleton Lake] (NP)
51°36'48"N 116°55'55"W
Status: Doubtful
Brook trout
Rainbow trout

Horseshoe Lake is located 6 km downstream from Douglas Lake, and is overlooked by most hikers because of the dangerous ford of the Red Deer River. However, a cablecar crossing of the Red Deer is found in the canyon just downstream from Horseshoe's outlet. This distinctly U-shaped lake once held plenty of brook and rainbow trout averaging 25–35 cm in length. A severe winterkill in the winter of 2017–18 appears to have done extreme damage to trout in Horseshoe Lake, and few, if any, remain.

■ Drummond Lake (NP)
51°35'16"N 116°59'15"W
Status: Devoid of fish
Drummond Lake is hidden in a side valley northwest of the Red Deer River. The lake has never been stocked and contains no fish.

■ Pipit Lake (NP)
51°37'01"N 116°51'48"W
Rainbow trout to 40 cm
This small, isolated lake sits west of the Cascade Fire Road on the northern side of Snow Creek Summit. It receives very few two-legged visitors each summer. Although the route is fairly obvious, a map and compass are recommended, as no formal trails lead to the lake. Reports indicate that Pipit holds a small population of rainbow trout averaging 20–30 cm in length.

■ Snowflake Lake (NP)
51°35'56"N 116°49'58"W
Status: Doubtful
Snowflake Lake is set in a beautiful alpine basin west of Snow Creek Summit. Snowflake Lake has been stocked several times, but has been unable to maintain a stable population of trout. Both rainbow and brook trout have been unsuccessfully planted in the past and reports now indicate that the lake is likely barren.

■ Snow Creek Summit ponds (NP)

Bull trout to 40 cm

This series of beaver ponds is located on the western side of Snow Creek Summit, overlooked by most parties passing through. The ponds, hidden in the brush at the summit of the pass, hold plenty of small bull trout averaging 20–30 cm in length.

■ Grouse Lake (NP)

51°35'52"N 116°46'40"W

Status: Devoid of fish

Grouse Lake lies hidden in a narrow side valley just east of the Cascade Fire Road. The brook trout stocked in the past failed to reproduce, and the lake is now devoid of fish.

■ Harrison Lake (NP)

51°33'16"N 116°48'40"W

Bull trout to 45 cm

Harrison Lake is nestled high on the flank of an unnamed peak at the south end of the Vermilion Range. Harrison is one of the area's hidden treasures, and it is accessed by a 3 km side trail from the Cascade Fire Road. Despite the long distances involved, Harrison Lake is visited by a few anglers each season. The lake has plenty of bull trout averaging 30–40 cm in length, making it worth the long distances traveled.

■ Panther River (NP-AB)

Bull trout to 70 cm (4.0 kg)
Whitefish to 40 cm
Brook trout to 35 cm
Rainbow trout to 35 cm

The Panther River flows east to its junction with the Red Deer River and offers average stream fishing at best. Bull trout and whitefish are found in pockets along the entire length of the river, but never in great numbers. Progressing downstream, the fishing generally picks up, and nearing the park boundary, the odd brook trout and rainbow can also be caught. Horse trails parallel the Panther, intersecting with the Cascade Fire Road at Wigmore Creek.

■ Ice Lake (AB)

51°39'22"N 115°35'00"W

Cutthroat trout to 40 cm

Ice Lake is located in a stark alpine basin just outside Banff National Park, approximately three kilometres above the Panther River-Ya Ha Tinda trail. Ice-out occurs well into the summer in most years. Ice Lake holds a good population of cutthroat in the 25–35 cm range.

Ice Lake and Ice Lake cutthroat trout

■ Prisoner Point Lake (AB)

51°40'11"N 115°37'14"W

Status: Devoid of fish

Prisoner Point Lake is a small body of water located in the valley immediately northeast of Ice Lake. Prisoner Point Lake has never been stocked and holds no fish.

■ Dormer Lake (AB)

51°35'27"N 115°29'56"W

Brook trout to 40 cm

Dormer Lake is a pretty green body of water set in heavy forest cover approximately four kilometres by trail south of the Panther River-Ya Ya Tinda trail. Many horse parties make their way to Dormer Lake. The trail into Dormer Lake suffered damage during recent major flooding. The lake holds plenty of brook trout in the 25–35 cm range.

Dormer Lake

Dormer Lake brook trout

■ Winchester Creek (AB)

Brook trout to 30 cm

Winchester Creek is the outlet stream for Dormer Lake and holds brook trout in small sizes along its entire length to the Panther River.

■ Dormer River (AB)

Bull trout to 60 cm (2.0 kg)
Whitefish to 30 cm
Brook trout to 30 cm
Rainbow trout to 30 cm

The Dormer River is a major tributary of the Panther River and holds the same variety of fish as the Panther.

■ Panther Lakes (aka Panther Lake) (NP)

51°27'51"N 116°52'11"W

Status: Doubtful

This series of interconnected lakes set amid spectacular scenery at the head of the Panther River has never been stocked. It is possible, although unlikely, that a few bull trout have worked their way into the lakes.

□ Wigmore Pond (NP)

Bull trout to 40 cm
Rainbow trout to 30 cm
Brook trout to 30 cm

Tiny Wigmore Pond sits alongside the Cascade Fire Road just north of Wigmore Summit. Although rainbow and brook trout have been stocked in the past and reports indicate they are still present, bull trout is the predominant species.

YOHO PARK REGION

This Region encompasses the entirety of spectacular Yoho National Park. The Trans-Canada Highway bisects the region and provides access. The tiny community of Field offers very limited services for visitors. There are few high-quality fisheries in the region. Most of the rivers are glacial, and run silted much of the year. Lakes tend to be small, backcountry lakes with very limited populations of trout. The Region is divided into three Sub-Regions: The area around exquisite Lake O'Hara; the area around Emerald Lake; and the main Kicking Horse River valley.

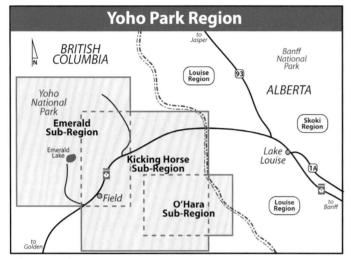

O'Hara Sub-Region

O'Hara's jeweled setting of pristine mountain lakes set beneath the spectacular peaks of the Continental Divide is equal to that of any area in the Rockies. The Lake O'Hara vicinity is renowned for its quality hiking and climbing opportunities, and not for fishing. However, prospective anglers coming to this corner of Yoho National Park will not be disappointed. Lake O'Hara, the focal point of the region, is reached via a 13 km limited access fire road from the Trans-Canada Highway. Arrangements can be made with Lake O'Hara Lodge to reserve a space on the shuttle bus during summer months (1-877-737-3783). Both Lake O'Hara Lodge and the Alpine Club of Canada's Elizabeth Parker Hut require reservations, as does the park campground, located a half kilometre below Lake O'Hara alongside Cataract Brook. From the shores of beautiful Lake O'Hara, trails radiate out to nearby lakes, including Mary, Schaeffer, McArthur, Morning Glory, Linda, Vera and Oesa lakes.

⬛ Lake O'Hara (NP)
51°21'20"N 116°19'49"W
Cutthroat trout to 55 cm (1.5 kg)
The aquamarine waters of Lake O'Hara are situated beneath the same impressive peaks that form the backdrop for Lake Louise. The O'Hara Sub-Region is a favourite destination of backcountry visitors. Unfortunately, while Lake O'Hara's fishing has never been able to match its beauty, it is worth tossing a line. The lake contains cutthroat trout in the 25–35 cm range in decent numbers. The tangle of sunken logs in the area of the lake's outlet is a popular spot that usually holds trout. Canoes can be rented from the Lake O'Hara Lodge, but fishing from a boat is not usually a great aid here, as the fish tend to stay close to shore due to the silted nature of the water.

Lake O'Hara

Lake O'Hara cutthroat trout

⬛ Lake Oesa (NP)
51°21'16"N 116°18'11"W
Status: Devoid of fish
Lake Oesa remains ice-covered for ten months each year. The lake was stocked in the past with rainbow trout, but they probably just froze to death! There are no fish in Lake Oesa.

Lake Oesa

⬛ Yukness Lake (NP)
51°21'25"N 116°19'15"W
⬛ Lake Victoria (NP)
51°21'29"N 116°18'52"W
⬛ Lefroy Lake (NP)
51°21'20"N 116°18'39"W
Status: Devoid of fish
These three small, silted bodies of water alongside the trail to Lake Oesa have never been stocked and contain no fish.

⬛ Hungabee Lake (NP)
51°20'36"N 116°19'09"W
⬛ Opabin Lake (NP)
51°20'27"N 116°18'42"W
⬛ Moor Lakes (NP)
51°20'38"N 116°19'16"W
Status: Devoid of fish

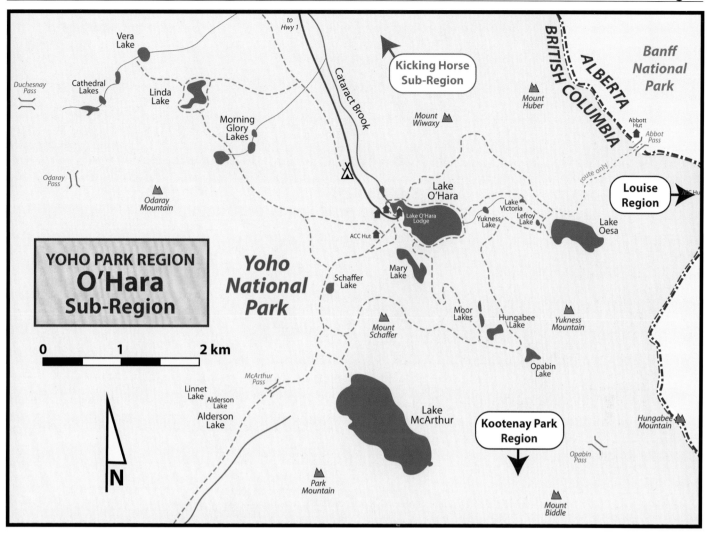

Set in the alpine environs of the Opabin Plateau, none of Hungabee, Opabin or Moor lakes has ever been stocked.

☐ Lake McArthur (NP)

51°20'02"N 116°20'26"W

Brook trout to 40 cm

Lake McArthur is the largest lake of the Sub-Region, and it lies hidden in a stunning hanging valley 3 km south of Lake O'Hara. It noted for its exceptional blue colouration, a result of heavy silting from nearby glaciers. Although the lake holds brook trout averaging 20–30 cm in length, anglers at McArthur have not enjoyed great success in recent years. Reports tend to indicate that a very small number of trout still exist in McArthur.

Lake McArthur

■ Schaeffer Lake (NP)

51°20'53"N 116°20'58"W

Status: Devoid of fish

Schaeffer Lake was stocked in the past with both rainbow and cutthroat trout, but no reproductive success has ever been recorded. It is very likely that Schaeffer Lake is devoid of fish.

Schaeffer Lake

■ Mary Lake (NP)

51°21'05"N 116°20'05"W

Status: Devoid of fish

Mary Lake is located on a bench just south of Lake O'Hara. It has never been stocked and contains no fish.

☐ Morning Glory Lakes (NP)

(upper lake) 51°21'46"N 116°22'11"W

Cutthroat trout to 30 cm

The Morning Glory Lakes are a series of three shallow lakes situated beneath the impressive north face of Mt. Odaray. All three contain very limited populations of small cutthroat trout. Most fish are in the 15–25 cm range. The fish spook easily due to the shallow nature of the water, making patience an important asset for anglers. For those fly fishing, there is plenty of fly casting room around all three lakes.

■ Linda Lake (NP)
51°22'11"N 116°22'26"W
Cutthroat trout to 45 cm
Linda Lake is set in a quiet subalpine basin northwest 3 km northwest of Lake O'Hara. Linda Lake offers the best potential of any lake in the area. Its clear blue waters hold plenty of cutthroat trout in the 20–30 cm range, with larger fish are taken regularly. Flies work very well here. Numerous openings in the forest cover along the shoreline allow for fly casting. No one area seems to be best and anglers are advised to keep a close eye on the water while working around the lake.

Linda Lake

□ Vera Lake (NP)
51°22'27"N 116°23'11"W
Cutthroat to 35 cm
Vera Lake is located a little over 4 km by trail from Lake O'Hara. It is seldom visited by anyone, as most hikers do not venture beyond nearby Linda Lake. Vera Lake's placid waters reportedly hold a small population of cutthroat trout averaging 15–25 cm in length. The areas around the inlet and outlet creeks are usually productive.

? Cathedral Lakes (NP)
51°22'20"N 116°23'21"W
Status: Unknown
The diminutive Cathedral Lakes are located half a kilometre above Vera Lake. They have never been stocked with trout. However, it is possible that fish could have migrated upstream over time from Vera Lake.

■ Cataract Brook (NP)
Cutthroat trout to 35 cm
Cataract Brook parallels the Lake O'Hara Fire Road. As its name indicates, Cataract Creek contains numerous falls and rapids. The creek holds small cutthroat trout in the 25–35 cm range in its upper section, particularly in the 2 km stretch below Lake O'Hara, where there are several large pools just below the lake's outlet.

Emerald Sub-Region

This Sub-Region encompasses the northern half of Yoho National Park. It possesses an abundance of superb scenery and a scarcity of good fishing opportunities. The main access is via the Yoho Valley Road or the Emerald Lake Road, both of which branch north off the Trans-Canada Highway. Charming Emerald Lake is a favourite with sightseers, and is the hub of hiking trails leading to Hamilton Lake and Yoho Lake. From the terminus of the Yoho Valley Road at magnificent 380m-high Takakkaw Falls, the main Yoho Valley trail leads past Celeste, Duchesnay and Marpole lakes, none of which hold much promise for anglers.

■ Emerald Lake (NP)
51°26'35"N 116°31'54"W
Brook trout to 45 cm
Rainbow trout to 40 cm
Bull trout to 60 cm (2.0 kg)
Emerald Lake's dazzling setting attracts hordes of visitors each summer, and its shoreline always seems to be busy with hikers and photographers. Although Emerald is not heavily fished despite the number of canoes on the lake at any one time, its rich green waters contain good numbers of both brook and rainbow trout averaging 20–30 cm in length, with brook trout in the majority. The occasional bull trout may also be present. As the water is silted, fish can generally be taken close to shore, particularly in the area around the outlet and bridge to Emerald Lake Lodge. From a canoe, which can be rented at the lake, the best tactic is to keep fairly close to shore while trolling a fly or lure.

Emerald Lake

Emerald Lake brook trout
Wayne Pierce photo

■ Peaceful Pond (NP)
51°26'15"N 116°32'12"W
Brook trout to 35 cm
Rainbow trout to 35 cm
Peaceful Pond is hidden in thick forest less than 200 metres southeast of the outlet of Emerald Lake. It is connected directly to the Emerald River and contains the same fish that are found in Emerald Lake, namely brook and rainbow trout in the 15–25 cm range.

■ Lone Duck Lake (NP)
51°25'51"N 116°31'53"W
Brook trout to 35 cm
Rainbow trout to 35 cm

Lone Duck Lake is simply a widening of the Emerald River approximately a kilometre downstream from Emerald Lake. It holds brook and rainbow trout in small sizes.

■ Emerald River (NP)

Brook trout to 35 cm
Rainbow trout to 35 cm
Bull trout to 60 cm (2.0 kg)
The Emerald River flows from Emerald Lake to the Kicking Horse River and possesses long stretches of fishable water. The river is never more than a short walk away from the Emerald Lake Road. Small brook and rainbow trout in the 20–30 cm range can be caught in the river. A few larger bull trout may be present in the deeper pools.

■ Hamilton Lake (NP)

51°27'19"N 116°34'41"W
Status: Devoid of fish
Delightful Hamilton Lake is located 5 km by trail above Emerald Lake and is set in a rocky cirque beneath Mount Carnarvon. Hamilton Lake has never been stocked and contains no trout.

Hamilton Lake

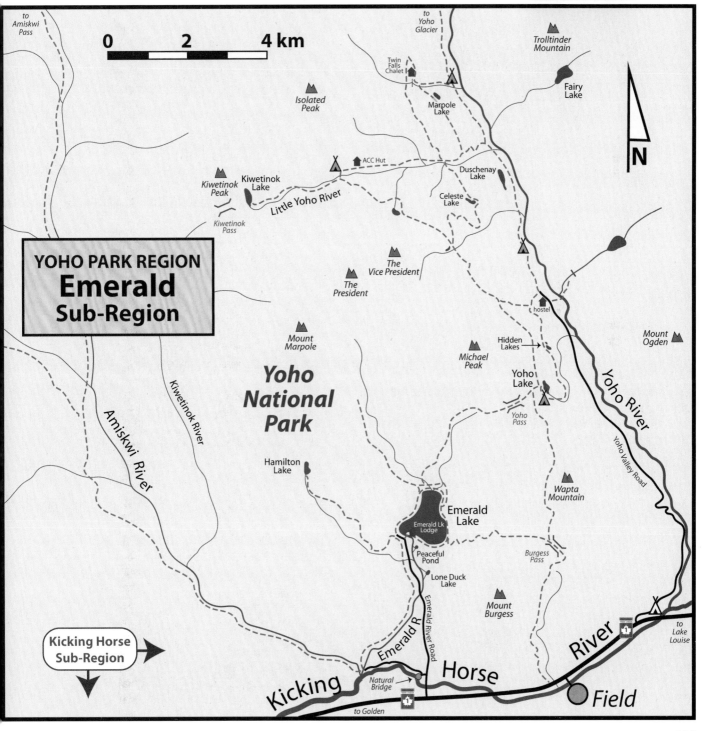

Amiskwi River (NP)

Brook trout to 35 cm
Bull trout to 60 cm (2.0 kg)

The Amiskwi River receives little attention from anglers, particularly in the upper sections. Access is along a seldom-hiked fire road that parallels the Amiskwi over its entire length. Small brook and bull trout in the 15-25 cm range are the normal catch, although larger bulls are taken on occasion. Due to high, silty water, the river is generally unfishable until late July.

Amiskwi River

Kiwetinok River (NP)

Bull trout to 40 cm

The Kiwetinok River is a tributary of the Amiskwi River. It contains bull trout in small numbers and sizes but is generally not worth the effort of the long approach up the Amiskwi Fire Road.

Yoho River (NP)

Status: Doubtful

The Yoho River, with its headwaters the Wapta and Yoho Glaciers, is extremely silted throughout the year. In addition to heavy silting, the river is excessively torrential over most of its course and it is very unlikely that trout would proliferate under these conditions. It is possible, however, that small bull trout may live in some pockets near the confluence of clearer running tributary streams.

Little Yoho River (NP)

Status: Devoid of fish

The Little Yoho River flows through the much-hiked Little Yoho Valley, but is too torrential and too silted to hold trout.

Yoho Lake (NP)

51°28'29"N 116°29'05"W
Status: Doubtful

Yoho Lake is situated less than a kilometre east of Yoho Pass, and 6.4 km by trail from the Emerald Lake trailhead. Lovely Yoho Lake is very popular with day hikers throughout the summer. The lake at one time held a good population of brook trout in smaller sizes, but it seems the trout in the lake have finally succumbed to harsh winters and a failure to reproduce. Very recent examination failed to spot any fish in the lake, although there could be still be a few holding out in the logs by the outlet stream. As this was always a favourite lake of the author, the demise of its trout population sits as a personal loss.

Yoho Lake

Hidden Lake (NP)

51°29'01"N 116°29'02"W
Status: Devoid of fish

Tiny Hidden Lake is located on the eastern side of the Yoho Lake-Takakkaw Falls trail. Hidden Lake has been stocked in the past with both brook and rainbow trout. However, the fish failed to reproduce, and it is very doubtful that any remain.

Fairy Lake (NP)

51°32'51"N 116°28'41"W
Status: Devoid of fish

Fairy Lake is tucked high on the flank of Trolltinder Mountain, protected by a 300 m high cliff. Fortunately for anglers, Fairy Lake has never been stocked and contains no fish.

Duchesnay Lake (NP)

51°31'25"N 116°30'04"W
Status: Devoid of fish

Forest-rimmed Duchesnay Lake is situated on the western side of the Yoho Valley trail, 4 km from the Takakkaw Falls trailhead. This shallow lake was stocked in the past with brook trout, but the fish succumbed to winterkill.

Celeste Lake (NP)

51°31'05"N 116°30'46"W
Status: Devoid of fish

This small, shallow body of water less than a kilometre due west of Duchesnay Lake has never been stocked and contains no fish.

Marpole Lake (NP)

51°32'35"N 116°31'40"W

Status: Doubtful

Diminutive Marpole Lake is located just south of Twin Falls Chalet. Marpole Lake was stocked several times in the past with brook, cutthroat and rainbow trout. It is very doubtful there are any trout remaining in the lake. Aside from reproductive failure, winterkill is also likely a major factor limiting numbers.

Kiwetinok Lake (NP)

51°31'09"N 116°36'01"W

Status: Devoid of fish

Kiwetinok Lake is set in the harsh alpine environs of Kiwetinok Pass and remains ice-covered much of the year. No fish are present.

Kicking Horse Sub-Region

The Kicking Horse River forms a deep valley bounded on the north and south by the imposing peaks of Yoho National Park. The Trans-Canada Highway parallels the river, cutting through the middle of the Sub-Region, connecting Golden and Lake Louise. The village of Field, housing the headquarters for Yoho National Park, offers little in the way of services beyond the essentials of gas and food. Sink, Summit and Ross lakes are located within a kilometre of Kicking Horse Pass and the continental divide. Farther west, Wapta Lake lies alongside the Trans-Canada Highway, while Sherbrooke and Narao lakes are only a short hike away.

Kicking Horse River (NP)

Bull trout to 65 cm (2.5 kg)

Brook trout to 40 cm

Whitefish to 35 cm

The Kicking Horse River forms the main artery through Yoho National Park, and its tributaries extend to the far corners of the park. The river is paralleled by the Trans-Canada Highway. It is readily accessible to anglers but unfortunately offers only poor fishing even on its best days. It is heavily silted most of the year, clearing up only in the late summer-early fall when bull trout and whitefish along with a few brook trout can be taken. Most fish are in the 20–30 cm range, although large bull trout to 60 cm can be caught on occasion. Fishing is best around the Kicking Horse's confluence with its tributary streams, particularly the larger ones such as the Emerald, Amiskwi, Ottertail and Otterhead rivers.

Kicking Horse River

Ross Lake (NP)

51°26'14"N 116°18'11"W

Brook trout to 35 cm

This small tree-fringed lake is 3 km by road walk and trail from the Lake O'Hara trailhead. It receives little fishing pressure due to its secluded location. Ross Lake's green waters hold brook trout averaging 20–30 cm in length. The best angling opportunities are found along the scree slopes on the south side of the lake.

Ross Lake

Ross Lake brook trout

Summit Lake (NP)

51°27'02"N 116°17'31"W

Brook trout to 30 cm

Summit Lake is a shallow lake located alongside the 1-A Highway just west of Kicking Horse Pass. It is no longer of much interest to fishermen since its ability to hold fish is entirely dependent on regular plantings, a practice that no longer occurs in Summit. Rainbow, cutthroat and brook trout were all been stocked in the past in Summit Lake, and all have had difficulty in maintaining viable populations. If anything, a few brook trout may still be present in Summit Lake.

Sink Lake (NP)

51°27'01"N 116°18'32"W

Status: Doubtful

Sink Lake possesses many of the same characteristics as nearby Summit Lake. Winter kill has been a major factor in the demise of fish in the lake over the years. Rainbow, brook and cutthroat trout, as well as splake, have all been planted in Sink Lake, but failed to take hold. Although quite unlikely, some remnants of brook trout plantings may still exist in the lake.

Wapta Lake (NP)

51°26'22"N 116°21'03"W

Lake trout to 60 cm (2.5 kg)

Brook trout to 40 cm

Rainbow trout to 40 cm

Wapta Lake receives relatively little fishing pressure despite its proximity to the Trans-Canada Highway. Rainbow, brook and lake trout are all present with most fish averaging 25–35 cm. As the lake is silted in nature, the area around the inlet and outlet generally produce the best.

Wapta Lake

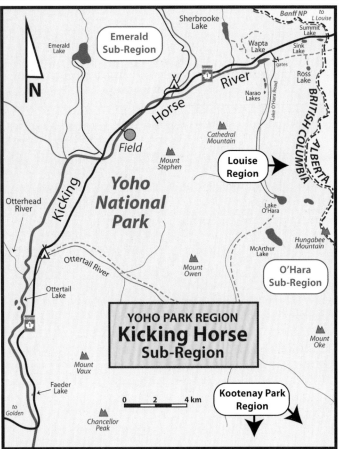

☐ Narao Lakes (NP)

51°25'30"N 116°20'51"W

Brook trout to 35 cm

The Narao Lakes are set amid marshy surroundings 2 km by trail south of Wapta Lake. The lakes are seldom visited by anglers since wet feet are unavoidable and few fish are present. Although the lakes were stocked in the past with brook trout, their reproductive success is suspect at best.

■ Sherbrooke Lake (NP)

51°27'26"N 116°23'15"W

Rainbow trout to 50 cm

Lake trout to 55 cm (1.5 kg)

Bull trout to 55 cm (1.5 kg)

The narrow valley between Paget Peak and Mount Ogden holds the elongated form of Sherbrooke Lake. Inlet streams flow from the Daly and Niles glaciers, and Sherbrooke Lake is quite silted. Fishing is slow for rainbow, bull and lake trout that average 25–35 cm in length. Anglers working around the shore can usually take rainbows in the shallow water, particularly in the area of the outlet that is strewn with deadfall. Anglers using lures will have an advantage over fly fishers in catching Sherbrooke's bull and lake trout.

Sherbrooke Lake

■ Otterhead River (NP)

Bull trout to 40 cm

Brook trout to 30 cm

Whitefish to 30 cm

The Otterhead River joins the Kicking Horse River as a major tributary approximately 5 km west of Field. It can be accessed from a fire road along the north side of the Kicking Horse River. The Otterhead River contains bull and brook trout along with whitefish in its lower reaches and bull trout in its upper waters. Most fish taken are small, averaging only 15–25 cm in length.

☐ Faeder Lake (NP)

51°14'21"N 116°34'52"W

Brook trout to 30 cm

Faeder Lake is a small pond alongside the Trans-Canada Highway. It at one time held small population of brook trout. A few trout may still be in the pond today.

Faeder Lake

■ Ottertail Lake (NP)

51°13'39"N 116°33'20"W

Brook trout to 35 cm

Ottertail Lake is located on the north side of the Kicking Horse River, just over a kilometre west of the river's confluence with the Otterhead River. Seldom fished, the lake holds brook trout in the 15–25 cm range.

■ Ottertail River (NP)

Bull trout to 40 cm

Brook trout to 30 cm

Whitefish to 30 cm

A fire road branching off the Trans-Canada Highway leads up the Ottertail drainage, where trails link to Lake O'Hara and Kootenay National Park. Whitefish, brook and bull trout all inhabit the lower stretches of the Ottertail River. Small bull trout can be caught in the headwaters.

Ottertail River

NORTH SASKATCHEWAN REGION

This Region takes in much of the upper North Saskatchewan River watershed. The Icefields Parkway (Highway 93) runs north-south and is the main access through the Region. The David Thompson Highway (Highway 11) connects to the Icefields Parkway at Saskatchewan Crossing, and provides a direct connection to Rocky Mountain House and central Alberta. Fishing opportunities in the region are limited, as fast-flowing rivers and glacial lakes are the norm. The North Saskatchewan Region is divided into three Sub-Regions. The most southerly Sub-Region covers the Mistaya River drainage. The northern Sub-Region includes the North Saskatchewan River valley within Banff National Park. The easternmost Sub-Region is centred on the Abraham Lake-Kootenay Plains area and is located outside the Banff Park boundary.

Mistaya Sub-Region

The Mistaya River is paralleled by the Icefields Parkway, and flows north through the core of the Sub-Region, from Peyto Lake to the North Saskatchewan River. The area is well-known for the magnificent views of the dazzling mountains and glaciers from the Icefields Parkway. The area offers only mediocre angling in its best lakes, notably Peyto Lake, the Waterfowl Lakes and nearby Cirque, Chephren and Mistaya lakes. The amazing colouration of the region's lakes is attributable to the presence of glacial silt, with the much-photographed blue waters of Peyto Lake being the most prominent example.

■ Peyto Lake (NP)
51°43'22"N 116°31'17"W
Cutthroat trout to 50 cm
Although it is admired by thousands of tourists from the viewpoint at Bow Summit each summer, Peyto Lake receives relatively few visitors to its shores. This is no doubt due to the steep 2 km trail which descends from the Icefields Parkway to lake level. Fishing in Peyto's delightful blue waters for cutthroat trout averaging 25–35 cm in length is usually slow. During the height of the summer, nearby glaciers deposit large amounts of silt into the lake. As the temperatures begins to drop by autumn, fishing in Peyto Lake improves somewhat. The area around the lake's outlet is the most productive.

Peyto Lake

■ Caldron Lake (NP)
51°41'49"N 116°33'53"W
Status: Devoid of fish
Caldron Lake lies hidden in an isolated hanging valley west of the Peyto Glacier and 5 km upstream from Peyto Lake. Caldron Lake has never been stocked and contains no fish.

■ Mistaya River (NP)
Cutthroat trout to 45 cm
Rainbow trout to 45 cm
Brook trout to 35 cm
Bull trout to 70 cm (4.0 kg)
Whitefish to 30 cm
The Mistaya River, flowing north from Peyto Lake to the North Saskatchewan River, possesses many long stretches of fishable water, especially in the area between Mistaya and Waterfowl lakes. The angling season is shortened by the long run-off which brings large amounts of silt down from the icefields to the west. Fishing tends to improve in the late season fishing on the Mistaya River, but still is only fair on its best days. Depending on which section of river is being fished, a variety of species can be caught. Cutthroat are dominant in the upper reaches and bull trout in the lower, while in the stretch from Mistaya Lake through to the Waterfowl Lakes, cutthroat and brook trout make up the greatest percentage, with a few rainbow trout likely present as well. Whitefish can also be taken from many spots along the river throughout its length. Although a short jaunt through the bush is usually required, the Mistaya is always within a kilometre or two of the Icefields Parkway.

■ Mistaya Lake (NP)
51°47'25"N 116°35'42"W
Cutthroat to 45 cm
Brook trout to 40 cm
Rainbow trout to 40 cm
Bull trout to 55 cm (1.5 kg)
Whitefish to 30 cm
Mistaya Lake is hidden by heavy forest, and goes unnoticed by most visitors, despite the crowded campground at Waterfowl Lakes, only 2 km distant. Cutthroat trout averaging 25–35 cm in length predominate in Mistaya, although the odd brook or rainbow trout occasionally makes its way in from Waterfowl Lakes. Its possible whitefish and bull trout may also be present

in limited numbers. As the lake is silted much of the summer, fish tend to keep to the shallower waters in search of food. The waters around the inlet are the most productive if silting isn't too heavy.

■ Capricorn Lake (NP)

51°46'20"N 116°37'36"W
Status: Devoid of fish
Capricorn Lake is set beneath the Capricorn Glacier in a cirque high above Mistaya Lake. Capricorn Lake has never been stocked and is devoid of fish.

■ Upper Waterfowl Lake (NP)

51°50'01"N 116°36'57"W

■ Lower Waterfowl Lake (NP)

51°50'59"N 116°38'01"W
Brook trout to 45 cm
Cutthroat trout to 45 cm
Rainbow trout to 45 cm
Upper and Lower Waterfowl are by far the most popular fishing spots in the Sub-Region. A major campground is situated between the two lakes. The Waterfowl Lakes are similar in character to most other major lakes along the Mistaya River. Heavy silting occurs, which accounts for the lake's appealing blue-green colouration. Cutthroat and brook trout averaging 25–35 cm in length are the normal catch. Areas around the inlets and outlets can be productive at times.

Lower Waterfowl Lake

☐ Cirque Lake (NP)

51°48'23"N 116°38'00"W
Brook trout to 40 cm
Rainbow trout to 40 cm
Cirque Lake lies tucked away in a side valley 5 km by trail from the Waterfowl Lakes campground. Cirque Lake is generally silty due to run-off from glaciers at the head of the lake. The lake fishes better in the late season for brook and rainbow trout averaging 20–30 cm in length. An extensive outlet strewn with deadfall usually holds trout, although many a fly or lure will be lost to snags.

Cirque Lake

☐ Chephren Lake (NP)

51°49'52"N 116°39'20"W
Brook trout to 40 cm
Cutthroat trout to 40 cm
Rainbow trout to 40 cm
Chephren Lake is lightly larger than Cirque Lake and occupies the next side valley to the north, 4 km by trail from the Waterfowl Lakes. Chephren Lake at one time offered fair fishing for brook,

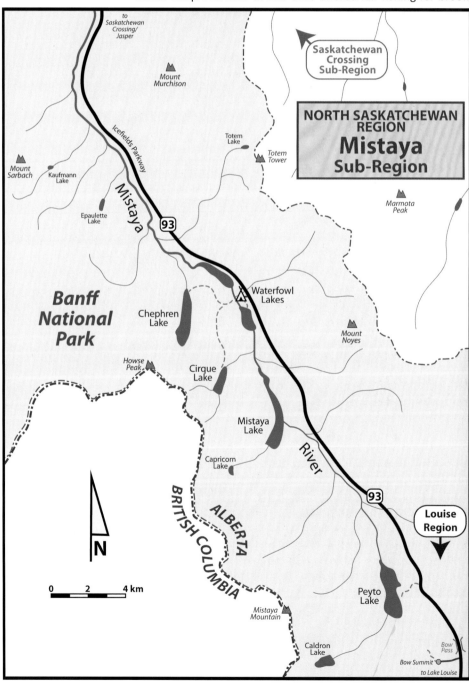

cutthroat and rainbow trout in the 25–35 cm range. Fish can usually be taken close to shore, and the large amount of sunken deadfall providing excellent cover for the trout. Flies work well, and fly casting is possible from many locations.

Chephren Lake

◼ Epaulette Lake (NP)
51°52'36"N 116°42'41"W
Status: Devoid of fish
Epaulette Lake is located 2 km west of the Mistaya River through heavy forest and is inaccessible to all but the most determined route-finders. Fortunately for anglers, Epaulette Lake has never been stocked and contains no fish.

◼ Kaufmann Lake (NP)
51°53'47"N 116°43'54"W
Status: Devoid of fish
No fish are present in this tiny glacial tarn set beneath the east face of Mt. Sarbach.

? Totem Lake (NP)
51°54'00"N 116°36'59"W
Status: Unknown
Totem Lake is set high in a stark, rocky basin on the flank of Mt. Murchison and is accessed by an ill-defined, difficult 6 km route from the Icefields Parkway. Totem Lake is far removed from fishing pressure. Although the lake was stocked in the past with rainbow trout, few confirmed reports about Totem ever make their way out, and it is unknown whether any fish remain.

Saskatchewan Crossing Sub-Region

This Sub-Region encompasses the north end of Banff National Park and is dominated geographically by the mighty North Saskatchewan River and its tributaries. The Icefields Parkway (Highway 93) provides the main access into the region, and is intersected by the David Thompson Highway (Highway 11) coming in from the east at Saskatchewan River Crossing. Limited tourist supplies of gas, food and lodging can be found at The Crossing. Hiking is required to reach the shores of most lakes in the area. The Howse River, a major tributary to the North Saskatchewan, contains David, Outram, Lagoon and Glacier lakes within its watershed while farther north the Alexandra River and Arctomys Creek flow west to join the North Saskatchewan.

◼ North Saskatchewan River (NP) (Headwaters to Banff Park boundary)
Bull trout to 70 cm (4.0 kg)
Lake trout to 65 cm (3.0 kg)
Whitefish to 40 cm
Brook trout to 40 cm
Rainbow trout to 40 cm
The North Saskatchewan River flows from its source at Saskatchewan Glacier and is joined by a number of other glacial rivers. The North Saskatchewan River is heavily silted much of the year, only clearing in late summer. During runoff, fishing is very slow, and usually confined to waters around clearer flowing tributary streams. When runoff is finally complete, fishing improves slightly along the entire length of the river. Large bull and lake trout, along with whitefish, make up the vast majority of fish in the river. Brook and rainbow trout are also caught on occasion. Fishing is usually productive near the mouths of the Mistaya, Howse and Alexandra rivers.

◼ Howse River (NP)
Bull trout to 65 cm (3.0 kg)
Lake trout to 60 cm (2.0 kg)
Whitefish to 40 cm
The Howse River flows from headwaters below historic Howse Pass to its junction with the North Saskatchewan River, just west of Saskatchewan River Crossing. Flowing through a broad valley over its final 10 km, the Howse River is characterized by wide gravel flats with extensive braiding where you can fish for bull trout in the 30-40 cm range, plus whitefish and the occasional lake trout. Generally, fishing is very slow in the Howse, picking up somewhat in late summer and early fall, when water levels recede and the river clears. A major horse trail leading to Howse Pass parallels the river for its entire length.

Howse River

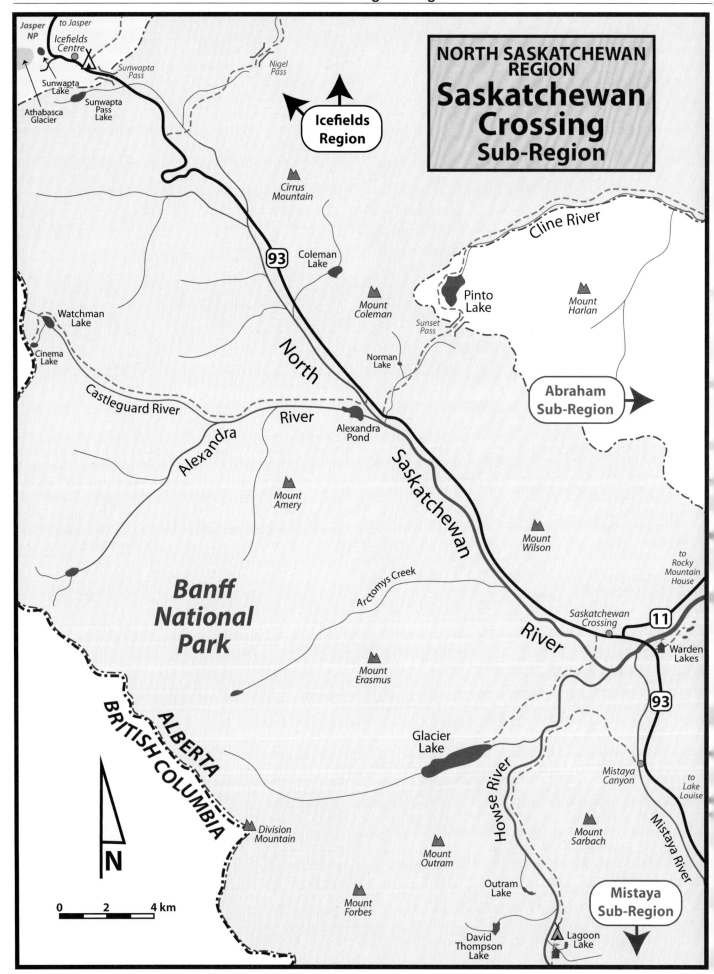

Jasper NP

to Jasper

Icefields Centre

Sunwapta Pass

Nigel Pass

Sunwapta Lake

Sunwapta Pass Lake

Athabasca Glacier

Icefields Region

Cirrus Mountain

93

Coleman Lake

Cline River

Pinto Lake

Mount Harlan

Watchman Lake

Cinema Lake

Mount Coleman

Sunset Pass

Norman Lake

Abraham Sub-Region

Castleguard River

North

River

Alexandra

Alexandra Pond

Saskatchewan

Mount Amery

Mount Wilson

to Rocky Mountain House

Banff National Park

Arctomys Creek

River

Saskatchewan Crossing

11

Warden Lakes

Mount Erasmus

93

ALBERTA

BRITISH COLUMBIA

Glacier Lake

Howse River

Mistaya Canyon

to Lake Louise

Division Mountain

Mount Sarbach

Mistaya River

N

Mount Outram

Outram Lake

Mistaya Sub-Region

0   2   4 km

Mount Forbes

David Thompson Lake

Lagoon Lake

■ Lagoon Lake (NP)

51°50'24"N 116°46'53"W
Bull trout to 65 cm (3.0 kg)
Whitefish to 30 cm

Lagoon Lake lies in marshy meadows east of the Howse River near a backcountry campground and warden's cabin, approximately 20 km by trail from the Icefields Parkway. Lagoon Lake was stocked in the past with rainbow trout that apparently failed to reproduce. At present, the lake contains bull trout and possibly a few whitefish, which have made their way in from the Howse River.

? David Thompson Lake (aka David Lake) (NP)

51°50'53"N 116°50'07"W
Rainbow trout to 35 cm

David Thompson Lake is set in a cirque directly beneath the north face of Mt. David. It is well protected by a major ford of the Howse River, and by steep and difficult terrain over its final 2 km of approach. Very few visitors reach the lake each year. Due to lack of information, it has never been determined whether the rainbow trout stocked a number of years ago still exist in good numbers.

■ Outram Lake (NP)

51°51'10"N 116°47'52"W
Bull trout to 60 cm (3.5 kg)
Whitefish to 35 cm
Rainbow trout to 35 cm

A ford of the Howse River, which is passable for hikers by late summer, is required to reach Outram Lake. Outram Lake is located on a bench above the west bank of the Howse River, opposite the Lagoon Lake warden cabin. The lake holds rainbow and bull trout in good numbers, as well as whitefish. Due to its lengthy and difficult access, Outram Lake offers the promise of solitude.

■ Glacier Lake (NP)

51°55'17"N 116°51'31"W
Lake trout to 80 cm (7.0 kg)
Bull trout to 70 cm (5.0 kg)
Whitefish to 50 cm

Glacier Lake is reached via a 8.5 km hike from the trailhead just north of Saskatchewan Crossing. Glacier Lake is the largest lake in the Region but has never gained a favourable reputation for fishing. This is due to runoff from the nearby Lyell Glacier, which ensures the water is heavily silted all year long. When the waters clear a bit in the late season, the area around the outlet is worth a look. Those using lures will have the best success in Glacier, which holds some lake and bull trout of gigantic proportions, as well as whitefish in fair numbers. Although fish can be taken from most locations along the shore, the sheer size of the lake will intimidate most anglers.

Glacier Lake

□ Warden Lakes (NP)

51°58'38"N 116°41'34"W
Brook trout to 35 cm
Rainbow trout to 35 cm

The two Warden Lakes are located on a bench south of the Saskatchewan River, 2 km east of the Icefields Parkway by trail. The Lower Lake was stocked in the past with both rainbow and brook trout, which failed to reproduce, and the lake is now devoid of fish. The larger Upper Lake is subject to winterkill. Upper Warden Lake has been stocked with rainbow, cutthroat, brook and splake. It is possible that a few brook or rainbow trout are still in the Upper Lake.

□ Arctomys Creek (NP)

51°51'... *Bull trout to 55 cm (1.5 kg)*
Whitefish to 35 cm

Arctomys Creek is born in the Lyell Glacier, high among the peaks of the Continental Divide. Arctomys Creek possesses the same characteristics as other major rivers of the region, as it runs very silty most of the year. It clears up marginally in late summer, when a limited population of bull trout and whitefish can be caught in its lower reaches. Access is difficult, requiring either a near-impossible ford of the North Saskatchewan River or a long, ill-defined approach from the Glacier Lake trail.

□ Norman Lake (NP)

52°05'30"N 116°54'08"W
Brook trout to 35 cm

Norman Lake is located 5 km along the Sunset Pass trail from the Icefields Parkway and is bypassed by most hikers on their way to Pinto Lake. Norman Lake is set in marshy and mosquito-infested meadows below Sunset Pass and holds a small population of brook trout averaging 20–30 cm in length. Flies are effective, and fly casting room is plentiful around the shoreline, although wet feet are a definite possibility.

Norman Lake

⊗ Pinto Lake (AB)

52°07′25″N 116°51′52″W
Status: Closed to angling
Bull trout

Pinto Lake is located on the north side of Sunset Pass, just outside the Banff National Park boundary. It is very popular destination for outfitters and backpackers during the summer. A 14 km trail from the Icefields Parkway is the usual route of approach for hikers, although outfitters tend to favour the longer access up the Cline River from the David Thompson Highway. Pinto Lake was renowned among anglers in the past for its large bull trout. Today, Pinto Lake is at present closed to fishing to protect this important bull trout habitat.

Pinto
Lake

◼ Alexandra Pond (NP)

52°04′21″N 116°56′49″W
Bull trout to 60 cm (3.0 kg)
Lake trout to 60 cm (3.0 kg)
Whitefish to 35 cm

Alexandra Pond, one of several ponds in the same area, is merely a widening of the Alexandra River located less than a kilometre upstream from the Alexandra's confluence with the North Saskatchewan River. It is reached by a trail that bridges the North Saskatchewan River but receives little fishing pressure. The early season is too silted for angling and even after runoff is over the fishing is very slow for lake trout, bull trout and whitefish.

◼ Alexandra River (NP)

Bull trout to 60 cm (3.0 kg)
Lake trout to 60 cm (3.0 kg)
Whitefish to 35 cm

The Alexandra River is a major tributary of the North Saskatchewan River, and offers poor fishing over its entire length. The lower reaches just above and below Alexandra Pond are the most productive with whitefish, lake trout and bull trout present in very limited numbers.

Alexandra
River

◼ Castleguard River (NP)

Bull trout to 55 cm (1.5 kg)
Whitefish to 30 cm
⊗ *Status: upper portion of river closed to angling*

The Castleguard River, a tributary of the upper Alexandra River, and presents very few opportunities for anglers. The upper portion of the Castleguard River, located in the Castleguard Caves Zone I Preservation Area in the east side of the upper drainage of the Castleguard River, is closed to fishing.

◼ Watchman Lake (NP)

52°04′39″N 117°15′51″W
Cutthroat trout to 40 cm

Two days of hiking from the Icefields Parkway are required to reach Watchman Lake. It is an attractive body of water set in subalpine forest 2 km northwest of seldom-visited Thompson Pass. Cutthroat trout averaging 20–30 cm in length are reported to be present in the lake.

◼ Cinema Lake (NP)

52°04′04″N 117°14′54″W
Status: Devoid of fish

Cinema Lake guards the northwest entrance to Thompson Pass. It has never been stocked and contains no fish.

◼ Coleman Lake (NP)

52°07′52″N 116°56′55″W
Status: Devoid of fish

Coleman Lake is reached by only the most enterprising of individuals. It is defended by a line of cliffs that parallel the Icefields Parkway. Coleman Lake has never been stocked, and no fish are present in its waters.

◼ Sunwapta Pass Lake (NP)

52°12′24″N 117°09′52″W
Status: Devoid of fish

Although it sits in a sparse forest less than a kilometre from the busy Icefields Parkway, the pretty green waters of Sunwapta Pass Lake receive little attention. A series of intermittent game trails lead in short order from the Sunwapta Pass parking area to the lake's shoreline. Sunwapta Pass Lake was once stocked with cutthroat and brook trout, but reports indicate no fish remain.

◼ Sunwapta Lake (NP)

51°12′53″N 116°14′06″W
Status: Devoid of fish

This small tarn at the toe of the awe-inspiring Athabasca Glacier is barren.

Abraham Sub-Region

This Sub-Region lies to the east of Banff National Park in the North Saskatchewan River valley. The Kootenay Plains and Lake Abraham are the most significant natural features. The David Thompson Highway (Highway 11) connects east to Rocky Mountain House and west to Banff National Park and the Icefields Parkway (Highway 93). Fishing opportunities in the Abraham Sub-Region are inconsistent. There are some excellent backcountry lakes, typified by Landslide Lake, Lake of the Falls, Coral Lake and Michelle Lakes. The more prominent waters, such as Abraham Lake and the North Saskatchewan River, offer only poor to fair angling.

◼ Abraham Lake (AB)
52°11'18"N 116°27'13"W
Bull trout to 75 cm (6.0 kg)
Brook trout to 55 cm (1.5 kg)
Lake trout to 70 cm (5.0 kg)
Rainbow trout to 60 cm (2.0 kg)
Whitefish to 50 cm

Abraham Lake was created by the construction of the Bighorn Dam on the North Saskatchewan River. Although Abraham Lake contains a wide variety of game fish, it has never been noted for its quality of angling. Hurricane force winds regularly whip down the length of the lake, making it very dangerous for boating. Fishing from shore is most productive where major streams or rivers enter the lake. This includes the Cline River and Tershishner Creek. Bull and brook trout are the most likely catch, although there are other species present.

Abraham Lake

◼ North Saskatchewan River (AB) (Banff Park boundary to Abraham Lake)
Bull trout to 75 cm (6.0 kg)
Brook trout to 40 cm
Lake trout to 65 cm (3.0 kg)
Whitefish to 40 cm

The North Saskatchewan River is paralleled by Highway 11 as it flows from Banff National Park to Abraham Lake. The river is very silted for most of the year, clearing up only in the fall. Fishing this section of the North Saskatchewan River is generally confined to September and October. Angling is poor to fair for bull, brook and lake trout as well as whitefish. Some of the deep pools can produce well.

North Saskatchewan River

◪ Landslide Lake (AB)
52°04'58"N 116°33'16"W
Cutthroat trout to 55 cm (1.5 kg)

Landslide Lake is situated 17 km by trail from Highway 11. Its pristine waters hold good numbers of large cutthroat trout. Most trout caught from Landslide Lake will average 30–40 cm in length. Angling is good around virtually the entire lake. The area near the outlet is popular due to its proximity to the main camping areas. The waters around the various inlet creeks at the south end of the lake are very productive.

Landslide Lake

Landslide Lake cutthroat lake

◼ Lake of the Falls (AB)
52°05'04"N 116°37'42"W
Cutthroat trout to 45 cm
Bull trout to 55 cm (1.5 kg)

Lake of the Falls is 17 km by trail from Highway 11, and the first two-thirds of the access trail are the same as for Landslide Lake. Lake of the Falls is set in a beautiful subalpine basin. It holds cutthroat and bull trout that average 25–35 cm in length. Flies and lures work well, and there is lots of fly casting room available along the shoreline.

Lake of the Falls

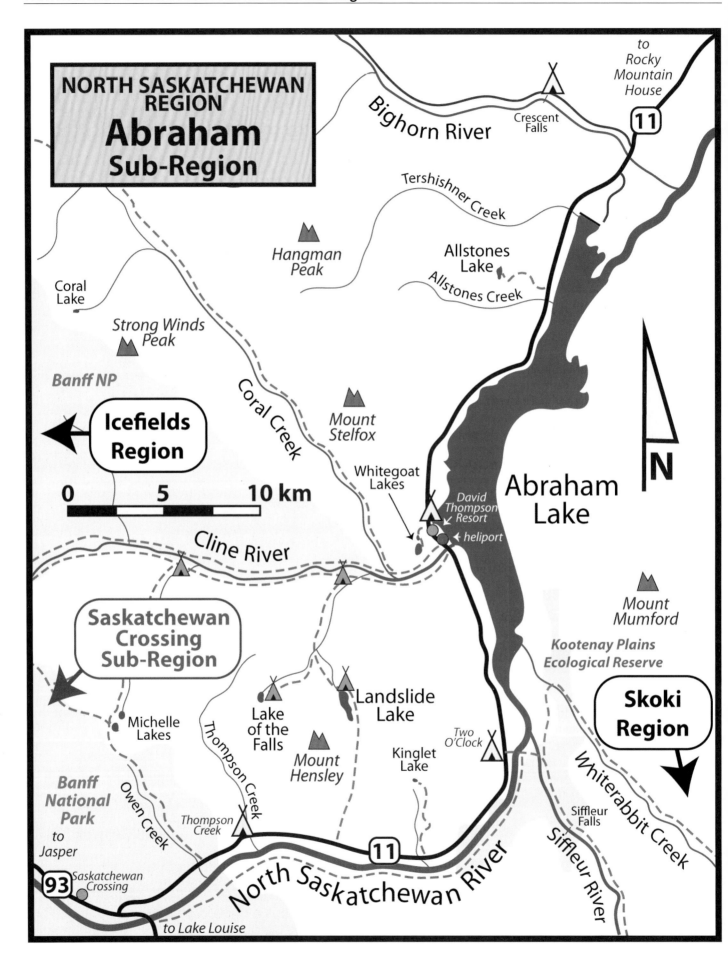

Lake of the Falls cutthroat trout

Steve Luethi photo

■ **Entry Lake (aka Hidden Lake) (AB)**
52°06'22"N 116°33'53"W
Cutthroat trout to 45 cm
Entry Lake is a small lake located east of the hiking trail into Landslide Lake. It holds small cutthroat trout, most in the 25–35 cm range.

■ **Entry Creek (AB)**
Cutthroat trout to 30 cm
Bull trout to 35 cm
Entry Creek is a tributary of the Cline River and collects its water from the Lake of the Falls and Landslide Creek. Entry Creek contains small cutthroat trout in its lower reaches, and bull trout as far upstream as the junction with Landslide Creek.

■ **Cline River (AB)**
Bull trout to 65 cm (3.0 kg)
Cutthroat trout to 55 cm (1.5 kg)
Brook trout to 50 cm
Whitefish to 40 cm
The Cline River is a major tributary of the North Saskatchewan River that eventually empties into Abraham Lake. There are three distinct sections on the Cline River. The first few kilometres above Abraham Lake is usually good for brook and bull trout. Continuing upstream, the river enters a major canyon, where fishing is difficult due to rough access. Above the canyon, the river is paralleled by a good horse trail. Cutthroat trout are present in good numbers above the canyon, with most in the 20–30 cm range. Fly fishing is the best method of angling on the upper Cline River.

Cline River

■ **Whitegoat Lakes (AB)**
52°02'59"N 116°28'23"W
Status: Doubtful
The Whitegoat Lakes are located a short distance off Highway 11, opposite the David Thompson Resort. Several short trails lead to the lakes. The Whitegoat Lakes are very shallow, and fish are likely unable to overwinter in the lakes. The occasional trout may make its way into the lakes each summer via the outlet creek.

Whitegoat Lakes

 Siffleur River (AB) (Banff Park boundary to North Saskatchewan River)
Status: Closed to angling
The section of the Siffleur River that flows from Banff National Park to the North Saskatchewan River is closed to angling. Siffleur Falls are located 4 km by trail from Highway 11 and are worth viewing.

□ **Kinglet Lake (AB)**
52°02'59"N 116°28'23"W
Cutthroat trout to 35 cm
Kinglet Lake is a small tarn set high in an alpine cirque north of Whirlpool Point on the North Saskatchewan River. Access is very difficult and requires a stiff trek up a rocky ridge from Highway 11. The lake has been stocked on several occasions and likely still holds a few small cutthroat trout.

■ **Allstones Lake (AB)**
52°18'11"N 116°25'07"W
Brook trout to 45 cm
Allstones Lake is set in a forested basin, and is reached by following a very steep 5 km hike up from Highway 11. The lake holds brook trout that average 25–35 cm in length. Lures and flies both work in Allstones Lake. Fly fishing is difficult in most locations because of the forest cover.

Allstones Lake

■ **Michelle Lakes (AB)**

(Upper lake) 52°04'07"N 116°45'11"W

Golden trout to 35 cm

The Michelle Lakes are reached after a long hike up the Cline River and then a torturous route up Waterfalls Creek. These lakes are for very determined anglers only. Fortunately, Rockies Heli Canada provides helicopter access from Highway 11 into Michelle Lake, as well as Coral Lake, Landslide Lake and Lake of the Falls. The Michelle Lakes are unique in that they hold golden trout, one of Alberta's rarest game fish. The golden trout in the lakes are neither large nor numerous. Most trout taken will be in the 20–30 size range and are normally taken in better numbers by fly fishers than spin casters.

Michelle Lakes

Michelle Lakes golden trout

□ **Coral Lake (AB)**

52°16'59"N 116°47'05"W

Golden trout to 35 cm

Each season Coral Lake attracts anglers in search of the elusive golden trout. Most arrive via helicopter from the Cline River Heliport on Highway 11. For those determined to hike into Coral Lake access is via a long and difficult trail up the Cline River and Coral Creek valleys. Those who reach Coral Lake, by whatever means they choose, can expect brightly coloured golden trout in the 20–30 cm range.

■ **Bighorn River (AB)**

Cutthroat trout to 40 cm

Brook trout to 40 cm

Brown trout to 50 cm

Bull trout to 70 cm (4.0 kg)

Whitefish to 40 cm

The Bighorn River is a major tributary of the North Saskatchewan River and enters downstream from Abraham Lake and the Bighorn Dam. The spectacular Crescent Falls are an impassable obstacle for fish. Below the falls, bull and brook trout are most likely to be caught. Brown trout and whitefish may be present as well. Above Crescent Falls, cutthroat trout are present in good numbers. Fly fishing is very effective on the upper Bighorn River.

Bighorn River

■ **Tershishner Creek (AB)**

Brook trout to 45 cm

Bull trout to 60 cm (3.0 kg)

Whitefish to 45 cm

Tershishner Creek joins the North Saskatchewan River at the north end Abraham Lake, near the Bighorn Dam. Fishing is generally good where Tershishner Creek enters Abraham Lake. Upstream from Abraham Lake, Tershishner Creek holds brook and bull trout in the 20–30 cm range, as well as whitefish.

ICEFIELDS REGION

This Region encompasses the southern half of Jasper National Park. It includes the watersheds of the upper Athabasca, Sunwapta and Brazeau Rivers. The Icefields Parkway (Highway 93) follows the course of the Athabasca and Sunwapta Rivers, and offers anglers direct access to several roadside locations. Beyond the Icefields Parkway, access to most of the rest of the region is very difficult and requires extended travel by trail. There are some outstanding lakes in the region, highlighted by Amethyst Lakes in Tonquin Valley and Fortress Lake in BC's Hamber Provincial Forest. The Region is divided into three Sub-Regions. The Upper Athabasca Sub-Region includes the main Athabasca valley upstream (south) of Athabasca Falls. The Brazeau Sub-Region is very remote and includes the Brazeau River drainage within Jasper National Park. The Tonquin Sub-Region includes the renowned Amethyst Lakes and Tonquin Valley and their outstanding backpacking opportunities.

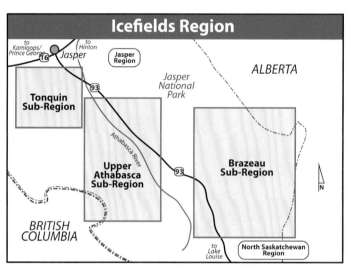

Upper Athabasca Sub-Region

This Sub-Region extends from Banff National Park in the south to Athabasca Falls in the north and includes the Sunwapta and upper Athabasca River valleys. The Icefields Parkway (Highway 93) is the sole highway access. Angling opportunities are limited to lakes that have been stocked in the past and now have stable trout populations. The best of the Sub-Region includes Moab and Fortress lakes.

◼ Sunwapta River (NP)
Bull trout to 70 cm (4.0 kg)
Rainbow trout to 45 cm
Brook trout to 45 cm
Whitefish to 45 cm
The Sunwapta River flows northwest from the Banff-Jasper Boundary at Sunwapta Pass, and joins the Athabasca River 3 km downstream from Sunwapta Falls. The river is readily accessible from the Icefields Parkway and offers poor fishing below the falls for bull, rainbow and brook trout. With its source high among the glaciers of the Continental Divide, the Sunwapta River runs silted for much of the year, clearing only in the fall.

◼ Athabasca River (NP) (Headwaters to Athabasca Falls)
Bull trout to 80 cm (7.0 kg)
Rainbow trout to 55 cm (1.5 kg)
Brook trout to 50 cm
Whitefish to 50 cm
The headwaters of the Athabasca River, upstream from Athabasca Falls, is typically silted much of the year. The river clears long enough in the fall to offer some fishing opportunities. Bull trout and whitefish are the main fare in the upper Athabasca River, with the occasional rainbow and brook trout taken. Anglers are advised to work areas around the confluence with clearer tributaries.

Athabasca River

Logan Urie photo

Athabasca River bull trout

◼ Gong Lake (NP)
52°23'15"N 117°35'29"W
Status: Devoid of trout
This large glacial lake near the headwaters of the Athabasca River has never been stocked and contains no fish.

☐ Dragon Lake (NP)
52°28'08"N 117°42'58"W
Brook trout to 40 cm
Dragon Lake is protected by a major ford of the Athabasca River and by poorly defined access routes. The lake was stocked in the past with brook trout, and recent reports indicate that some trout still exist although their numbers are limited.

Fishing Nirvana

Fortress Lake is tucked away in a stunning, remote valley of the Canadian Rockies and is dominated by peaks and glaciers that tower above the lake in all directions, creating a 360-degree "Fortress." The brilliant waters of Fortress Lake hold some of the largest brook trout on the planet. A 30-minute helicopter flight through some of the Rockies' most breath-taking scenery ends at Fortress Lake Wilderness Retreat (*fortresslake.com*), a backcountry wilderness lodge that provides full-service accommodation. Fishing for the monster brook trout that inhabit Fortress Lake is paradise to anglers. Brook trout in the 2–3 kg range are commonplace, with much larger trout caught regularly. From the lodge, the Fortress Lake valley also provides hikers, canoeists and kayakers with a backcountry oasis to discover.

■ Fortress Lake (BC)

52°22'08"N 117°47'01"W

Brook trout to 70 cm (4.0 kg)

Fortress Lake is an incredibly magnificent 10-km long body of water situated just west of the Alberta-BC boundary at Fortress Pass in Hamber Provincial Forest in BC. Fortress Lake is renowned for its massive brook trout, many of which will top the 3 kg mark. There are two ways to get to Fortress Lake. One is a daunting 25 km hike that includes a major ford of the Chaba River. The other way is to helicopter into the lodge at Fortress Lake Wilderness Retreat. The lodge been popular among helicopter-in anglers for many years and is complete with boats and guides. Fortress Lake's remote location ensures that the quality of fishing should remain high for many years to come.

Fortress Lake

Fortress Lake brook trout

Fortress Lake Wilderness Lodge photo

Fortress Lake Wilderness Lodge photo

□ Buck Lake (NP)

52°33'06"N 117°39'43"W

Brook trout to 40

Rainbow trout to 50 cm (1.5 kg)

Buck Lake is surrounded by heavy forest and sits less than a kilometre by trail from the Icefields Parkway. Buck Lake likely still holds a few rainbow and brook trout, averaging 25–35 cm in length. The lake's ability to hold trout has generally been dependent on regular stockings, and as such the quality of fishing has declined over the years.

Buck Lake

⊗ Osprey Lake (NP)

52°33'32"N 117°40'12"W

Status: Closed to angling

This small reed-fringed lake is a short 15-minute trail walk from the Icefields Parkway. Osprey at one time contained both rainbow and brook trout, but is presently closed to angling.

□ Honeymoon Lake (NP)

52°33'23"N 117°40'40"W

Rainbow trout to 40 cm

Honeymoon Lake is situated immediately east of the Icefields Parkway and has a nice campground on its shore. A limited number of rainbow trout averaging 25–35 cm in length inhabit Honeymoon's waters. Reports indicate that the quality of fishing has declined somewhat in the past few years and the lake's ability to hold fish is somewhat in question.

■ Little Honeymoon Lake (NP)

52°33'36"N 117°41'04"W

Status: Devoid of fish

Little Honeymoon Lake is located just north of Honeymoon Lake. It was stocked in the past with brook trout, but it is unlikely that any fish remain in the lake.

■ Leach Lake (NP)

52°41'38"N 117°54'71"W

Rainbow trout to 50 cm

Leach Lake is located alongside Highway 93A and gained a reputation over the years of harbouring some large fish. Rainbow trout in the 25–35 cm range are reportedly still present in the lake. Shallows extending far out into the lake make fishing from shore a difficult proposition. During low light conditions when many of the larger fish make their way into the shallows to feed, patient fly fishers can be rewarded with large rainbows 40 cm or more. Boats are available through rental arrangements made at sporting goods stores in Jasper. Working the distinct margin that separates the shallow water from the deep from a boat is usually very effective.

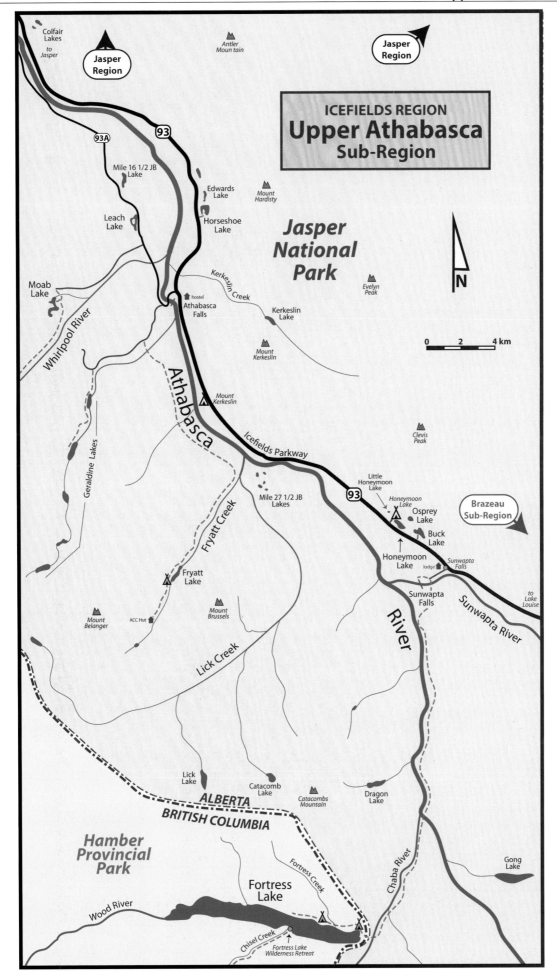

ICEFIELDS REGION
Upper Athabasca
Sub-Region

Colfair Lakes

to Jasper

Jasper Region

Jasper Region

93A

93

Mile 16 1/2 JB Lake

Edwards Lake

Antler Mountain

Mount Hardisty

Leach Lake

Horseshoe Lake

Jasper National Park

Moab Lake

Kerkeslin Creek

hostel
Athabasca Falls

Kerkeslin Lake

Evelyn Peak

N

Whirlpool River

Mount Kerkeslin

0 2 4 km

Athabasca

Mount Kerkeslin

Icefields Parkway

Clevis Peak

Geraldine Lakes

Mile 27 1/2 JB Lakes

Little Honeymoon Lake

Fryatt Creek

93

Honeymoon Lake

Osprey Lake

Brazeau Sub-Region

Buck Lake

Fryatt Lake

Honeymoon Lake

lodge

Sunwapta Falls

Mount Belanger

ACC Hut

Mount Brussels

Sunwapta Falls

River

Sunwapta River

to Lake Louise

Lick Creek

Lick Lake

Catacomb Lake

Catacombs Mountain

Dragon Lake

ALBERTA
BRITISH COLUMBIA

Chaba River

Gong Lake

Hamber Provincial Park

Fortress Creek

Fortress Lake

Wood River

Chisel Creek

Fortress Lake Wilderness Retreat

209

Leach Lake

■ Mile 16 1/2 Lake (Jasper-Banff) (NP)

52°42'33"N 117°54'37"W

Rainbow trout to 50 cm

Brook trout to 50 cm

Mile 16 1/2 Lake is situated less than a kilometre north of Leach Lake on the opposite side of Highway 93A and in the past drew high praise from anglers. Mile 16 1/2 Lake is shallow and similar in character to Leach. It at one time contained large rainbow and brook trout averaging 30–40 cm in length. Current populations are limited in number and size. The lake is best fished from a boat, which can be rented from sporting goods stores in Jasper. Consistent with other lakes of this nature, the zone between the shallow and deep waters usually holds fish. Slowly trolling a lure or wet fly through the deeper water has also proved effective.

■ Lick Lake (NP)

52°27'29"N 117°51'36"W

■ Catacomb Lake (NP)

52°26'09"N 117°47'06"W

Status: Devoid of fish

These two glacial lakes are set high among the peaks of the Continental Divide at the head of Lick Creek, a minor tributary of the Athabasca River. The lakes have never been stocked and contain no fish.

◬ Moab Lake (NP)

52°39'49"N 117°57'33"W

Lake trout to 75 cm (5.0 kg)

Rainbow trout to 45 cm

Pretty Moab Lake is reached via a short 1 km hike at the end of a 7 km-long fire road off Highway 93A. Moab Lake is popular with anglers, and its clear waters hold rainbow trout along with large lake trout. Although the lake's distinctive shape allows for fishing from along much of the shoreline, a boat is strongly recommended. Boats are available for rent on Moab Lake through prior arrangements made with one of Jasper's sporting goods stores. Lure fishers and those trolling generally have good success with Moab's lake trout, especially in the first part of the season after ice-out. Stick to the deep drop-offs near the many cliffs. Fly fishing is effective on the rainbow trout population, especially in the first bay on the lake (where you reach the lake from the trail). ✖ Be sure to check fishing regulations, as the area around the lake's outlet and the outlet stream are permanently closed to angling.

Moab Lake

Logan Urie with Moab Lake lake trout

Logan Urie photo

■ Whirlpool River (NP)

Bull trout to 60 cm (2.5 kg)

Rainbow trout to 40 cm

Whitefish to 30 cm

The Whirlpool River is paralleled for its entire distance by the historic Athabasca Pass trail. The river receives little pressure from anglers above its confluence with the Athabasca River. Small bull trout are present in the river's upper reaches with bull and rainbow trout along with in the lower river. The waters near the Whirlpool's confluence with the Athabasca are usually productive.

◬ Geraldine Lakes (NP)

(Lower (first) lake) 52°36'57"N 117°55'44"W

Brook trout to 60 cm (2.5 kg)

These five exquisite lakes strung like pearls in a series of basins separated by short headwalls provide one of the Sub-Region's more popular day hikes. The first lake lies less than 2 km from the trailhead on the Geraldine Lakes Fire Road, while the upper, or fifth, lake lies another 6 km distant. The first two lakes contain good numbers of brook trout ranging from 25–35 cm in length that can often be sighted well out into the clear waters. Some very large brookies in the 2-3 kg range are pulled from the first lake each season. Sunken deadfall provides cover in the waters near shore, particularly in the first lake, and anglers are advised to work these areas. Fish may be present in the upper three lakes.

☐ **Horseshoe Lake (NP)**
52°41'55"N 117°51'55"W
Rainbow trout to 40 cm
Appropriately-shaped Horseshoe Lake sits alongside the Icefields Parkway 20 km south of Jasper. Although Horseshoe Lake's ability to sustain trout over time has long been questioned, its sparkling blue waters likely still hold a few rainbow trout averaging 25–35 cm in length. The lakeshore is made up of rock rubble that will present problems for those who will be fly casting. More likely you will encounter a cliff jumper than a trout.

Horseshoe Lake

☐ **Edwards Lake (NP)**
52°42'14"N 117°51'58"W
Brook trout to 35 cm
Edwards Lake is located approximately a few hundred metres north of Horseshoe Lake, hidden in the forest just to the east of Highway 93. Edwards is generally overlooked by the area's anglers, if for no other reason than it is a little bit hidden. Edwards Lake holds brook trout in the 25–35 cm range, which can be taken the deeper water found around much of the lake.

Tyler Ambrosi photo

Edwards Lake

Logan Urie photo

Edwards Lake brook trout

Lower Geraldine Lake

Lower Geraldine Lake brook trout

☐ **Fryatt Lake (NP)**
52°31'11"N 117°51'58"W
Rainbow trout to 40 cm
Fryatt Lake is pinched in a narrow valley between Brussels Peak and Mt. Fryatt, and is accessed by a tiring 17 km hike from the Geraldine Lakes Fire Road. While the upper Fryatt Creek valley is a favourite haunt of climbers, anglers are more likely to be enticed by Fryatt Lake and its limited population of rainbow trout. The lake is almost completely encircled by heavy timber that will cause problems for most of those fly fishing.

☐ **Colfair Lakes (NP)**
52°45'55"N 117°57'48"W
Status: Doubtful
These two small lakes set in the heavily wooded hills north of Hardisty Creek once offered good rainbow trout fishing to those who reached their shores. Although a number of very ill-defined trails connect the Colfair Lakes to the Icefields Parkway 2 km distant, finding a trailhead may be a problem. Your best bet is to carry a map and compass. Although unlikely, there may still be a few rainbow trout in the Colfair Lakes.

☐ **Mile 27 1/2 Lakes J-B (NP)**
52°39'14"N 117°46'55"W
Brook trout to 40 cm
This series of ponds is located on the western side of the Icefields Parkway approximately 2 km north of Horseshoe Lake. Brook trout are likely present in the ponds, averaging 20-30 cm in length.

⍰ **Kerkeslin Lake (aka Hardisty Lake) (NP)**
52°39'14"N 117°51'59"W
Status: Unknown
The pristine waters of Kerkeslin Lake are located high in an isolated valley north of Mt. Kerkeslin, and remain virtually untouched. Reliable reports seldom make their way out, but it is possible that Kerkeslin Lake holds a limited population of bull trout that have worked their way in over a period of time from the Athabasca River.

☐ **Kerkeslin Creek (NP)**
Rainbow trout to 35 cm
Bull trout to 40 cm
The outlet of Kerkeslin Lake flows into the Athabasca River. Small rainbow and bull trout can be found in the better pools along the creek.

Brazeau Sub-Region

The Brazeau River watershed constitutes the major portion of this Sub-Region, located in the remote southeast corner of Jasper National Park. Extended backpacking trips are required to reach most potential fishing spots in the district, which include Brazeau Lake, the Brazeau River and its major tributaries, the Southesk and Cairn rivers. To the southeast and outside the Jasper National Park boundary are Job and Obstruction lakes, which can be reached via extended trails from the David Thompson Highway (Highway 11).

■ **Brazeau Lake (NP)**
52°24'12"N 117°03'09"W
Rainbow trout to 60 cm (2.0 kg)
Bull trout to 75 cm (5.0 kg)
Majestic Brazeau Lake is set in a deep valley west of the Brazeau River and is a remote 30 km by trail away from the Icefields Parkway. As a consequence, Brazeau Lake receives very little attention from anglers. The lake's silted waters contain both rainbow and bull trout in limited numbers. Lures fished deep are often effective in Brazeau Lake, and the area around the outlet can be productive.

Brazeau Lake

■ **Brazeau River (NP/AB)**
Bull trout to 70 cm (4.0 kg)
Whitefish to 40 cm
Rainbow trout to 40 cm
The Brazeau River is a major tributary of the North Saskatchewan River. It has never been noted for the quality of angling in its upper reaches. Access is by trails that parallel the upper river. The Brazeau River is very silted much of the summer. Fishing improves somewhat in late August and early September when bull trout and whitefish and the occasional rainbow trout can be taken. Where the Brazeau River forms the boundary of Jasper National Park, national park fishing regulations are in effect.

Brazeau River

■ **Azote Lake, Wisht Lake, Poboktan Lake, Upperslate Lake, Lowerslate Lake, Wolverine Pond, Cloudy Lake, Oreamnos Lake (NP)**
(general area) 52°25'55"N 117°16'39"W
Status: Devoid of fish
This cluster of lakes is located in the valley above Brazeau Lake. None has lakes have ever been stocked.

⊗ **Job Lake (aka Wilson Lake, Blue Lake) (AB)**
52°22'04"N 117°51'00"W
Status: Closed to angling
Cutthroat trout
Job Lake is exceptional in terms of both beauty and fish habitat. The lake has been popular with outfitters for many years, despite the long 40 km trail from the David Thompson Highway and the even longer 50+ km approach from the Icefields Parkway. For anglers, cutthroat trout in large sizes and good numbers were Job Lake's main attraction. At present, Job is closed to fishing to protect native cutthroat trout stocks.

☐ **Obstruction Lakes (AB)**
52°25'07"N 117°51'37"W
Cutthroat trout to 40 cm
Tiny Obstruction Lakes are located 4 km southwest of Job Creek by ill-defined trail and receive little attention from anglers each season. The lakes hold cutthroat trout in the 20–30 cm range.

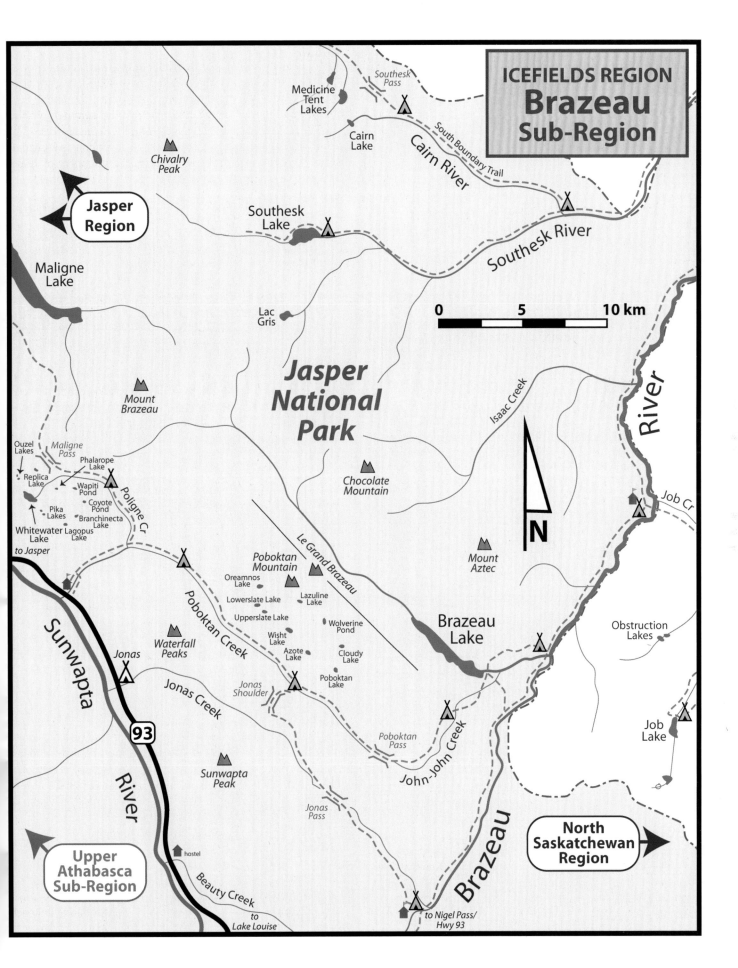

☐ **Southesk River (NP)**
Bull trout to 65 cm (2.5 kg)
Whitefish to 35 cm
The Southesk River flows east from its headwaters in Southesk Lake and joins the Brazeau River at the Jasper National Park boundary. The Southesk River is seldom fished due to lengthy access routes. The river holds limited numbers of bull trout and whitefish.

☐ **Southesk Lake (NP)**
52°38'32"N 117°11'59"W
Bull trout to 65 cm (2.5 kg)
Poor trails and restricted access limit travel into Southesk Lake, which is situated in one of the most remote corners of Jasper National Park. Bull trout are present in Southesk, although not in substantial numbers.

■ **Lac Gris (NP)**
52°35'51"N 117°13'06"W
Status: Devoid of fish
Lac Gris is a silted body of water located in the valley south of Southesk Lake. Lac Gris has never been stocked, and contains no fish.

☐ **Cairn River (NP)**
Bull trout to 50 cm
The Cairn River is a tributary to the Southesk River and receives virtually no angling pressure. Bull trout are present in small numbers in the river, which begins on the east side of Southesk Pass.

■ **Cairn Lake (NP)**
52°42'18"N 117°09'31"W
Status: Devoid of fish
Cairn Lake is the headwaters of the Cairn River. It has never been stocked and is reported to be devoid of fish.

■ **Medicine Tent Lakes (NP)**
52°43'09"N 117°09'50"W
Status: Devoid of fish
The Medicine Tent Lakes are set in alpine terrain on the west side of Southesk Pass. The lakes are the source of the Medicine Tent River, which flows northwest to join the Rocky River. The Medicine Tent Lakes have never been stocked and contain no fish.

■ **Whitewater Lake (NP)**
52°29'43"N 117°27'31"W
Status: Devoid of fish
Whitewater Lake is the largest of the lakes in the immediate Maligne Pass vicinity. It has never been stocked and is devoid of fish.

■ **Pika Lakes (North and South), Phalarope Lake, Lagopus Pond, Brachinecta Pond, Coyote Pond, Wapiti Pond, Replica Lake, Ouzel Lakes (Upper and Lower) (NP)**
(general area) 52°29'58"N 117°27'14"W
Status: Devoid of fish
This network of small lakes and ponds is located in the alpine environs of Maligne Pass. All of the lakes are devoid of fish.

Tonquin Sub-Region

The resplendent Tonquin Valley is one of Jasper National Park's most popular backcountry destinations. This glorious area is comparable to any area in the Rockies in terms of scenery. Two 20 km-long trails lead into Tonquin Valley, one via the Astoria River and the other via Portal and Maccarib creeks. Visitors to the area are able to choose from several fine backcountry campsites as well as permanent outfitters camps, and an Alpine Club of Canada hut at Outpost Lake. The centerpiece of the Sub-Region is Amethyst Lakes, which are set beneath the spectacular castellate summits of the Ramparts. Amethyst Lakes are truly one of the jewels of the Canadian Rockies. Sparkling waters are home to huge rainbow and brook trout, yet its location is remote enough to ensure the quality of fishing remains high. Many of the other waters in the Tonquin area are devoid of fish, although Moat Lake and the Astoria River hold the promise of good fishing.

⬂ **Amethyst Lakes (NP)**
52°42'32"N 118°16'44"W
Rainbow trout to 65 cm (3.0 kg)
Brook trout to 60 cm (2.0 kg)
Fortunately for anglers, fishing in Amethyst Lakes rivals the area's scenic splendour. Large rainbow and brook trout, averaging 40-60 cm in length, can be taken in good numbers all summer long. As the lakes are sizable, fishing from shore can be an intimidating proposition. Anglers staying at one of the valley's two lodges have the advantage of fishing from boats. Fishing from a boat increases fishing potential exponentially, and just trolling a wet fly or lure while admiring the scenery will usually produce results. Fish can be taken any time during the day. Having recently stayed at the Tonquin Valley Lodge, I can highly recommend the accommodations, the food, the staff, and, of course, the fishing! ⊗ The stretch of the Astoria River between its outlet and a point 400 m downstream is permanently closed to angling. Check regulations before fishing. Be forewarned that the marshy environs of Amethyst Lakes support a ravenous mosquito population.

Tyler Ambrosi with Amethyst Lakes rainbow trout

(northern) Amethyst Lake

Amethyst Lake brook trout

Logan Urie photo

◢ Moat Lake (NP)

52°43'21"N 118°19'40"W

Rainbow trout to 40 cm

Moat Lake is reached by a short 2 km side trail from Amethyst Lakes. Moat Lake is set amid very marshy meadows, which contribute to the area's large insect population. The lake holds plenty of rainbow trout averaging 25–35 cm in length. Trout in the lake feed actively on the surface on most days, and a dry fly is usually very effective. Fly casting room is adequate around most of the shoreline. Moat Lake's long, narrow shape is favourable to fly fishing, since a large portion of the fishable water can be

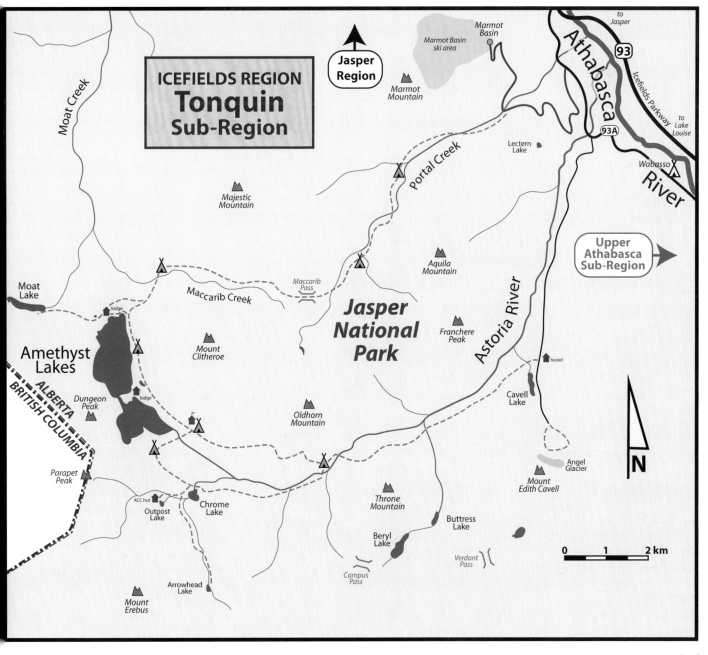

reached by shorebound anglers. Boats are available for rent through arrangements with outfitters on Amethyst Lakes.

Moat Lake

◼ Moat Creek (NP)
Rainbow trout to 35 cm

Moat Creek is the outlet stream for Moat Lake, and it flows north into Meadow Creek before eventually emptying into the Miette River. In the waters immediately downstream from Moat Lake, the creek holds good numbers of rainbow trout, most averaging 15–25 cm in length.

◼ Maccarib Creek (NP)
Rainbow trout to 30 cm

Maccarib Creek meanders through open meadows below Maccarib Pass before flowing into Moat Creek. It holds small rainbow trout in the 15–25 cm range over its entire length. The best fishing is in the waters above the Maccarib campground on the Maccarib Pass trail.

Maccarib Creek

◼ Portal Creek (NP)
Rainbow trout to 35 cm
Brook trout to 35 cm

Portal Creek flows east from the heights of Maccarib Pass to the Athabasca River. Portal Creek has plenty of fine pools that contain small rainbow and brook trout. The upper Portal Creek valley is also prime grizzly habitat, and anglers should be aware at all times.

◼ Astoria River (NP)
Rainbow trout to 40 cm
Bull trout to 60 cm (2.0 kg)
Brook trout to 35 cm
Whitefish to 35 cm

The turbulent Astoria River flows from the Amethyst Lakes to the Athabasca River. The Astoria River possesses several fine stretches of fishable water. Most fishing activity takes place in the area of the confluence with the Athabasca and in the upper reaches, within 10 km of Amethyst Lakes. Rainbow trout in the 20–30 cm range are caught in greater numbers than bull and brook trout in the upper section. Near the Athabasca River bull trout tend to predominate, and the odd whitefish may also be taken.

☐ Chrome Lake (NP)
52°39'46"N 118°14'14"W
Rainbow trout to 40 cm

Chrome Lake is located 2 km south of Amethyst Lakes by trail and is surrounded by a pleasant combination of forest and meadow. It reportedly still holds a small population of rainbow trout averaging 25–30 cm in length. Chrome Lake is generally overlooked by anglers, due to its proximity to the more renowned waters of Amethyst Lakes. It is often very silty due to glacial runoff, and fish are generally taken in the shallower waters close to shore.

◼ Outpost Lake (NP)
52°39'42"N 118°15'15"W
Status: Devoid of fish

The Alpine Club of Canada's Waites-Gibson Hut is located on the shore of tiny Outpost Lake. Outpost Lake has never been stocked and contains no fish.

◼ Arrowhead Lake (NP)
52°38'08"N 118°13'47"W
Status: Devoid of fish

Appropriately shaped Arrowhead Lake lies at the base of Eremite Glacier in Eremite Valley, 3 km south of Chrome Lake. Arrowhead has never been stocked, and is likely too silted for fish to thrive.

◼ Buttress Lake (NP)
52°39'25"N 118°06'41"W
◼ Beryl Lake (NP)
52°38'52"N 118°07'52"W
Status: Doubtful

Buttress and Beryl Lakes have never been stocked with trout. Their isolated location in a remote valley off Verdant Creek makes it highly improbable that they contain any fish.

☐ Cavell Lake (NP)
52°41'54"N 118°03'42"W
Brook trout to 30 cm
Cutthroat trout to 30 cm

The emerald-green waters of charming Cavell Lake are most famous as a foreground in photographs of Mt. Edith Cavell. The lake is seldom fished, and reports indicate very poor fishing for a few brook and cutthroat trout in the 15–25 cm range.

Cavell Lake

☐ Lectern Lake (NP)
52°46'17"N 118°03'26"W
Rainbow trout to 30 cm

Lectern Lake is hidden in a forested basin above the Marmot Basin road, midway between Portal Creek and the Astoria River. The lake was stocked in the past with rainbow trout. Few reliable reports are available on Lectern Lake, but it is likely to hold a few rainbow trout in small sizes.

JASPER REGION

This popular Region offers excellent fishing opportunities in and around the Jasper townsite. The Icefields Parkway (Highway 93) and Yellowhead Highway (Highway 16) provide the primary access to the region. Tourist facilities and fishing equipment are available in Jasper. Large trout are the main angling attraction, and they can be taken from a number of lakes, including Maligne, Medicine, Annette, Edith, Pyramid and Patricia. The Athabasca, Miette and Maligne rivers provide some excellent river fishing. The Region is divided into three Sub-Regions. The first is the area west of the Jasper townsite and includes the Miette River and waters west along the Yellowhead Highway. The Skyline Sub-Region includes the Athabasca River and the areas south of Jasper along the Icefields Parkway and east along the Yellowhead Highway. The Maligne Sub-Region includes the Maligne River watershed, southeast of Jasper.

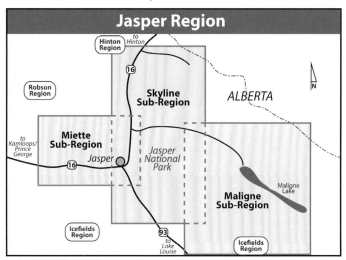

Miette Sub-Region

This Sub-Region also includes the Jasper townsite and extends north to Pyramid and Patricia Lakes. These two lakes are very popular with anglers throughout the summer. To the west of Jasper a series of hiking trails radiates out from townsite and from the Pyramid Lake Road, leading to Riley, Mina, Marjorie, Hibernia, Caledonia, Minnow, High and Saturday Night lakes. The Miette River and valley stretch to the west and the BC border. From Highway 16 west of Jasper, a short trail leads to Dorothy, Christine, Iris and Virl lakes.

Pyramid Lake (NP)
52°55'14"N 118°05'55"W
Lake trout to 60 cm (3.0 kg)
Rainbow trout to 55 cm (1.5 kg)
Brook trout to 50 cm
Whitefish to 45 cm
Pyramid Lake is located six kilometres from Jasper by road, and is the Sub-Region's most popular fishing spot. It is busy with anglers from opening to closing day. Although both rainbow and brook trout are plentiful, it's the lake trout that attract the attention. In the early season, lake trout can be taken in the shallower waters simply by slowly trolling a flatfish behind some kind of flasher. The lake trout migrate to the colder waters as soon as the lake begins to warm. By mid-summer, rainbow become the standard fare, with some nice ones taken each season. Lake trout are still

caught by those anglers fishing the lake's very depths. Rental boats are available at the lake.

Pyramid Lake

Tyler Ambrosi with Pyramid Lake lake trout

Patricia Lake (NP)
52°54'13"N 118°06'04"W
Rainbow trout to 60 cm (3.0 kg)
Lake trout to 60 cm (3.0 kg)
The striking blue waters of Patricia Lake are situated alongside the Pyramid Lake Road, 5 km from Jasper. Patricia Lake is often overlooked by anglers intent on fishing nearby Pyramid Lake. Patricia Lake holds a limited population of large rainbow trout, with most caught in the 40–50 cm range. There are also large lake trout in the lake and they tend to be more aggressive in the early season. Trolling a lure or large wet fly is the standard technique on Patricia, whether for rainbows or lakers. Boats are available for rent through Jasper sporting goods stores.

Patricia Lake

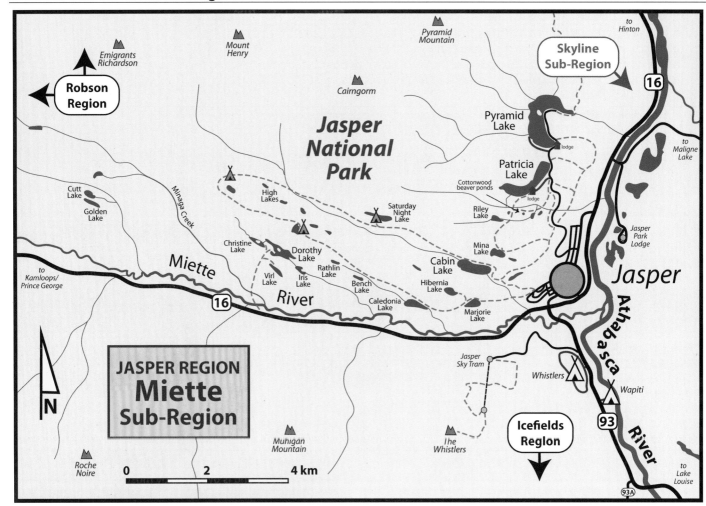

Patricia Lake rainbow trout

☐ **Cottonwood beaver ponds (NP)**
52°53'38"N 118°05'32"W
Brook trout to 35 cm
This series of beaver ponds extends west from Pyramid Lake Road, 3 km from Jasper. The ponds hold brook trout in the 15–25 cm range. The marshy setting of the ponds, complete with heavy vegetation growth, makes access difficult and fly casting even more difficult.

The End of Fish Stocking

The late 1980s saw the end of fish stocking in most lakes in National Parks in the Rocky Mountains. Many lakes had sustained their populations only through regular plantings. Many fish populations were unable to propagate in lakes with no inlet or outlet streams. The last fish in these lakes grew to large sizes but then started to die off from old age. Without any new fish in the lakes to replace the existing populations, these waters were soon devoid of fish. Many of the lakes in the immediate Jasper vicinity suffered this fate. Lakes that not so many years ago held decent populations of trout are now completely without fish. Although this lack of fish in these lakes negatively affects the quality of angling in the parks, it has positively affected ecosystems in these lakes, returning them to their natural state.

■ **Riley Lake (NP)**
52°53'36"N 118°07'17"W
Status: Doubtful
Riley Lake is a small reed-encircled lake, 3 km by trail from the Pyramid Lake Road. Riley Lake at one time good fishing for rainbow trout. It is likely that few, if any, trout remain in Riley Lake.

■ **Mina Lake (NP)**
52°52'59"N 118°07'14"W
Status: Doubtful
Mina Lake is located on the Mina-Riley loop trail, 3 km from the Pyramid Lake Road. Mina Lake is typical of many of the smaller lakes on the bench west of Jasper. Both rainbow and brook trout were present in the lake at one time. Today, it is doubtful that any trout remain in Mina Lake.

■ **Cabin Lake (NP)**
52°52'41"N 118°07'54"W
Rainbow trout to 40 cm
Cabin Lake is the source of Jasper's water supply, and was closed to angling for many years. Cabin Lake is now open to fishing, and

it is one of the few lakes in the area where the trout population has flourished. Rainbow trout can be taken from Cabin Lake in good numbers, most in the 15–25 cm range. There is usually good fishing off the dam at the east end of the lake.

Cabin Lake

Marjorie Lake (NP)
52°52'04"N 118°07'54"W
Status: Doubtful
Marjorie Lake was a popular fishing destination, as it is an easy 15 to 20 minute walk from Jasper townsite along the Saturday Night loop. Marjorie Lake held both rainbow and brook trout in good numbers, but it is likely that no fish remain in the lake.

Hibernia Lake (NP)
52°52'16"N 118°08'37"W
Status: Doubtful
Hibernia Lake is located on a spur trail, less than a kilometre off the main Saturday Night loop. Hibernia Lake used to attract anglers in search of its rainbow trout. Today, it's unlikely that any trout remain in Hibernia.

Caledonia Lake (NP)
52°52'02"N 118°09'44"W
Rainbow trout to 40 cm
Brook trout to 40 cm
Caledonia Lake is set on a forested bench, 2 km by trail beyond Marjorie Lake, and 5 km from Jasper. Both rainbow and brook trout were both stocked in the past but it seems that the rainbow won out and are present in good numbers.

Caledonia Lake

Rathlin Lake (NP)
52°52'31"N 118°11'31"W
Bench Lake (NP)
52°52'50"N 118°12'22"W
Status: Doubtful
These two small lakes are located alongside the Saturday Night loop between Caledonia and Minnow lakes. Both lakes contained brook trout at one time. It's likely no fish remain in either lake.

Minnow Lake (NP)
52°53'25"N 118°13'23"W
Status: Doubtful
Minnow Lake is situated near the upper end of the Saturday Night loop. Rainbow and brook trout were stocked in the past. It's doubtful that any fish are present in Minnow Lake

High Lakes (NP)
52°53'53"N 118°13'47"W
Status: Doubtful
This series of shallow lakes is located at the upper end of the Saturday Night loop. The seven High Lakes were stocked at one time with both rainbow and brook trout, but it's unlikely that any trout remain in any of the High Lakes.

Saturday Night Lake (NP)
52°53'38"N 118°10'48"W
Status: Doubtful
Saturday Night Lake was the usual destination for anglers undertaking the Saturday Night loop trail. The lake's shimmering blue waters at one time held plenty of rainbow and brook trout. There may be a few fish in Saturday Night Lake, but their numbers will be very limited.

Saturday Night Lake

Dorothy Lake (NP)
52°52'58"N 118°13'48"W
Status: Doubtful
Dorothy Lake is accessed by a 4 km trail from the Yellowhead Highway west of Jasper. Dorothy was stocked with both rainbow and brook trout at one time. Similar to other lakes in the area, once the regular stocking stopped, the number of fish in the lake plummeted and it is unlikely there are any trout in the lake today.

Dorothy Lake

Christine Lake (NP)

52°53'09"N 118°14'29"W

Status: Doubtful

Christine Lake is located less than half a kilometre by trail from Dorothy Lake. Brook and rainbow trout were both planted in the past. It is doubtful that any trout remain in Christine Lake.

Iris Lake (NP)

52°52'40"N 118°13'19"W

Status: Doubtful

Iris Lake is located less than a kilometre below the east end of Dorothy Lake and is reached by ill-defined trails winding around Dorothy Lake. Rainbow trout used to be the normal catch, but it's questionable if any remain today.

Virl Lake (NP)

52°52'37"N 118°13'58"W

Status: Doubtful

Virl Lake is set in an opening in heavy forest just east of the main Dorothy Lake trail. Brook and rainbow trout averaging were once plentiful in Virl. It is unlikely that any trout remain in Virl Lake.

Virl Lake

Miette River (NP)

Rainbow trout to 45 cm

Brook trout to 40 cm

Bull trout to 70 cm (3.0 kg)

Whitefish to 50 cm (1.5 kg)

The Miette River is a major tributary of the Athabasca River. It flows east from the Alberta-B.C. boundary to its junction with the Athabasca at Jasper. The Yellowhead Highway (Highway 16) closely parallels the Miette River for virtually its entire length. The Miette River is very muddy each year during run-off, but it generally clears somewhat by mid-summer. Rainbow, brook and bull trout can all be caught from the river's many fine pools. Large whitefish in good numbers can be taken in the fall, when the fishing on the Miette is at its best.

Miette River

Minaga Creek (NP)

Rainbow trout to 35 cm

Brook trout to 35 cm

This minor tributary of the Miette River is crossed by the Dorothy Lake trail approximately 1 km from Highway 16. Minaga Creek holds both rainbow and brook trout in the 20–30 cm range.

Cutt Lake (NP)

52°54'02"N 118°19'50"W

Status: Doubtful

Cutt Lake is reached from trails on upper Minaga Creek. This small lake was stocked long ago with cutthroat trout, and more recently with rainbow trout. It's unlikely that any trout remain in Cutt Lake.

Golden Lake (NP)

52°53'53"N 118°19'44"W

Status: Doubtful

Golden Lake is located less than a kilometre from Cutt Lake. It was originally stocked with golden trout, then later with rainbow trout. It is doubtful that there any trout remaining in Golden Lake.

Skyline Sub-Region

The Jasper townsite is the focal point of the Sub-Region. The Sub-Region includes the Athabasca River and the Jasper Park Lodge environs on the eastern side of the Athabasca River. Roads or short trails reach most fish-holding waters. The Athabasca River is popular with anglers in the spring and autumn, especially for its giant bull trout. Lac Beauvert, Edith, Annette and Trefoil lakes are located on the bench east of the Athabasca. To the south, along the Icefields Parkway and Highway 93A, short trails lead to the Valley of the Five Lakes. East of Jasper, the Athabasca and Rocky Rivers, along with Jasper, Talbot, Edna and Mile 14 lakes present plenty of opportunities for anglers.

Athabasca River (NP)

Bull trout to 80 cm (7.0 kg)

Rainbow trout to 55 cm (1.5 kg)

Brook trout to 50 cm

Whitefish to 50 cm

Northern pike to 70 cm (5.0 kg)

Jasper National Park's major river flows from the Columbia Icefields north to Jasper. It then swings east and exits the park, eventually turning north on its route to the Arctic Ocean. South of Jasper, the Icefields Parkway (Highway 93) follows the course of the upper Athabasca closely and provides easy access. Although it is very turbulent and muddy for much of the summer, the river does present fishing opportunities in the late season in the waters below Athabasca Falls, where large bull trout and northern pike, along with rainbow and brook trout and whitefish can all be caught in fair numbers. The whitefish from the river are particularly large. The best fishing in the Athabasca will always be when the main river is clear. Areas around the Athabasca's confluence with both major and minor tributaries generally hold fish, especially when the main river is muddy. The Athabasca's confluences with the Maligne, Snaring and Rocky rivers are choice spots.

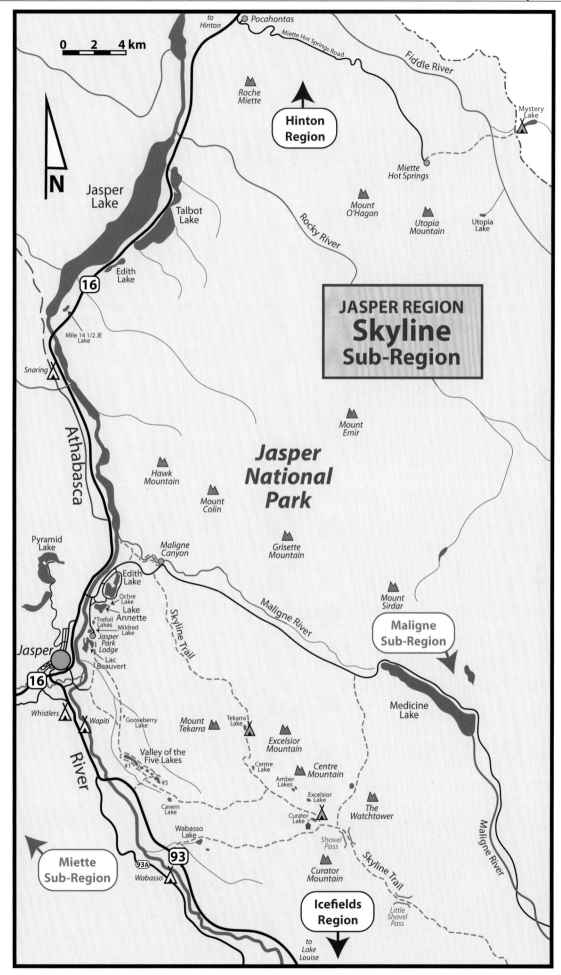

Logan Urie with Athabasca River bull trout

Logan Urie photo

◼ Maligne River (downstream from Maligne Canyon)

Bull trout to 70 cm (4.0 kg)
Brook trout to 35 cm
Whitefish to 45 cm
Northern pike to 65 cm (2.5 kg)

The best fishing on the lower Maligne River is near its confluence with the Athabasca River. Good-sized bull trout can be taken from this section of the river. Fishing quality declines as one moves upstream towards Maligne Canyon.

☐ Edith Lake (NP)

52°54'35"N 118°02'27"W
Rainbow trout to 60 cm (2.0 kg)
Brook trout to 60 cm (2.0 kg)

Edith Lake is located just east of the Maligne Lake Road, some 6 km from Jasper townsite. The translucent blue waters of Edith Lake hold some large rainbow and brook trout, although their numbers are limited. Edith Lake is a large lake with a bottom that drops off sharply in most locations and fishing is better from a boat. Boats are available for rent through arrangements made with sporting goods stores in Jasper. Trolling is generally productive, especially along the zone around the many deep holes in Edith.

◼ Annette Lake (NP)

52°54'06"N 118°02'53"W
Brook trout to 60 cm (2.0 kg)
Rainbow trout to 60 cm (2.0 kg)

This very pretty lake is set amid quiet woods east of the Jasper Park Lodge Road and attracts plenty of picnickers as well as anglers. The extremely clear waters hold brook and rainbow trout averaging 25–35 cm in length. Boats can be rented through arrangements made in one of Jasper's sporting goods stores, a move that greatly enhances the quality of fishing. Trolling a fly or lure while admiring the scenery is a superb way to get the most out of Annette Lake.

◼ Ochre Lake (NP)

52°54'12"N 118°02'31"W
Status: Devoid of fish

This small pond is located off the east side of Annette Lake. There are no fish in Ochre Lake.

Annette Lake

◻ Trefoil Lakes (NP)

52°53'38"N 118°03'15"W
Status: Doubtful

In the past, the fishing potential of three small lakes on the grounds of Jasper Park Lodge was been directly related to artificial stocking. It is possible that the two larger lakes (Trefoil #1 and #2), still contain limited populations of rainbow or brook trout.

◼ Mildred Lake (NP)

52°53'23"N 118°03'27"W
Status: Devoid of fish

This over-sized duck pond on the western side of the Jasper Park Lodge Road was stocked in the past, but the fish failed to reproduce.

☐ Lac Beauvert (NP)

52°52'54"N 118°03'41"W
Rainbow trout to 40 cm
Brook trout to 40 cm

The sparkling green waters of Lac Beauvert, the scenic centerpiece of the Jasper Park Lodge grounds, have never been renowned for a high quality of fishing. Although a variety of fish were stocked in the past, it is likely that a very limited number of rainbow and brook trout are all that are still present.

Lac Beauvert

◮ Valley of the Five Lakes (NP)

(#1) 52°49'22"N 118°01'15"W
(#5) 52°48'49"N 118°00'03"W
Brook trout to 45 cm

The Valley of the Five Lakes is 2 km by trail east of the Icefields Parkway. The lakes are a favourite spot with local anglers. Lakes

#3, #4 and #5 hold brook trout in good numbers. Some enormous rainbow trout, in the 5–6 kg range, have been taken from Lake #1 the past, although it is doubtful if any trout are in the lake today. Lakes #4 and #5 hold the most promise for anglers. As all of the lakes are fairly narrow, casting the fish-holding waters with a lure or fly is usually not a major problem. Boats are available on Lake #5, and arrangements for their rental can be made in sporting goods stores in Jasper.

Valley of the Five Lakes (First Lake)

Valley of the Five Lakes (Fifth Lake)

Valley of the Five Lakes (Fifth Lake) brook trout

■ Wabasso Lake (NP)
52°46'51"N 117°57'47"W
Rainbow trout to 40 cm
Brook trout to 40 cm
The quiet waters of Wabasso Lake lie less than 3 km by trail from the busy Icefields Parkway. Wabasso Lake is a popular destination for family hikes. It also holds promise for anglers since it reportedly contains both rainbow and brook trout in decent numbers. For those fly fishing, fly casting is somewhat restricted around much of the shoreline due to heavy reed growth and the proximity of the forest cover.

Wabasso Lake

? Gooseberry Lake (NP)
52°50'48"N 118°02'03"W
Status: Unknown
Gooseberry Lake is located 2 km north of the Valley of the Five Lakes by trail. Gooseberry Lake was stocked in the past with brook trout, but it is unlikely that any fish remain today.

? Cavern Lake (NP)
52°48'09"N 117°59'07"W
Status: Unknown
Cavern Lake is located south of the Valley of the Five Lakes, near the head of Tekarra Creek. Cavern Lake held a few brook trout at one time, but it's doubtful if any remain.

■ Curator Lake (NP)
52°47'35"N 117°51'52"W
■ Excelsior Lake (NP)
52°48'30"N 117°52'53"W
■ Tekarra Lake (NP)
52°50'26"N 117°55'26"W
■ Center Lake (NP)
52°49'27"N 117°54'40"W
■ Amber Lakes (NP)
52°48'48"N 117°53'31"W
Status: Devoid of fish
Curator, Excelsior, Tekarra, Center and Amber lakes are companions to hikers on the Skyline Trail from Maligne Lake to Jasper. They have never been stocked and contain no fish.

Centre Lake

■ Jasper Lake (NP)
53°07'27"N 118°00'16"W
Bull trout to 70 cm (4.0 kg)
Rainbow trout to 50 cm (1.5 kg)
Brook trout to 50 cm (1.5 kg)
Whitefish to 50 cm (1.5 kg)
Northern pike to 60 cm (2.5 kg)
The shallow waters of Jasper Lake are merely a widening of the mighty Athabasca River. Jasper Lake attract little attention from anglers despite its impressive variety of fish which includes whitefish, bull, rainbow and brook trout, as well as pike, ling, chub and suckers. Fishing is generally restricted to the river's main channels, but unfortunately these areas are usually near-impossible to reach because extensive shallows make up the vast majority of the lake. Anglers are advised to work the waters in and around the lake's inlet and outlet where the Athabasca is reduced to a more reasonable width.

Jasper Lake

☐ **Mile 14 Lake J-E [Jasper-Edmonton] (NP)**
53°04'30"N 118°03'45"W
Rainbow trout to 40 cm
Brook trout to 40 cm
This lake is located, appropriately enough, 14 miles (or 23 km) from Jasper on the north side of the Yellowhead Highway. Mile 14 Lake receives little pressure each summer for limited numbers of brook and rainbow trout in the 20–30 cm range.

Local Knowledge

Whenever fishing new waters, it is always best to get the best knowledge available regarding the fish, the lures, the tactics and the locations. Local sporting goods stores will often provide some general information, but nothing very specific. Some stores, such as On-Line Sports & Tackle in Jasper, go out of their way to give you all the information and equipment you need to take your fishing to the next level. They know that if you catch fish and are happy, you will be back. With information from guys like Mike Merilovich at On-Line, you no longer feel like a visitor; you start to feel like a local! Your chances of catching fish will go up exponentially. PS: Mike, thanks for the froggie-lure tip for Talbot Lake!

🔼 **Talbot Lake (NP)**
53°05'52"N 117°59'37"W
Northern pike to 1 m (8.0 kg)
Whitefish to 40 cm
The clear waters of Talbot Lake stand in stark contrast to the silted waters of Jasper Lake, separated only by the Yellowhead Highway. Northern pike are the fish of choice at Talbot Lake, and there are generally a few anglers working the lake at any given time. Boats are available for rent through prior arrangements with sporting good stores in Jasper. Anglers using a variety of pike-targeting lures, including frogs and yellow and red five-of-diamonds, are normally more successful than those fly fishing at Talbot, although fly fishing for pike has become very popular in recent years. Prime time on Talbot Lake is in the first few weeks after the season opens. This is when the large pike are in the shallower waters for spawning and they are very aggressive. Work the areas along the edge of the reeds and be prepared for a big hit.

Talbot Lake northern pike

Talbot Lake

◼ **Edna Lake (NP)**
53°08'56"N 118°02'30"W
Rainbow trout to 40 cm
Brook trout to 40 cm
Edna Lake is situated less than a kilometre west of Talbot Lake, and is similar in character to other lakes along the Athabasca River. It holds both brook and rainbow trout ranging from 20–30 cm in length. Fish can be taken fairly close to shore during low light conditions.

◼ **Rocky River (NP)**
Bull trout to 65 cm (2.5 kg)
Rainbow trout to 40 cm
Brook trout to 40 cm
Whitefish to 45 cm
The Rocky River joins the Athabasca River as a major tributary just east of Talbot Lake. The Rocky River generally clears sooner than the Athabasca, offering fine river fishing from mid-summer on for bull, rainbow and brook trout, along with whitefish. Fish can be taken in good numbers from the lower reaches of the river, within easy walking distance of the Yellowhead Highway. Of particular interest to anglers are the waters around the Rocky River's confluence with the Athabasca, a short hike downstream from Highway 16. Bull trout predominate in the remote upper sections of the Rocky River accessed by trail from Jacques Lake.

◼ **Fiddle River (NP)**
Bull trout to 60 cm (2.0 kg)
Rainbow trout to 40 cm
Whitefish to 40 cm
The Fiddle River begins high in the Miette Range and joins the Athabasca River as a minor tributary just inside the eastern boundary of Jasper National Park. The lower reaches are accessible from both the Yellowhead Highway and from the Miette Hot Springs Road. The upper Fiddle is accessed from trails beginning at Miette Hot Springs. Whitefish, bull trout and rainbow trout are all present, with bull trout becoming the dominant species the farther upstream you fish.

Utopia Lake (NP)

53°04'59"N 117°45'00"W

Cutthroat trout to 40 cm

Utopia Lake is hidden high on the flank of Utopia Mountain, and receives few, if any, visitors each year. The lake was stocked in the past with cutthroat trout and recent reports indicate that a healthy population of cutthroat thrives in the lake, the only location in Jasper Park where cutthroat trout are present. Most fish taken will be in the 20–30 cm range. Access is for route-finders, and Utopia Lake is recommended for only the most hardy of souls, outfitted with a map and compass.

Mystery Lake (AB)

53°08'56"N 117°40'25"W

Status: Doubtful

Mystery Lake, at the end of a 10 km hike and protected by a troublesome ford of the Fiddle River, is located just outside the Jasper National Park boundary. The ford of the Fiddle River can be very dangerous in the early season and during periods of rainy weather. Although it is becoming more popular as a backpacking destination, Mystery Lake is still far removed from the crowds. At one time, the lake was stocked with both rainbow and brook trout. The level of water in the lake fluctuates significantly from year to year and season to season, and it is likely that no trout remain in the lake today.

Maligne Sub-Region

Remarkable Maligne Lake is set amid some of the most impressive mountain scenery the Rockies has to offer. It stands out as the centerpiece of the Sub-Region. Maligne Lake's world-class rainbow trout attract anglers from far and wide. The lake is easily accessible via a 45 km-long paved road that leads southeast from the Yellowhead Highway (Highway 16), five kilometres east of Jasper. Lorraine, Moose, Mona and Evelyn lakes are all located within easy hiking distance from the Maligne Lake Road terminus. Medicine Lake is situated downstream from Maligne Lake on the Maligne River and offers superb late-summer and autumn fishing for large rainbow trout.

Maligne Lake (NP)

52°40'32"N 117°33'14"W

Rainbow trout to 75 cm (5.0 kg)

Brook trout to 65 cm (2.5 kg)

Maligne Lake is situated at the head of the beautiful Maligne Valley and attracts crowds of visitors to its shores each summer. Tour boats make daily sightseeing excursions down the lake. Maligne Lake is regarded as an excellent fishing lake, one of the best in the Rockies, and contains large rainbow and brook trout. Monster rainbow trout over 7 kg have been caught In Maligne Lake in the past, but few fish reach those spectacular sizes these days. Boats and canoes can be rented at the lake, which increases fishing potential enormously. Trolling a lure or wet fly is very effective, particularly in the famed "Rainbow Alley" which extends from near the outlet of the Maligne River for the first few kilometres down the lake. Almost 10 km from the dock, the Sampson Narrows have also gained renown for fishing, although it is a long trip if you're rowing or paddling. Thankfully for anglers, electric motors can be used on Maligne. For those who are shore bound the area around the outlet holds some promise. In most

years, Maligne Lake is not usually free of ice until mid-June, often after its season opening date.

Maligne Lake

Logan Urie photo

Logan Urie with Maligne Lake rainbow trout

Maligne Lake brook trout

Moose Lake (NP)

52°43'00"N 117°38'34"W

Status: Doubtful

Tiny Moose Lake is less than a kilometre from the Maligne Pass trailhead and draws little attention from anglers. Brook trout were stocked in the past, but recent reports indicate they are present in very limited numbers at best.

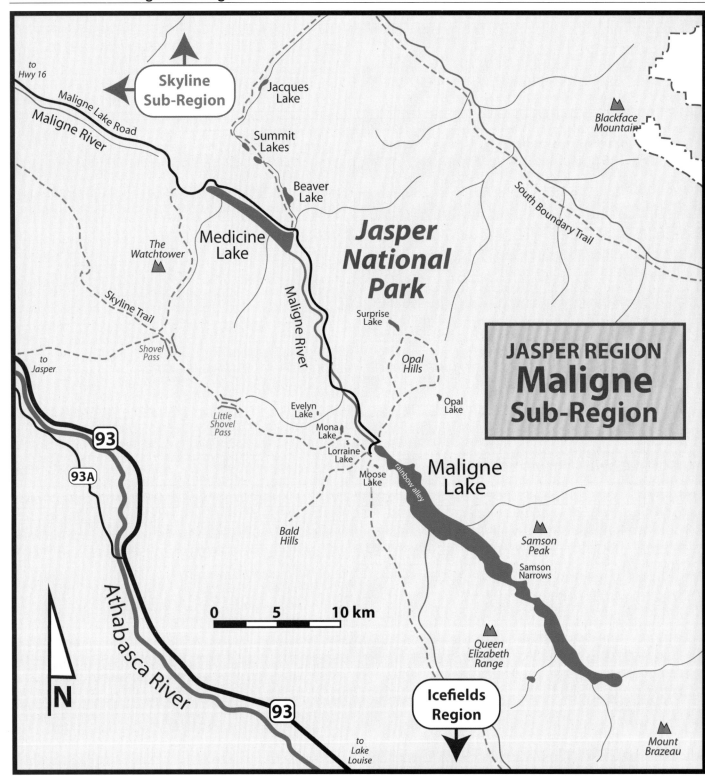

□ **Mona Lake (NP)**

52°44'10"N 117°40'27"W

Brook trout to 45 cm

Mona Lake is situated 2 km along the Skyline Trail from Maligne Lake and is the largest of the lakes located to the west of Maligne Lake. Mona Lake's clear waters hold brook trout in limited numbers averaging 20–30 cm in length. Mona Lake is ringed by forest, and presents casting problems for those who will be fly casting.

Mona Lake

☐ Lorraine Lake (NP)

52°43'48"N 117°40'05"W

Brook trout to 35 cm

Lorraine Lake is situated opposite Mona Lake, approximately 2 km along the Skyline Trail. This lake attracts hikers from nearby Maligne Lake. Anglers can expect reduced numbers of brook trout in the 20–30 cm range. Heavy reed growth and extended shallows extend around much of the lake. During low light periods, however, the trout tend to work the shallows extensively for food, and patient anglers are often rewarded at these times.

Lorraine Lake

■ Evelyn Lake (NP)

52°44'47"N 117°41'31"W

Status: Doubtful

This small lake is located less than a kilometre northwest of Mona Lake. Evelyn Lake may still hold a small population of both brook and rainbow trout in small sizes.

■ Surprise Lake (NP)

52°47'42"N 117°37'26"W

Status: Devoid of fish

Only experienced route finders armed with map and compass find their way into secluded Surprise Lake, located some 4 km east of the Maligne Lake Road. Surprise Lake was stocked in the past with brook trout, which apparently failed to take hold. If any fish were found today in Surprise Lake, it would definitely be a surprise.

■ Opal Lake (aka Summit Lake) (NP)

52°45'17"N 117°34'59"W

Status: Devoid of fish

This small lake is set in the Opal Hills to the northeast of Maligne Lake. Opal Lake has never been stocked and contains no fish.

Felt-soled waders and the fight against whirling disease

Whirling disease, which can decimate trout populations, has been detected in several Alberta watersheds. Anglers and boaters can help stop the spread of whirling disease by cleaning, draining and drying all gear after each use. The microscopic parasite that causes the disease lives in mud and is easily transferred through felt-soled waders. For that reason, Parks Canada has banned the use of felt-soled waders in all of the mountain parks. Other jurisdictions will likely soon follow suit. Anglers can stay ahead of the curve by no longer using felt-soled waders and making sure that they clean, drain and dry all of their other equipment after every use.

■ Medicine Lake (NP)

52°52'03"N 117°47'21"W

Rainbow trout to 60 cm (2.5 kg)

Brook trout to 55 cm (1.5 kg)

Medicine Lake is located alongside the Maligne Lake Road, approximately 10 km downstream from Maligne Lake. When fishing is hot, Medicine Lake ranks favourably with the better fishing lakes in the Rockies. At times during the year, the lake holds good numbers of large rainbow and brook trout. Rainbow trout taken from the lake will average 35–45 cm in length. Water levels on Medicine Lake fluctuate dramatically during the year, with the lake nearly doubling in size at the height of the runoff in early July. As the lake level recedes in the beginning in August, fishing picks up considerably, and continues to improve into September. In the fall, the upper portion of the lake is little more than a mud flat, crisscrossed by various channels of the Maligne River. During this time of the year, there is excellent fly fishing for large rainbows in Medicine Lake from the riverbank in the mud flats. Be cautioned that if standing in one spot for any length of time, it will be difficult to pull your feet from the muck. I was told of a story where the angler made it out, but one wader still resides in the mud. If fishing earlier in the season when there is actually water in Medicine Lake, boats are available for rent through prior arrangement with sporting goods stores in Jasper. In the early season, stick to the channel formed by the Maligne River.

Tyler Ambrosi photo

Medicine Lake   *Medicine Lake mud flats*

Logan Urie photo

Nick Nace with Medicine Lake rainbow trout

◼ Maligne River (Maligne Lake to Medicine Lake) (NP)

Rainbow trout to 60 cm (2.0 kg)
Brook trout to 50 cm

The Maligne River between Maligne Lake and Medicine Lake offers several stretches of outstanding angling for plentiful numbers of rainbow and brook trout in the 25–35 cm range. Regulations permit fly fishing only on this section of the river. The best areas are found just downstream from Maligne Lake and just above the inlet on Medicine Lake. ⊗ Take note of the angling closure from a 100 m radius out into Maligne Lake at the outlet to a point 420 m downstream from the Maligne Lake outlet bridge.

◼ Beaver Lake (NP)

52°51'58"N 117°43'27"W
Brook trout to 55 cm (1.5 kg)

Shallow Beaver Lake is set in a pleasant valley less than 2 km from the Maligne Lake Road. It is a popular spot for family picnics, as well as for fishing. At one time, extremely large brook trout, in the 3–4 kg range, inhabited the lake. Overharvest of the big brookies took its toll, and today it's unlikely there are trout of that size in the lake. Brook trout are still plentiful, but most are 20–25 cm in length. The entire shoreline is made up of heavy reed growth, a strong deterrent to fly casting. Boats are available for rent, and can be reserved through sporting goods stores in Jasper. Larger trout can be taken from the lake's deeper waters. When conditions are right Beaver Lake offers some excellent dry fly fishing. ⊗ The outlet stream from Beaver Lake to its junction with the Maligne Lake Road is permanently closed to fishing.

Beaver Lake

Logan Urie photo

Beaver Lake brook trout

◼ Summit Lakes (NP)

52°51'55"N 117°43'26"W
Status: Devoid of fish

These two small lakes are situated at the height of land on the Jacques Lake trail. They have been stocked in the past with brook trout, which failed to reproduce. At present, no fish exist in the lakes.

⊗ Jacques Lake (NP)

52°55'46"N 117°45'00"W
Status: Closed to angling
Bull trout

Pretty Jacques Lake is a popular backpacking destination, 12 km by trail from the Maligne Lake Road. The lake is closed to angling to protect its healthy population of bull trout.

ROBSON REGION

This Region is dominated by awe-inspiring Mt. Robson, the highest point in the Canadian Rockies and represents the pinnacle in mountain scenery. Glacier-mantled peaks towering over pristine lakes attract visitors from all corners of the world. The Yellowhead Highway (Highway 16) is the primary transportation route through the Region. The Region's fishing potential has never gained the stature of the surrounding physical beauty. Berg Lake, set at the base of Mt. Robson, is a classic backpacking destination but attracts no anglers. Beyond Berg Lake, Jasper National Park's noted North Boundary Trail leads adventuresome hikers past Adolphus, Beatrix and Twintree lakes and the Smoky River, before crossing Snake Indian Pass into the Snake Indian River drainage. The Region is divided into two Sub-Regions: the Yellowhead Sub-Region, encompassing the immediate Mt. Robson area; and a second Sub-Region shadowing the North Boundary Trail.

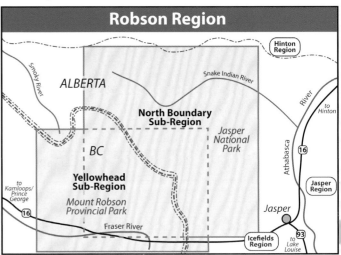

Yellowhead Sub-Region

Mighty Mt. Robson stands guard over the Sub-Region, which stretches out along the Yellowhead Highway (Highway 16) west from Yellowhead Pass and the BC-Alberta boundary. The best fishing opportunities are in the string of lakes that parallel the highway and include Moose and Yellowhead lakes. Berg and Kinney lakes are popular with hikers but are of little value to anglers.

◮ Portal Lake (aka Flora Lake) (BC)

52°53'01"N 118°27'11"W
Rainbow trout to 30 cm

Portal Lake is located alongside the Yellowhead, just west of the BC-Alberta border. There is a large parking area and a picnic site beside the lake. Rainbow trout are present in the lake in good numbers, with most averaging 15–25 cm in length. Flies and lures will work well, although those who are fly fishing may have some difficulty finding backcasting room anywhere but the picnic area. Spin casters may have a few issues with the large lily pad population.

Portal Lake rainbow trout

Tyler Ambrosi at Portal Lake

Yellowhead Lake (BC)

52°51'40"N 118°32'40"W
Lake trout to 75 cm (5.0 kg)
Rainbow trout to 55 cm (1.5 kg)
Whitefish to 40 cm

Yellowhead Lake is situated alongside the Yellowhead Highway a few kilometres west of the Continental Divide at Yellowhead Pass. The lake holds large lake trout averaging 40–50 cm in length, as well as plenty of rainbow trout and whitefish. In the early season, lake trout can be taken in good numbers in the shallower waters, but as the season progresses, rainbows and whitefish become the normal catch. Due to the size of the lake, the best tactic is trolling from boats, which are available through rental arrangements made with sporting goods stores in Jasper. Yellowhead Lake narrows and has a downstream extension near the Lucerne campground. Fishing from shore is possible here at several locations near the inlet and outlet creek.

Yellowhead Lake

Yellowhead Lake lake trout

Witney Lake (BC)

52°51'15"N 118°33'17"W
Rainbow trout to 50 cm

Witney Lake is right beside the highway between the main portion Yellowhead Lake and the Lucerne campground. Despite its easy access, this small lake does not receive much angling pressure. Witney Lake holds stocked rainbow trout in the 25–35 cm range.

Witney Lake

Kettle Lakes (BC)

52°50'57"N 118°35'37"W
Status: Doubtful

The two Kettle Lakes, which are indeed kettle lakes, are located south of the Yellowhead Highway (Highway 16) just east of Yellowhead Lake. It is unlikely that there are any fish in either lake.

Rink Lake (NP)

52°54'11"N 118°35'18"W
Status: Devoid of fish

Rink Lake is located in a side valley to the west of the Miette River, beneath the peaks that form the BC-Alberta boundary. It has never been stocked and contains no fish.

Moren Lakes (NP)

53°00'39"N 118°32'28"W
Status: Devoid of fish

The two small Moren Lakes are set in an isolated valley to the east of the upper Miette Valley. The lakes have never been stocked, and reportedly contain no fish.

? Mahood Lake (NP)

53°01'22"N 118°33'24"W
Status: Unknown

This large lake is set in a side valley west of the Miette River headwaters and has never been stocked. Due to its isolated position, few anglers ever make their way into Mahood Lake. It is possible that a few bull trout have made their way into the lake from the Miette River.

Miette Lake (NP)

53°01'08"N 118°37'43"W
Bull trout to 55 cm (1.5 kg)

Miette Lake is at the headwaters of the Miette River, an arduous 25 km hike from the Yellowhead Highway. The lake is reached only by a few outfitter parties and intrepid hikers each summer. Miette Lake reportedly holds a limited number of bull trout averaging 30–40 cm in length.

Miette Lake

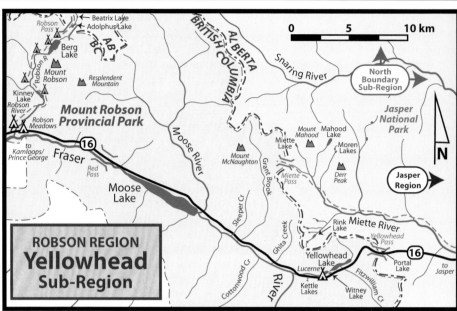

■ Moose Lake (BC)
52°57'04"N 118°54'00"W
Lake trout to 1 m (10 kg)
Bull trout to 80 cm (8 kg)
Rainbow trout to 60 cm (2.5 kg)
Kokanee to 50 cm
Whitefish to 50 cm

Moose Lake is almost 10 km in length and is a companion to people driving the Yellowhead Highway. Moose Lake is essentially a filter for the Fraser River. Muddy waters from the upper Fraser enter the lake's east end and clear waters depart the lake's western end. Moose Lake's waters, which remain silted much of the season, hold a variety of fish with large lake and bull trout predominating. Lake and bull trout in excess of 5 kg in weight are caught regularly. Trolling is the most effective method of angling on Moose Lake. A good area is near where the Fraser enters, particularly along the dividing line between the river's cloudy waters and the lake's clear waters. Be aware of strong winds that occasionally sweep through Yellowhead Pass.

Moose Lake

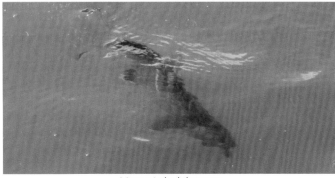

Moose Lake lake trout

■ Moose River (BC)
Bull trout to 65 cm (2.5 kg)
Rainbow trout to 50 cm
Whitefish to 45 cm

Moose River has its source high among the peaks that straddle the Continental Divide. It flows south from humble beginnings to join the upper Fraser River as a major tributary just east of Moose Lake. Much of the upper Moose River lies far beyond the reach of most hikers and remains the domain of grizzly bears, interrupted only by the occasional horse party. Bull and rainbow trout in the 25–35 cm range as well as a few whitefish can be taken along the entire length of the river. Fishing pressure is light in the lower reaches and virtually non-existent along the remote upper Moose River.

Moose River

□ Grant Brook (BC)
Bull trout to 55 cm (1.5 kg)
Whitefish to 40 cm

Grant Brook is a tributary of the Fraser, joining midway between Yellowhead Lake and the Moose River. Grant Brook holds a few bull trout and whitefish.

■ Fraser River (Headwaters to Robson River) (BC)
Bull trout to 80 cm (5.0 kg)
Rainbow trout to 55 cm (1.5 kg)
Whitefish to 45 cm
Kokanee to 45 cm

The upper Fraser River, between Yellowhead Lake and the Robson River, possesses long stretches of fishable water. Bull and rainbow trout predominate, with whitefish and kokanee present in fair numbers as well. This entire section of the Fraser is paralleled by the Yellowhead Highway (Highway 16), which affords decent access to the better fishing spots. Runoff is usually complete by mid-summer when fishing begins to pick up appreciably. Salmon runs in the fall are spectacular to watch. Above Moose Lake, the Fraser River runs very muddy in the early season, but Moose Lake absorbs the silt and the Fraser runs crystal clear below Moose Lake even in early season.

Fraser River

■ **Cottonwood Creek, Ghita Creek, Sleeper Creek (BC)**
Bull trout to 40 cm
Rainbow trout to 30 cm
Whitefish to 30 cm
These tributaries of the upper Fraser River all hold fish in small sizes in their lower reaches.

☐ **Robson River (BC)**
Bull trout to 65 cm (2.5 kg)
Rainbow trout to 40 cm
Whitefish to 35 cm
Kokanee to 35 cm
From its source at Berg Lake, the Robson roars through the Valley of a Thousand Falls into Kinney Lake, before finally emptying into the Fraser River. The upper section is far too torrential to hold fish, and any angling on the Robson River should be confined to the final 6 km before its confluence with the Fraser. Whitefish, kokanee, bull and rainbow trout can be taken in limited numbers. Due to its glacial source, the Robson River runs silted much longer than most rivers, generally clearing only for a few short weeks in the fall.

Robson River

 Kinney Lake (BC)
53°04'56"N 119°11'30"W
Rainbow trout
Kinney Lake is perpetually silted due to the inflow of the Robson River. The lake is situated 5 km along the Berg Lake trail and has never been able to sustain a respectable fish population. Rainbow trout in limited numbers are reported to inhabit the lake. The outlet area is likely to be the best option, particularly later in the season when the lake's silt levels are lowest.

Kinney Lake

■ **Berg Lake (BC)**
53°08'43"N 119°09'28"W
Status: Doubtful
Berg Lake is blessed with one of the most exquisite settings anywhere in the mountain world and is busy with backpackers, photographers and helicopter-in sightseers throughout the summer months. The stunning, glacier-clad north face of Mt. Robson towering above the lake is a sight few people forget. Despite being a strenuous 17 km hike-in from the Yellowhead Highway, the access trail remains one of the most popular backpacking routes in the Rockies. Unfortunately, fishing in the ever-silted Berg Lake can be regarded as dismal at best, with rumours of rainbow trout in the lake in small numbers.

Berg Lake and Mount Robson

■ **Adolphus Lake (NP)**
53°10'14"N 119°07'04"W
Rainbow trout to 45 cm
Brook trout to 45 cm
Adolphus Lake is set in open subalpine forest less than 1 km north of Robson Pass in Jasper National Park. Adolphus Lake offers some respite from the crowds at nearby Berg Lake. This headwater of the Smoky River holds rainbow and brook trout

231

averaging 25-35 cm in its clear waters. Flies and lures are both effective in Adolphus Lake.

Adolphus Lake and Mount Robson

☐ Beatrix Lake (NP)
53°10'46"N 119°06'53"W
Rainbow trout to 35 cm
Brook trout to 30 cm
Tiny Beatrix Lake is located less than 1 km downstream from Adolphus Lake and is little more than a widening of the Smoky River. Rainbow trout in the 20–30 cm range are present as well as the odd brook trout that makes its way from Adolphus Lake from time to time. Heavy brush around the lake will cause problems for those fly casting.

North Boundary Sub-Region

This isolated Sub-Region is located in the remote, rugged north end of Jasper National Park. The Sub-Region is bounded on the west by Mt. Robson Provincial Park and on the north by Willmore Wilderness Provincial Park. Jasper's famed North Boundary Trail cuts through the core of the Sub-Region and provides access for horse parties and hardy backpackers. The Snake Indian River parallels the North Boundary Trail from the eastern trailhead at Celestine Lake to the alpine environs of Snake Indian Pass. To the south of this drainage, the Snaring River makes its way east from the heights of the Continental Divide. Like much of the rest of the territory, it remains virtually untouched.

■ Snaring River (NP)
Bull trout to 65 cm (2.5 kg)
Rainbow trout to 40 cm
Whitefish to 40 cm
This major tributary to the Athabasca River joins the Athabasca 17 km east of Jasper and offers fine fishing in its lower reaches for bull and rainbow trout. Whitefish are plentiful in the fall. While its upper sections are located far beyond the reach of the average angler, the lower Snaring is easily accessed from the Celestine Lake Road.

⊗ Mile 9 Lake J-E [Jasper-Edmonton] (NP)
53°10'46"N 119°06'53"W
Status: Closed to angling
Northern pike
Whitefish
Mile 9 Lake is located alongside the access road to the Snaring Overflow camping area. The lake is closed to protect pike and whitefish spawning habitat.

Mile 9 Lake J-E

■ Vine Creek (NP)
Rainbow trout to 30 cm
Brook trout to 30 cm
Vine Creek is a very minor tributary of the Athabasca River and joins it just west of Jasper Lake. Vine Creek reportedly holds both rainbow and brook trout.

■ Vine Creek beaver dams (NP)
Status: Doubtful
There is a series of beaver dams on Vine Creek, within easy walking distance of the Celestine Lake Road. These dams have been stocked in the past with both rainbow and brook trout. However, reproductive success among the trout planted has been limited at best, and fish, if any, are present in small numbers.

Note: To reach the Celestine and Princess lakes and North Boundary Trail trailheads, the upper portion of Celestine Lake Road must be driven. Due to narrow and dangerous corners, travel is limited to one direction for specific hours during the day. Check with the Parks Canada Information Centre in Jasper or on the Parks Canada website for details.

■ Celestine Lake (NP)
53°11'13"N 118°02'48"W
Rainbow trout to 65 cm (2.0 kg)
Celestine Lake is a short 2 km hike from the end of the rough and sometimes hair-raising 33 km-long Celestine Lake Road. Despite the long access, the lake attracts numerous anglers and sightseers alike each summer. The lake's appealing green waters hold rainbow trout averaging 25–35 cm in length, but due to extended shallows around much of the lake and heavy forest cover, those fly fishing will encounter problems. Boats are available for rent through prior arrangement with one of Jasper's sporting goods stores.

Celestine Lake

Princess Lake (NP)

53°11'19"N 118°04'07"W

Brook trout to 50 cm

The long, narrow form of Princess Lake is located alongside the Celestine Lake trail. Anglers generally bypass Princess Lake on their way to Celestine Lake. However, Princess Lake has offered decent fishing in the past, and with brook trout ranging from 20–35 cm in length.

Princess Lake

Snake Indian River (NP)

Bull trout to 60 cm (2.0 kg)
Rainbow trout to 40 cm
Whitefish to 40 cm

The Snake Indian River is a constant companion to those hiking the eastern half of the North Boundary Trail. The Snake Indian River runs muddy much of the summer and offers little in the way of fishing until early August. At that time, rainbows, bull trout and whitefish can be taken along the entire length of the river. The areas at the confluence with tributaries usually offer the best fishing. Many of the river's overflow lakes hold trout, although marsh generally accompanies these areas. Dedicated long-distance backpackers and horse parties make their way beyond thunderous Snake Indian Falls located 21 km from the eastern trailhead at Celestine Lake. The distance from Celestine Lake to the Berg Lake trailhead via the North Boundary Trail is a staggering 175 km.

Snake Indian Falls

Haultain Lake (NP)

53°09'47"N 118°16'11"W

Status: Unknown

Secluded Haultain Lake is set in a valley to the southwest of the Snake Indian River, and remains virtually untouched by civilization. Although the lake was stocked in the past with both cutthroat and rainbow trout, there are no recent reports on the status of fish in the lake.

Harvey Lake (NP)

53°09'22"N 118°27'02"W

Status: Unknown

Harvey Lake lies hidden deep within the Snaring River drainage, and remains a mystery to most anglers. It was stocked in the past with rainbow trout, but it has never been determined whether fish are still present. Due to difficult access, Harvey Lake is likely to keep its secrets for many years to come.

Nellie Lake (NP)

53°18'55"N 118°34'13"W

Bull trout to 55 cm (1.5 kg)
Rainbow trout to 35 cm

This large, shallow lake is located 50 km from the Celestine Lake trailhead. It offers only limited opportunities for anglers. The marshy shoreline, complete with reeds, makes access very difficult. Bull and rainbow trout along with the odd whitefish tend to make their way to and from the nearby Snake Indian River, but never seem to be present in large numbers in the lake.

Nellie Lake

Topaz Lake (NP)

53°23'21"N 118°51'06"W

Rainbow trout to 55 cm (2.0 kg)

Topaz Lake is set in the Blue Creek drainage, the most scenically impressive corner of the entire North Boundary region. Topaz Lake attracts only a limited number of visitors due to the extremely long access of over 60 km from the Celestine Lake trailhead. Topaz Lake holds rainbow trout in the 30–40 cm range, ample reward for the few anglers who do make it there.

Caribou Lakes (NP)

53°24'58"N 118°56'21"W

Rainbow trout to 55 cm (1.5 kg)
Bull trout to 70 cm (4.0 kg)

The Caribou Lakes are another link in the chain of sparkling lakes to the west of Blue Creek. The Caribou Lakes contain plenty of good-sized rainbow and bull trout. Angling quality should remain high in these lakes for many years to come, as fishing pressure will undoubtedly be light.

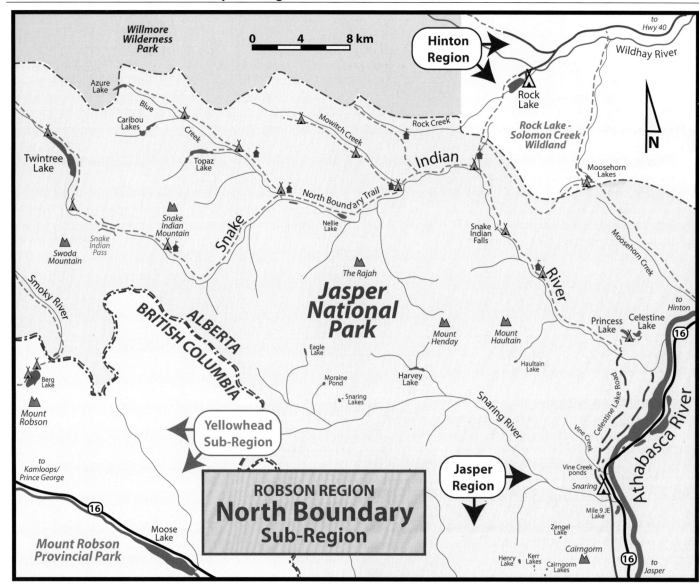

Azure Lake (aka Indigo Lake) (NP)

53°25'01"N 118°56'27"W

Status: Doubtful

Beautifully coloured Azure Lake is much alike in colour to Topaz and Caribou lakes to the south, but does not offer much in the way of fishing opportunities. This relatively shallow lake held rainbow and bull trout in the past, but recent reports indicate there are few, if any, fish in the lake.

Twintree Lake (NP)

53°22'47"N 119°05'41"W

Rainbow trout to 70 cm (4.0 kg)

Twintree Lake is located in the most remote corner of Jasper National Park and is reached via the North Boundary Trail. Twintree Lake is a distant 65 km hike from the Berg Lake trailhead, and an even more distant 105 km hike from the Celestine Lake Road trailhead. Suffice to say that Twintree Lake receives very little fishing pressure each year. Twintree is a large lake and is normally silted for much of the summer. The fishing picks up only as the lake begins to clear in August. Large rainbow trout, many in the 40–50 cm range, are present in Twintree Lake, although their numbers are not overwhelming. Due to the size of the lake, anglers are advised to work the waters around any inlet creeks where the water is liable to be clearer.

Twintree Lake

Smoky River (NP)

Bull trout to 70 cm (4.0 kg)

Rainbow trout to 35 cm

Whitefish to 40 cm

The upper Smoky River offers several kilometres of fine stream fishing as it flows north from Adolphus Lake. Meandering quietly back and forth across the broad valley north of Robson Pass, it possesses plenty of fine holes where bull and rainbow trout are present in fair numbers. Progressing downstream, the Smoky begins to accumulate tributaries and increases appreciably in size, and rainbow trout decrease in number. Bull trout and whitefish become predominant. Access is via the North Boundary Trail, which follows the course of the Smoky River to a point approximately 10 km from the northern boundary of Jasper National Park, whereupon the main trail swings east, away from the Smoky River and towards Twintree Lake.

■ Kerr Lakes, Cairngorm Lakes, Zengel Lake, Henry Lake (NP)
(general area) 53°01'10"N 118°28'18"W
Status: Devoid of fish
This cluster of lakes is located in remote backcountry northwest of Jasper. Access is very difficult, and the area is for explorers only. None of the lakes have ever been stocked, and it is unlikely that any contain fish.

■ Eagle Lake, Moraine Pond, Snaring Lakes (NP)
(general area) 53°08'29"N 118°38'15"W
Status: Devoid of fish
These lakes are found in the upper Snaring River drainage. They are very isolated and access is extremely arduous. They have not been stocked and contain no fish.

Backcountry buddy

HINTON REGION

The Hinton Region takes in the area to the east of Jasper National Park to the Town of Hinton and north to include William A. Switzer Provincial Park and Rock Lake-Solomon Creek Wildland. The Yellowhead Highway (Highway 16) is the main east-west transportation route through the Region. Highway 40 provides north-south transportation in the Region, crossing Highway 16 just west of Hinton. Fishing is good and varies between stocked trout lakes and pike/whitefish/perch lakes. The Region divides into two Sub-Regions. The Switzer Park Sub-Region includes waters in William A. Switzer Provincial Park and outside the park, up to and including Rock Lake. The second Sub-Region lies north of Highway 16, between the national park boundary and Hinton and includes all of the lakes in the Wildhorse Lakes Provincial Recreation Area, the namesake of the region.

Switzer Park Sub-Region

Rock Lake and its healthy population of lake, bull and rainbow trout is the primary focus of serious anglers in the Sub-Region. The Wildhay River provides excellent stream fishing for arctic grayling, particularly in the fall. William A. Switzer Provincial Park holds myriad of good fishing lakes, including Gregg, Jarvis, Blue, Cache and Graveyard. Access to Switzer Park is via Highway 40 north of Highway 16.

■ Rock Lake (AB)
53°27'36"N 118°15'53"W
Lake trout to 80 cm (8.0 kg)
Bull trout to 70 cm (3.0 kg)
Whitefish to 50 cm
Rainbow trout to 55 cm (1.5 kg)
Northern pike to 60 (3.0 kg)
Rock Lake is situated in a heavily wooded valley just west of the Wildhay River, approximately 70 km northwest of Hinton (40 km north on Highway 40, then 35 km west on the gravel Rock Lake/ Willmore Wilderness Park road). Rock Lake attracts many anglers each season. The lake's waters hold some lake trout of immense proportions as well as whitefish, bull trout, rainbow trout and the odd pike. Lake trout taken from Rock Lake will average 40–50 cm in length. Although it is possible to fish from shore from a number of locations, a boat is strongly recommended since trolling deep can be very effective. Springtime is usually the big

charge on the lakers that come into the shallower water and are quite aggressive. The campground at Rock Lake is very popular and is usually filled to capacity each weekend during the summer.

Rock Lake

Rock Lake lake trout

Moosehorn Lakes (aka Busby Lake) (AB)
53°22′09″N 118°08′49″W
Cutthroat trout to 40 cm

The Moosehorn Lakes are located just outside the north boundary of Jasper National Park. These seldom-visited lakes are accessed by two main trails, one from the Celestine Lake Road and the other from Rock Lake, both over 30 km in length. The lakes are reported to contain cutthroat trout in good numbers averaging 25–35 cm in length. The lower Moosehorn Lake is sometimes referred to as Busby Lake.

Wildhay River (AB)
Rainbow trout to 40 cm
Arctic grayling to 40 cm
Whitefish to 55 cm (1.5 kg)
Bull trout to 65 cm (3.0 kg)

The Wildhay River flows approximately 80 km from above Rock Lake downstream to join the Berland River. Above Rock Lake, the Wildhay River is quite small and does not gain river status until it accepts the outflow from Rock Lake. There is reasonable access to the river along the Rock Lake/Willmore Wilderness Park road, which branches west off Highway 40 about 40 kilometres northwest of Hinton. The Wildhay has innumerable fine pools along its course, and the pools are home to rainbow and bull trout, whitefish and arctic grayling. The grayling are of particular interest to fly fishers, especially in the fall when the grayling tend to gather in some of the larger pools on the river. Finding one of these loaded holes will make any angler's day. The grayling population in the Wildhay has recovered significantly from overharvest. Special regulations apply on the river.

Wildhay River

Moberly Creek (AB)
Rainbow trout to 35 cm
Bull trout to 55 cm (1.5 kg)
Whitefish to 35 cm

Mumm Creek (AB)
Status: Doubtful

These two tributaries of the Wildhay River join the main river downstream from Rock Lake. Expect to catch small rainbow and bull trout as well as whitefish in Moberly Creek. Mumm Creek dries up completely in most years and does not hold fish.

Gregg Lake (AB)
53°31′54″N 117°48′02″W
Northern pike to 70 cm (5.0 kg)
Whitefish to 60 cm (2.0 kg)
Walleye to 55 cm (1.5 kg)
Brown trout to 60 cm (2.0 kg)
Yellow perch

Gregg Lake is a large body of water located at the north end of William A. Switzer Provincial Park. The park is accessed off Highway 40 approximately 26 km north of Hinton. A large campground is at the lake and it is busy throughout the summer. Northern pike is the focus of most anglers, and large fish upwards of 4 kg are taken with regularity. Most pike from the lake will be in the 40–50 cm range. There are a number of other species in the lake, including large whitefish, walleye and brown trout. Targeting each usually requires different tactics, but it can be fun to try to guess what you have on the line before you pull it up.

Gregg Lake

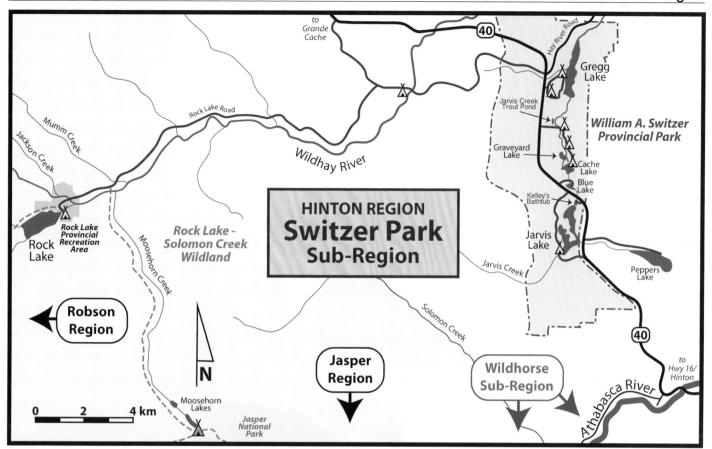

Gregg Lake northern pike

Jarvis Creek
Trout Pond

◼ Jarvis Creek Trout Pond (AB)

53°30'32"N 117°48'36"W

Rainbow trout to 45 cm

The parking lot for the Jarvis Creek Trout Pond is about 800 m in off Highway 40 on the access road to Cache Lake campground in Switzer Park. A short 200 m trail leads down to the shore of the pond. The readily accessible dock will attract most anglers hoping to gain an advantage in getting their lures out farther in the lake. Stocked rainbow trout in the 20–30 cm range are the normal catch and they can be taken from most locations around the pond.

◼ Cache Lake (AB)

53°29'20"N 117°47'58"W

Northern pike to 75 cm (6.0 kg)

Whitefish to 55 cm (1.5 kg)

Yellow perch

Cache Lake is located in Switzer Park, less than a kilometre past the Cache Lake parking area, which in turn is about one kilometre past the Cache Lake campground. To reach the lakeshore one must follow along the banks of Jarvis Creek. Wet feet are a certainty. Taking a canoe on Jarvis Creek to reach Cache Lake will work well. Northern pike in Cache Lake will average 40–50 cm in length. Some good-sized whitefish are taken from the lake each year as well.

Cache Lake
and
Jarvis Creek

Graveyard Lake (AB)
53°29'43"N 117°48'19"W
Northern pike to 75 cm (6.0 kg)
Whitefish to 55 cm (1.5 kg)
Yellow perch
Graveyard Lake is reached by a short 1 km trail from the Cache Lake parking area. Viewing Graveyard Lake from above on the access trail, one can readily see the dividing line between the shallow and deep water in the lake. Large pike can be taken from the shallow waters, especially in the springtime. Most pike caught will be 40–50 cm in length.

Graveyard Lake

Blue Lake (AB)
53°28'51"N 117°47'56"W
Northern Pike to 65 cm (4.0 kg)
Whitefish to 50 cm
Yellow perch
The road off Highway 40 to Blue Lake leads to the Blue Lake Centre, which when open offers group accommodation for organization/company retreats. From the parking area at the end of the access road, it is a short walk down to Blue Lake. The lake holds pike, whitefish and perch, with pike from the lake averaging 35–45 cm in length. A few points jut out into the lake and offer the best shore angling spots.

Blue Lake

Jarvis Lake (AB)
53°27'05"N 117°47'55"W
Northern pike to 70 km (4.0 kg)
Walleye to 65 cm (2.0 kg)
Whitefish to 55 cm (1.5 kg)
Yellow perch
Pretty Jarvis Lake is located at the south end of William A. Switzer Provincial Park on the west side of Highway 40 approximately 20 km north of Hinton. Two access roads lead to Jarvis Lake, one at

the south end and one at the north end of the lake. The south access leads to the main Jarvis Lake campground. The north access leads to Kelley's Bathtub Visitor Centre and Day Use Area. Jarvis Lake is very large with many bays and inlets. Fish can be taken from most locations around the lake if fishing from a boat. Northern pike in the 35–45 cm range and walleye in the 25–35 cm range are the normal catch at Jarvis Lake.

Kelley's Bathtub and Jarvis Lake

Jarvis Lake northern pike

Jarvis Creek (AB)
Rainbow trout to 50 cm
Brown trout to 60 cm (2.0 kg)
Whitefish
Jarvis Creek runs either through or close to most of the lakes in William A. Switzer Provincial Park. Although it is a relatively small creek, a canoe can be taken on the creek from the launch point off Highway 40, just before the entrance to Kelley's Bathtub Visitor Centre. You can then canoe downstream past Blue Lake to the take-out point at Cache Lake parking area. Jarvis Lake holds a few rainbow and brown trout as well as whitefish along its course.

Peppers Lake (AB)
53°26'35"N 117°43'15"W
Status: Doubtful
Peppers Lake is located 4 km east of Highway 40, approximately 20 km north of Hinton. This shallow lake probably holds no fish.

238

Wildhorse Sub-Region

This Sub-Region covers the area to the west of Hinton just north of the Yellowhead Highway (Highway 16), up to the Jasper Park boundary. The Athabasca River is the main water feature of the Sub-Region. Most fishing in the Sub-Region takes place in the Wildhorse Lakes Provincial Recreation Area, which holds several good trout lakes, including the two Wildhorse lakes, Kinky Lake and Kia Nea Lake. A nice campground is located in the Recreation Area that is 14 km west of Hinton, followed by a short 3 km gravel road to reach the lakes.

Solomon Creek

◼ Athabasca River (AB) (Jasper Park to Hinton)
Bull trout to 1 m (10 kg)
Rainbow trout to 55 cm (1.5 kg)
Whitefish to 55 cm (1.5 kg)
The mighty Athabasca leaves Jasper National Park on its journey east then north to the Arctic Ocean. From the park boundary downstream, bull and rainbow trout plus whitefish can be taken from the river. The Athabasca is very silty for virtually the entire year, so the best fishing opportunities occur where clearer tributary streams enter the main river.

Logan Urie photo
Athabasca River bull trout

◼ Brule Lake (AB)
53°17'29"N 117°50'58"W
Bull trout to 1 m (10 kg)
Rainbow trout to 55 cm (1.5 kg)
Whitefish to 55 cm (1.5 kg)
Brule Lake is simply a downstream widening of the Athabasca River that begins at the Jasper Park boundary. Fishing is difficult at Brule Lake because the Athabasca River is now many times wider than its normal width, but just as silty. The same variety of fish that are in the main river can be taken from Brule Lake, namely bull and rainbow trout and whitefish.

◼ Solomon Creek (AB)
Bull trout to 70 cm (4.0 kg)
Rainbow trout to 40 cm
Whitefish to 40 cm
Solomon Creek is a tributary to the Athabasca River and joins the main river at the east end of Brule Lake. It can be accessed by the secondary road to Brule, just after crossing the Athabasca River on Highway 40. Solomon Creek holds bull and rainbow trout and whitefish in decent numbers. There are some nice beaver ponds on Solomon Creek above the Brule road.

◼ Hinton Fish and Game Pond (AB)
53°17'29"N 117°50'58"W
Rainbow trout to 40 cm
The Hinton Fish and Game Pond is located in a borrow pit approximately 3 km south of Highway 16 on Highway 40. Catchable rainbow trout in the 20–25 cm range are stocked each year. Steady fishing pressure usually reduces the trout population to near zero by the end of the season. In the early season, after the fish have been stocked, they can be taken from any location around the pond.

Hinton Fish and Game Pond

◼ Hardisty Creek (AB)
Rainbow trout to 30 cm
Brook trout to 30 cm
This little creek flows through Hinton and is a popular fishing spot for local youngsters. Small rainbow and brook trout in the 15–25 cm range are taken from the creek.

◼ Thompson Lake (AB)
53°23'45"N 117°33'43"W
Rainbow trout to 35 cm
This small lake is located in the forested hills at the east end of Hinton off Sawyer Drive. Thompson Lake is stocked annually with catchable rainbow trout in the 20–25 cm range, few of whom survive the fishing pressure of the season. Lily pads and weeds are ever-present in Thompson Lake

Thompson Lake

■ **Maxwell Lake (AB)**
53°23'14"N 117°35'10"W
Status: Devoid of fish
The second of Hinton's small urban lakes does not contain any fish.

■ **Kinky Lake (AB)**
53°16'50"N 117°47'01"W
Brook trout to 45 cm
Kinky Lake is the first lake encountered when entering Wildhorse Lakes Provincial Recreation Area. The Rec Area is reached by following a short 3 km gravel road north off of the Yellowhead Highway (Highway 16) approximately 14 km west of Hinton. Brook trout are stocked regularly in Kinky Lake and most average 20–30 cm in length. Fishing from shore is possible but difficult. A boat or float tube will help a lot. Electric motors only on Kinky Lake.

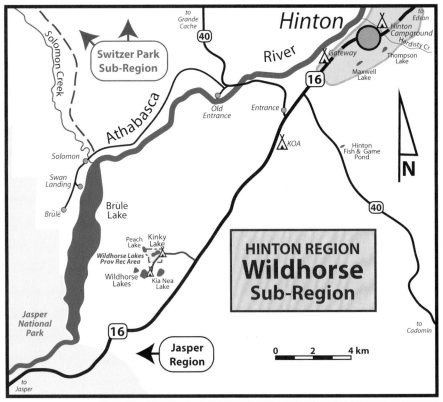

Kinky Lake

■ **Peach Lake (AB)**
53°16'59"N 117°47'35"W
Status: Doubtful
Peach Lake is located less than 250 m northwest of Kinky Lake. Although it has never been stocked, Peach Lake may hold the odd brook trout.

▲ **Wildhorse Lake #1 (AB) (aka Lower Wildhorse Lake)**
53°16'11"N 117°47'35"W
Rainbow trout to 55 cm (1.5 kg)
Brook trout to 40 cm
Brown trout
Wildhorse #1 is not far past Kinky Lake. It is accessed from the Recreation Area road and has a boat launch. Wildhorse #1 is the larger of the two Wildhorse lakes and has a wide margin of shallow water, making shore fishing difficult. Rainbow trout are stocked regularly in the lake and average 25–35 cm in length. There are also brook trout in the lake and reports of the odd large brown trout still present. Lures and flies will both work well at Wildhorse #1, especially if fishing from a boat.

Wildhorse Lake #1

Wildhorse Lake brook trout

■ **Wildhorse Lake #2 (AB) (aka Upper Wildhorse Lake)**
53°16'17"N 117°48'04"W
Brook trout to 50 cm
Wildhorse Lake #2 is located less than 100 m northwest of Wildhorse #1 but is not road accessible. Wildhorse #2 holds plenty of brook trout which are stocked regularly. Brookies in the lake will average 20–30 cm in length and can be taken from shore by those with good casting skills.

□ **Kia Nea Lake (AB)**
53°16'14"N 117°46'42"W
Brook trout to 40 cm
Kia Nea Lake is similar in character to all of the other lakes in the Wildhorse Rec Area. The lake is located about 300 m southwest of the Wildhorse Lakes campground at Wildhorse #1. Kia Nea may hold a few brook trout.

Index to
Lakes, Rivers and Streams
of the Canadian Rockies

ABOUT THE AUTHOR

Joey Ambrosi (B.A., M.A., M.Des.) still enjoys life in the Canadian Rockies. Fishing and hiking continue to be his particular passions, although the hikes tend to be shorter and shorter. He has hiked over 22,000 kilometres in the Rockies and has personally visited and fished the vast majority of waters in this book. When not fishing, travel with his family is a favourite activity and he has been to many countries all around the globe. He has previously authored six books: *Hiking Alberta's Southwest*, *Fly Fishing the Canadian Rockies*, *The Courthouse*, *Hiking the Southern Rockies*, *Fishing the Canadian Rockies*, and *Southern Rockies Trail Guide*. The author currently lives in Crowsnest Pass in the southern Rockies with his wife, Valerie.

CONTRIBUTORS

Older But Wiser

Jason Godkin is an avid backcountry enthusiast and fisherman. He continues to explore and enjoy the Alberta and British Columbia Rockies whether via hiking, backpacking, mountain biking or skiing and of course fishing wherever possible. He maintains *Outdooralberta.com* in order to share fishing information with the public.

Vic Bergman claims to be "just a fisherman" but is much, much more. In addition to operating his own fishing shop and guiding service (*crowsnestangler.com*), Vic is a renowned professional photographer and outdoor writer.

"There is nothing more sad or glorious than generations changing hands."

John Mellencamp

The Young Guns

Tyler Ambrosi is a lifelong angler who has covered much of the Rockies, usually at his father's side. Tyler is a graduate of the College of the Rockies' Mountain Adventure Skill Training Program and currently lives in Jasper where he enjoys skiing and hockey in the winter and fishing and hiking in the summer.

Curtis Hall is also a graduate of the College of the Rockies' Mountain Adventure Skill Training Program and currently works for Fernie Wilderness Adventures as a fishing guide in the summer and in their cat-skiing operations in the winter. Curtis is a very talented professional photographer and videographer who has produced a number of excellent short films.

Logan Urie is a born-and-raised Jasper resident with a particular passion for fishing. In any spare time he can muster, Logan will be found with a rod in his hand testing some local waters. In just a few short years, he has accumulated an incredible collection of fishing images of waters in the northern Rockies.

other fishing titles from Hancock House Publishers

From the same author

Fishing the Canadian Rockies
First Edition 2001
Joey Ambrosi
978-0-88839-900-7
8.5 x 11, 240pp
100 maps, 520 photos
$24.95

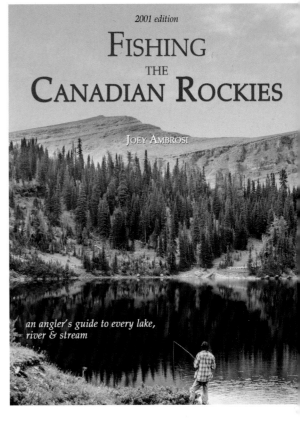

West Coast Fly Fisher
Brian Chan *et al*, 1998
978-0-8883-944-0
5.5 x 8.5, 152 color pages
$19.95

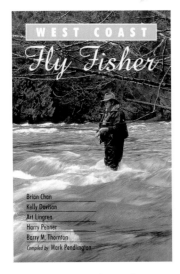

West Coast Steelheader
Mark Peddlington *et al*, 2000
978-0-88839-459-0
5.5 x 8.5, 96 color pages
$12.95

Trout Fishing
Ed Rychkun, 1994
978-0-88839-338-8
5.5 x 8.5, 120 pages
$16.95

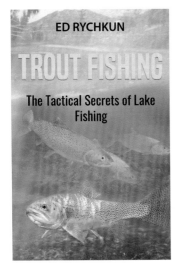

12 Basic Skills of Fly Fishing
Ted Peck & Ed Rychkun, *2000*
978-0-88839-459-0
5.5 x 8.5, 96 color pages
$12.95

Steelhead
Barry Thornton, *1995*
978-0-88839-370-8
5.5 x 8.5, 192 pages
$17.95

Hancock House Publishers
19313 0 Ave, Surrey, BC, Canada V3Z 9R9
#104 4550 Birch Bay-Lynden Rd, Blaine, WA, USA 98230
www.hancockhouse.com
sales@hancockhouse.com
1-800-938-1114

hancock
house